HOUGHTON MIFFLIN

SOCIAL STUDIES

★ NORTH AMERICA ★

REGIONS AND PEOPLE

Visit **Education Place**
www.eduplace.com/kids

HOUGHTON MIFFLIN   BOSTON

OHIO

★ AUTHORS ★

Senior Author
Dr. Herman J. Viola
Curator Emeritus
Smithsonian Institution

Dr. Cheryl Jennings
Project Director
Florida Institute of
 Education
University of North
 Florida

Dr. Sarah Witham Bednarz
Associate Professor,
 Geography
Texas A&M University

Dr. Mark C. Schug
Professor and Director
Center for Economic
 Education
University of Wisconsin,
 Milwaukee

Dr. Carlos E. Cortés
Professor Emeritus, History
University of California,
Riverside

Dr. Charles S. White
Associate Professor
School of Education
Boston University

Consulting Authors
Dr. Dolores Beltran
Assistant Professor
Curriculum Instruction
California State University, Los Angeles
(Support for English Language Learners)

Dr. MaryEllen Vogt
Co-Director
California State University Center
for the Advancement of Reading
(Reading in the Content Area)

Consultants

Patricia Clayton
Summit County Education
   Service Center
Cuyahoga Falls, Ohio

Philip J. Deloria
Associate Professor
Department of History
   and Program in
   American Studies
University of Michigan

Lucien Ellington
UC Professor of Education
   and Asia Program
   Co-Director
University of Tennessee,
   Chattanooga

Thelma Wills Foote
Associate Professor
University of California

Stephen J. Fugita
Distinguished Professor
Psychology and Ethnic
   Studies
Santa Clara University

Charles C. Haynes
Senior Scholar
First Amendment Center

Ted Hemmingway
Professor of History
The Florida Agricultural &
   Mechanical University

Douglas Monroy
Professor of History
The Colorado College

Lynette K. Oshima
Assistant Professor
Department of Language,
   Literacy and Sociocultural
   Studies and Social Studies
   Program Coordinator
University of New Mexico

Jeffrey Strickland
Assistant Professor, History
University of Texas Pan
   American

Clifford E. Trafzer
Professor of History and
   American Indian Studies
University of California

Teacher Reviewers

Skip Bayliss
Surfside Elementary
Satellite Beach, FL

Annette Bomba
Schenevus Central School
Schenevus, NY

Amy Clark
Gateway Elementary
Travelers Rest, SC

Melissa Cook
Machado Elementary
Lake Elsinore, CA

Kelli Dunn
Lindop School
Broadview, IL

Peggy Greene
Upson-Lee North
   Elementary
Thomaston, GA

Elyce Kaplan
Kumeyaay Elementary
San Diego, CA

Julia McNeal
Webster Elementary
Dayton, OH

Lesa Roberts
Hampton Cove Middle School
Huntsville, AL

Lynn Schew
Leila G. Davis Elementary
Clearwater, FL

Linda Whitford
Manning Oaks Elementary
Alpharetta, GA

Lisa Yingling
Round Hills Elementary
Williamsport, PA

ISBN: 0-618-90972-9
ISBN: 978-0-618-90972-8

56789   0914   13 12 11 10 09

North American Handbook

**Broad Street Bridge
in Columbus, Ohio**

UNIT 1

Regions of North America

v

UNIT 2

Regions of the United States

Coast of Mount Desert Island, Maine

Farmers pull hay bales in Ohio

UNIT 3

Settlement

SunWatch Indian Village in Dayton, Ohio

UNIT 4

Growth and Immigration

Fort Washington, Cincinnati, Ohio

UNIT 5

Citizenship and Government

**National Underground Railroad
Freedom Center, Cincinnati, Ohio**

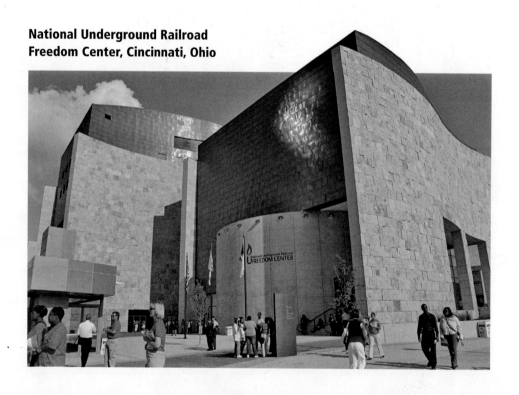

Ohio state flag

References

Citizenship Handbook

Resources

Extend Lessons

Connect the core lesson to an important concept and dig into it. Extend your social studies knowledge!

Readers' Theater

Geography

Economics

Citizenship

Technology

Biography

Primary Sources

History

Culture

Skill Lessons

Take a step-by-step approach to learning and practicing key social studies skills.

Visual Learning

Become skilled at reading visuals. Graphs, maps, and fine art help you put all the information together.

Maps

Charts and Graphs

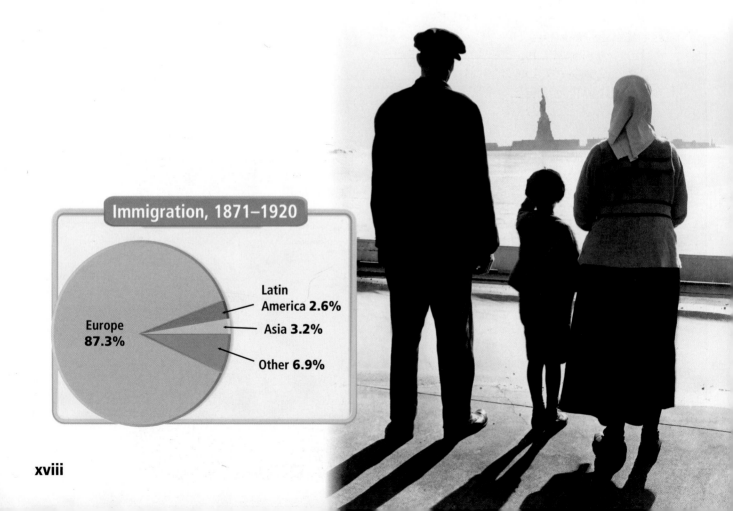

Immigration, 1871–1920

Europe 87.3%

Latin America 2.6%

Asia 3.2%

Other 6.9%

Constitution Day

★ ★

"We the people of the United States, in order to form a more perfect union . . ." These are the words that begin the United States Constitution, the plan for our national government. The leaders who wrote this document in 1787 wanted to create a good government for United States citizens. Today, we celebrate the Constitution during the week of September 17. We call this day Constitution Day and Citizenship Day.

The words "We the people" show that the people are the source of the government's authority. For the government to work, citizens must take part. They do this by voting, serving on juries, paying taxes, registering for the selective service, and working as community and national leaders.

Alexander Hamilton

James Madison

George Washington

National Constitution Center This exhibit in Philadelphia shows delegates debating at the Constitutional Convention.

The first and fourth pages of the Constitution are displayed in the National Archives Building in Washington, D.C. September 17 is the only day the whole Constitution is on display.

Famous leaders of the Revolution, such as George Washington and Alexander Hamilton, traveled to Philadelphia to write the Constitution.

Though the framers, or people who wrote the Constitution, spent just four months writing the document, it has lasted over 200 years.

Activity

IN YOUR OWN WORDS Look up the beginning, or Preamble, of the Constitution in the back of your textbook. Make a glossary of difficult terms used in the Preamble. Then rewrite the sentence in your own words.

North American
Countries

The three largest countries of North America are Canada, the United States, and Mexico. Many geographers think of Greenland, the countries of Central America, and the islands of the Caribbean as part of North America, too. Hawaii is part of the United States, so it is also shown on this map.

The United States and Mexico are divided into states. Canada is divided into provinces and territories.

The map on page xxiii is a political map. Political maps show the borders of countries. They may also show smaller areas of government such as states, provinces, and cities.

Use the maps on pages R102–R103 to learn more about the states of the United States and on pages 277 and 279 to learn about the provinces of Canada and the states of Mexico.

Provinces and States

Canada
Capital: Ottawa
10 provinces
3 territories

Mexico
Capital: Mexico City
31 states

United States
Capital: Washington, D.C.
50 states

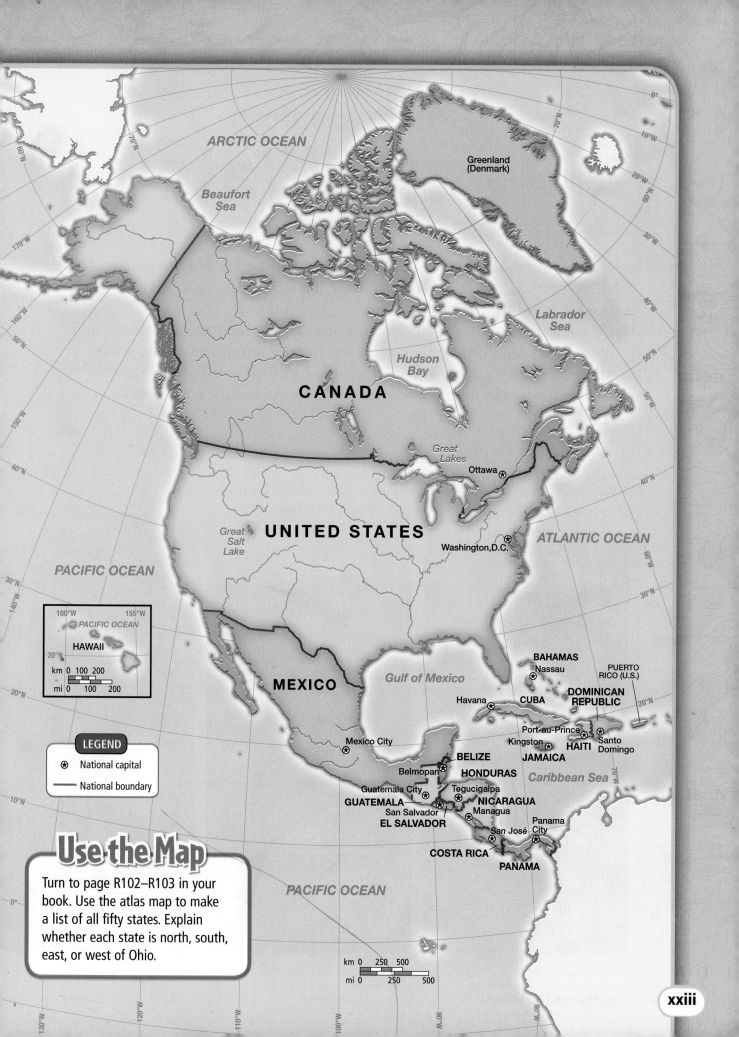

ARCTIC OCEAN

Beaufort
Sea

Greenland
(Denmark)

CANADA

Hudson
Bay

Labrador
Sea

Great
Lakes

Ottawa ⊛

PACIFIC OCEAN

Great
Salt
Lake

UNITED STATES

Washington, D.C. ⊛

ATLANTIC OCEAN

160°W   155°W

PACIFIC OCEAN

HAWAII

km 0 100 200

mi 0   100   200

MEXICO

Gulf of Mexico

BAHAMAS
Nassau ⊛

PUERTO
RICO (U.S.)

Havana ⊛   CUBA

DOMINICAN
REPUBLIC

Port-au-Prince ⊛   Santo
Kingston ⊛   Domingo ⊛

Mexico City ⊛   HAITI

JAMAICA

BELIZE

Belmopan ⊛   HONDURAS   Caribbean Sea

Guatemala City ⊛   Tegucigalpa ⊛

GUATEMALA   NICARAGUA

San Salvador ⊛   Managua ⊛

EL SALVADOR   Panama
                                   City ⊛

San José ⊛

COSTA RICA

PANAMA

PACIFIC OCEAN

LEGEND

⊛ National capital

— National boundary

Use the Map

Turn to page R102–R103 in your book. Use the atlas map to make a list of all fifty states. Explain whether each state is north, south, east, or west of Ohio.

km 0   250   500

mi 0   250   500

North American
Land and Water

A landform is a feature on the surface of Earth, such as a mountain, valley, or plain. North America has towering mountains, spacious plains, and majestic canyons.

Canada, Mexico, and the United States all have mountains, plateaus, and rivers. Some landforms extend from one country into the next. The Rocky Mountains run from northern Canada through the United States. The Rio Grande forms part of the border between Mexico and the United States.

A Varied Continent The landforms of North America include the mountains of Canada (left), Ohio's plains (center), and canyons in Mexico (right).

ARCTIC OCEAN

Beaufort
Sea

Brooks Range

Mt. McKinley
20,320 ft.
(6,194 m)

Mt. Logan
19,551 ft.
(5,959 m)

Mackenzie River

PACIFIC OCEAN

Hudson
Bay

Labrador
Sea

Fraser R.

Columbia R.

Saskatchewan River

Lake
Winnipeg

Lake
Manitoba

St. Lawrence
River

Great Lakes

R O C K Y   M O U N T A I N S

Coast Ranges

Sierra Nevada

Great
Salt
Lake

Missouri
River

Arkansas
River

Mississippi River

Ohio R.

A P P A L A C H I A N   M T S.

ATLANTIC OCEAN

Colorado R.

Rio Grande

Sierra Madre Occidental

Sierra Madre Oriental

Gulf of Mexico

Pico de Orizaba
18,410 ft.
(5,610 m)

Caribbean Sea

160°W   155°W

PACIFIC OCEAN

HAWAII

20°N

km 0   100   200
mi 0   100   200

LEGEND

15,000 ft. (4,500 m)
6,560 ft. (2,000 m)
3,280 ft. (1,000 m)
1,640 ft. (500 m)
650 ft. (200 m)
0 ft. (0 m)
Below sea level

——— National boundary

▲ Highest point

km 0   250   500
mi 0   250   500

Use the Map

Describe the location of the Rocky Mountains and the Appalachian Mountains so that someone who doesn't know where they are could find them.

North American
Climate

Geographers divide the world into climate regions. Climate is the type of weather a place has over a long period of time. Climate regions are areas that have about the same temperature and amounts of rain or snow. North America includes many different climate regions.

Use the Map

Make a three-column chart to show which climate regions are found in Canada, Mexico, and in the United States.

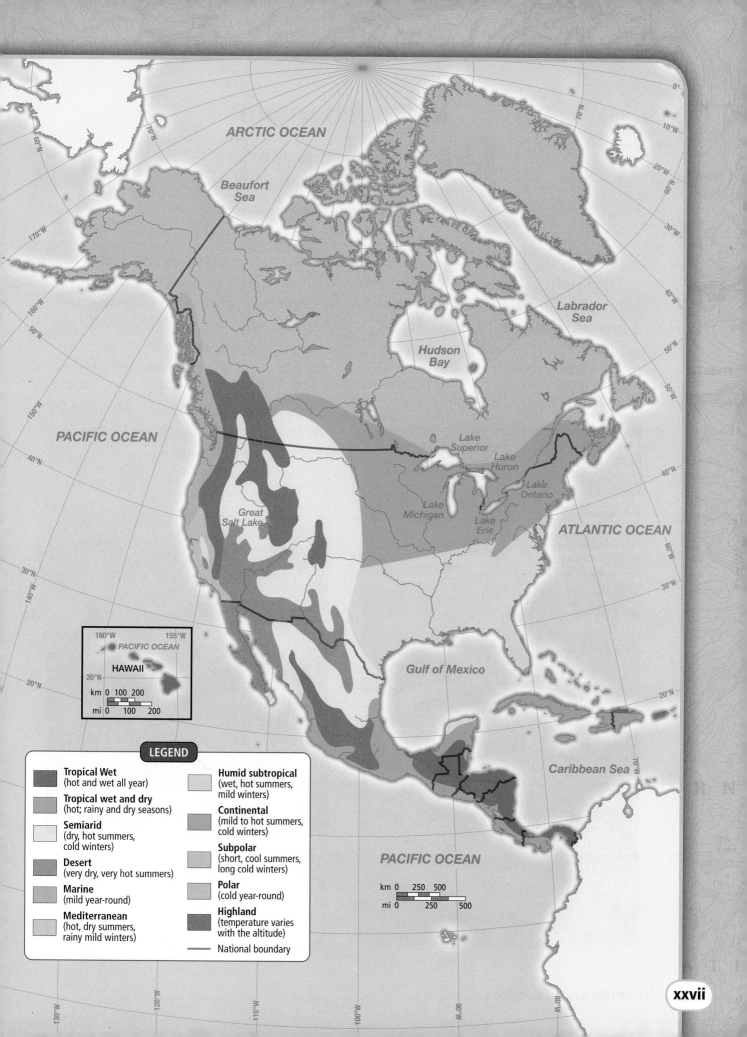

ARCTIC OCEAN

Beaufort
Sea

Labrador
Sea

Hudson
Bay

PACIFIC OCEAN

Lake
Superior
Lake
Huron
Lake
Ontario
Lake
Michigan
Lake
Erie

Great
Salt Lake

ATLANTIC OCEAN

Gulf of Mexico

Caribbean Sea

PACIFIC OCEAN

160°W   155°W
PACIFIC OCEAN
HAWAII
km 0 100 200
mi 0 100 200

LEGEND

Tropical Wet
(hot and wet all year)

Tropical wet and dry
(hot; rainy and dry seasons)

Semiarid
(dry, hot summers,
cold winters)

Desert
(very dry, very hot summers)

Marine
(mild year-round)

Mediterranean
(hot, dry summers,
rainy mild winters)

Humid subtropical
(wet, hot summers,
mild winters)

Continental
(mild to hot summers,
cold winters)

Subpolar
(short, cool summers,
long cold winters)

Polar
(cold year-round)

Highland
(temperature varies
with the altitude)

National boundary

km 0   250   500
mi 0   250   500

North American Products

Farmers throughout North America use rich soil and rainwater to grow farm products such as corn and wheat. A product is something made from natural resources. North America has many natural resources, or materials from nature, such as soil and trees.

Businesses in the United States, Canada, and Mexico create products that provide people with food, shelter, fuel, and ways to earn a living. Products such as clothing, automobiles, and machines are made in factories. Other products, such as soybeans, corn, and cotton, are grown on farms. Almost half the land in the United States is used to raise crops and livestock.

Car Factory

Sweet Corn Farm

Use the Map

Make a Venn diagram to compare farm products of Canada and Mexico.

ARCTIC OCEAN

Beaufort
Sea

Greenland
(Denmark)

Gulf of
Alaska

Labrador
Sea

Hudson
Bay

CANADA

Great
Lakes

UNITED STATES

ATLANTIC OCEAN

PACIFIC OCEAN

BAHAMAS

Gulf of Mexico

MEXICO

CUBA

PUERTO
RICO
(U.S.)

Caribbean Sea

160°W   155°W

PACIFIC OCEAN

HAWAII

20°N

km 0   100 200
mi 0   100 200

LEGEND

Cattle	Fishing	Poultry	
Coal	Fruit	Sheep	
Copper	Gold	Silver	
Corn	Iron/Steel	Soybeans	
Cotton	Natural gas	Timber	
Dairy products	Oil	Wheat	

km 0   250   500
mi 0   250   500

PACIFIC OCEAN

North American
Population

Almost 450 million people live in the North American countries of Canada, Mexico, and the United States. Some areas of North America are more densely populated than others. Population density is the average number of people who live in a square mile. The population is most dense in and around cities. Many people also live in suburbs outside of cities. Rural areas are not very densely populated. People live farther apart from one another.

Rural Area In Alaska, the population density is very low. It is higher in cities such as New York and Cleveland.

In the United States, people live in cities, suburbs, and small towns. Many big cities are located along the coast of the Atlantic and Pacific oceans and the Great Lakes. Most cities in Canada are located along the coasts and the southern border. In Mexico, the central and southern areas are more densely populated than the north.

People in North America

Earth at Night This satellite photograph shows North America at night. The lights of densely populated areas can be seen from outer space. Red borders have been added to help you identify countries of North America.

Use the Map

What regions of the United States are most brightly lit?

UNIT 1

Regions of North America

The Big Idea

What effects have people had on the physical environment where you live?

 Unit 1 Benchmarks

As you study this unit, you will cover these Ohio Social Studies benchmarks:

Geography C Identify and explain ways people have affected the physical environment of North America and analyze the positive and negative consequences.

Economics A Explain the opportunity costs involved in the allocation of scarce productive resources.

Economics C Explain how competition affects producers and consumers in a market economy and why specialization facilitates trade.

Skills and Methods D Use problem-solving skills to make decisions individually and in groups.

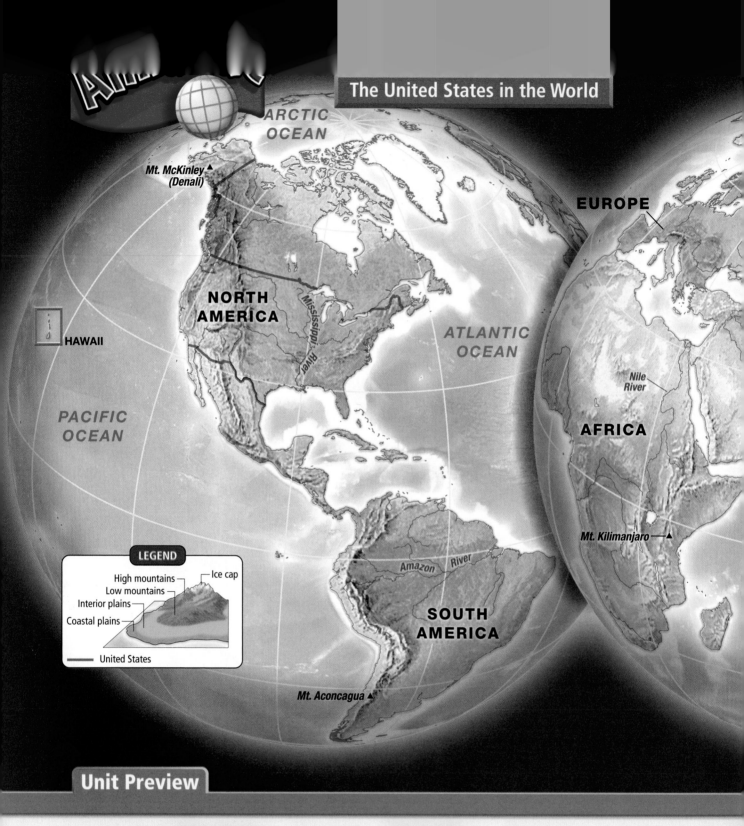

ARCTIC OCEAN

Mt. McKinley ▲
(Denali)

EUROPE

NORTH AMERICA

Mississippi River

ATLANTIC OCEAN

HAWAII

Nile River

PACIFIC OCEAN

AFRICA

Mt. Kilimanjaro ▲

LEGEND

High mountains — Ice cap
Low mountains
Interior plains
Coastal plains

── United States

Amazon River

SOUTH AMERICA

Mt. Aconcagua ▲

Unit Preview

Natural Resources
Resources such as trees can be replaced
Chapter 1, p. 6

Landforms
People define regions by physical features
Chapter 1, p. 16

People and Environment
Environment affects where people live
Chapter 2, p. 26

ARCTIC OCEAN

ASIA

Chang Jiang

Mt. Everest

PACIFIC OCEAN

INDIAN OCEAN

AUSTRALIA

Connect to...
Your World

Mountains of North America

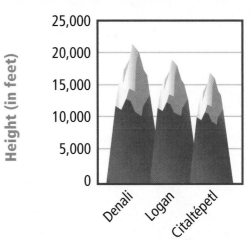

Height (in feet)

25,000
20,000
15,000
10,000
5,000
0

Denali   Logan   Citaltépetl

Rivers of North America

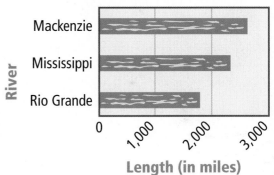

River

Mackenzie

Mississippi

Rio Grande

0   1,000   2,000   3,000

Length (in miles)

Think about mountains and rivers near you. What is the highest point in Ohio? What is the longest river that runs through Ohio?

Supply and Demand
Prices depend on what goods people want
Chapter 2, p. 32

Vocabulary Preview

Technology

e • **glossary**
e • **word games**
www.eduplace.com/kids/hmss/

natural resource

Ohioans use their state's **natural resources** every day. They farm its soil, mine its minerals, and drink its fresh water. **page 6**

conservation

When people save natural resources, they are working for **conservation.** Recycling reduces the amount of resources people need to use. **page 10**

Reading Strategy

Predict and Infer

As you read each lesson, use this strategy.

Quick Tip   Look at the pictures in a lesson to predict what it will be about. What will you read about?

region

People think of canyons as a feature of the **region** called the West. Landforms are one feature that can define regions. **page 16**

specialization

Fertile soil is a resource that Minnesota farmers use to grow corn. Each region has certain resources that lead to **specialization.** **page 18**

Resources of North America

VOCABULARY

natural resource
scarcity
opportunity cost
conservation

Vocabulary Strategy

conservation

A synonym for **conservation** is "saving." Conservation saves resources for the future.

READING SKILL

Draw Conclusions Use details from the lesson to decide whether protecting resources is important.

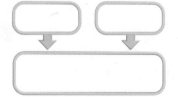

BENCHMARKS
GEO B   Places and regions
ECON A   Scarcity and resource allocation

GRADE LEVEL INDICATORS
GEO 6   Patterns of resources
GEO 7   Regional conflict and cooperation

Build on What You Know Think about where the food you eat, the clothes you wear, and the building you live in come from. Almost everything we use starts with materials from nature, but that is just the beginning.

Natural Resources

Main Idea Natural resources in North America include renewable, nonrenewable, and flow resources.

Many of the things we use every day come from nature. The water you drink may come from rivers or lakes. The gasoline to run your school bus may have come from oil wells in Mexico. The bus itself began as iron ore that may have come from Minnesota.

Water, oil, and iron ore are natural resources. A **natural resource** is a useful material that comes from nature. Air to breathe and soil and sunshine for growing crops are also found in nature. Without natural resources, human beings would not be able to survive.

Ohio's Resources At a farmer's market in Toledo, people shop for natural resources such as fruits and vegetables.

Renewable Resources

Natural resources are found all over North America—in the mountains, on the plains, and in the rivers and lakes. Some natural resources are renewable. They can be replaced, or renewed. Other resources are nonrenewable. Once they are used, they cannot be replaced. Some resources are flow resources. They can be used only at a certain time or place.

Trees are an example of a renewable resource. People use wood from trees to make paper, pencils, furniture, and hundreds of other products. In many places in North America, farmers grow trees as a crop. When loggers cut down trees, they plant new trees to replace the ones they cut down.

People need to use renewable resources wisely. It can take a long time to replace some resources, such as trees. Other resources must be protected or they may not replace themselves at all. Fisheries, for example, are places where fish are caught. If people catch too many fish, new fish won't be able to hatch and grow.

The map on page 9 shows patterns in the locations of some renewable resources. Farms are usually located on flat land, where it is easier to plant and raise crops. Forests, however, can grow near different kinds of landforms, such as mountains or plains. The location of forests usually depends on whether the area has enough rain for trees to grow.

REVIEW What makes a resource renewable?

Ohio Corn Fields Natural resources such as sun, soil, and water are needed to raise corn and other crops. Because corn is a renewable resource, Ohio farmers can harvest it every year.

Types of Natural Resources

Renewable	Nonrenewable	Flow

Wind Power Windmills, also known as turbines, use moving air to create electricity. **SKILL Reading Charts** What kind of natural resource is wind?

Nonrenewable Resources

Nonrenewable resources cannot be replaced after they are used up. Oil is one of the United States' nonrenewable resources. After oil is removed from the ground, no new oil will take its place. Look at the map on the next page. What pattern do you see in the location of oil in North America?

Oil, iron ore, and copper are mineral resources. They are mined, or taken from the ground. Some mineral resources, such as oil and coal, are turned into energy to heat homes, run cars, and cook food. Iron ore is used to produce steel, which is an important building material. All mineral resources are nonrenewable.

Flow Resources

Wind, sunlight, and water are flow resources. Strong winds, sunlight, and running water produce energy that can be made into electricity.

Flow resources can only be used at a certain time or place. People can only use the power of the wind while it is blowing. The wind turns the blades of a windmill, which changes the wind's power into electricity. Special panels can turn sunlight into electricity, but only when the sun shines. As the map on the next page shows, major rivers are the source of flowing water, which can run machines that make electricity.

REVIEW What is the difference between nonrenewable and flow resources?

Natural Resources

PACIFIC OCEAN

ATLANTIC OCEAN

CANADA

UNITED STATES

MEXICO

Gulf of Mexico

Lake Superior
Lake Huron
Lake Michigan
Lake Ontario
Lake Erie

HAWAII

PACIFIC OCEAN

km 0 100 200
mi 0 100 200

km 0 250 500
mi 0 250 500

LEGEND

Forests	Coal
Farmland	Oil
Other	Iron Ore
	Source of water power

Resources Across the Continent Resources such as coal and oil are found underground. Other resources, such as forests, are above ground.

SKILL **Reading Maps** Where are most of North America's forests found?

Making Choices

Although there are many types of resources, there are not enough resources to provide all that people want. This problem is called scarcity. **Scarcity** means not having as much of something as people would like.

The problem of scarcity means that people have to make decisions about what they want most. For example, your teacher might want to buy a wall map and a video. The school may not have enough money to buy both. If your teacher chooses to buy the video, he or she gives up the opportunity to buy the map. The map is called an opportunity cost. An **opportunity cost** is the thing you give up when you decide to do or have something else. Every choice people make about how to spend their money or their time has an opportunity cost.

Conservation and Cooperation

Another choice that people make is how to use resources. People must balance the needs of today with care for the future through conservation. **Conservation** is the protection and wise use of natural resources.

The United States cooperates with Mexico and Canada to solve problems of conservation. For example, the countries identify animals that are in danger across North America. Their solution is to share knowledge and work together to protect those animals and their homelands.

The Great Lakes are part of the border between the United States and Canada. People from both countries use the lakes for shipping, fishing, building power plants, and getting fresh water. The United States and Canada work together to set rules for the uses of the lakes. They also try to keep the lakes clean.

Protecting the Environment This Ottawa County girl fishes in Lake Erie. Canada and the United States cooperate to keep this lake clean and to use its resources wisely.

People Make a Difference

The United States government supports conservation in many ways. The government has passed laws to keep the air and water clean. Laws also protect animals that are in danger of becoming extinct. Extinct means that a species no longer exists.

Recycling The material in paper, cans, and plastic can be used again to conserve resources.

Individuals also cooperate to practice conservation. People can use water, gas, or electricity carefully so these resources are not wasted. Recycling paper, cans, and bottles means the material used to make these products can be used again. Everyone can help conserve natural resources for the future.

REVIEW What can people do to solve the problem of resources being wasted?

Lesson Summary

- Natural resources are materials found in nature that people use.
- Because of scarcity, people make decisions about what they want most and what they can do without.
- Conservation is one important way to preserve natural resources and use them wisely.

Why It Matters...

Today and in the future, Americans will face many important decisions about how to use and protect natural resources.

Lesson Review

❶ **VOCABULARY** Write a short paragraph about resources in North America, using **scarcity** and **conservation.**

❷ **READING SKILL** Why can you **conclude** that nonrenewable resources need to be used wisely?

❸ **MAIN IDEA: Geography** What is one example of each kind of resource: renewable, nonrenewable, and flow?

❹ **MAIN IDEA: Economics** Why does scarcity force people to make choices?

❺ **CRITICAL THINKING: Decision Making** Describe the opportunity cost if you decide to check out a mystery book instead of a science video from the library.

❻ **CRITICAL THINKING: Analyze** Why do you think nations in North America cooperate to conserve resources?

HANDS ON

ART ACTIVITY Resources are necessary for businesses. Create a poster for a T-shirt company, showing the different types of resources the business uses to make its product.

Save the Animals

All over North America, animals need food, water, and places to raise their young. Animals such as the leatherback turtle and the burrowing owl travel the continent and the waters around it to find what they need. North American people and governments cooperate to protect these and other animals as they journey across borders.

In southern Mexico, students from Mexico, Canada, and the United States release baby leatherback turtles. The students protect the young turtles until they are old enough to defend themselves in the wild.

Wildlife organizations teach ship captains about the routes whales travel. Ships such as this one, near Hawaii, can avoid hitting whales.

Volunteers in Mexico, Canada, and the United States use plastic tubes to create burrows like the one in Tucson, Arizona, pictured here. They replace burrowing owl homes destroyed by construction.

Activities

1. **TALK ABOUT IT** Why do you think Canada, Mexico, and the United States cooperate to save animals?

2. **WRITE ABOUT IT** Write a readers' theater about people cooperating in the conservation effort shown in one of the pictures.

Solve a Problem

In Lesson 1, you read about how nations cooperate. However, conflicts or problems can occur if groups or nations have different goals. The steps below can help to solve problems.

Learn the Skill

Step 1: Identify the problem.

A class needs money to visit a science museum.

Step 2: Gather information that can help solve the problem.

Going to the museum costs $130. The class had a bake sale that raised only $70.

Step 3: List and consider options.

The class could hold another bake sale to raise more money, or choose a less expensive trip.

Step 4: Consider the advantages and disadvantages of each option.

The bake sale would take a lot of time and work. A less expensive trip might be just as much fun.

Step 5: Choose a solution and implement it, or put it into action.

They decide to visit a nature center, which costs only $60.

Step 6: Create criteria, or guidelines, to decide whether the solution was effective.

The solution was effective if the trip to the nature center was interesting and fun.

Step 7: Evaluate whether or not the solution was effective.

The trip was interesting and fun, so it was effective.

Practice the Skill

Read about a problem that the United States and Canada faced. Then answer the questions about how they cooperated to solve it.

> The governments of Canada and the United States wanted a way for large ships to travel from the Atlantic Ocean to the Great Lakes. In the early 1950s, Canada began building dams and canals on the St. Lawrence River. However, it became too expensive for Canada to complete the work alone. The United States agreed to help but wanted to control the project. Canada did not want the United States to have complete control.
>
> The two governments compromised. Each country agreed to build different parts of the waterway. Each government would then take part of the profits from the project. In June, 1959, Queen Elizabeth of Great Britain and President Eisenhower opened the St. Lawrence Seaway.

1 What problem did Canada and the United States face?

2 What did the two nations do to solve the problem?

3 How would you evaluate whether or not their solution was effective?

Apply the Skill

Identify a disagreement in your community. Gather information and write a paragraph describing advantages and disadvantages of several possible solutions. How could you determine which one would be most effective?

Regions and Trade

VOCABULARY

region
economy
specialization
trade
interdependence

Vocabulary Strategy

interdependence

Find the word **depend** in **interdependence**. People depending on each other leads to interdependence.

READING SKILL

Problem and Solution As you read, note how regions have solved the problem of lack of resources.

PROBLEM   SOLUTION

BENCHMARKS

GEO B   Places and regions
ECON C Markets

GRADE LEVEL INDICATORS

GEO 3   Characteristics of places and regions
GEO 4   Influences on climate
GEO 5   North American regions
ECON 4 Interdependence and specialization

Build on What You Know Imagine a school with different classrooms. Each class is different from the others, but together they make a whole. We can use features to divide North America into sections, too.

What Is a Region?

Main Idea Geographers divide the United States into many types of regions.

To learn more about the world around us, geographers divide it into regions. A **region** is an area that has one or more features in common. Those physical or human features make the region different from other regions.

One way to divide North America into regions is to look at political regions. Canada, the United States, and Mexico are each a political region. Each country is divided into states, provinces, or territories.

Physical characteristics, such as landforms or climate, can also be used to divide North America into regions. These regions cross the borders of the three countries. The western part of the continent has mountain regions. The center of the continent is flatter. There are low mountains and the coastal lowlands in the East.

Deserts These regions are dry and often hot. This desert is in Mexico, near San Carlos.

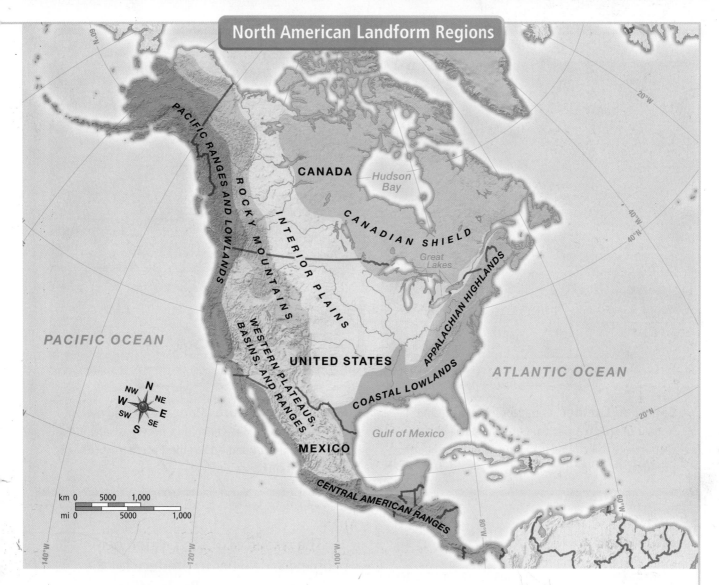

North American Landform Regions

PACIFIC RANGES AND LOWLANDS

ROCKY MOUNTAINS

INTERIOR PLAINS

CANADA

Hudson Bay

CANADIAN SHIELD

Great Lakes

APPALACHIAN HIGHLANDS

WESTERN PLATEAUS, BASINS, AND RANGES

UNITED STATES

COASTAL LOWLANDS

PACIFIC OCEAN

ATLANTIC OCEAN

Gulf of Mexico

MEXICO

CENTRAL AMERICAN RANGES

km 0   5000   1,000
mi 0   5000   1,000

A Varied Continent This map shows the major landform regions of North America.

SKILL **Reading Maps** Which region extends through Canada, the United States, and Mexico?

Characteristics of Regions

Regions can be defined by the activities of people in an area. For example, the cultures of the people who live in North America or the languages they speak can be used to divide the continent into regions. Regions can also be based on economic characteristics, such as the work that people do. The Silver Belt is a region in central Mexico where people mined large amounts of silver in the 1700s. Today silver is still mined in this region, along with many other minerals.

Human characteristics of regions can change over time. The Great Plains region is located in the Interior Lowlands, covering much of the central United States and southern Canada. People once called this region "the Great American Desert" because crops did not grow well there. When farmers learned new farming methods, though, the plains blossomed with crops. Today, much of the wheat grown in the United States and Canada comes from this region.

REVIEW What human characteristics can be used to define regions?

Canadian Lumber

Mexican Agriculture

Canadian Lumber Canada's forests are the largest in North America. Canadians use this resource to specialize in selling wood and wood products to other nations.

Mexican Agriculture Mexicans take advantage of their warm climate and long growing season to specialize in growing and selling a wide variety of crops, such as bananas.

Regions and Resources

Main Idea Each region uses its resources to focus on producing certain goods and services.

Another way to define a region is by its resources. Most regions have plenty of some resources and a scarcity of others. For example, Kentucky's Eastern Coal Field region has a large amount of coal. The region lacks other resources, though, such as fertile soil.

Resources are important for the growth of a region's economy. An **economy** is the system people use to produce goods and services. These goods and services include the things people buy and sell and the work that people do for others. Through the economy, people get the food, clothing, shelter, and other things they need or want.

The resources of each region help people decide what to produce for the economy. The Grand Banks off the east coast of Canada are one of the world's best sources of fish. Canadians in this region catch and sell large amounts of fish. The southern United States has rich soil and a warm climate. Farmers in the South use these resources to grow millions of tons of cotton. Mexicans use their country's rich deposits of petroleum to produce and sell oil around the world.

A region that makes a lot of one product is using specialization. **Specialization** happens when people make the goods they are best able to produce with the resources they have. By specializing, people can usually produce more goods and services at a lower cost and earn more money.

Interdependence and Trade

When regions specialize in certain products, they do not produce all the goods and services that consumers may want. A consumer is someone who buys and uses goods and services.

People and businesses in different regions trade with each other to make more goods available to consumers. **Trade** is the buying and selling of goods. For example, oil and natural gas from the Gulf of Mexico are sold beyond that region. People in the Gulf area use money they make from selling oil and other products to buy goods from other regions.

Trade among regions in North America leads to interdependence. **Interdependence** means depending, or relying, on each other. The economies of Canada, Mexico, and the United States all depend on specializing in certain goods and then trading with each other and with other countries.

Interdependence increases the amount and variety of goods available. For example, the United States sells many machines and machine parts to people in Mexico, giving Mexican consumers more choices about the products they can buy.

REVIEW What problem does trade between regions solve?

Lesson Summary

Regions share physical or human features

Regions specialize

Regions trade

Why It Matters . . .

Specialization and trade increase the amount and variety of goods and services people produce.

Lesson Review

1 VOCABULARY Write a short description of where you live, using **region** and **economy.**

2 READING SKILL If a region doesn't have resources that it needs, what is one **solution** to the **problem?**

3 MAIN IDEA: Geography Why did people's ideas about the Great Plains change?

4 MAIN IDEA: Economics How do the natural resources in a region affect which products people make?

5 PLACES TO KNOW: Where is the Silver Belt region?

6 CRITICAL THINKING: Cause and Effect What effect does specialization have on regions?

WRITING ACTIVITY Write a poem that describes the natural resources, climate, landforms, foods, customs, or other features that make your region of the United States different from the rest of the country.

What Makes CLIMATE?

Why is Ohio warmer than Alaska, but not as warm as Mexico? The climate of Ohio, and of every other place on Earth, is influenced by Earth-Sun relationships, landforms, and vegetation.

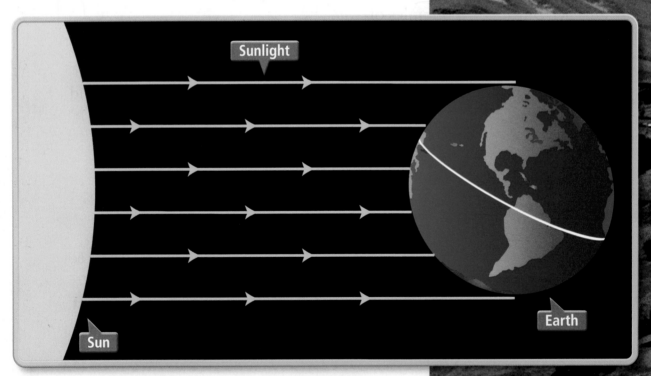

Sunlight

Earth

Sun

Earth-Sun Relationships Regions near the equator get direct sunlight and are warm year-round. Farther north or south, sunlight strikes at an angle, so the same amount of light warms a larger area. In general, the farther a region is from the equator, the cooler its climate.

Mt. Chimborazo, Ecuador: 14°F

Vegetation In the Central American rainforest, vegetation makes the climate humid, or wet. Plants hold moisture in the soil and release moisture into the air.

Landforms At high elevations, air holds less heat. Mountain regions are cooler than regions with low elevations. Even mountains near the equator, such as those in Ecuador, are covered with snow and ice.

Activities

1. **TALK ABOUT IT** Look at the pictures of the mountain and the rainforest. Which region would be easier for people to settle? Explain your answer.

2. **DRAW IT** Draw a picture that shows what the climate is like in your region. Explain why your region has this type of climate.

Visual Summary

1. – 3. Describe and write a brief example for the words below.

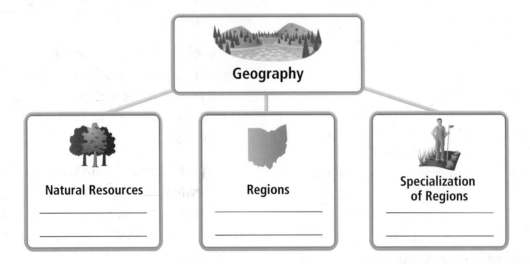

Geography

Natural Resources
_____
_____

Regions
_____
_____

Specialization of Regions
_____
_____

Facts and Main Ideas

✔ **TEST PREP** Answer each question with information from the chapter.

4. **Geography** Why are mineral resources nonrenewable?

5. **Economics** Explain what would be the opportunity cost if you chose to buy a book instead of a shirt.

6. **Citizenship** Name two ways people can conserve resources.

7. **Geography** Name two kinds of regions.

8. **Economics** Why do regions trade?

Vocabulary

✔ **TEST PREP** Choose the correct word from the list below to complete each sentence.

natural resource, p. 6
opportunity cost, p. 10
specialization, p. 18

9. _____ allows people to produce more goods at lower prices.

10. The thing you give up when you buy something is the _____.

11. Coal mined in Ohio is a(n) _____.

Apply Skills

TEST PREP **Citizenship Skill** Read the paragraph below and use what you have learned about solving problems to answer each question.

> Rivers are part of the border between the United States and Mexico. Floods and pollution affect cities in both countries. The International Boundary and Water Commission works in both countries to prevent floods and to build centers for cleaning the water. By cooperating, the countries make sure they both have clean water.

12. What issue might cause a problem between the United States and Mexico?

A. Flood and pollution affect the United States.

B. Floods and pollution affect both countries.

C. Floods and pollution affect neither country.

D. Both are blamed for floods and pollution in other countries.

13. Why is an international organization a good way to solve a problem?

A. It does what is best for the United States.

B. It does what is best for Mexico.

C. It does what is best for both countries.

D. It does what is best for other countries.

Extended Response

TEST PREP Write a short paragraph to answer the question.

14. People in Ohio use renewable, nonrenewable, and flow resources every day. These resources provide food, clothing, building materials, and electricity.

In your **Answer Document,** identify two renewable resources, two nonrenewable resources, and two flow resources, and explain how people in Ohio use them.

Activities

Research Activity Use library or Internet resources to learn about and explain one way that regions of North America cooperate on the environment or trade. Write a report explaining what you learn.

Writing Activity Think about a time when you had to make an economic decision that involved an opportunity cost. Write a personal essay explaining your decision and the opportunity cost.

Technology

Writing Process Tips
Get help with your essay at
www.eduplace.com/kids/hmss

People of North America

Technology

e • **glossary**
e • **word games**
www.eduplace.com/kids/hmss/

Vocabulary Preview

environment

Air, water, land, plants, and animals are part of North America's **environment.** People depend on the environment, but they also change it. **page 27**

erosion

Erosion is the wearing away of land by wind, water, or ice. It can happen very slowly and gradually. It can also happen quickly during a severe storm or flood. **page 28**

Reading Strategy

Monitor and Clarify

Use this strategy to check your understanding of the information in this chapter.

Quick Tip

If you are confused about something in this lesson, reread or read ahead.

ecosystem

The soil, air, and plant and animal communities of a wetland area make up an **ecosystem.** Every part of this ecosystem needs the other parts. **page 29**

economic system

Every nation must find a way to use its resources and produce goods. The **economic system** of the United States leaves these decisions to individuals and businesses. **page 30**

People and the Land

Build on What You Know What makes the area where you live a good place for people? Maybe it is the geography. Geography affects where people live and the work they do.

How Land Affects People

Main Idea The land and its resources affect where and how people live.

Why do cities grow in certain places? Cincinnati, Ohio, grew along the Ohio River, in the southwestern corner of the state. The city's river location was the main reason for its growth. In the early 1800s, people traveled there on boats that could float along the river. Later, steamboats moved people and goods in and out of Cincinnati. Today, more goods travel along the Ohio River than along any other inland waterway in the world.

Railroads and other new forms of transportation helped the city continue to grow. Because of its location in the middle of the United States, Cincinnati has become a center for air, bus, railroad, and river travel.

Cincinnati The Ohio River helped make this city a transportation center.

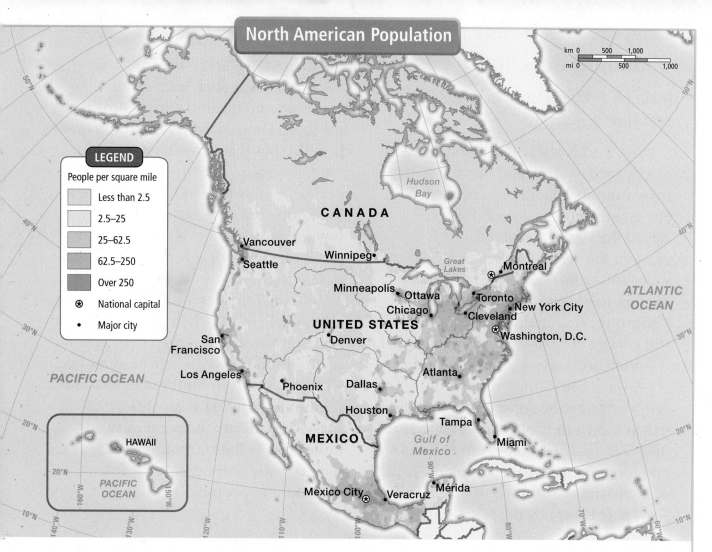

North American Population

LEGEND

People per square mile

- Less than 2.5
- 2.5–25
- 25–62.5
- 62.5–250
- Over 250
- ⊛ National capital
- • Major city

CANADA

Vancouver
Seattle
Winnipeg
Minneapolis
Ottawa
Chicago
Toronto
Cleveland
New York City
Montreal
Washington, D.C.
Denver
San Francisco
Los Angeles
Phoenix
Dallas
Atlanta
Houston
Tampa
Miami

UNITED STATES

MEXICO

Mexico City
Veracruz
Mérida

Hudson Bay
Great Lakes
ATLANTIC OCEAN
PACIFIC OCEAN
Gulf of Mexico

HAWAII
PACIFIC OCEAN

Where People Live This map shows that some areas have many people and other areas have very few. **SKILL** **Reading Maps** Do more people live in the eastern half or in the western half of the United States?

Where People Live

A strong economy is another reason why places grow. People choose to live in places where they can find good jobs. Monterrey, Mexico, for example, has a rapidly growing population because it is a growing center for business.

Monterrey is in the state of Nuevo Leon, which is close to the United States border. Many businesses in this city trade with United States businesses. As more businesses trade, more jobs are created. Those new jobs bring more people to Monterrey, because people settle in places where they can earn a living.

People also settle in places they enjoy. Geography can push people out of their area or pull them into a new location. Cold and gray skies often push people to search for a better climate. Millions of people have been pulled to states such as Florida and Arizona. A warm, sunny climate is part of the environment in these places. The **environment** is the surroundings in which people, plants, and animals live. It is an example of a push or pull factor which causes people to move.

REVIEW What is a solution to the problem of living in a region with few jobs?

Changing the Land

Main Idea Natural forces and human activities both affect the land.

The land is always changing. Natural forces, such as wind and moving water, constantly shape and reshape the land. For example, the Colorado River has carved the Grand Canyon through erosion. **Erosion** is the process by which water and wind wear away the land. Erosion has been shaping the Grand Canyon for several million years, and it is still cutting the canyon deeper and wider.

Wind and water change the land in other ways, too. Strong wind and rushing water can carry bits of soil for miles. Soil that is blown or washed away collects in other places. Over time it can build up and form whole new areas of land. Much of Louisiana was formed from soil that was carried there by the Mississippi River.

Human Activities

Human activities, such as building highways and digging mines, also change the land. These activities can bring many benefits, but they often have costs, too. Big projects can hurt the environment or change how the land may be used in the future. Building highways provides a way for people to travel, but the land cannot be used for other purposes, such as farming.

Mining provides jobs and resources that people want. When people dig mines, however, they often destroy plant life and places where animals live. Chemicals used in mining can also create pollution. **Pollution** is anything that makes the soil, air, or water dirty and unhealthy. Pollution from mines may make nearby rivers unsafe for fish, wildlife, and people.

Human Activities Highways make travel easier, but they take up a lot of land. Erosion from strip mining can carry pollution into rivers and wetlands.

Changes to the Environment

Humans sometimes make small changes to the environment that have big effects. The environment is made up of many ecosystems. An **ecosystem** is a community of plants and animals along with the surrounding soil, air, and water. Each part of an ecosystem affects the health of all the other parts.

Human activity can affect an ecosystem in ways people never expected. Ships have accidentally carried plants and animals from one ecosystem to another. In their new ecosystems, these plants and animals sometimes spread quickly. This happened in the Great Lakes. The zebra mussel, a type of shellfish, came to the Great Lakes attached to ships. Because there are few animals in North America that eat them, the mussels have spread throughout the Great Lakes and many of the country's rivers. Zebra mussels can cause big problems. They form groups that clog pipes, and they eat the food that local fish depend on.

People also affect the environment when they move soil from the bottom of the Great Lakes. They do this to make the lakes deep enough for large ships to navigate. This process can stir up pollution that is in the soil. Today, people are aware that what they do always has an effect on the environment.

REVIEW What is one example of how people can change the environment?

Lesson Summary

Landforms, natural resources, environment, and other features of the land affect where and how people live. People change the environment to meet their needs. When people change the environment, the effects can be surprising.

Why It Matters . . .

People's lives are always connected to the land, so learning about the environment is important.

Lesson Review

1. **VOCABULARY** Write a sample e-mail to the editor of your local newspaper, using **environment** and **pollution.**

2. **READING SKILL** Would you **classify** pollution as a result of natural or human changes? Why?

3. **MAIN IDEA: Geography** How does climate influence where people live?

4. **MAIN IDEA: Economics** Give an example from the lesson of how people change the environment, and explain why they do it.

5. **CRITICAL THINKING: Draw Conclusions** What is the relationship between the geography in your region and the activities people there do for fun?

6. **CRITICAL THINKING: Cause and Effect** What effect did the spread of zebra mussels have on the Great Lakes?

SPEAKING ACTIVITY Find out about a way people have changed the environment near where you live. Prepare a short talk on the change and its positive and negative consequences.

Economies in North America

VOCABULARY

economic system
demand
supply
competition

Vocabulary Strategy

| demand |

When you make a **demand,** you say you want something. In economics, **demand** is the number of consumers who want a product or service.

 READING SKILL

Cause and Effect As you read, take notes about what causes prices to change.

BENCHMARKS
ECON A   Scarcity and resource allocation
ECON C   Markets

GRADE LEVEL INDICATORS
ECON 2   Economic production questions
ECON 5   Supply, demand, and price

Goods and Services Businesses decide what to sell and people decide what to buy at the 2nd Street Public Market in Dayton.

Build on What You Know You know that people need to make decisions about what jobs they want or how to use their money. Countries also make decisions about how to use their resources.

Three Economic Questions

Main Idea There are many different ways a country can use its resources and organize its economy.

Everyone has to make economic decisions. For example, business owners decide what to produce. Workers decide what to buy with the money they earn.

Countries have to make economic decisions too. No country has enough natural resources to produce everything its people want. To solve this problem, each country has an economic system. An **economic system** is a set of ideas that guides how a country will use its resources and produce its goods. Every economic system offers ways to answer three basic questions.

- What goods will be produced?
- How will those goods be produced?
- Who will receive or buy the goods?

Making Cars The owners of this car factory in Anna, Ohio, make the decisions about what and how many goods to produce.

The United States Economic System

The United States has a wide variety of workers and businesses. Some provide services, and others produce goods. The products made in the United States range from applesauce and cars to computers and cookware. The services people provide include teaching, providing medical care, and preparing food.

In the economic system of the United States, individuals and businesses make the decisions that answer the three economic questions. People and businesses are free to decide what to produce. To make this decision, businesses try to find out what buyers want.

Individuals in the United States also decide how to produce goods and services. The producer can choose which resources to use to make the goods. Producers often choose resources that are least expensive or easiest to find. A business may decide to produce quickly, or at low cost, or with great care. Businesses ask questions such as how much of a product they think people will buy.

The third economic question asks who will use or buy the goods that are produced. A company that produces warm boots will find most of its customers in regions that have cold climates, and not in warmer states such as New Mexico.

REVIEW What are the three basic economic questions?

Supply, Demand, and Price

Main Idea Supply and demand affect prices in the United States economic system.

Consumers in the United States help decide what will be produced. If people buy a lot of a product or service, more companies will make it. However, if consumers do not buy a certain good or service, the producer will need to provide something else or go out of business.

Consumers also affect the price that producers charge for their goods. For example, suppose a company produces canned tomato soup and canned onion soup. The company tries to sell each for $1.00 a can.

Tomato soup turns out to be popular. The cans of tomato soup sell quickly because demand for them is high. **Demand** is the amount of something that people want to buy for a certain price. When demand for a product is high, its price usually goes up. The company will probably produce more tomato soup and may raise the price.

Not many people buy the onion soup, however. The company has too large a supply of onion soup. **Supply** is the amount of something that producers want to make at a certain price. When supply is high, prices generally fall. In this case, the company will probably make less onion soup and may lower the price.

Free Market Prices are affected by how much of a good there is and by how many people want the good.

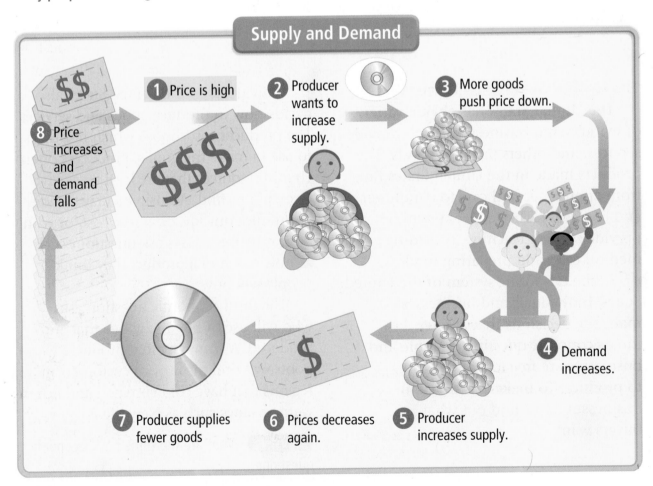

Supply and Demand

1. Price is high
2. Producer wants to increase supply.
3. More goods push price down.
4. Demand increases.
5. Producer increases supply.
6. Prices decreases again.
7. Producer supplies fewer goods
8. Price increases and demand falls

Competition

Competition influences prices as well. **Competition** occurs when businesses that sell similar goods and services try to attract the most consumers and make the most money. When there is a lot of competition, consumers have many choices of where to buy what they need and want. One way companies win customers is to keep prices low and quality high.

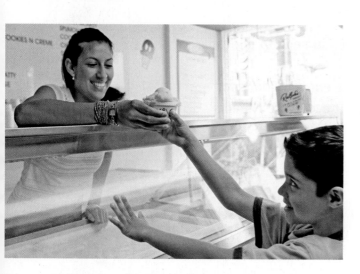

Competing for Business Providing good customer service is one way sellers compete with one another.

Sometimes goods become scarce. When that happens, competition can occur among consumers. Consumers compete when there is not enough of a product for every consumer who wants it. There are many different ways to allocate, or divide up, scarce goods. One way is by price. For example, if there is not enough soup for all the people who wanted it, some consumers might be willing to pay more to get it.

REVIEW What can companies do to solve the problem of low demand?

Lesson Summary

- Societies use different economic systems to answer the three basic economic questions.
- In the United States economic system, supply and demand help determine prices and amounts of goods produced.
- Competition occurs among producers and among consumers.

Why It Matters . . .

The United States economic system has made the country a world economic leader.

Lesson Review

1 **VOCABULARY** Write a description of the United States **economic system.**

2 **READING SKILL** What **effect** does competition among producers have on prices?

3 **MAIN IDEA: Economics** What is the purpose of an economic system?

4 **MAIN IDEA: Economics** When might consumers compete to buy a product or service?

5 **CRITICAL THINKING: Synthesize** Suppose you have an idea for a new product. Why would it be a good idea to do research on how many people might want to buy your product?

WRITING ACTIVITY In the United States, it is illegal for only one company to make and sell certain products. For example, one company is not allowed to produce all the steel in the country. Write a paragraph that explains how competition helps consumers.

Sharing Resources

You and seven friends have made a pizza. You slice it into eight pieces, and then two more friends arrive. Now you have a **scarcity** of pizza, because you don't have as much as people would like. You need to allocate, or divide up, the pizza that you have.

Countries have a similar problem. They do not have enough goods for everyone to have as much as they would like. Different economic systems use different methods to allocate scarce goods and services. You could choose one or more of these methods to divide your pizza.

Allocation Methods

Price

The person who is willing to pay the most for each slice of pizza is the one who gets it. The United States economic system uses price to allocate most resources.

Command

An adult, or someone in charge, could decide who gets the pizza. In countries with command economies, the government makes many decisions about who gets resources.

First-come, first-served

The eight people who were there first get the eight slices. This method of allocating resources isn't useful for an entire country, but it can work for a specific event, such as a concert with free tickets or items at a store.

Sharing Equally

You might cut your slices into more pieces, so that each person gets the same amount of pizza. Sometimes a government gives everyone the same benefit, such as a free education.

Rationing

To ration means to limit the amount of pizza each person can have. If each person takes only half a slice, there will be enough for everyone. During times of great shortages, governments may ration certain goods.

Lottery

You and your friends could pick numbers out of a hat to decide who gets the slices of pizza. A community might use this method to distribute a small number of items, such as permits to use parking spaces.

Activities

1. **TALK ABOUT IT** Which method would you choose to divide the eight slices? Explain why you chose this method.

2. **CHART IT** Create a chart comparing the methods of allocating pizza. For each method, show how many people get pizza, how much pizza each person gets, and whether or not the method seems fair to you.

Skillbuilder

Make a Decision

You have learned about the steps of making a decision to solve a problem. When people use the decision-making process, they have to think about the consequences of their choices. A **consequence** is a result of a decision or an action. It can be positive or negative. People also need to come up with criteria to evaluate whether their decision was effective. **Criteria** are guidelines.

▶ **VOCABULARY**

consequence

criteria

Learn the Skill

Step 1: Identify and describe the decision to be made.

Step 2: Gather information.

Step 3: Think of and list your options.

Step 4: Consider the positive or negative consequences of each option.

Step 5: Choose an option.

Step 6: Develop criteria for judging whether the decision was effective. Based on the information you gathered, what do you expect the outcome to be?

Step 7: Use your criteria to evaluate whether the decision was effective. If it wasn't, you may have needed to gather more information.

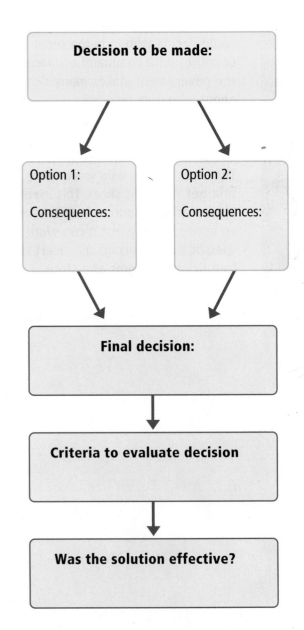

Decision to be made:

Option 1:

Consequences:

Option 2:

Consequences:

Final decision:

Criteria to evaluate decision

Was the solution effective?

Practice the Skill

Think about the economic choices people make when deciding what to produce, sell, or buy. Consider each person described below. Decide what each one should do. Use a chart like the one on page 36 as you think about the positive and negative consequences of each person's options. Also think about what criteria they might use to evaluate whether their decisions are effective.

1. Producer making a product for which there is a high demand
2. Consumer who has many choices about where to buy a product or service
3. Consumer who wants a scarce good

Apply the Skill

Choose a current issue about which people must make a decision. You might choose a topic about business, the environment, an upcoming election, or some other important issue. Fill out a chart like the one on page 36. Then write a paragraph explaining what you think the right decision is, and what criteria you would use to evaluate it.

Visual Summary

1. – 3. Write a description of how each of the three economic questions is answered in the United States.

What goods will be produced?

_____
_____
_____
_____

How will those goods be produced?

_____
_____
_____
_____

Who will receive or buy the goods?

_____
_____
_____
_____

Facts and Main Ideas

✓ **TEST PREP** Answer each question with information from the chapter.

4. **History** In what way did Cincinnati's location on the Ohio River help it grow economically and in population?

5. **Geography** Describe the natural forces that formed much of Louisiana's land.

6. **Geography** What consequences could result from moving soil at the bottom of the Great Lakes to make room for larger ships?

7. **Economics** What usually happens when there is too much of one type of item for sale?

8. **Economics** What is one way companies compete to win customers?

Vocabulary

✓ **TEST PREP** Choose the correct word from the list below to complete each sentence.

environment, p. 27
economic system, p. 30
competition, p. 33

9. In the _____ of the United States, individuals and businesses decide what to produce.

10. The warm climate of Florida is part of its _____.

11. Consumers often have more choices when businesses are in _____ with each other.

✓ **TEST PREP** **Citizenship Skill** Use the information below and what you have learned about making decisions to answer each question.

> The Brown family has lived in Frosty all their lives. They have many friends and relatives in the town. However, there are few jobs in Frosty, and Mr. and Mrs. Brown are having a hard time finding work. The weather in Frosty is often cold, too. The Browns are thinking about moving to California.

12. What is one piece of information the Browns would need to decide whether to move?

   A. whether there are more jobs in California
   B. the price of coats in California
   C. how long the trip would take
   D. the average temperature in California

13. What would be a negative consequence of moving?

   A. The weather would be warmer.
   B. They would make new friends.
   C. California is west of Frosty.
   D. They would miss their friends and family.

✓ **TEST PREP** Write a short paragraph to answer each question.

14. In your **Answer Document,** explain how competition, supply, and demand affect the cost of items.

15. Suppose your town has only one grocery store. People in the town feel they are paying too much for groceries, and that the groceries are not very good. Then a second grocery store opens.

   In your **Answer Document,** explain what effect the second grocery store might have on prices and quality at the first store.

Activities

Art Activity Make a diagram showing what happens to the price of a good if there is competition among producers, and what happens if there is competition among consumers.

Writing Activity Use library or Internet resources to find out ways Ohioans have affected the environment. Use your research to write a report that describes this change.

Technology
Writing Process Tips
Get help with your essay at
www.eduplace.com/kids/hmss/

Review and Test Prep

Vocabulary and Main Ideas

✔ TEST PREP Write a sentence to answer each question.

1. Why do people need **natural resources?**

2. In what way does **specialization** affect **trade?**

3. Explain how **interdependence** can happen between two different regions.

4. How can **pollution** harm the **environment?**

5. If one part of an **ecosystem** becomes polluted, what may happen to the other parts?

6. Why might **supply** of a product rise if **demand** is high and prices are high?

Critical Thinking

✔ TEST PREP Write a short paragraph to answer each question.

7. **Infer** Silicon Valley and the Corn Belt are names for regions in the United States. What is a region that Ohio is part of?

8. **Draw Conclusions** What would happen to the price of milk if there were a shortage of milk? Write a short paragraph explaining your conclusion.

Unit Activity

Play a Place Card Game

- Choose a region in the United States to research.

- Write one fact card about the region for each of the following topics: resources; physical and human characteristics; ways people and the land affect each other; and economy.

- Mix up the cards. With a group of four, take turns picking a card from the pile.

- The first person to pick two cards about the same place wins.

At the Library

You may find these books at your library.

United States of America
by Christine and David Petersen
This book gives an overview of United States geography, history, people, and culture.

Places in Time: A New Atlas of American History
by E. Leacock and S. Buckley
The authors put a geographical spin on United States history.

Apply Skills

✔️ **TEST PREP** Read the paragraph below. Then use what you have learned about solving problems to answer each question.

> Mr. Dawson's fifth-grade class want to go on a field trip in Cleveland. They all agreed about the importance of seeing something outside of school, but they disagree about where they will spend their time and money. Some students want to visit the Cleveland Museum of Art. Others think going to the Nature Center at Shaker Lakes would be more valuable. Still others want to see a play.

9. What is the first step the class should take to solve the problem?

   A. Try to convince each other that one field trip is the best.
   B. Identify the conflict.
   C. Ask the principal to decide.
   D. Forget about going on a field trip.

10. In your **Answer Document,** list the remaining steps in the problem-solving process and explain what the class could do at each step.

✔️ **TEST PREP** Answer each question below.

11. Smith Company has made special running shoes for many years. Then Feet Incorporated begins to make running shoes that cost less than the shoes Smith Company makes. What can Smith Company do to compete?

    A. raise prices and lower quality
    B. lower prices and quality
    C. raise prices and quality
    D. lower prices and raise quality

12. Regions can be defined in many ways, such as by physical or human characteristics. What is one human characteristic that can be used to define a region?

    A. economy
    B. mountains
    C. climate
    D. natural resources

13. Coal is a valuable natural resource that people use to make heat and electricity. Eastern Ohio has many coal mines.

    In your **Answer Document,** explain possible positive and negative consequences of mining for coal.

UNIT 2

Regions of the United States

The Big Idea

What are the physical and human features of the place where you live?

 Unit 2 Benchmarks

As you study this unit, you will cover these Ohio Social Studies benchmarks:

History A Construct time lines to demonstrate an understanding of units of time and chronological order.

Geography A Use map elements or coordinates to locate physical and human features of North America.

Geography B Identify the physical and human characteristics of places and regions in North America.

Skills and Methods C Communicate social studies information using graphs or tables.

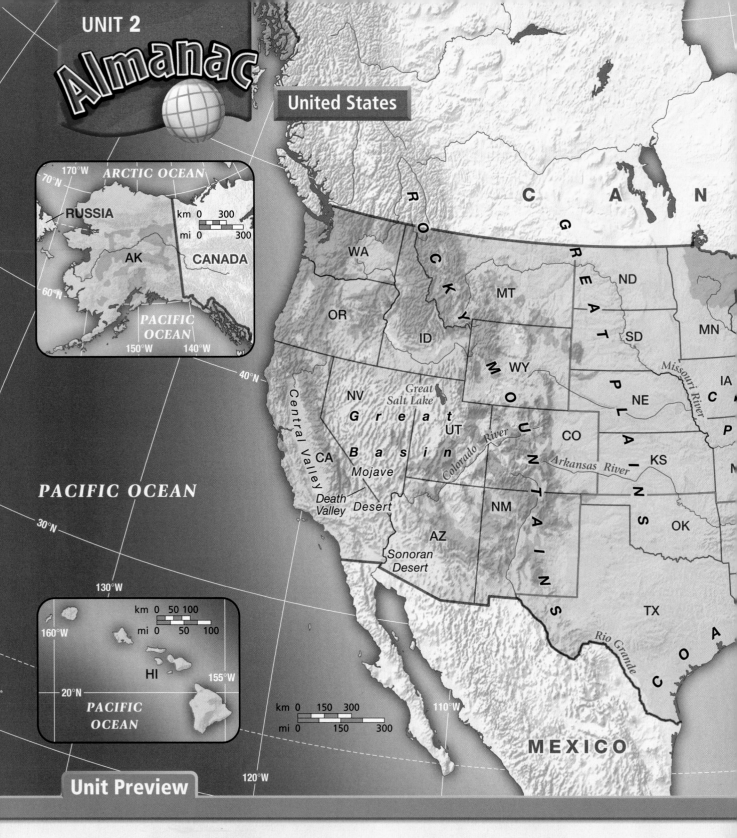

United States

ARCTIC OCEAN

70°N
170°W

RUSSIA

km 0   300
mi 0   300

AK

CANADA

60°N

150°W   140°W

PACIFIC
OCEAN

PACIFIC OCEAN

40°N

30°N

130°W

160°W

km 0   50 100
mi 0   50   100

HI

20°N

155°W

PACIFIC
OCEAN

120°W

WA

OR

ID

MT

WY

NV

Great
Salt Lake

UT

Great
Basin

Mojave

Death
Valley   Desert

CA

Central Valley

AZ

Sonoran
Desert

NM

Colorado River

CO

Arkansas River

ND

SD

NE

Missouri River

MN

IA

KS

OK

TX

Rio Grande

MEXICO

km 0   150 300
mi 0   150   300

110°W

R O C K Y   M O U N T A I N S

G R E A T   P L A I N S

C A N

C O A

Unit Preview

Mineral Resources
Coal is mined in the East
Chapter 3, page 52

Dams
Many southerners get their electricity from dams
Chapter 3, page 66

Farmland
Much of the country's farmland is in the Midwest
Chapter 4, page 85

Map labels:

A D A

L. Superior

WI

L. Michigan

MI

L. Huron

L. Ontario

L. Erie

ME

VT

NH

MA

NY

RI

CT

PA

NJ

MD DE

OH

WV

VA

NTRAL

IL

IN

AINS

Ohio River

KY

TN

NC

APPALACHIAN MOUNTAINS

SC

A I N

ATLANTIC
OCEAN

MS

AL

GA

P

L

T

A L

LA

FL

Mississippi River

Gulf of Mexico

50°N

60°W

40°N

30°N

70°W

80°W

90°W

Compass: N NE E SE S SW W NW

Death Valley

This desert is in the West **Chapter 4, page 94**

LEGEND
— National border
— State border
— Regional border
▢ Evergreen forest
▢ Mixed forest
▢ Grassland
▢ Arid
▢ Tundra

Connect to

The Nation

U.S. Land Area

The area of the East is 174,045 square miles.

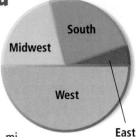

South
Midwest
West
East

East	174,045	sq. mi
West	1,752,951	sq. mi
Midwest	751,426	sq. mi
South	859,016	sq. mi

U.S. Population

The population of the East is 61,792,086 people.

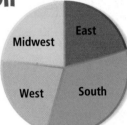

East
Midwest
West
South

East	61,792,068 people
South	102,033,019 people
West	69,355,643 people
Midwest	66,217,736 people

Compare the East with other regions. The East has a smaller land area, but about the same population. What might this mean for people and where they live in the East?

CURRENT EVENTS

WEEKLY (WR) READER

Current events on the web!

Read social studies articles about current events at:
www.eduplace.com/kids/hmss/

Chapter 3

The East and South

Vocabulary Preview

Technology

e • **glossary**
e • **word games**
www.eduplace.com/kids/hmss/

coast

Many people enjoy beaches along the **coast.** The United States has a long east coast, a long west coast, and a southern coast along the Gulf of Mexico. **page 48**

human resources

Human resources are a very important part of any company. Workers provide needed skills that help the company produce goods and services. **page 56**

Reading Strategy

Summarize As you read, use the summarize strategy to focus on important ideas.

Review the main ideas to get started. Then look for important details that support the main idea.

producer

A **producer** uses workers, resources, and equipment to make products. For example, a farmer uses seeds, soil, and tractors to raise corn. **page 67**

consumer

A **consumer** buys and uses products made by a producer. If the product is peanut butter, the consumer will probably eat it! **page 67**

Land of the East

VOCABULARY

coast
coastal plain
cape
bay

Vocabulary Strategy

coastal plain

A **coast** is land next to an ocean. A **coastal plain** is a plain next to an ocean.

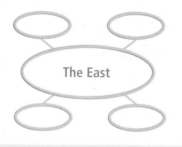

READING SKILL

Main Idea and Details
List details about the land and water of the East.

The East

BENCHMARKS
GEO B   Places and regions

GRADE LEVEL INDICATORS
GEO 2   Use maps to identify locations
GEO 3   Characteristics of places and regions

Build on What You Know When a road cuts through a mountain, it reveals many layers of rock. Scientists can tell the age of mountains by looking at these layers. The Appalachian Mountains are hundreds of millions of years old.

Land and Water of the East

Main Idea The East has many landforms and bodies of water.

The region between the Atlantic Ocean and the Great Lakes is known as the East. Canada borders the region to the north. Our nation's capital, Washington, D.C., is at the southern tip. The Appalachian Mountains run through this region.

The East includes six states in New England and five Mid-Atlantic states. The nation's largest city, New York, is in the Mid-Atlantic region.

Nine states in the East are on the coast. A **coast** is land that borders an ocean. Coastal areas form a landform region called the coastal plain. A **coastal plain** is flat, level land along a coast.

Western New York The Genesee River flows between steep cliffs and thick forests. The cliffs show layers of rock.

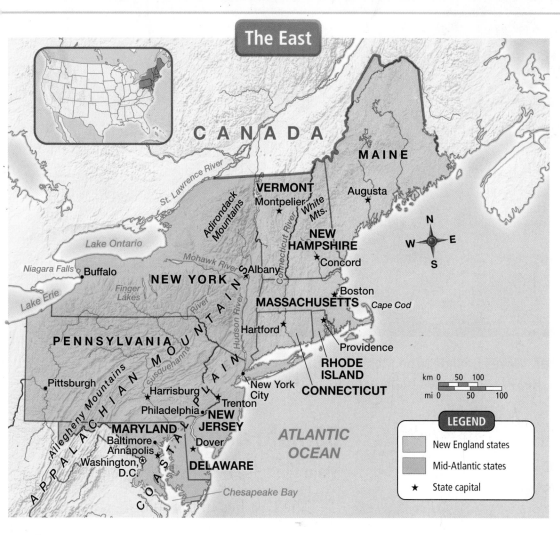

The East

C A N A D A

MAINE

VERMONT
Montpelier ★
Augusta ★

Adirondack Mountains

St. Lawrence River

NEW HAMPSHIRE
Concord ★

White Mts.

Lake Ontario

Niagara Falls • Buffalo

NEW YORK

Albany ★

Mohawk River

Connecticut River

Boston •

MASSACHUSETTS
Cape Cod

Finger Lakes

Lake Erie

Hartford ★

Providence •

PENNSYLVANIA

Hudson River

RHODE ISLAND

CONNECTICUT

Pittsburgh •

Susquehanna River

Harrisburg ★

New York City

Allegheny Mountains

APPALACHIAN MOUNTAIN

Philadelphia •

Trenton ★

NEW JERSEY

ATLANTIC OCEAN

MARYLAND

Baltimore •
Annapolis ★

Dover ★

Washington, D.C. ⊛

COASTAL PLAIN

DELAWARE

Chesapeake Bay

N
W E
S

km 0   50   100
mi 0   50   100

LEGEND

New England states

Mid-Atlantic states

★ State capital

The East Two main landform regions are the Appalachian Mountains and the coastal plain.

SKILL **Reading Maps** Find three states in the East through which the Appalachian Mountains pass.

Physical Features of the East

The Appalachian Mountains were formed by the movement of the earth. Over millions of years, two moving continents came together. The land between them slowly buckled and rose up. These huge piles of rocks became the Appalachians.

Wind, weather, and the water flowing in rivers slowly wore the Appalachians down. Glaciers also changed the mountains' shape. They carved out valleys or leveled the land with the rocks and dirt they left behind.

East of the Appalachians is the coastal plain. In northern New England, this plain lies mostly underwater.

It is wider from Massachusetts to Florida. Here, the plain has major cities, farms, and factories. Rock and sand left from glaciers formed islands with sandy beaches, such as Long Island. They also formed capes, such as Cape Cod. A **cape** is a point of land that sticks out into the water.

Many of the landforms in the East can be found in eastern Canada as well. The Appalachians extend north into Canadian regions such as Quebec and New Brunswick. Like parts of New England, these are rocky areas with many capes and islands.

REVIEW What effects have glaciers had on the East?

Winter Nor'easter Waves pounded the Massachusetts coast in this March 2001 storm. Heavy snow forced many schools to close.

Bodies of Water

The East is a land of lakes, rivers, and the ocean. Some rivers, such as the St. Lawrence River, are part of state or national borders. As rivers flow down to the plain, sudden changes in elevation create waterfalls. People built dams to use the water's force to power machines in mills and factories. Dams and water-powered mills led to the growth of other human features, such as major cities, highways, and railroads.

People built settlements near the best harbors along the Atlantic coast. Ships carrying people and goods from other continents arrived in the harbors and bays. A **bay** is a body of water partly surrounded by land but open to the sea. The Chesapeake Bay, which reaches into Maryland, is important for shipping. It also supports thousands of plants and animals.

Climate and Its Effects

Main Idea The East has a temperate climate.

The East lies in the middle latitudes, about halfway between the North Pole and the equator. This location gives it four seasons and a temperate climate. Temperate means without extremes, such as the very cold weather in the Arctic or the very hot weather near the equator. Cool breezes blow from the Atlantic Ocean on hot days, and warm breezes blow on cold days. Winters in the East are cold and snowy, though, and summers are warm and humid.

The East sometimes has storms called "nor'easters." These storms bring strong winds from the northeast. Nor'easters also bring high ocean waves and heavy snow or rain. People need warm clothing and snow shovels to help them cope with winter conditions.

Plants and Animals

Climate affects the plants and animals that can live in a region. In the East, trees such as maple, birch, hickory, and oak drop their leaves before winter. This helps them survive the lack of water in the frozen soil.

Eastern animals must cope with both cold winters and changing food supplies. Squirrels bury nuts during the warmer months. In the winter, when food is hard to find, they can dig up the nuts and eat them. Other animals, such as black bears, hibernate during the winter. They use leaves and twigs to make a den in a cave or other shelter. Then they sleep for up to 100 days. Raccoons, skunks, and chipmunks also hibernate during the winter.

REVIEW What problem do people in the East solve by wearing warm clothing?

Lesson Summary

- The landforms of the East include mountains and plains.

- Rivers, harbors, and bays are important for development.

- The climate of the East is temperate, but winters are cold and snowy.

Why It Matters ...

Water power, travel routes, and a temperate climate helped the East develop.

Black Bear Bears sleep through the coldest part of eastern winters.

Lesson Review

1 VOCABULARY Write a paragraph about the east **coast.** Include **capes** and **bays** in your paragraph.

2 READING SKILL List two **details** that support this **main idea:** People learned to use bodies of water in the East.

3 MAIN IDEA: Geography Describe two landforms and two waterways that a visitor to the East might see.

4 MAIN IDEA: Culture Explain one effect of the climate on people's lives in the East.

5 CRITICAL THINKING: Fact and Opinion Write one fact about New England. Then write an opinion based on that fact.

MAP ACTIVITY Use an atlas to research the geography of the eastern United States and eastern Canada. Draw a map of the areas, showing what landforms they share.

Resources of the East

VOCABULARY

market economy
profit
human resources
capital resources

Vocabulary Strategy

| market economy |

A **market** is a place where you can choose what to buy. A **market economy** lets people choose what they buy, make, and sell.

READING SKILL

Classify Use a chart to list some natural resources of the East.

Natural resources

BENCHMARKS

ECON B Production, distribution, and consumption
ECON C Markets.

GRADE LEVEL INDICATORS

GEO 3 Characteristics of places and regions
ECON 3 Effects on productive resources
ECON 4 Interdependence and specialization

Build on What You Know Suppose you want to sell lemonade in your neighborhood. What price will you charge? Every business owner must choose what to sell, where to sell it, and for how much.

Natural Resources

Main Idea The natural resources of the East include forests, soil, and minerals.

The East has less of some natural resources than other regions. However, the East has rivers, forests, farmland, fish, and the ocean. People specialize in using these resources to make goods. People in other regions and countries buy these goods, making them interdependent with the East.

The Appalachian Mountains contain coal. Workers mine coal in Pennsylvania. Power plants burn it to make electricity.

Coal Mine Workers take coal from mine shafts dug deep into the ground.

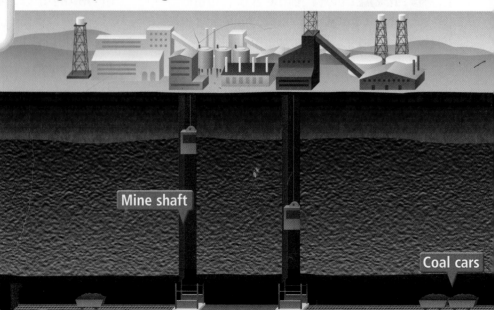

Mine shaft

Coal cars

Natural Resources of the East

Resource	Uses
Granite	Stones for building
Marble	Monuments, parts of buildings
Coal	Fuel to make electricity, steel, iron, glass, stone, paper
Forests/Wood	Building materials, furniture, paper, fuel, maple syrup
Soil	Fruits, vegetables, grain, dairy cows
Fish	Food, fertilizer
Rivers/Ocean	Moving goods or people, source of water and power, fish

SKILL **Reading Charts** Which resources are used for fuel or power?

Apple Picking in New York In the fall, Easterners can pick their own apples.

Environment Affects Human Activity

The resources in the East, as in all regions, affect the kinds of work people do and the homes they live in. Forests provide wood for homes, paper, furniture, and fuel. Wood can also be used to make chemicals for many other products, including plastics and textiles.

Do you like pancakes with syrup for breakfast? Maple syrup comes from sugar maple trees. Vermont produces more maple syrup than any other state.

The soil and climate of the East allow farmers to use their land in different ways. Blueberries grow well in the soil of Maine and New Hampshire. The soil of the Aroostook Valley in Maine is perfect for potatoes.

Massachusetts and New Jersey have sandy marshes where farmers grow cranberries. The warm, rainy summers in New York and Vermont make grasses grow well. These conditions are good for dairy cows, which eat the grasses. Eastern farmers also grow vegetables such as tomatoes, corn, and beans. Some farmers raise fruit trees, including apple and peach trees.

The Atlantic Ocean is an important resource for the East. From Maine to Maryland, as well as in eastern Canada, people catch lobsters, sardines, flounder, and bass. Maryland and Delaware produce many blue crabs.

REVIEW Why is the farmland of the East an important natural resource?

Economy of the East

Main Idea In a market economy, people decide what to make, buy, and sell.

A nation's economy is the system by which it uses resources to meet its needs and wants. The United States has a market economy. In a **market economy,** people are free to decide how to answer the three economic questions of what to make, how to make it, and for whom to make it.

A market economy is different from a command economy. In a command economy, the government decides what to make, who will make it, and who will get it. The government also sets the prices for goods.

Business owners keep their profits in a market economy. **Profit** is the money left over after a business pays its expenses. Some businesses make profits by selling natural resources. Others make goods from resources. Then they sell the goods. Paper, maple syrup, and furniture are goods.

Some businesses sell services. A service is any kind of work that one person does for another person as a job. Lawyers, plumbers, and engineers all provide services. In recent years, more and more people have worked in service businesses. In a competitive market, businesses often try to improve their goods and services to attract more customers.

Market Economy In a market economy, people have many choices.

Trading Resources

Businesses use trade to get the resources they want. Trade begins when one person has what another wants. These people exchange resources or money for goods or services. Through this interdependence, both people get what they want.

Moving goods is important for interdependence and trade. Imagine that a chemical factory in Delaware needs to buy raw materials from an owner in another region. The factory must pay a trucking company to bring the materials to the factory. Many businesses settle near big cities because the roads, waterways, and airports in these cities make trade easier.

Factories in the East specialize in different kinds of goods. For example, New Jersey businesses make chemicals, medicines, machinery, and clothing. In Connecticut, factory workers make sewing machines, jet engines, and clocks. By specializing in one product, these factories can produce more of that product.

Many eastern businesses provide services. For example, banks offer a safe place for people to keep their money. Banks also lend money to people. Many banks started in eastern cities. In banks, people can work as bank tellers, loan officers, and even computer programmers.

REVIEW How is making goods different from performing services?

Service Businesses in the East

Banking	Insurance
Communication	Legal services
Education	Recreation
Engineering	Repairs
Health care	Restaurants
Hotels	Tourism

Services Restaurants perform a service. The chart shows other service businesses that provide jobs in the East.

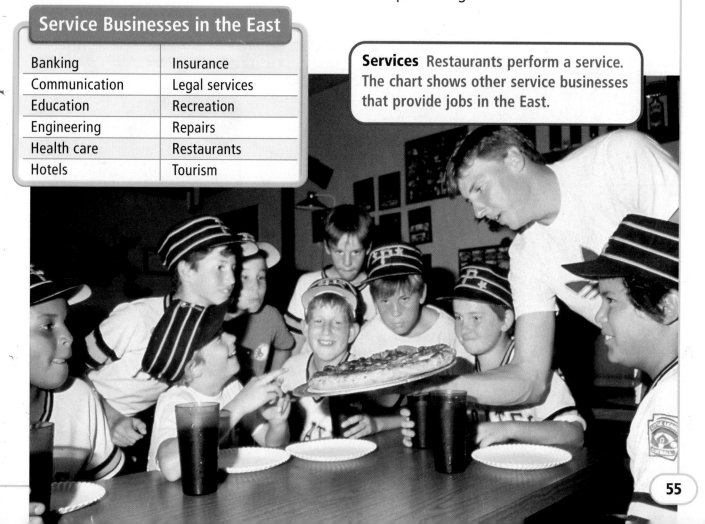

Elements of Business

Main Idea In a system of private ownership, individuals own the factors of production.

A business needs equipment, workers, and often some raw materials. These are productive resources. Productive resources are the people and materials needed to make goods or provide services. The four productive resources are natural and human resources, capital goods, and entrepreneurship (ahn truh pruh NUHR ship).

Productive Resources Skilled workers are needed to make sap into maple syrup.

SKILL **Reading Visuals** What capital goods do you see in the pictures below?

Human resources are the services, knowledge, skills, education, and intelligence that workers provide. **Capital resources,** also called capital goods, are the tools, machines, buildings, and other equipment that a business uses. Entrepreneurs are people who are willing to take the risk of starting a new business.

Businesses look for better ways to use resources. Workers with the right education and skills, who can work quickly and do a good job, make a business more productive. Capital goods, such as machines that do things more quickly, can also help businesses make more of a good or service.

Maple Syrup Production

Natural and capital resources + Human resource = Product

Entrepreneurs and Ownership

Entrepreneurs use productive resources to start new businesses. They take risks by investing their time and money in their businesses. However, people might not want to buy their goods or services. Then, instead of making a profit, the entrepreneurs could lose money. Entrepreneurs must plan carefully and work hard to have the best chance of earning a profit.

Entrepreneurs own their own businesses. Private ownership is an important part of a market economy. Private ownership means that individual people, not the government, own the productive resources. Individuals also make their own business decisions, hoping to earn a profit.

REVIEW What might an entrepreneur's solution to the risk of losing money be?

Entrepreneurship A person who opens a new store is an entrepreneur.

Lesson Summary

- People use the natural resources of the East to make products and trade with businesses in other areas.

- Businesses make profits by selling resources, goods, and services.

- Entrepreneurship and resources—natural, human, and capital—are necessary in any business.

Why It Matters ...

A market economy can give people more freedom to choose how they work and live.

Lesson Review

1 **VOCABULARY** Explain how **human resources** and **capital resoures** are used to make goods.

2 **READING SKILL** List two things that can be **classified** as human resources and two that can be classified as capital resources.

3 **MAIN IDEA: Geography** What are two natural resources of the East, and how are they used?

4 **MAIN IDEA: Economics** In what way is a market economy different from a command economy?

5 **CRITICAL THINKING: Analyze** Why might someone start a business in or near a city?

HANDS ON **INTERVIEW ACTIVITY** Interview several adults who work in different jobs. Ask each person if his or her job involves making a product or providing a service. Make a chart of these products and services.

Graph and Chart Skills

Skillbuilder

Make a Time Line

▶ **VOCABULARY**
decade
century

Placing dates on a time line can help you organize and understand what you read. You can also use time lines to identify cause and effect relationships. The time line below shows the years in which early businesses of the East started. Time lines are usually divided by years, decades, or centuries. A **decade** is a period of 10 years. A **century** is a period of 100 years.

Learn the Skill

Step 1: Some time lines have titles. If there is a title, read it to find out the subject of the time line.

Step 2: Look at the beginning date and the ending date to find out how much time the time line covers.

Step 3: Look at the events described in the time line. Read the dates on the time line to find out when the events happened. Figure out how the events are related to each other.

Early Businesses of the East

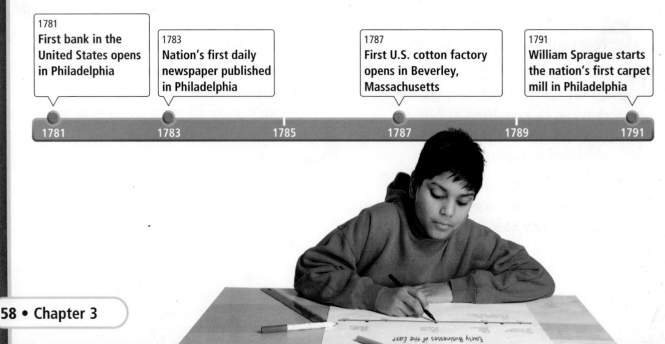

1781
First bank in the United States opens in Philadelphia

1783
Nation's first daily newspaper published in Philadelphia

1787
First U.S. cotton factory opens in Beverley, Massachusetts

1791
William Sprague starts the nation's first carpet mill in Philadelphia

1781   1783   1785   1787   1789   1791

Practice the Skill

Use the time line on page 58 to answer the questions.

1 What does the title tell you about the events in the time line?

2 How many years does the time line cover?

3 Where did the first carpet mill start, and when?

4 When did the first daily newspaper in the United States begin publication?

5 When was the first bank in the United States established?

Apply the Skill

Read the paragraph below. List the events and their dates in the order in which they happened. Then use your list to create a time line.

The *Pennsylvania Evening Post*, printed in 1783, was the nation's first daily newspaper, but there was a long history of newspapers before it. The first newspaper in the United States was published in 1690. The *Boston News-Letter* began in 1704. In 1721, James Franklin published the *New England Courant*. Eight years later, his brother, Benjamin Franklin, started the *Pennsylvania Gazette* in Philadelphia.

Land of the South

VOCABULARY

peninsula
interior
delta
adapt

Vocabulary Strategy

interior

Interior is a synonym for inland. Both words describe a place that is away from a coast.

READING SKILL
Compare and Contrast
Use a chart to compare and contrast the Upper South and the Lower South.

Upper South   Lower South

GRADE LEVEL INDICATORS
GEO 2   Use maps to identify locations
GEO 3   Characteristics of places and regions
GEO 8   Effects of physical environments

Build on What You Know What does the land look like where you live? Does it have many different landforms? The South has a little bit of everything, from rugged mountains to low, swampy wetlands.

Physical Features of the South

Main Idea The South has many different landforms and waterways, including mountains, plains, rivers, and wetlands.

Fourteen states make up the South. This region can be divided into two smaller regions—the Upper South and the Lower South.

The South has many kinds of landforms, or physical features. For example, the Upper South has plateaus, hills, and valleys. Plateaus are high, flat areas. They can be found in Arkansas, Virginia, and West Virginia. Kentucky, Virginia, and Tennessee have rolling hills and rich river valleys.

Both the Upper South and the Lower South have low coastal plains and wetlands. Parts of Florida, Alabama, Mississippi, and Louisiana are at sea level. These lowland states have beaches, swamps, and marshes. Many rivers also flow through the South.

Wetlands in the South support wildlife, including alligators.

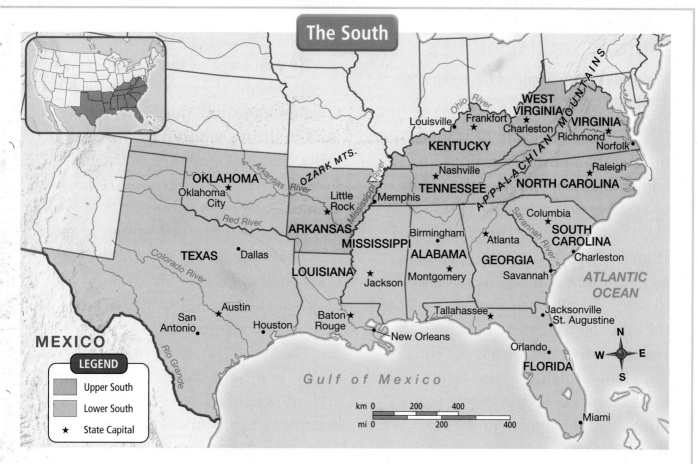

The South

The South Waterways are a central physical feature of this region.

SKILL **Reading Maps** What river forms the border between Texas and Mexico?

Coastal Plains and Highlands

The South's coastline is formed by the Gulf and Atlantic coastal plains. These coastal plains are lowlands. The Gulf coastal plain stretches from the mouth of the Rio Grande in Texas to the tip of the Florida peninsula in the Gulf of Mexico. A **peninsula** is a piece of land surrounded by water on three sides. The Atlantic coastal plain extends from Florida along the Atlantic Ocean to Virginia.

The Appalachians and the Ozark Plateau are the highest landforms in the South. These highlands are in the interior. An **interior** place is away from a coast or border.

Wetlands and Water

The South's largest river—the Mississippi—fans out into a huge delta at the Gulf of Mexico. A **delta** is a triangle-shaped area at the mouth of a river. The river brings rich soil to the delta. Swamps and marshes are other wetlands. Wetlands, like the Everglades in Florida, have water on or near the surface of the soil.

Water affects where people live. Big cities are one example of a human feature that has grown near coasts and rivers because people use water to travel and to move goods.

REVIEW In what ways is the Gulf coastal plain different from the Ozark Plateau?

Climate and Wildlife

Main Idea The climate of the South is warm, but it varies across the region.

The South tends to be warmer and moister than northern regions. In winter, many people visit the South to avoid cold northern temperatures.

The South has more than one climate. Factors that control climate are latitude, elevation, and closeness to water. Because the South is closer to the equator, its climate is warmer than regions farther away from the equator. The southern latitude also results in a longer growing season than regions farther north. Farmers in coastal regions of the South can grow crops for most of the year.

Seasons and Severe Weather

Coastal areas of the South are usually warm. The ocean helps keep the air temperature steady. Winter is mild in the lowlands of the Mississippi Delta. Summer, however, is hot and humid. Humid means moist, or having a lot of water vapor in the air.

At higher elevations, winter is not as warm as in the coastal plains. The Ozark highlands can have severe weather. Frequent tornadoes strike in Texas, Oklahoma, and Florida.

The South has many tropical storms that can cause heavy flooding and other damage. Most start in the Atlantic Ocean. Some grow into hurricanes. Between 1900 and 1996, Texas had 36 hurricanes. Florida had 57.

Hurricane Damage Hurricanes bring strong winds, heavy rain, and large ocean waves. When these tropical storms hit land, they can cause damage to buildings, trees, and anything else in their path.

Plants and Animals

Plants and animals have adapted to the climate in the South. To **adapt** means to change in order to better fit the environment. For example, mangrove trees have adapted over the centuries to survive in salty Florida swamps. They've developed broad roots that arch above the muddy soil. These roots work like snorkels. They help provide oxygen to the tree as water levels rise and fall.

Animals adapt to life in their environment, too. Some sea turtles have adapted and survived since the time of the dinosaurs. These turtles nest on beaches. The females bury their eggs in the sand. The turtles have learned to dig nests above the reach of high tides to protect their eggs.

REVIEW Why does the South have such a variety of climates?

Mangrove Tree Several root systems can support one mangrove tree.

Lesson Summary

The South has a long coastline and many rivers. Most people live on the coastal plains. The warm climate gives the South a long growing season. Plants and animals have adapted to the environment and the climate.

Why It Matters ...

The warm climate and rich natural resources have allowed people to build a successful economy in the South.

Lesson Review

① VOCABULARY Choose the best word to fill in the blank:
delta   interior   peninsula

Florida is a(n) _____.

② READING SKILL In what ways does the climate of the South **contrast** with the climate of northern regions?

③ MAIN IDEA: Geography Describe one major landform and one kind of waterway found in the South.

④ MAIN IDEA: Geography In what ways can the climate of the South make life difficult at times?

⑤ CRITICAL THINKING: Analyze What might people do to adapt to the climate of the South?

HANDS ON

RESEARCH ACTIVITY Use library or Internet resources to learn about northern Mexico. Write a description comparing its landforms to those in the South.

Cooperating for the Environment

Preventing pollution costs less than cleaning it up.
An electric company in El Paso, Texas, is cooperating with
brick makers in Ciudad Juárez (see-eu-DAHD WAHR-ehz),
Mexico, to control air pollution. Ciudad Juárez is just across
the Rio Grande from El Paso.

Brick makers use large ovens called kilns to
fire, or harden, the bricks. Old kilns in Ciudad
Juárez put smoke and dust into the air.
El Paso Electric is replacing 60 old kilns
with new kilns that cycle smoke to help
remove pollution.

The new system is better for the
environment and for people. It cuts the
amount of toxic gases put into the air
by four fifths, or 80 percent. The brick
makers are healthier and safer.

Air pollution from traditional kilns can
cause serious health problems for
people living nearby.

Chimney

Bricks being fired

1 Fuel is burned here.
The heat fires the bricks
loaded above.

Cleaner smoke

3 These raw bricks filter air pollution created by the burning fuels. They will be fired later.

Bricks filtering out pollution

2 An underground tunnel sends gases and heat to the second kiln.

Activities

1. **DRAW IT** Suppose a fire is lit in the kiln on the right. Show where the heat and gases would travel to reach the bricks in the other kiln.

2. **TALK ABOUT IT** Why would a company from the United States want to help brick makers in Mexico? Discuss why the new kilns are good for people on both sides of the border.

Resources of the South

VOCABULARY

dam
producer
consumer

Vocabulary Strategy

producer, consumer

Producer and **consumer** end with **-er.** This ending can mean a person who does something.

READING SKILL

Categorize As you read, sort the resources of the South into three groups.

Natural resources	Goods	Services

GRADE LEVEL INDICATORS
ECON 4   Interdependence and specialization
ECON 5   Supply, demand, and price

Build on What You Know What snacks do you like? Some people enjoy chicken wings. Others like peanut butter or orange juice. The raw materials for these products are grown in the South.

Production in the South

Main Idea People use the natural resources of the South to fuel a strong economy.

Like people everywhere, southerners use resources to produce goods and services. For example, they use water moving through dams to make electricity. A **dam** is a barrier built across a waterway to control the flow and level of water. Dams are one human feature that changes the physical environment. The positive consequence of dams is that they produce electricity. The Tennessee Valley Authority, or TVA, has 29 dams that make power.

Fort Loudoun Dam This TVA dam is in Knoxville, Tennessee. The TVA is the largest power company in the United States.

Capital resource: dam

Natural resource: water

Goods and Services from Natural Resources

Natural Resource	Goods and Services
Rich soil	Cotton fabric, orange juice, peaches, pecans, peanuts
Waterways	Fish sticks, sea salt, boating, water power
Warm climate	Amusement parks, golf, vacation hotels
Oil and gas	Gasoline, plastics
Coal deposits	Coal, electricity
Forests	Paper, lumber

Georgia Peanuts Southerners use natural resources to create many goods and services. For example, farmers grow peanuts. Factory workers turn them into peanut butter.

Producers and Consumers

In manufacturing, producers turn raw materials into goods. A **producer** is someone who makes or sells goods or services for consumers. A **consumer** is someone who buys or uses goods and services. Raw materials in the South include coal and oil below the ground and fish in the waters.

People can be both producers and consumers. Suppose a manufacturer in North Carolina produces chairs. Before making a chair, the manufacturer will consume wood, glue, and labor. That manufacturer is both a consumer and a producer.

The South's environment affects what goods producers specialize in making. People grow more peanuts, cotton, rice, and sugar cane here than in any other region. Producers use all of these resources. Every year, for example, Texas produces nearly five million bales of raw cotton. In other southern states, workers in textile mills spin the cotton. They produce cotton yarn. Then other manufacturers use the yarn to produce cloth, t-shirts, towels, and other cotton products.

REVIEW What productive resources are needed to create cotton t-shirts?

A Diverse Economy

Main Idea Producers and consumers make choices about how to use resources.

The South's economy once relied mainly on farming. Farming is still very important. Texas, North Carolina, Georgia, and Florida rank in the top ten states for farm income. Leading products include rice, cotton, tobacco, sugar cane, oranges, chickens, hogs, and cattle. In today's economy, many other industries also thrive in a region rich with natural and human resources.

The manufacturing and service industries in the South rely on the human resources of the region. Many people in the Piedmont work in textile mills. In North Carolina alone, the cotton industry employs nearly 75,000 people to make yarn, cloth, and rugs.

Top coal mining states include West Virginia, Kentucky, and Texas. Coal and other resources help create power and energy. Many businesses in the South specialize in the oil industry. These businesses are interdependent with consumers in other areas. For example, people in Ohio need oil from the South to heat their homes in winter. Oil workers need to sell oil to people in other regions to make money. By specializing and trading, the regions can increase the amount and variety of goods and services available.

Thousands of southerners work for the government. The U.S. government is one of the largest employers in the South. Most government employees in the South live in Texas, Virginia, and Florida.

The Cotton Industry Cotton creates many jobs in the South.

SKILL **Reading Graphs** Which state has the most jobs from cotton?

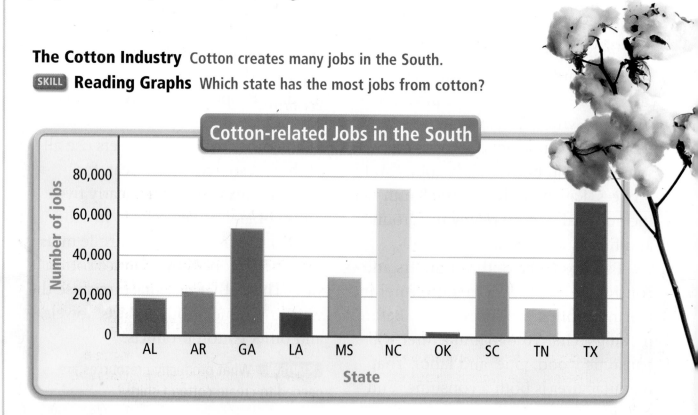

Cotton-related Jobs in the South

Making Economic Choices

Consumers decide whether or not to buy southern products such as oranges. Producers in the South try to provide goods and services that consumers will want to buy. Producers decide what resources to use. They also set prices for their goods and services.

Scarcity of supply affects prices. Scarcity means there are not enough resources to provide a product or service that people want. For example, suppose a winter frost hurt orange groves in Florida. With a scarcity of oranges, the price of orange juice would go up.

As a consumer, you could decide to buy a cheaper kind of juice. If you buy expensive orange juice, you will have less money to spend on something else. This is an example of opportunity cost. An opportunity cost is what someone gives up to get something else.

Like consumers, businesses also face opportunity cost. Suppose an orange juice company buys new equipment. The company would have less money to spend on other things, such as a new building.

REVIEW What problem does scarcity create for consumers?

Lesson Summary

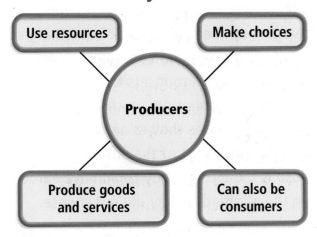

Why It Matters ...

The choices that producers and consumers make determine how resources are used in the nation's economy.

Lesson Review

❶ **VOCABULARY** Write a short paragraph using **producer** and **consumer.**

❷ **READING SKILL** How would you **categorize** orange juice? Is it a natural resource, a manufactured good, or a service?

❸ **MAIN IDEA: Economics** Give two examples of how producers and consumers use natural resources.

❹ **MAIN IDEA: Economics** Why is opportunity cost important to consumers?

❺ **CRITICAL THINKING: Evaluate** What three basic economic questions affect producers' decisions about what goods and services to provide?

WRITING ACTIVITY Write a paragraph describing some goods and services that you consume.

Making Choices

People never have enough time or money to do everything they want. They must make choices. When people choose one thing, they often give up the chance to do something else.

Both producers and consumers make economic choices. Producers try to plan the best way to earn income from producing goods and services. They make choices among alternatives. The opportunity cost of the alternative they choose is the income they could have earned from the alternative they did not choose.

Consumers have opportunity costs, too. Let's look at Pedro. He has been helping his mom take care of his younger brother and has earned $12. The first choice he makes is whether to save his money or spend it now.

Pedro likes these action figures. However, he is saving for a robot construction kit, which costs almost $50. If he buys the action figures now, it will take him longer to save for the kit. In other words, the opportunity cost of buying the action figures now would be the chance to get a robot kit in the future.

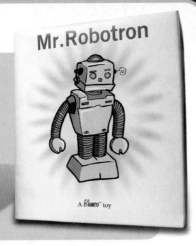

Pedro decides to save more money. He walks pets for neighbors and earns $10. When he has saved enough to buy a kit, he goes to several stores to find the best price. The kit he likes best costs $5 more than all the others.

Pedro decides to get a less expensive kit that is almost as good. He saves the extra $5 to spend or save for something else. He can't have everything, but he's happy about the choices he made with his money!

Activities

1. **TALK ABOUT IT** Explain why Pedro didn't buy the action figures when he had $12.

2. **WRITE ABOUT IT** Write about a time when you chose between two things. Explain the opportunity cost of the choice you made.

Skillbuilder

Use Latitude and Longitude

▶ **VOCABULARY**
absolute location
latitude lines
longitude lines

Lines of latitude and longitude are imaginary lines drawn on a globe or map. Using these lines can help you give the **absolute location,** or exact position, of any place in the world. **Latitude lines,** or parallels, run east and west and measure distances north and south of the equator. **Longitude lines,** or meridians, run north and south and measure distances east and west of the prime meridian.

Learn the Skill

Step 1: Study the latitude lines circling this globe. The parallel in the middle of the globe is called the equator. The equator is located at 0° (zero degrees) latitude.

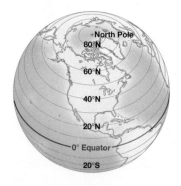

Step 2: Look at the longitude lines circling this globe. The prime meridian is located at 0° longitude.

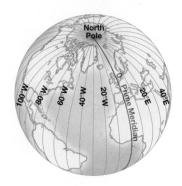

Step 3: Look at the map. You can record the absolute location of a place by identifying the parallel and the meridian on which it lies. For example, New Orleans, Louisiana, is found at 30°N, 90°W. These numbers are the coordinates of New Orleans.

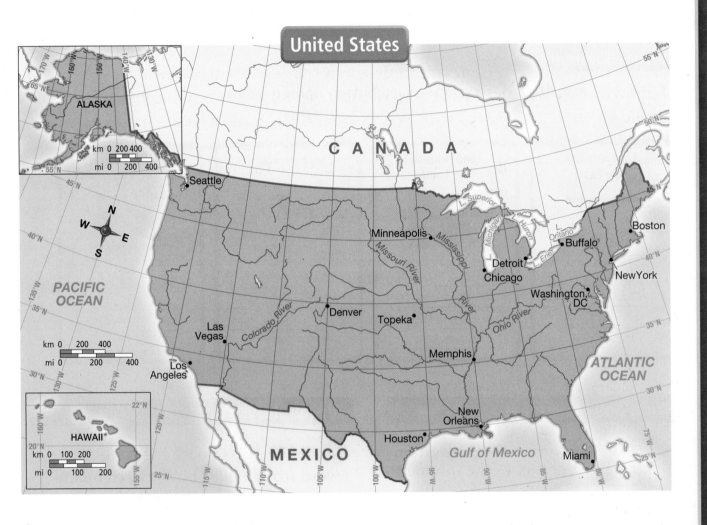

United States

Practice the Skill

Use the map to answer the questions.

1. What is the absolute location of Memphis?

2. What city is located close to 40°N, 105°W?

Apply the Skill

Use latitude and longitude to identify the absolute locations, or coordinates, of three other places in the South.

Visual Summary

1. – 4. Write a description of each item named below.

Landforms of the East	Landforms of the South	Eastern Resources	Southern Resources
	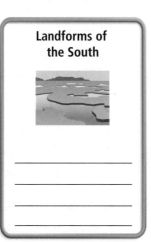		
_____	_____	_____	_____

Facts and Main Ideas

TEST PREP Answer each question below.

5. **Geography** In what way is the land of the East similar to eastern Canada?

6. **Economics** What economic questions are people free to answer in a market economy?

7. **Geography** What are three physical characteristics that can be used to define the Upper South?

8. **Geography** Explain how climate has affected the way people live in the South.

9. **Economics** In what ways do the choices of producers and consumers affect the economy?

Vocabulary

TEST PREP Choose the correct word from the list below to complete each sentence.

bay, p. 50
peninsula, p. 61
consumer, p. 67

10. A _____ is surrounded on three sides by water.

11. A _____ buys or uses goods and services.

12. A body of water that is protected but open to the seas is a _____.

☑ **TEST PREP** **Chart and Graph Skill**
Read the paragraph below. Then use what you have learned about time lines to answer each question.

> The earliest states in the United States are in the East and the South. Delaware, Pennsylvania, and New Jersey were the first three. They all became states in December of 1787. In January 1788, Georgia became the first southern state. Virginia became a state in June of that year, the same month as New York. The last state in the East and the South was Oklahoma, which did not become a state until November of 1907.

13. In what month did New York become a state?

   A. December 1787
   B. January 1788
   C. June 1788
   D. November 1907

14. In your **Answer Document,** construct a time line that has evenly spaced intervals of time and label them. Place the events on the time line in the correct order.

☑ **TEST PREP** Write a short paragraph to answer each question below.

15. Nonrenewable resources, such as coal and oil, are found in the East and South. People must use mining to get these resources out of the ground.

In your **Answer Document,** analyze the positive and negative consequences of mining for coal and oil.

16. Because of a machine problem, a company that owns a factory has to choose whether to make cars or trucks. It chooses to make cars.

In your **Answer Document,** identify and explain the opportunity cost of the company's decision.

Activities

Art Activity Draw pictures of some of the natural resources of the East and South to show how people have used them.

Writing Activity Use library or Internet resources to learn more about eastern Canada. Write a report describing and comparing the East or the South with eastern Canada.

Technology
Writing Process Tips
Get help with your report at:
www.eduplace.com/kids/hmss/

The Midwest and West

Technology

e • **glossary**
e • **word games**
www.eduplace.com/kids/hmss/

Vocabulary Preview

prairie

On the wide, flat **prairie** of the Midwest, people have replaced most of the tall grasses with farmland. **page 78**

tributary

A **tributary** is a smaller river or stream that flows into a larger river or stream. Each major river has many tributaries that flow into it. **page 79**

Reading Strategy

Predict and Infer Use this strategy before you read.

Quick Tip Look at the titles and pictures. What can you tell about the places you will read about?

geothermal

When a volcano erupts, it sends out **geothermal** energy in the form of lava and gas. Volcanic eruptions can cause a great deal of damage. **page 93**

national park

Yosemite is a **national park** in the West. Parks like this one are set aside by the federal government for people to visit and enjoy. **page 97**

Land of the Midwest

VOCABULARY

prairie
tributary
levee
lock

Vocabulary Strategy

tributary

Tributary and **contribute** have the same root. **Contribute** means to give or add to something. A **tributary** adds water to a river.

READING SKILL

Cause and Effect
How did waterways affect settlement in the Midwest? List causes on the chart.

Cause	Effect

BENCHMARKS
GEO B   Places and regions
GEO C   Human environment interaction

GRADE LEVEL INDICATORS
GEO 3   Characteristics of places and regions
GEO 8   Environment affects humans
GEO 9   Human changes to environment

Build on What You Know Does wind seem harsher out in the open than in a forest? The Midwest has lots of flat, open plains. What might the wind feel like there?

Physical Features of the Midwest

Main Idea The Midwest is a central region of wide open plains, thick woods, and huge waterways.

The Midwest lies in the middle of the country. Canada lies to the north. The Rocky Mountains and the Appalachian Mountains lie on either side of it.

The eastern part of this region features the Great Lakes. The land is mostly flat, with some hilly areas. The rainfall here supports deep forests. Pine forests in the north can withstand the harsh climate.

West of the Great Lakes are the Great Plains, which stretch from Canada to Texas. The climate is drier here. Prairie grasses cover much of the land. A **prairie** is a dry, mostly flat grassland with few trees. People have turned prairies into farmland. Much of the country's wheat and corn is grown here.

Iowa Farmland Midwestern farmers have turned grasslands into farms.

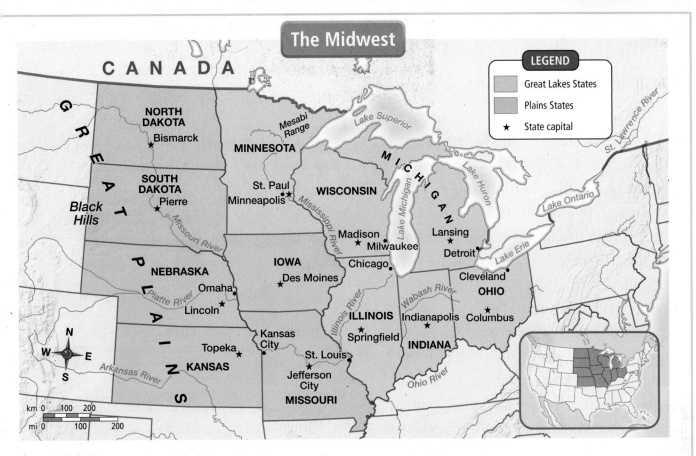

The Midwest

LEGEND
- Great Lakes States
- Plains States
- ★ State capital

CANADA

GREAT PLAINS

NORTH DAKOTA
★ Bismarck

Mesabi Range

MINNESOTA

Lake Superior

MICHIGAN

St. Lawrence River

SOUTH DAKOTA
★ Pierre

St. Paul
Minneapolis ★

WISCONSIN

Lake Huron

Black Hills

Missouri River

Madison
★ Milwaukee

Lansing ★
Detroit

Lake Michigan

Lake Ontario

Lake Erie

NEBRASKA

IOWA
★ Des Moines

Chicago

Cleveland

OHIO

Platte River

Omaha

Illinois River

Wabash River

Indianapolis ★ Columbus ★

Lincoln

ILLINOIS

Springfield ★

INDIANA

Kansas City

Topeka ★

St. Louis

Arkansas River

KANSAS

Jefferson City ★

Ohio River

MISSOURI

N W E S

km 0   100   200
mi 0   100   200

Midwest Regions The Midwest includes the Plains States and the Great Lakes States.

Water Resources

The Midwest has two main waterways. The Great Lakes area is one of them. The lakes form the world's largest body of fresh water. Rivers and canals connect the lakes to the Atlantic Ocean and the Gulf of Mexico. Water from the Great Lakes flows into the St. Lawrence River.

By building canals and removing soil from the routes that ships use, people can make Great Lakes navigation easier. Altering the environment can have negative consequences as well, however. Canals change the ecology of the lakes by allowing fish to travel from lake to lake. The large ships on the Great Lakes also create more pollution.

The Mississippi River is the second main waterway. With its major tributaries, the Missouri and Ohio rivers, it forms the nation's largest river system. A **tributary** is a river or stream that flows into another river. Dams and levees help limit floods on these rivers. A **levee** is a high river bank that stops the river from overflowing.

Waterfalls can make river travel difficult. Locks can help ships get past waterfalls. A **lock** is a part of a waterway closed off by gates. Ships enter a lock. Then, people let water into or out of it. As the water level goes up or down, so does the ship.

REVIEW What are the major regions and waterways of the Midwest?

Climate, Plants, Animals

Main Idea The Midwest can have severe weather.

The location of the Midwest affects its climate. There is no ocean nearby to warm the land in winter and cool it in summer. As a result, the climate varies more than in coastal regions. In parts of the Midwest, the temperature can change as much as 100°F between winter and summer.

The Great Lakes are not as big as an ocean, but they affect the climate by adding moisture to the air. In winter, this moisture causes lake effect snow.

Fierce snowstorms often strike the region. This weather can affect people's activities. They wear layers of clothing. They use covered walkways to get from one building to another. People also find ways to enjoy winter. They go skiing, skating, and icefishing. They hold winter festivals.

Tornadoes often hit the Midwest in warmer weather. Tornadoes are strong, spinning storms with high winds.

SKILL **Reading Charts** Which two states have had the greatest change in temperature?

Extreme Temperatures in the Midwest

State	Highest	Lowest
Illinois	117°F	−36°F
Indiana	116°F	−36°F
Iowa	118°F	−47°F
Kansas	121°F	−40°F
Michigan	112°F	−51°F
Minnesota	114°F	−60°F
Missouri	118°F	−40°F
Nebraska	118°F	−47°F
North Dakota	121°F	−60°F
Ohio	113°F	−39°F
South Dakota	120°F	−58°F
Wisconsin	114°F	−55°F

Lake Effect Snow

1 Warm, moist air rises from the lake and meets cold, dry air.

2 The cold air freezes the moisture and drops it as snow over the land.

Midwestern Plants and Animals

Plants and animals have adapted to the region's climate extremes. For example, some prairie grasses have deep roots. They help the plants find moisture. Pine trees keep their needles for years. This saves energy and helps the trees survive harsh weather.

Animals have also adapted. Some birds migrate to warmer places. Prairie dogs dig underground dens that protect them from severe weather.

Millions of bison, or buffalo, once roamed the Great Plains. Thick coats of fur kept them warm. Hunters wanted this fur. By 1885, they had killed all but a few hundred bison. Then people started protecting bison. Today, about 150,000 bison live in the United States.

REVIEW What are some options for solving the problem of cold weather?

Lesson Summary

- Landforms of the Midwest include prairies, hills, and forests.
- The region's two main waterways are the Great Lakes and the Mississippi River system.
- The Midwest is very hot in summer and very cold in winter.

Why It Matters . . .

People, plants, and animals have adapted to the Midwest's climate and made it their home.

Prairie Dog The prairie dog, found in the Midwest, is not really a dog. It is a rodent.

Lesson Review

❶ **VOCABULARY** Write a paragraph showing that you know what **levee** and **lock** mean.

❷ **READING SKILL** Explain two **effects** of improving Great Lakes navigation.

❸ **MAIN IDEA: Geography** Name the major midwestern landforms.

❹ **MAIN IDEA: Geography** How does location affect climate in the Midwest?

❺ **CRITICAL THINKING: Evaluate** In what ways might the Midwest be different without its large rivers and tributaries?

WRITING ACTIVITY Look at a physical map of Canada and the United States. What features does the Midwest share with Canada? Write a description comparing the two regions.

The **Mighty** Mississippi

The Mississippi River flows through ten of the fifty states. It starts in Minnesota and ends in Louisiana at the Gulf of Mexico. People use the river for many purposes. Its water is used for drinking, for making electricity, and for transporting people and goods. Barges on the Mississippi carry grain, coal, gravel, petroleum products, chemicals, paper, wood, coffee, iron, and steel. This powerful river provides many benefits, but people can never completely tame it.

Water
The Mississippi is a source of fresh water for millions of people who live in nearby towns and cities.

Agriculture
Farmers use water from the Mississippi to grow cotton, corn, soybeans, and rice. Others use the water to raise catfish.

Transportation
For hundreds of years, the river has been like a highway. Today, there is more traffic than ever. Each year, people ship about 500 million tons of cargo on the river.

Recreation

Every year, more than 12 million people visit the upper Mississippi to boat, fish, and enjoy the scenery. These visitors create jobs for people who live near the river.

Floods and Levees

The U.S. government has built **levees** and other structures to try to control the river's yearly floods. However, levees prevent natural wetlands from soaking up extra water. This may make flooding worse downstream.

Towns

Many towns are along the river. When people built levees, they thought it was safe to build near the river's edge. However, flooding still takes place sometimes. Some people think that homes should be built on higher ground.

Activities

1. **DRAW YOUR OWN** Draw a picture of life on the Mississippi. Show people using the river in at least three ways.

2. **RESEARCH IT** Find out about dams and locks. How do they work? Why are they used? How many are there on the Mississippi? Write about your findings.

Resources of the Midwest

VOCABULARY

mineral
service

Vocabulary Strategy

mineral

Look for **mine** in **mineral.** People dig mines underground to find minerals.

READING SKILL

Classify Use a chart to classify the goods and services produced by midwestern businesses.

Manu- factured products	Farm products	Services

BENCHMARKS
GEO B   Places and regions
ECON C   Markets

GRADE LEVEL INDICATORS
GEO 3   Characteristics of places and regions
GEO 9   Human changes to environment
ECON 5   Supply, demand, and price
ECON 6   Competition among producers
ECON 7   Competition among consumers

Build on What You Know How often do you go to the market? Do they have many kinds of cereal, cheese, and bread? These foods come from the Midwest.

Using Midwestern Resources

Main Idea Resources provide products and jobs.

The Midwest has many natural resources. Water, rich soil, and minerals helped the region become a major farming and manufacturing center.

People use the Midwest's water resources in many ways. Farmers water their crops. More than 26 million people drink water from the Great Lakes. Rivers and lakes provide transportation. Barges and ships carry resources, such as coal. Human features such as large manufacturing centers have grown along waterways.

In parts of the Midwest, the soil and climate support dense forests. Forests provide lumber and wood products, such as plywood and paper.

Wakeboarding Midwesterners enjoy many activities on the region's lakes and rivers.

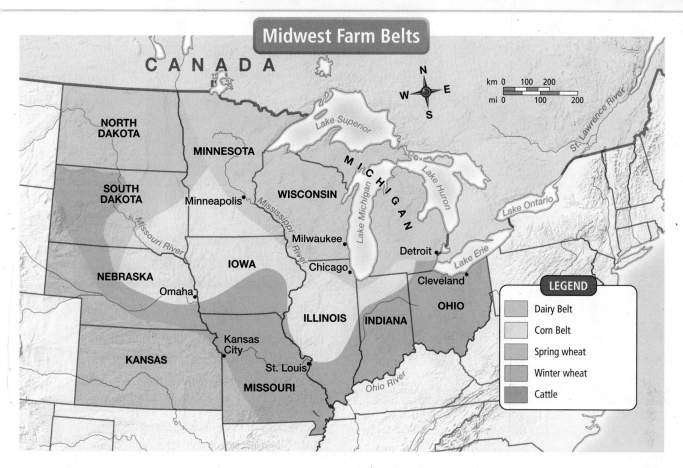

Midwest Farm Belts

CANADA

NORTH DAKOTA

MINNESOTA

SOUTH DAKOTA

Minneapolis

WISCONSIN

Lake Superior

MICHIGAN

Lake Huron

St. Lawrence River

Lake Ontario

NEBRASKA

Omaha

IOWA

Milwaukee

Chicago

Detroit

Lake Erie

Cleveland

OHIO

ILLINOIS

INDIANA

KANSAS

Kansas City

St. Louis

MISSOURI

Ohio River

Lake Michigan

Mississippi River

Missouri River

km 0   100   200
mi 0   100   200

LEGEND

Dairy Belt
Corn Belt
Spring wheat
Winter wheat
Cattle

Midwest Farm Belts The Midwest has rich soil, hot summers, and plenty of rain. **SKILL** **Reading Maps** What states have the same products on the map as Ohio?

A Farming Region

The Midwest's rich soil has attracted many farmers. The human feature of wheat, corn, and soybean farms stretch for miles. Iowa, Illinois, and Nebraska grow more corn than any other states. Farmers in Manitoba, Canada, grow many of the same crops.

Midwestern farmers also grow hay, fruits, and vegetables. They raise hogs and dairy cows. Wisconsin is called America's Dairyland. Ohio is home to more than one million cattle.

Many people work in farm-related industries. Some build tractors. Others ship food around the world.

Mining and Other Industries

Valuable minerals lie below the Midwest's soil. **Minerals** are natural substances that lie deep underground. Lead is one valuable mineral. People use it to make batteries and computers. Ohio and Illinois are important in the coal industry. Much of the nation's iron ore comes from Minnesota and Michigan. Workers use iron ore to make steel.

Steel is used to make products that include tools, planes, boats, bridges, and cars. Detroit, Michigan, is famous for its automobile industry. Its nickname is "Motor City."

REVIEW Name two midwestern industries.

Some Goods and Services from the Midwest	
Region	**Goods and Services**
Plains States	banking, health care, chemical products, insurance, houses, telephone services, auto sales, real estate, tires, hotels
Great Lakes States	health care, banking, airlines, electronic equipment, medicines, engineering, business services, cars and trucks

SKILL **Reading Charts** Which goods and services might a traveler use?

The Midwest's Economy

Main Idea The Midwest's economy was built around its natural resources and the laws of supply and demand.

If you were a manufacturer, you might want to build your factory in the Midwest. The region has many natural resources and skilled workers. It also has waterways for moving goods. Factories in the Midwest that make products such as cars are one human feature that has resulted from these resources.

Service industries have also grown in the Midwest. A **service** is an activity a person or company does for someone else. For example, the transportation industry provides a service. It brings raw materials to factories and ships finished goods to consumers.

Many midwestern cities have good railroads, streets, and waterways to serve consumers. Cleveland, Chicago, Kansas City, and other cities in the region are transportation hubs.

People and businesses also want banking, health, and communication services. Services such as these do not come directly from natural resources. If someone wants to buy or sell a home, the person can talk to a real estate agent. These services and others have become major industries in the Midwest.

Supply and Demand

The laws of supply and demand can help you understand the Midwest's economy. Supply is how much of a product producers will make at different prices. Demand is how much of a product consumers will buy at different prices. Supply, demand, and price affect each other.

Suppose a Midwestern company makes a delicious new cereal. Many people want to buy it. In a market economy, when demand for the cereal rises, the price also rises. That is because people are willing to pay a higher price for what they want. At the higher price, the cereal maker will make more of its new cereal. Over time, the higher price will attract more producers. As more suppliers enter the market, the supply increases to meet demand. Producers compete by lowering prices and improving the quality of their cereal.

Midwestern farmers supply many products, including milk, corn, and meat. When there is an increase in demand, prices rise. Farmers earn more income, but consumers pay higher prices. When there is an increase in supply, prices fall. Farmers earn less income, but consumers pay lower prices.

REVIEW What can producers do to solve the problem of competition?

Lesson Summary

The Midwest has many natural and human resources. As a result, farming and manufacturing industries have grown there. Like industries everywhere, they are affected by supply and demand.

Why It Matters ...

Midwestern businesses grow when there is demand for their products.

Lesson Review

1 VOCABULARY Describe the economy of the Midwest, using **mineral** and **service.**

2 READING SKILL Which industries did you **classify** as services?

3 MAIN IDEA: Geography Name three farm industries of the Midwest.

4 MAIN IDEA: Economics How might low demand affect producers?

5 CRITICAL THINKING: Draw Conclusions What makes iron ore such an important mineral?

HANDS ON

ART ACTIVITY Find out more about the economy of the Midwest and Manitoba, Canada. Use what you learn to draw pictures of jobs people do in the Midwest and in Manitoba.

Extend Lesson 2

Economics

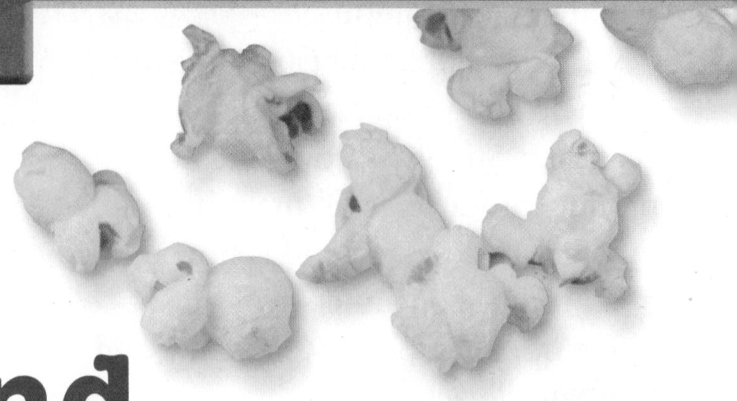

Supply and Demand

Most of the world's popcorn is grown in the Midwest. Selling popcorn is a good way for movie theaters to earn money. Theater owners must decide how much popcorn to make each day and what to charge for each box.

Supply

The **supply** of popcorn is how much theater owners are willing and able to sell at different prices. Look at the chart and think about how the price affects the supply.

Supply of Popcorn

Price of one box of popcorn	Amount owners will produce at each price
50 cents	10 boxes
$1	50 boxes
$4	300 boxes
$7	600 boxes
$10	800 boxes

Demand

The **demand** for popcorn is how much people are willing and able to buy at different prices. If the popcorn's price is low, many people will buy it. However, when the price goes up, people will buy less. The chart shows how price affects demand.

Demand of Popcorn

Price of one box of popcorn	Amount people will buy at each price
50 cents	800 boxes
$1	600 boxes
$4	300 boxes
$7	50 boxes
$10	10 boxes

Supply Greater Than Demand	Demand Greater Than Supply	Supply Equals Demand

Too Much Popcorn

The seller has set a high price. He planned to sell 600 boxes of popcorn. But at this high price, people demanded only a few boxes.

Not Enough Popcorn

The seller has set a low price. He planned to sell only a few boxes of popcorn. But at this low price, people demanded a lot of boxes.

Just Enough Popcorn

The seller has the right amount of popcorn and customers. According to the charts on page 200, the seller is making 300 boxes of popcorn and charging $4 per box.

Activities

1. **TALK ABOUT IT** Why will the theater owners sell less popcorn if the price rises above $4 per box?

2. **CHART IT** Make your own supply and demand charts for a product.

Skillbuilder

Identify Primary and Secondary Sources

▶ **VOCABULARY**

primary source
secondary source

A **primary source** comes from a person who witnessed an event. A **secondary source** is written by someone who did not see the event. Primary and secondary sources can offer different points of view on the same topic. As you read sources, you should differentiate between primary and secondary sources. The sources below are about the journey of an explorer, Meriwether Lewis, who traveled through the Midwest in 1805.

Passage A

I saw immense quantities [large numbers] of buffalo in every direction, also some elk, deer, and goats; having an abundance [lots] of meat on hand I passed them without firing on them. They are extremely gentle . . . I passed several in the open plain within fifty paces, they viewed me for a moment as something novel [unusual] and then . . . continued to feed.

—The Lewis and Clark Journals,
May 4, 1805

Passage B

The group led by Meriwether Lewis saw thousands of buffalo as they explored the Great Plains. During their journey they killed buffalo for food when they ran out of other meat. Throughout the 1800s, people hunted so many buffalo that the animals almost became extinct.

Learn the Skill

Step 1: Read the sources carefully. What is their subject?

Step 2: Identify the primary source. Look for words such as **I**, **my**, **we**, and **our**. Also look for personal details. These hint that the writer was actually at the event being described.

Step 3: Find the secondary source. Secondary sources do not include personal information about the event. Often, secondary sources summarize or analyze an event.

Practice the Skill

Use the passages on page 90 to answer the questions.

1 Which is the primary source, and which is the secondary source? How do you know?

2 Which facts are the same in both sources?

3 What do you learn from the secondary source that was not included in the primary source?

Apply the Skill

Using a newspaper, find one example of a primary source and one example of a secondary source. Write a paragraph to explain how the two sources are similar and how they are different.

Land of the West

Build on What You Know Many movies show hot and dusty areas of the West. The West has cool and rainy areas, too.

Physical Features of the West

Main Idea The West is divided by mountain ranges and rivers.

The West is a huge region of 13 states. Land and water separate two of these states from the others. The other 11 states lie east of the Pacific Ocean and between Canada and Mexico. The map shows how we divide these states into three regions. The regions are the Southwest, Mountain, and Pacific states.

Because the West is so big, its land and climate vary greatly. The region has towering mountains and deep valleys. It has dry deserts and tropical forests. It has frozen glaciers and smoking volcanoes. Many of these features extend into western Canada and Mexico.

Western Coastline Much of the western coastline is rugged and rocky. Sea otters live in these areas.

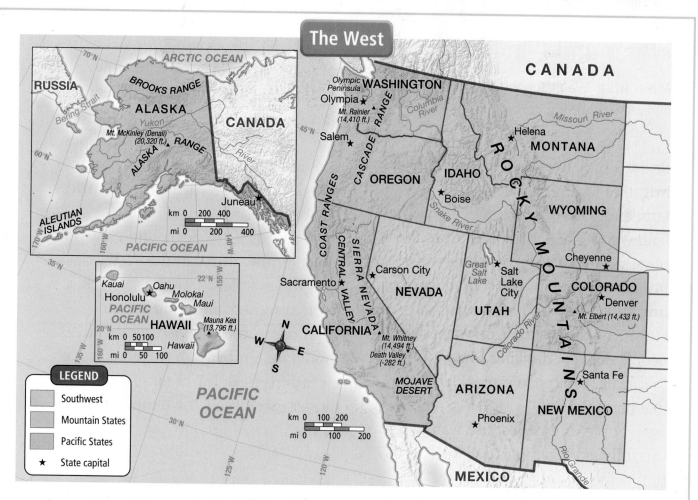

The West Three regions make up the West.

SKILL **Reading Maps** What mountains run through Montana, Wyoming, and Colorado?

Mountains in the West

Four mountain systems run north and south in the West. The Rocky Mountains formed as tectonic plates pushed against each other, causing the earth's crust to fold. The Rockies extend from northern Canada, through the United States, and into Mexico.

Other mountains, like the volcanoes in the Cascades Range, formed when melted rock, or lava, bubbled up from openings in the earth's crust and hardened. Volcanoes release geothermal energy in the form of lava and gas. **Geothermal** refers to heat from beneath the earth's crust.

Between the mountains lie valleys, basins, and raised, flat areas called plateaus. Glaciers created some valleys, such as Yosemite Valley. Rivers carved out deep, steep-sided valleys called canyons. One example is the Grand Canyon in Arizona.

The landscape between the Rockies and the western ranges is rugged yet beautiful. It has ranching and mining businesses. Many tourists visit the area to ski and hike. Much of the land is set aside for people to enjoy nature.

REVIEW What are three major landforms found in the West?

Water and Climate

Main Idea Water supports people, plants, and animals of the West.

Many rivers flow west from the Rocky Mountains. These rivers provide irrigation for millions of acres of farmland. **Irrigation** means supplying land with water. Irrigation changes the physical environment by taking water from rivers. The positive consequence of irrigation is that it supplies water to crops. However, it can also use up water that people need for drinking. The water used to irrigate crops often carries chemicals that harm the soil.

People in the West use water carefully. For example, they use dams to produce hydroelectric power. **Hydroelectric power** is electricity produced from flowing water. Some dams create lakes, such as Lake Mead in the Mojave (moh HAH vee) Desert.

The Pacific Ocean affects climates in the West. Cool, moist air flows east from the northwest Pacific. As the air rises over the western ranges, it drops rain and snow on the western slopes. Dry air then flows down the eastern slopes, creating an arid climate. Arid means very dry.

Latitude, the ocean, and elevation affect temperatures in the West. Alaska is in the northern latitudes, so it has short summers and long winters. Cool ocean breezes give coastal areas moderate temperatures. Places at high elevations have lower temperatures. On Mt. McKinley, the temperature can fall below −95°F.

Elevation Extremes Mount McKinley (small photo) is the highest spot in North America. Death Valley is the lowest. Summer temperatures there can reach 120°F.

Plants and Animals of the West

Plant life varies with the climate. In Hawaii, orchids and other tropical plants thrive. Plants that need little water, such as cactus and mesquite (meh SKEET), grow in arid areas. Mesquite's deep roots can reach underground water. Giant redwood trees grow in wet coastal areas. In the mountains are some of Earth's oldest living things—bristlecone pine trees.

A variety of animals live in the West. The huge Alaskan brown bear can weigh 1,700 pounds. The moose is another large animal of the West. The California condor is the largest flying bird in North America. Elk, bighorn sheep, and cougars roam the mountains. Lizards, scorpions, tarantulas, and snakes have adapted to the dry heat of the Southwest.

REVIEW What problems are created by irrigation?

Lesson Summary

- Landforms in the West include mountains, valleys, plateaus, canyons, and basins.

- Westerners use rivers for power and for irrigation.

- The West has many climates.

- Plants and animals have adapted to the different climates.

Why It Matters ...

Almost half the land in our country lies in the vast spaces of the West.

Cougar The cougar is an animal found in the West.

Lesson Review

1. **VOCABULARY** Write two sentences using **irrigation** and **hydroelectric power** to describe how westerners use rivers.

2. **READING SKILL** What **details** tell how plants and animals in the West adapt to the amount of water available?

3. **MAIN IDEA: Technology** Why have people built dams on western rivers?

4. **MAIN IDEA: Geography** Why is the land so varied in the West?

5. **CRITICAL THINKING: Summarize** Describe the physical and human features of the West.

HANDS ON **SCIENCE ACTIVITY** Make a diagram to show how the Rocky Mountains change in height as they run from Canada to Mexico.

Resources of the West

VOCABULARY

national park
wages

Vocabulary Strategy

wages

A synonym for **wages** is salary. Both words mean payment for working.

READING SKILL

Draw Conclusions Chart facts that lead you to the conclusion below.

Natural resources help support many industries.

BENCHMARKS
ECON B   Production, distribution, and consumption

GRADE LEVEL INDICATORS
GEO 3   Characteristics of regions
ECON 3   Effects on productive capacity
ECON 4   Interdependence and specialization

Build on What You Know If you were going to make a movie, where would you do it? Many filmmakers choose the West.

Specialization in the West

Main Idea Westerners use their land, climate, water, and minerals.

Natural resources affect the jobs of people in the West. For example, farmers use fertile soil and a warm climate to specialize in certain crops. By specializing, they can produce more. Some crops, such as pineapples, avocados, and peas, are in great demand around the world. Farmers in the West sell these crops and then use the money they earn to buy products made in other regions, where people specialize in other goods. This trade increases productivity and the variety of goods available. It also makes farmers in the West interdependent with people in other regions.

Huge forests in the West create jobs. People use trees to make wood and paper. Oceans, rivers, and lakes are another important part of western life. Workers in the fishing industry bring seafood from coastal waters.

Orange Harvest People in many other regions eat food grown in the West.

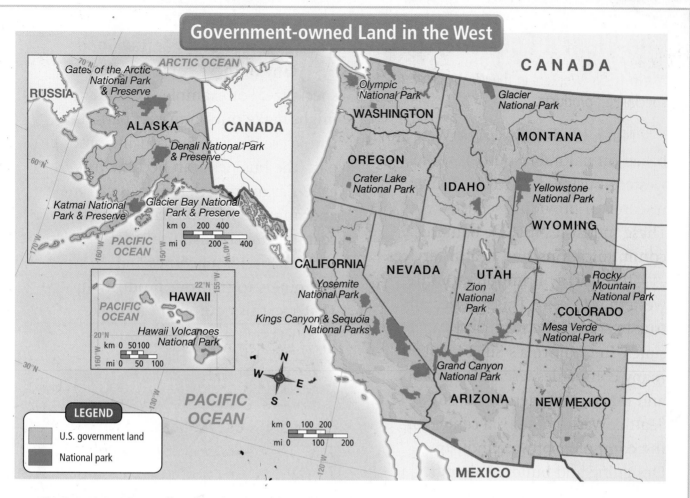

Government-owned Land in the West

Government Land Large areas of land in the West are protected by the federal government.

Movies and Mines

Other industries depend on the West's climate. Aircraft companies came west because of the fine flying conditions. The movie industry came to Los Angeles because of the pleasant climate. Many tourists visit the West to enjoy the scenery and outdoor activities.

The West contains many mineral resources. Arizona and Utah supply much of the nation's copper. Western mines also produce gold, uranium, and coal. People work in mines to dig these minerals from the ground. Others work in industries that make products from minerals.

The U.S. government owns more than 600 million acres of land in the West. It has created national parks to preserve some areas. A **national park** is an area set aside by the federal government. Examples include Glacier, Yellowstone, and Grand Canyon.

Mining, logging, and livestock companies lease, or rent, some public land. The government lets them use the land's resources. They set rules for the use of public lands. People who own land privately can use it as they choose, as long as they obey the law.

REVIEW What are two ways that people use resources in the West?

The West's Economy

Main Idea Workers in the West make specialized products.

Not all industries in the West are based on natural resources. Many western businesses involve doing research or providing services. These industries include banking, communications, and health services.

Technology is important in the western economy. This is especially true in some Southwest and Pacific states. In California's Silicon Valley, many companies research, develop, and make computer products. Seattle, Washington, is a center for the computer software industry. Designing and building aircraft is another leading industry.

Software Development Computer software designed in the West is used all over the world.

Specialization and Capital Goods

Many of these companies specialize. For example, a company might make one computer part, not whole computers. By focusing on one part, the business can become more expert at making that part. It can make and improve its product at a lower cost. Businesses also use capital goods such as special machines and computers to improve productivity. They use this equipment to make products better and more quickly.

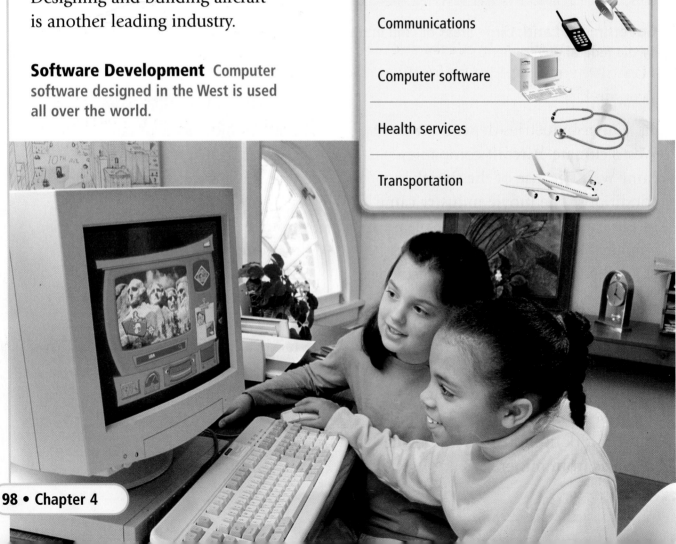

Service Industries in the West

Banking

Communications

Computer software

Health services

Transportation

Education and Workers

Many industries hire skilled workers. A skilled worker is someone who has received special training or education. For example, many people in the computer industry have advanced computer training. Educated workers can make a business more productive. They usually receive higher wages than unskilled workers. **Wages** are the money that people are paid for working.

The Mountain States contain fewer urban areas and less industry than the Pacific and Southwest states. However, there are some technology jobs in the Mountain States. For example, Colorado has a medical equipment industry. People throughout the West work in service jobs, such as health care or construction. In Alaska and Hawaii, many people work for the government.

REVIEW What could a worker do to solve the problem of low wages?

Phoenix Aerospace Workers Many industries in the West need skilled workers.

Lesson Summary

Farming, logging, and mining industries depend on the West's natural resources. Natural resources help the tourism industry, too. Most of the West's technology industries rely on skilled workers, not natural resources.

Why It Matters ...

Industries and consumers across the country depend on the West's natural and human resources.

Lesson Review

❶ **VOCABULARY** Use **national park** in a paragraph about the West.

❷ **READING SKILL** What **conclusions** can you **draw** about the economy in the West?

❸ **MAIN IDEA: Government** How do private businesses use public land?

❹ **MAIN IDEA: Economics** Explain how companies specialize.

❺ **CRITICAL THINKING: Infer** Why do you think skilled workers usually get higher pay than unskilled workers?

WRITING ACTIVITY Write a news report. Tell how people use a natural resource in your area.

Visual Summary

1. – 3. Write a description of each item named below.

Prairies of the Midwest

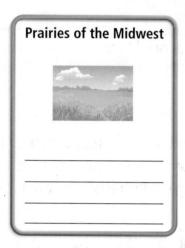

_____
_____
_____
_____

Mountains of the West

_____
_____
_____
_____

Mineral Resources

_____
_____
_____
_____

Facts and Main Ideas

✔️ **TEST PREP** Answer each question below.

4. **Geography** Why are the Great Lakes and the Mississippi River important?

5. **Economics** What usually happens to prices when there is great demand for a product?

6. **Geography** What effect do landforms, such as mountains, have on climate in the West?

7. **Geography** What are two factors that affect human activities in the West, such as where people settle?

8. **Economics** What do businesses in the West do to make products better and faster?

Vocabulary

✔️ **TEST PREP** Choose the correct word from the list below to complete each sentence.

tributary, p. 73
irrigation, p. 84
service, p. 86
national park, p. 87

9. A(n) _____ is an area set aside by the federal government.

10. A(n) _____ is a river or stream that flows into another river.

11. Some companies in the Midwest provide a(n) _____, such as banking.

12. _____ brings water to crops in dry areas.

✔ **TEST PREP** **Study Skill** Read the passage below and use what you have learned about primary and secondary sources to answer each question.

> After reaching the Pacific Ocean, Lewis and Clark's expedition set up camp in the present-day Washington town of Chinook. Ten days later, the group held a vote. They needed to decide whether to remain where they were, or move to the more sheltered Oregon side of the Columbia River. They voted to cross the river.

13. What kind of source is this passage?

   A. a primary source

   B. a secondary source

   C. a dictionary entry

   D. a quotation

14. Which word is a clue that tells you a passage is a secondary source?

   A. they

   B. because

   C. I

   D. my

✔ **TEST PREP** Write a short paragraph to answer each question below.

15. Large ships need to reach Great Lakes ports such as Toledo. To make navigation on the lakes easier, people remove soil from the lake bottoms and dig canals.

In your **Answer Document,** analyze the positive and negative consequences of this change to the physical environment.

16. Suppose two clothing stores open up across the street from each other.

In your **Answer Document,** use what you have learned about competition between businesses to describe how the price and quality of each store's products will be affected.

Activities

Speaking Activity Use library or Internet resources to learn more about Mexico. Give a report comparing the Midwest or West with Mexico.

Writing Activity Research a specialized product made in Ohio. Write a report describing this product, what resources are needed to make it, and where it is made.

Technology
Writing Process Tips
Get help with your report at:
www.eduplace.com/kids/hmss/

Vocabulary and Main Ideas

✔ **TEST PREP** Write a sentence to answer each question.

1. What are some of the physical characteristics of the **coastal plain?**

2. What is the difference between a **market economy** and a command economy?

3. Why might a **delta** be a good place for farming?

4. Name one positive consequence of building **dams.**

5. What are two things that might cause **demand** for a product to rise?

6. What effect does **irrigation** have on the physical environment?

Critical Thinking

✔ **TEST PREP** Write a short paragraph to answer each question.

7. **Cause and Effect** What are some natural resources of the East? How do they help determine the jobs that people do?

8. **Draw Conclusions** Identify ways people in the Midwest have affected the physical environment and analyze possible positive and negative consequences.

Unit Activity

Make a Travel Brochure

- Choose a part of the country that has physical and human characteristics you want to know more about.

- Fold a sheet of paper in half. Write the name of the place on the front cover. Draw a picture or map of the region.

- Research facts about the physical and human characteristics of the region. List the facts inside the brochure.

- Find or draw pictures of the region. Include captions.

- Post your brochure in your classroom.

At the Library

Look for this book at your school or public library.

Hottest Coldest Highest Deepest
by Steve Jenkins

Illustrations and brief text highlights some of the unique places on Earth.

✔ **TEST PREP** Use the two sources to answer each question below.

> *After traveling up the Missouri River, Lewis and Clark had to make a decision. The Missouri became two rivers. They thought that only one would take them to the Pacific Ocean. Before deciding which river to follow, Lewis and some men explored the river to the right.*

> *The whole of my party to a man except myself was fully persuaded that this river [the one on the right] was the Missouri . . .*
>
> *-The Lewis and Clark Journals*
> *June 8, 1805*

9. What piece of information tells you that the second passage is a primary source?

   A. the use of "my" and "myself"
   B. the description of people's opinions
   C. the fact that it is shorter
   D. the use of "persuaded"

10. In your **Answer Document,** explain how the two passages are similar and how they are different.

Multiple Choice and Short Response

✔ **TEST PREP** Answer each question below.

11. What physical feature extends from the South through the East and into Canada?

    A. Rocky Mountains
    B. Cascade Range
    C. Appalachian Mountains
    D. Grand Canyon

12. What is one nonrenewable resource found in both the South and the Midwest?

    A. coal
    B. copper
    C. iron
    D. gold

13. Many people in the Midwest specialize in growing wheat, corn, or soybeans. People in other parts of the country don't grow as much of those crops, but make goods that people in the Midwest want, such as computers.

    In your **Answer Document,** explain how this interdependence between regions of North America increases the amount and variety of goods and services available in both places.

UNIT 3

Settlement

The Big Idea

What were the effects of colonization on North America?

 Unit 3 Benchmarks

As you study this unit, you will cover these Ohio Social Studies benchmarks:

History B Describe the cultural patterns that are evident in North America today as a result of exploration, colonization, and conflict.

People in Societies B Explain the reasons people from various cultural groups came to North America and the consequences of their interactions with each other.

Geography D Analyze ways that transportation and communication relate to patterns of settlement and economic activity.

Government A Identify the responsibilities of the branches of the U.S. government and explain why they are necessary.

Government B Give examples of documents that specify the structure of state and national governments in the United States and explain how these documents foster self-government in a democracy.

Christopher Columbus
1451–1506

This explorer had a bold plan to sail west to Asia. Although he never reached his goal, his journeys to the Americas changed history for millions of people.
page 119

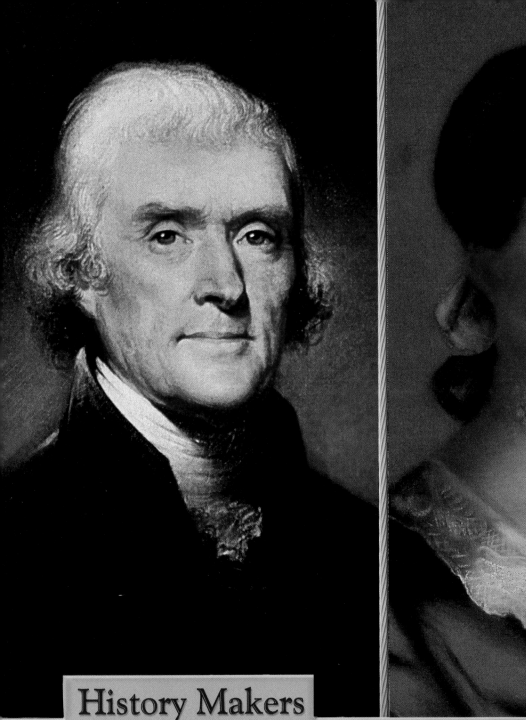

History Makers

Thomas Jefferson
1743–1826

Thomas Jefferson wrote words that are known all around the world—the Declaration of Independence. This document described essential characteristics of democracy. **page 153**

Abigail Adams
1744–1818

While her husband planned the new nation, Adams wrote to him about liberty. "Remember the Ladies," she urged. She also said that people who owned slaves could not value liberty. **page 154**

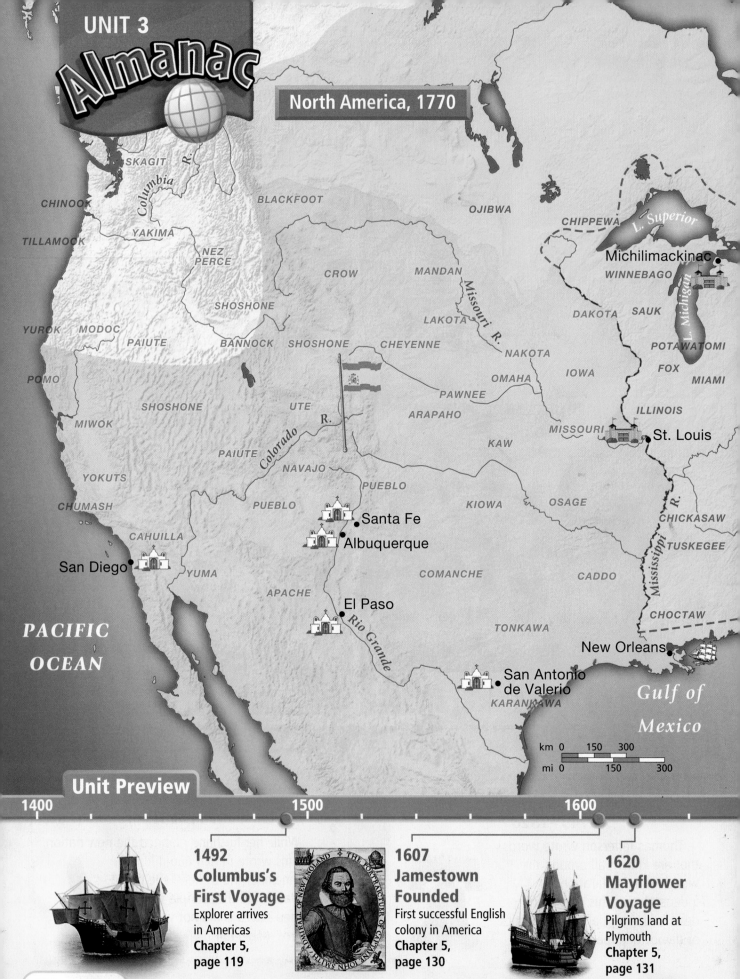

Almanac

North America, 1770

CHINOOK

TILLAMOCK

SKAGIT

Columbia R.

YAKIMA

BLACKFOOT

OJIBWA

CHIPPEWA

L. Superior

Michilimackinac

WINNEBAGO

L. Michigan

NEZ PERCE

YUROK

MODOC

CROW

MANDAN

DAKOTA

SAUK

PAIUTE

SHOSHONE

Missouri R.

LAKOTA

POTAWATOMI

BANNOCK

SHOSHONE

CHEYENNE

NAKOTA

IOWA

FOX

MIAMI

POMO

SHOSHONE

UTE

OMAHA

PAWNEE

ILLINOIS

MIWOK

Colorado R.

ARAPAHO

MISSOURI

St. Louis

YOKUTS

PAIUTE

NAVAJO

KAW

OSAGE

Mississippi R.

CHICKASAW

CHUMASH

PUEBLO

KIOWA

TUSKEGEE

CAHUILLA

PUEBLO

Santa Fe

Albuquerque

San Diego

YUMA

COMANCHE

CADDO

CHOCTAW

APACHE

El Paso

Rio Grande

TONKAWA

New Orleans

PACIFIC OCEAN

San Antonio de Valerio

KARANKAWA

Gulf of Mexico

km 0   150   300
mi 0   150   300

Unit Preview

1400   1500   1600

1492
Columbus's First Voyage
Explorer arrives in Americas
Chapter 5, page 119

1607
Jamestown Founded
First successful English colony in America
Chapter 5, page 130

1620
Mayflower Voyage
Pilgrims land at Plymouth
Chapter 5, page 131

Montreal

ABENAKI

HURON

IROQUOIS NATIONS

Huron

L. Ontario

Niagara

ERIE

L. Erie

etroit

• Boston

SUSQUEHANNOCK

New York

• Philadelphia

DELAWARE

Ohio R.

POWHATAN

SHAWNEE

N
NW   NE
W   E
SW   SE
S

TUSCARORA

CHEROKEE

CATAWBA

REEK

YAMASEE

ATLANTIC

OCEAN

• Charleston

TIMUCUA

CALUSA

• St. Augustine

LEGEND

	The Thirteen Colonies
	Other British territory
	Spanish territory
⌐ ⌐	Reserved for American Indians
⛵	Port
⛪	Mission
⌂	Trading post
HURON	American Indians

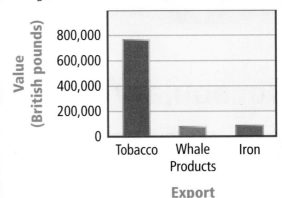

Exports to Britain in 1770s

Value (British pounds)

800,000
600,000
400,000
200,000
0

Tobacco   Whale Products   Iron

Export

In the 1770s, the colonies' top exports were raw materials.

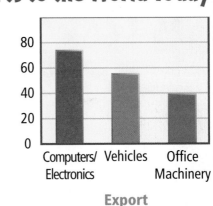

Exports to the World Today

Value (billions of dollars)

80
60
40
20
0

Computers/ Electronics   Vehicles   Office Machinery

Export

Today, the United States' top exports are manufactured products, such as computers. Why do you think the kinds of exports have changed from the 1770s to today?

CURRENT   EVENTS

WEEKLY (WR) READER

Current events on the web!

For a selection of social studies articles about current events, go to Education Place:
www.eduplace.com/kids/hmss/

1700   1800

1776 Liberty Declared
Declaration of Independence
Chapter 6, page 153

CONSTITUTION UNITED STATES

1787 Constitution
U.S. system of government is established
Chapter 6, page 162

Technology

e • **glossary**
e • **word games**
www.eduplace.com/kids/hmss

Vocabulary Preview

migration

Scientists believe that the first people to arrive in the Americas came from Asia. This early **migration** of people happened many thousands of years ago. **page 110**

navigation

In the 1400s, inventions in **navigation** allowed sailors to control the direction in which they traveled. Explorers traveled farther than before. **page 119**

Chapter Time Line

1535
New Spain founded

1607
Jamestown founded

| 1500 | 1550 | 1600 |

Reading Strategy

Summarize As you read, use the summarize strategy to focus on important ideas.

Quick Tip Review the main ideas to get started. Then look for important details that support them.

empire

The Aztecs ruled large areas of land and many people. Their **empire** included much of present-day Mexico.
page 124

self-government

Many settlers in the English colonies wanted to make laws for themselves. They believed that **self-government** was best for them.
page 135

1620
Plymouth founded

1664
English gain New York

1650

1700

First Americans

30,000 years ago   20,000   10,000   Today

27,000 years ago–500 years ago

VOCABULARY

migration
agriculture
culture

Vocabulary Strategy

culture

The oldest meaning of **culture** is to take care of something. In a **culture,** people take care of their traditions and pass them on.

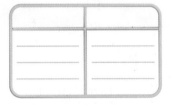

READING SKILL

Compare and Contrast
Chart similarities between two of the North American Indian groups in this lesson.

BENCHMARKS
HIS B   Settlement
PS B   Interaction

GRADE LEVEL INDICATORS
HIS 2   American Indian settlement and life
PS 1   Cultural practices and products
PS 2   Cultural practices of the past and today

Build on What You Know Have you ever seen a raccoon or a canoe? Do you know where Ohio and Massachusetts are? These words and place names, like many others, come from American Indian languages.

People Arrive in the Americas

Main Idea People may have first come to the Americas from Asia.

Thousands of years ago, the Earth was much colder than it is today. Large amounts of water were frozen in thick sheets of ice that covered almost half the world.

In some areas, the ocean floor was no longer covered by water. At the Bering Strait, west of what is now Alaska, the ocean floor turned into land covered by grasses. The grassland formed a bridge between Asia and North America. We call this land bridge Beringia.

Crossing into North America

Many scientists believe that the first people to come to North America crossed this land bridge 10,000 to 30,000 years ago. The people who crossed Beringia were hunters following big animals. Scientists think they traveled in groups from Asia over many thousands of years. Movement like this, from one region to another, is called **migration.** The migration over land to North America would have ended about 10,000 years ago, when the ice melted and water covered Beringia.

Other scientists disagree, however. Some think people also arrived by boats from Asia or Europe.

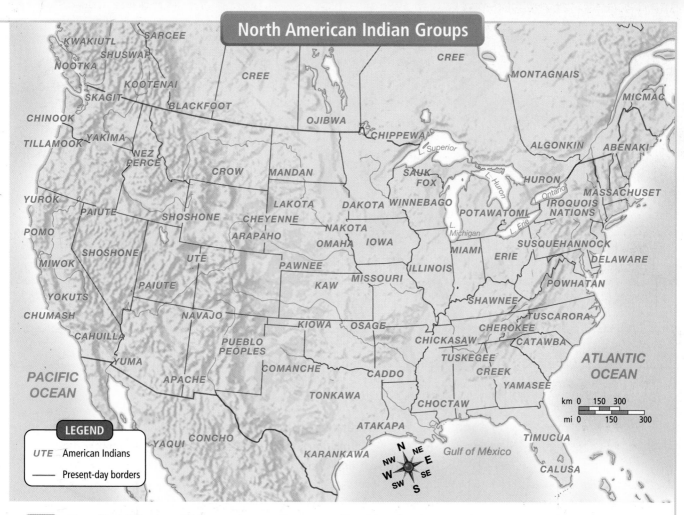

North American Indian Groups

KWAKIUTL
SARCEE
SHUSWAP
NOOTKA
KOOTENAI
SKAGIT
BLACKFOOT
CHINOOK
YAKIMA
TILLAMOOK
NEZ PERCE
CROW
MANDAN
YUROK
PAIUTE
SHOSHONE
CHEYENNE
POMO
ARAPAHO
SHOSHONE
UTE
MIWOK
PAWNEE
PAIUTE
YOKUTS
KAW
CHUMASH
NAVAJO
KIOWA
OSAGE
CAHUILLA
PUEBLO PEOPLES
YUMA
APACHE
COMANCHE
CADDO
PACIFIC OCEAN
CONCHO
YAQUI
TONKAWA
KARANKAWA
ATAKAPA
CHOCTAW

CREE
CREE
MONTAGNAIS
OJIBWA
MICMAC
CHIPPEWA
L. Superior
ALGONKIN
ABENAKI
SAUK FOX
L. Huron
HURON
L. Ontario
MASSACHUSET
LAKOTA
DAKOTA
WINNEBAGO
POTAWATOMI
IROQUOIS NATIONS
NAKOTA
L. Michigan
L. Erie
OMAHA
IOWA
MIAMI
ERIE
SUSQUEHANNOCK
DELAWARE
MISSOURI
ILLINOIS
POWHATAN
SHAWNEE
TUSCARORA
CHEROKEE
CHICKASAW
CATAWBA
TUSKEGEE
ATLANTIC OCEAN
CREEK
YAMASEE
TIMUCUA
Gulf of Mexico
CALUSA

LEGEND

UTE American Indians

—— Present-day borders

km 0 150 300
mi 0 150 300

N NE E SE S SW W NW

SKILL Reading Maps Which American Indian group lived in what is now Ohio?

Over time, American Indians migrated to all parts of the Americas. Around 9,000 years ago, people in present-day Mexico began to grow wild plants from seeds. This was the beginning of **agriculture,** or farming, in the Americas. As agriculture spread, some American Indian groups stopped moving around to follow the animals they hunted. They lived in one place all year round to care for the crops. Other groups continued to move.

As they adapted to their environment, American Indian groups created their own cultures. A **culture** is the way of life that people create for themselves and pass on to their children, including languages, beliefs, foods, and tools.

North America in 1500

Main Idea Over time, American Indians developed many different ways of life.

The cultures of American Indians depended in part on their environment. American Indian groups such as the Kiowa (KY uh wuh) traveled across the Western Great Plains. They hunted bison for food. Large herds of these woolly animals roamed the Plains.

Western Plains Indians depended on the bison for almost all of their needs. They ate bison meat and made shelter and clothing out of bison hides. They carved the bones into tools and weapons.

REVIEW What is the significance of Beringia?

Creek Village The Creek built their houses in groups of four. Each family had a winter house, a summer house, and two storehouses.

The Eastern Woodlands

In the forests of the East, American Indians lived very differently. The mild weather and plentiful rainfall were good for farming. Groups such as the Erie and Creek grew corn, beans, squash, and other crops.

Woodland Indians usually lived in villages near their fields. Some groups surrounded their villages with walls made of logs for protection. A Cherokee village might have 50 homes, some buildings to store food, and a central open area for public events.

Unlike the Great Plains, the Eastern Woodlands has mountains and valleys, rivers, swamps, and forests. Woodland Indians hunted the many animals that lived there, such as deer and bears. They also fished in the rivers and gathered wild plants for food.

The Northwest and Southwest

American Indians in other parts of North America also depended upon the environment for their survival. Along the Pacific Northwest coast, people lived near forests and along the sea. The region had many natural resources. Northwest Indian groups such as the Chinook (shih NOOK) caught salmon, hunted deer and other animals, and gathered berries and plants. They built homes and canoes with wood from the forests.

In the Southwest, American Indian groups such as the Diné, or Navajo (NAH vuh hoe), lived in a very dry climate with little rain and few trees. These groups learned how to farm by making the most of the scarce rainfall and water. They built homes with materials such as clay and stones, gathered from the surrounding land.

In all American Indian cultures, spiritual beliefs were very important. Plains Indians held ceremonies to show respect for the bison spirit and ask for a successful hunt. Southeast groups held the Green Corn Ceremony to give thanks for a good harvest. Indians of the Pacific Northwest honored the salmon in their spiritual practices. Southwest Indians held ceremonies to pray for rain and a good harvest. Though each group's beliefs were different, nature was important in the religious beliefs of all.

REVIEW What was the Diné solution to the problem of a dry environment?

Plains Indian Shield Warriors carried shields made from thick bison hide. These shields were strong enough to stop arrows.

Lesson Summary

Most scientists believe that people first came to the Americas when hunters crossed the Beringia land bridge. Others think people also came by boat. These people migrated across the Americas and adapted to the environments they found. The cultures of American Indian groups differed from region to region.

Why It Matters ...

American Indians started the first civilizations in the Americas. Their cultures are an important part of the history of the United States.

Lesson Review

❶ **VOCABULARY** Choose the correct word to complete the sentence.

> migration   culture   agriculture

People practiced _____ to grow plants for food.

❷ 📖 **READING SKILL Compare** and **contrast** the way Great Plains and Eastern Woodland Indians got their food.

❸ **MAIN IDEA: History** What effect did agriculture have on American Indian groups?

❹ **MAIN IDEA: Culture** Why was the salmon important to Northwest Indians?

❺ **PLACES TO REMEMBER** Where did people first start farming in the Americas?

❻ **CRITICAL THINKING: Cause and Effect** Think about the climate and geography where you live. How might they have affected the lives of American Indian groups who lived there?

❼ **CRITICAL THINKING: Infer** Why did the ceremonies of American Indian groups differ from region to region?

HANDS ON

RESEARCH ACTIVITY Choose one American Indian group from the map on page 111 and find information about it. Make a fact sheet with drawings and captions about that group's culture.

Ancient Traditions, Modern Lives

Many American Indians of the Southwest stay connected to their heritage by living and working on reservations. They want to keep alive the values and traditions of the past. Read about how a Laguna writer, a Diné scientist, and a Hopi filmmaker share their traditions with others.

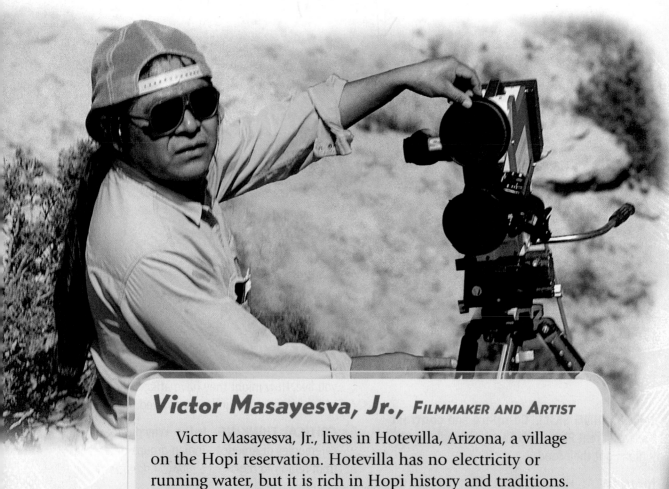

Victor Masayesva, Jr., FILMMAKER AND ARTIST

Victor Masayesva, Jr., lives in Hotevilla, Arizona, a village on the Hopi reservation. Hotevilla has no electricity or running water, but it is rich in Hopi history and traditions. Masayesva became a filmmaker as a way to teach others about Hopi culture. His film *Hopiit* follows everyday Hopi rituals and ceremonies.

Fred Begay, NUCLEAR PHYSICIST

Fred Begay believes that the Diné, or Navajo, traditions he learned as a boy helped prepare him for his career as a scientist. He grew up on the Ute Mountain Indian Reservation, where he learned Diné prayers and songs that explain the natural world. Begay saw a connection between Diné beliefs and the math and science he studied in college. He became a nuclear scientist at the Los Alamos National Laboratory. He also teaches science on the Diné reservation.

Leslie Marmon Silko, WRITER

Author Leslie Marmon Silko was raised on the Laguna Pueblo Reservation in New Mexico. As a child, she spent many hours listening to her great-grandmother tell stories about the earth and sky. Silko felt a strong pull toward the Laguna tradition of storytelling. She became a writer and teacher. Silko says, "What I know is the Laguna. This place I am from is everything I am . . ."

Activities

1. **TALK ABOUT IT** What questions would you like to ask each of these people about their traditions?

2. **COMPARE** Compare life on a reservation today with the cultural traditions of American Indians before the reservation system.

 Technology Visit Education Place for more biographies. www.eduplace.com/kids/hmss/

Summarize

▶ **VOCABULARY**

summary

A **summary** is a short description of the main points in a piece of writing. Knowing how to take notes to write a summary can help you to understand and remember the main ideas of what you read. The steps below will help you take notes to summarize the paragraph below.

> Western Plains people ate bison meat. They made bison hide into tepee covers, blankets, clothing, drums, and shields. They carved the bones into tools and wove the hair into rope. They even turned the tail into a fly swatter!

Learn the Skill

Step 1: Identify the topic of the piece of writing. Write the topic in the top box of the diagram.

Step 2: Identify the main points of the piece of writing. Write each main point in a box.

Step 3: Use your own words to write a summary of the information. Combine the important ideas into one or two sentences.

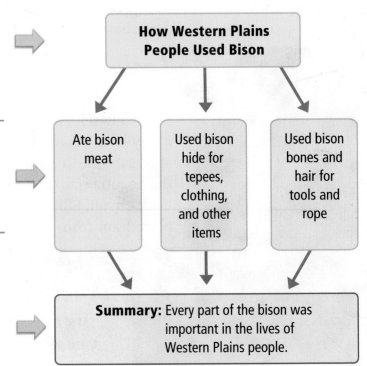

How Western Plains People Used Bison

Ate bison meat

Used bison hide for tepees, clothing, and other items

Used bison bones and hair for tools and rope

Summary: Every part of the bison was important in the lives of Western Plains people.

Practice the Skill

Write a summary of the following paragraph. Make a diagram like the one on page 116 to help you identify the main points.

The Lakota once lived along the Mississippi River. Fighting with the Ojibwa forced the Lakota to move west, onto the Great Plains. They met other American Indian nations already living there, such as the Cheyenne, Arapaho, and Crow. Later, settlers from the eastern United States arrived. Competition for land and resources increased. The Lakota felt they were being pushed off the land. They went to war against the settlers and other Plains Indians.

Apply the Skill

Read the information in Lesson 1 about how American Indians adapted to the resources around them. Fill out a diagram like the one on page 116. Then write a summary of the information.

Europeans in America

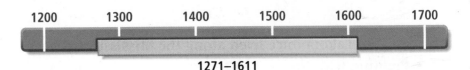

1200   1300   1400   1500   1600   1700

1271–1611

Build on What You Know Have you ever read a book that made you want to visit a new place? Around the year 1300, some Europeans read a book by Marco Polo that sparked their interest in a distant land.

The Age of Exploration

Main Idea European explorers began to travel great distances in search of trade routes to Asia.

Marco Polo was an Italian merchant. A **merchant** buys and sells goods to earn money. In 1271, he began a journey from Italy across Europe and Asia to China to trade goods. When he returned, he told his story in a book describing the wonders he saw while traveling. This book increased Europeans' interest in Asia.

Over the next 100 years, other European merchants set up trade routes to Asia. They bought goods such as silk and spices from traders in Asian cities. The merchants sold these goods at higher prices in Europe. They earned large profits from this trade. A profit is the money left over after expenses have been paid. The routes were slow and dangerous, however. European rulers tried to solve this problem by finding faster and safer trade routes to Asia to increase their nations' wealth and power.

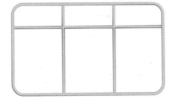

Astrolabe
Sailors used astrolabes to find their way on ocean voyages.

VOCABULARY

merchant
navigation
expedition
Columbian Exchange

Vocabulary Strategy

expedition

Expedition begins with the prefix **ex-,** just like "exit." On an expedition, people go out to achieve a goal.

 READING SKILL
Categorize As you read, categorize the explorers by country, places they explored, and reason for the exploration.

 BENCHMARKS

HIS B	Settlement
PS A	Cultures
GEO D	Movement

GRADE LEVEL INDICATORS

HIS 3	Europeans colonization and exploration
HIS 4	Influence of Spanish, French, and English colonies
PS 1	Cultural practices and products
GEO 10	Use maps of European influence

Portugal Leads the Way

European merchants knew that traveling by sea was faster than traveling by land. **Prince Henry** of Portugal believed that sailors could find a new route to Asia by sailing south around the tip of Africa and then northeast to India. To help meet this goal, he started a school for navigation. **Navigation** is the science of planning and guiding the route of a ship at sea.

Sailors at this school developed new, faster ships called caravels to send on expeditions. An **expedition** is a journey with an important goal. With improvements in navigation and shipbuilding, expeditions became safer as well as faster.

In 1498, Portuguese explorer **Vasco da Gama** became the first European to sail around Africa to Asia. His ships landed on the coast of India. This new sea route helped Portugal become rich from its trade with Asia.

Columbus's Ships Columbus and his sailors crossed the Atlantic on ships less than 100 feet long. This copy of Columbus's flagship, the *Santa Maria*, is in Columbus, Ohio.

Arriving in the Americas

Main Idea Christopher Columbus and other explorers searched for trade routes to Asia.

An Italian sailor named **Christopher Columbus** thought he could reach Asia by sailing west across the Atlantic Ocean. At that time, Europeans did not know that the Americas existed.

In the late 1400s, Spain's rulers, **Queen Isabella** and **King Ferdinand** wanted to expand Spain's power. They also wanted to spread Christianity to other parts of the world. The pull factors of economic opportunity and political gain led Queen Isabella to pay Columbus to lead an expedition west over the Atlantic. Columbus sailed from Spain in 1492 with three ships.

Two months later, the ships arrived at an island that Columbus named San Salvador. This island is in the Caribbean Sea between North and South America. Columbus wrongly believed he had reached the Indies, a group of islands off the Asian coast. He called the people he met there Indians.

REVIEW What problem led to European exploration?

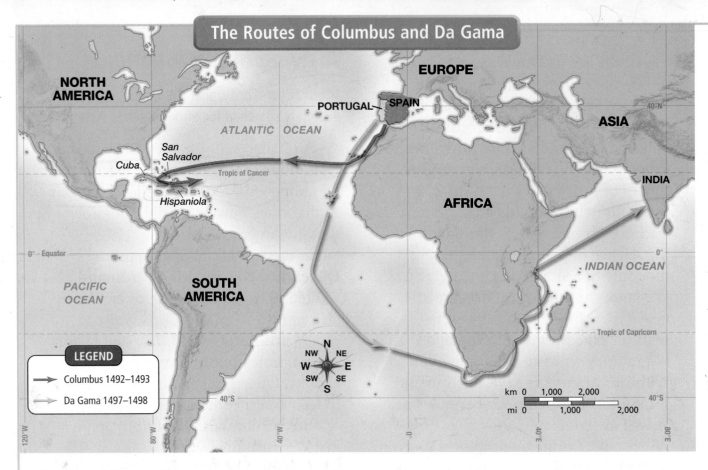

The Routes of Columbus and Da Gama

EUROPE

NORTH AMERICA

ATLANTIC OCEAN

PORTUGAL — SPAIN

ASIA

San Salvador

Cuba

Tropic of Cancer

INDIA

Hispaniola

AFRICA

Equator

INDIAN OCEAN

PACIFIC OCEAN

SOUTH AMERICA

Tropic of Capricorn

LEGEND

→ Columbus 1492–1493
→ Da Gama 1497–1498

km 0   1,000   2,000
mi 0   1,000   2,000

Routes of Exploration Columbus and da Gama both looked for new trade routes to Asia. **SKILL** **Reading Maps** Use cardinal and intermediate directions to describe da Gama's route to India.

More Voyages to the Americas

Columbus sailed back to Spain, but he returned three times to the Americas. He claimed all the lands he explored for Spain. In time, other Spanish explorers and settlers sailed to the Americas. Each journey increased Spain's power there.

England, Portugal, and France also joined the search for a western trade route to Asia. England hired a sea captain named **John Cabot** to lead an expedition. In 1497, he landed in Newfoundland on the coast of present-day Canada. He claimed this land for England.

Portugal hired **Pedro Álvares Cabral** to find a new route to India. On his expedition he found a land that was unknown to Europe—present-day Brazil. Cabral claimed this land for Portugal.

About forty years later, French explorer **Jacques Cartier** (kahr TYAY) explored part of the St. Lawrence River. He claimed the surrounding land for France. That land is now part of Canada.

English explorer **Henry Hudson** was hired by the Dutch and then by the English to find a water route across North America to Asia. Between 1609 and 1611, he explored a wide river in present-day New York and a large bay in northern Canada. Both were later named after him.

The Columbian Exchange

Once Europeans reached America's shores, both Europe and the Americas were changed. Europeans found benefits such as crops they had never seen before, including corn, potatoes, and tomatoes. They took these plants back to Europe.

Europeans brought new plants and animals to the Americas. These included wheat, sugar, horses, cattle, and pigs. This movement of goods between the Western Hemisphere and the Eastern Hemisphere is named after Columbus. It is called the **Columbian Exchange.**

The exchange had costs, as well. One unintended consequence was that Europeans carried diseases that were new to the Americas, such as smallpox and measles. Over time, European diseases killed millions of American Indians.

The Columbian Exchange made life better for American Indians in some ways, however. Plains Indians began using horses to hunt and travel. Many European plants and animals provided American Indians with new sources of food and clothing.

REVIEW What was a benefit of the Columbian Exchange for Europeans?

Lesson Summary

> Marco Polo's book led to European interest in Asian trade.

> In search of a new route to Asia, Christopher Columbus sailed to the Americas.

> French, Portuguese, and English explorers came to the Americas after Columbus.

> The Columbian Exchange carried plants, animals, and diseases between the Western and Eastern Hemispheres.

Why It Matters ...

Economic opportunity pulled Europeans to the Americas, where they had contact with American Indians for the first time. This contact changed life in both places forever. People today are pulled to the United States by economic opportunity.

Lesson Review

	1271 Marco Polo's journey	1492 Columbus's first trip	1609 Hudson explores Hudson River

1200   1300   1400   1500   1600   1700

1 **VOCABULARY** Why is **navigation** important to an **expedition?** Write a brief explanation using both words.

2 **READING SKILL** Review the **categories** you used for your chart. Write a paragraph about one of the explorers in this lesson, using information you have gathered.

3 **MAIN IDEA: History** In what ways did Prince Henry help European exploration?

4 **MAIN IDEA: Economics** What was the importance of the Columbian Exchange?

5 **TIME LINE SKILL** How many years after Marco Polo's journey did Columbus sail to the Americas?

6 **CRITICAL THINKING: Infer** European explorers found continents they had never known before. Why do you think they began claiming land there for their countries?

HANDS ON **GRAPH ACTIVITY** Using the map of European explorers' travel routes in the lesson, estimate the distance each traveled to their destination. Create a bar graph to show your results.

Spanish Influence

A Spanish colonist might feel right at home today in Santa Fe, New Mexico. Many churches, houses, stores, and government buildings here look like the buildings Spanish colonists built 400 years ago.

Today, you can see the lasting effects of Spanish culture on the traditions, language, food, and architecture of the regions Spain once ruled.

Language Spanish is spoken throughout much of the region that was once part of New Spain. This science museum in New Mexico uses Spanish and English in its exhibits.

New Spain

NORTH AMERICA

Missouri R.
Great Lakes
Mississippi R.
Colorado R.
Arkansas R.
Ohio R.

NEW SPAIN

Rio Grande

ATLANTIC OCEAN

PACIFIC OCEAN

Gulf of Mexico

LEGEND
Spanish territory

km 0   500
mi 0   500

Land Claims For centuries, Spain ruled a large area of North America known as New Spain.

Food Spanish explorers and settlers brought the first oranges to North America. This fruit is a common crop in states such as Florida and California.

Architecture Spanish colonists built structures, including this mission in Arizona, with towers, arches, windows, and doors much like those used in Spain.

Activities

1. **MAP IT** Use the map on page 122 to identify countries and states that were once part of New Spain.

2. **SHOW IT** Create a fold-out display showing the lasting effects of Spanish rule in North America.

123

New Settlements

1500   1550   1600   1650   1700   1750   1800

1519–1664

VOCABULARY

empire
colony
convert
mission

Vocabulary Strategy

mission

The word **mission** has more than one meaning. In this lesson, it means a religious community.

 READING SKILL

Predict Outcomes Note what you think will happen as a result of the European explorations.

PREDICTION:

OUTCOME:

BENCHMARKS

HIS B   Settlement
GEO D   Movement

GRADE LEVEL INDICATORS

HIS 3   European colonization and exploration
HIS 4   Influence of Spanish, French, and English colonies
GEO 10   Use maps of European influence

Build on What You Know When have you competed against others for something you really wanted? During the 1500s and 1600s, European countries competed with each other to gain land in North America.

New Spain

Main Idea After the Spanish conquered the Aztec Empire in present-day Mexico, they started the colony of New Spain.

In the early 1500s, the Aztecs ruled an empire that covered much of present-day Mexico. An **empire** is a group of nations or territories ruled by a single government or leader. The Aztecs built their empire by conquering nearby Indian nations. Many Aztec people lived in the capital city of Tenochtitlán (teh nawch tee TLAHN).

The Aztecs and Cortés

In 1519, the powerful Aztecs faced a new challenge. **Hernán Cortés** (kohr TEHS), a Spanish explorer, landed on the east coast of Mexico. Cortés and his 600 soldiers planned to conquer the region, claim land for Spain, and take gold back to their home country.

The Aztec ruler **Moctezuma** (mock teh zoo mah) welcomed Cortés at first. The Spanish explorer's greed for gold soon angered Moctezuma. The Aztecs attacked the Spanish and drove them from Tenochtitlán.

Moctezuma He was the last leader of the Aztecs, ruling from 1502 to 1520.

Defeat of the Aztecs

Cortés returned with an army that included thousands of men from nearby Indian nations. The Spanish also had horses, guns, and steel armor, and the Aztecs did not. With the Aztecs weakened by smallpox, a European disease, Cortés was able to defeat them in 1521.

Cortés took gold and other Aztec treasures back to Spain. His expedition encouraged more Spanish people to come to the Americas. In 1535, the king of Spain made Mexico a colony called New Spain. A **colony** is a territory that is ruled by a distant country.

In 1540, **Francisco Vásquez de Coronado** (kor oh NAH doh) led an expedition north of Mexico in search of gold. Coronado did not find gold, but he claimed large areas of what is now the southwestern United States for Spain. **Hernando de Soto**'s exploration in present-day Florida led to Spanish claims there as well.

Effects of Colonization

New Spain attracted thousands of Spanish settlers. The Spanish government gave land to the first settlers. The government also allowed colonists to force Indians to work for them without pay. Indians worked under harsh conditions on Spanish farms and in Spanish mines.

Priests followed the explorers into the Southwest. They believed they could improve the lives of American Indians by converting them to Roman Catholicism. To **convert** means to convince someone to change his or her religion or beliefs. To do this, the priests built missions throughout New Spain. A **mission** was a religious community where priests taught Christianity. Through the missions, the Spanish tried to change the religions of American Indians. They also tried to change their culture, language, and farming methods.

REVIEW Why was Cortés able to defeat the Aztecs?

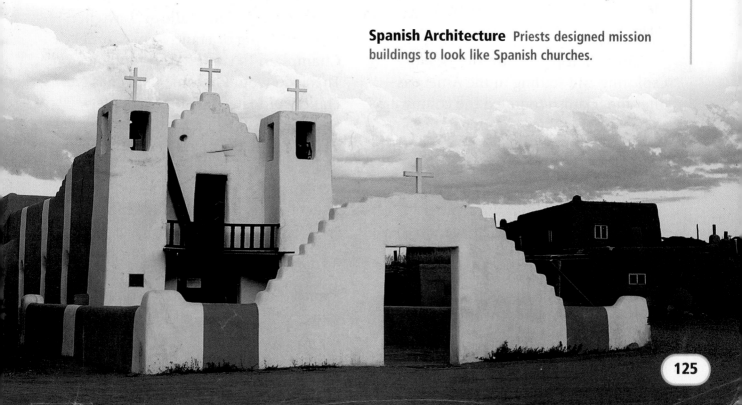

Spanish Architecture Priests designed mission buildings to look like Spanish churches.

Settlements in North America before 1650

NORTH

AMERICA

ROCKY MOUNTAINS

Lake Superior

Quebec 1608

Montreal 1642

St. Lawrence R.

Lake Ontario

Lake Michigan

Lake Huron

Lake Erie

Salem 1626

Fort Orange (Albany) 1623

Boston 1630

Providence 1636

New Amsterdam (New York) 1623

New Haven 1638

GREAT PLAINS

Missouri River

Ohio River

APPALACHIAN MOUNTAINS

Jamestown 1607

Roanoke Island 1585

Santa Fe 1609

Colorado River

Arkansas River

Mississippi River

Rio Grande

St. Augustine 1565

ATLANTIC OCEAN

PACIFIC OCEAN

LEGEND

● British settlement

● Dutch settlement

● French settlement

● Spanish settlement

Monterrey 1579

Gulf of Mexico

Havana 1515

Santo Domingo 1496

Mexico City (Tenochtitlán until 1521)

km 0 250 500

mi 0 250 500

N E S W

European Colonies Four European countries claimed different parts of North America. **SKILL** **Reading Maps** Which country settled farthest south?

French Colonization

Main Idea European countries explored and claimed land in North America.

Other European countries began exploring and settling in the Americas after the Spanish founded the colony of New Spain. France, Portugal, the Netherlands, and England wanted a share of the riches that had made Spain the most powerful country in the world.

When settlers from these other nations arrived, a new age began in the Americas. Spain now had to compete with other Europeans for land and wealth. New languages, religions, and customs were brought to North America.

New France

About 75 years after **Jacques Cartier** claimed land around the St. Lawrence River, the king of France sent **Samuel de Champlain** (sham PLAYN) to the region. This land would become known as New France, and later as Canada. But few French settlers had arrived since Cartier's journey, and Champlain found no major towns when he arrived.

Champlain started a fur-trading settlement on the St. Lawrence River in 1608. He named it Quebec. Later, it became the capital of the colony of New France.

Far fewer colonists came to New France than to New Spain. Those who came often worked in the fur trade or made a living fishing.

The French traded with the Huron and other American Indians living near the Great Lakes. Many traders learned American Indian languages and customs.

Over the next 100 years, French traders and explorers traveled across large parts of North America. They claimed much of it for France, including the Mississippi River and its surrounding lands. French traders and settlers brought their language, traditions, food, and architecture to North America.

New Netherland

The Dutch claimed all the land along the Hudson River. They called it New Netherland. Many settlers lived in New Amsterdam, which was the largest city in the colony.

Dutch control of New Netherland lasted only 42 years. In 1664, English ships sailed into the harbor at New Amsterdam to attack the colony.

The Dutch colony of New Netherland became an English colony. The English renamed New Amsterdam, calling it New York.

REVIEW What country did New France become?

Lesson Summary

- After Cortés's defeat of the Aztecs, Spain created the colony of New Spain.
- The Spanish forced many American Indians to work for them. They also built missions to teach Christianity to American Indians.
- The French and Dutch started colonies in North America. The settlers there fished, traded for furs, and farmed.

Why It Matters...

The creation of colonies brought European languages and cultures to the Americas.

Lesson Review

| 1521 Cortés defeats Aztecs | 1608 Champlain founds Quebec | 1664 English control New York |

1500   1600   1700

1. **VOCABULARY** Describe New Spain in a short paragraph, using the words **colony** and **mission.**

2. **READING SKILL** Did your **predictions** agree with the actual outcomes of the explorations? Explain why or why not.

3. **MAIN IDEA: History** Why did settlers come to New Spain?

4. **MAIN IDEA: Geography** Why did other European nations start colonies in North America after Spain?

5. **PEOPLE TO KNOW** Who was **Hernán Cortés** and what was the result of his voyage?

6. **TIME LINE SKILL** How many years passed between Cortés's defeat of the Aztecs and the founding of Quebec?

7. **CRITICAL THINKING: Cause and Effect** What effect did the Spanish have on the lives of American Indians in New Spain?

HANDS ON

MAP ACTIVITY Use library or Internet resources to learn about where Europeans explored and settled in North America. Construct a map to show what you have learned.

FRENCH INFLUENCE

What do New Orleans, Montreal, and St. Louis have in common? They were all founded by the French more than 200 years ago. France once claimed a large part of North America. French traders, missionaries, and settlers traveled this territory by canoe, using the Mississippi, Ohio, Missouri, and St. Lawrence rivers. France no longer rules this land, known as New France, but its influence is visible in the cultural patterns of many parts of the United States and Canada.

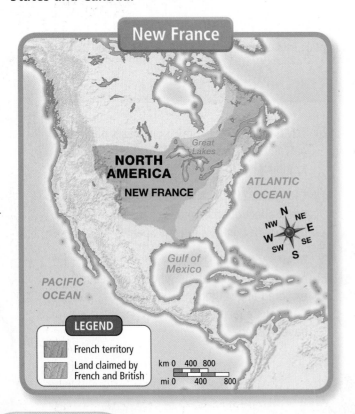

New France

NORTH AMERICA

NEW FRANCE

Great Lakes

ATLANTIC OCEAN

N NE
NW E
W SE
SW S

Gulf of Mexico

PACIFIC OCEAN

LEGEND

French territory

Land claimed by French and British

km 0   400 800
mi 0   400   800

Food New Orleans is famous for its food. Many dishes show French influence, for example by using ingredients and techniques that were common in France.

Architecture St. Louis, Missouri, still honors its French origins. Union Station, a train station built in the 1890s, was built to look like a French castle.

Tradition Events such as the Festival International de Louisiane celebrate French cultural heritage. Here, dancers in Lafayette, Louisiana, perform a traditional French dance.

Activities

1. **THINK ABOUT IT** Why do you think people enjoy dressing in the styles of the past and dancing in traditional ways?

2. **RESEARCH IT** Find a French bakery or restaurant in or near your community. Ask someone who bakes or cooks there questions about French foods.

English Colonies

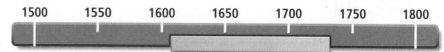

1500   1550   1600   1650   1700   1750   1800

1607–1732

VOCABULARY

cash crop
proprietor
tolerance
plantation
self-government

Vocabulary Strategy

proprietor

To remember **proprietor,** think of the word property. A proprietor owns property, often land.

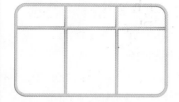

READING SKILL
Compare and Contrast
Take notes on ways the New England Colonies, Middle Colonies, and Southern Colonies were alike and different.

BENCHMARKS
HIS B   Settlement
PS B   Interaction
GEO D   Movement

GRADE LEVEL INDICATORS
HIS 3   European colonization and exploration
HIS 4   Influence of Spanish, French, and English colonies
PS 3   Experiences under slavery
GEO 10   Use maps of European influence

Build on What You Know Have you ever grown a plant from a seed? If so, you probably found that the soil and climate had to be just right for the plant to grow. When English colonists moved to North America, they had to learn which crops grew best in their new lands.

The First English Settlements

Main Idea The first successful English settlements in North America were in Virginia and Massachusetts.

When English settlers came to North America in the late 1500s and early 1600s, they hoped to find gold, silver, and other riches. These first settlers did not find riches, but they did claim land for England on the east coast of what is now the United States.

The first successful English colony in North America was Jamestown, in present-day Virginia. Jamestown was founded in 1607 by a group of English men and boys who came for economic opportunity. They were looking for gold.

Most of the Jamestown settlers did not know how to farm. Many colonists died from disease or lack of food.

John Smith He was the leader of the settlement at Jamestown. He helped the colony survive its difficult early years.

Plimoth Plantation At Plimoth Plantation (as it was originally spelled), actors show the way early settlers lived. **SKILL** **Reading Visuals** What activities are the settlers doing?

A Jamestown settler named **John Rolfe** began to grow tobacco in 1612. The crop grew well in Virginia's hot, humid climate. Before long, Jamestown merchants were selling thousands of pounds of tobacco to England. Tobacco became Jamestown's first cash crop. A **cash crop** is a crop that is grown and sold to earn income. The sale of tobacco gave the colony enough money to buy much-needed food and supplies from England.

In 1620, another group of English settlers sailed to North America on a ship called the *Mayflower*. These settlers became known as the Pilgrims. Their group was part of the Puritan movement in England. The Puritans were people who wanted to change and purify the Church of England.

The Church of England was the only legal church in England at that time. This oppression pushed the Pilgrims to leave England and form a settlement where they could live and worship freely. They founded the colony of Plymouth, in present-day Massachusetts.

During the first winter in Plymouth, nearly half of the Pilgrims died from lack of food. The following spring, the Pilgrims met an American Indian named **Squanto** (SKWAHN toh). Squanto taught the colonists how to raise crops such as maize (corn), pumpkins, and beans. He also guided them in hunting and fishing. Squanto's lessons helped the Pilgrims survive.

REVIEW How did tobacco contribute to Jamestown becoming a lasting settlement?

Three Regions

Main Idea Colonists built settlements and adapted to the different climates and resources in their regions.

During the 1600s, many more English settlers moved to North America. They started new colonies in the three regions of New England, the Middle Colonies, and the Southern Colonies.

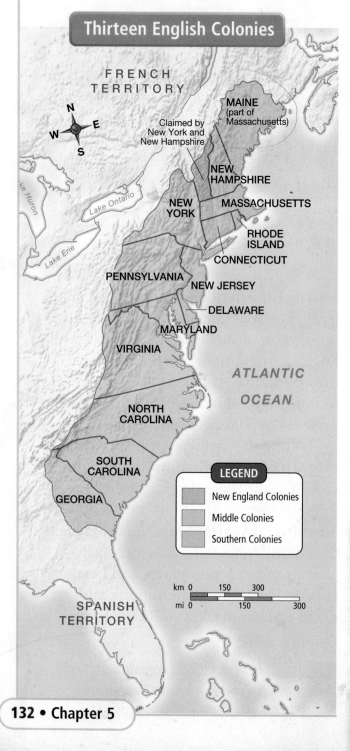

Thirteen English Colonies

FRENCH TERRITORY

MAINE (part of Massachusetts)

Claimed by New York and New Hampshire

NEW HAMPSHIRE

Lake Huron

Lake Ontario

Lake Erie

NEW YORK

MASSACHUSETTS

RHODE ISLAND

CONNECTICUT

PENNSYLVANIA

NEW JERSEY

DELAWARE

MARYLAND

VIRGINIA

ATLANTIC OCEAN

NORTH CAROLINA

SOUTH CAROLINA

GEORGIA

SPANISH TERRITORY

LEGEND
- New England Colonies
- Middle Colonies
- Southern Colonies

km 0   150   300
mi 0   150   300

New England

After the Pilgrims founded Plymouth, the hope for religious freedom pulled other groups of Puritans to the region. These new settlers also disagreed with the Church of England and hoped to start a community based on their religious beliefs. These Puritans settled north of Plymouth. The Puritan settlement was known as the Massachusetts Bay Colony and included the town of Boston.

In the Massachusetts Bay Colony, religion shaped the government. Only church members could vote or serve in town government. Many towns made laws that controlled the way people worshiped. Some colonists did not like these laws and were forced to leave the colony.

Roger Williams was a Puritan minister who wanted more religious freedom in the Massachusetts Bay Colony. Puritan leaders forced him out of the colony because of his beliefs. In 1636, Williams started a new colony that became known as Rhode Island.

Along the Coast England's thirteen colonies stretched along the Atlantic coast. People in cities such as Philadelphia (below) used rivers to ship goods to the coast.

The Massachusetts Bay Colony and other nearby colonies grew quickly. The area became known as New England. Most New England colonists were farmers. Farming was difficult in New England, because the area had rocky soil, long cold winters, and a short summer for growing crops. Farm families usually grew only enough food to feed themselves.

New England colonists found other ways to answer the economic question of what to produce. Some caught fish or hunted whales in the nearby Atlantic Ocean. Others used lumber from the region's forests to build ships. New England became a center for fishing, whaling, shipbuilding, and trading.

Middle Colonies

English settlements also spread through the area south and west of New England. They divided the land into several colonies. The region became known as the Middle Colonies.

Proprietors owned the Middle Colonies. A **proprietor** was a person who owned and controlled all the land of a colony. In Pennsylvania, **William Penn** was the proprietor. Penn was a member of a religious group called the Society of Friends, or Quakers. Quakers practiced religious tolerance. To practice **tolerance** is to respect beliefs that are different from your own.

Quakers believed that all Christians should be free to worship in their own ways. Some Quakers in England were put in jail or killed because they did not share the beliefs of the Church of England. Penn wanted Pennsylvania to be a place of religious tolerance for all Christians.

As in New England, most people in the Middle Colonies were farmers. The Middle Colonies, however, had better soil and a warmer climate than New England. Farmers there could grow enough crops to feed their families and still have plenty to sell.

REVIEW What influence did geography have on New England colonists earning a living?

The Plantation This painting of a Southern plantation shows the main house at the top of the hill where the owners lived. Ships brought goods to the plantation and carried cash crops and other products away.

Southern Colonies

While colonies were being founded in New England and the Middle Colonies, Virginia continued to grow. Several other colonies were founded near Virginia on the rich lands of the South.

In 1632, **Cecilius Calvert,** who was also known as **Lord Baltimore,** founded Maryland. He wanted to establish a colony where Catholics could worship freely. Like Quakers, Catholics in England were punished for their religious beliefs.

In 1663, **King Charles II** of England decided to start a new colony south of Virginia. He hoped the new colony would increase England's power in the area. This colony was later split into North Carolina and South Carolina.

James Oglethorpe founded the colony of Georgia in 1732. Oglethorpe wanted Georgia to be a place where poor English people could start new lives.

The warm, damp climate of the Southern Colonies made the region perfect for growing tobacco and rice. Indigo, a plant used to make a blue dye for cloth, also grew well in the South. These crops were grown in large amounts on plantations. A **plantation** is a big farm on which crops are raised by workers who live there.

Many workers did the hard labor that kept a plantation running. Plantation owners often used enslaved Africans for this work. Slavery was a cruel system that treated slaves as property instead of people. Although enslaved Africans lived in all the English colonies, most were in the Southern Colonies.

The South was known for its large plantations, but small farms were much more common. Most southern colonists lived on family farms with few slaves or none at all.

The Beginnings of Democracy

Main Idea Many of the colonies had some form of democratic government.

Settlers throughout the English colonies believed in self-government. **Self-government** happens when a group of people make laws for themselves.

In 1619, Virginia colonists formed the House of Burgesses (BUR jihs iz). The House of Burgesses was the first representative government in the English colonies. In a representative government, voters elect people to run the government.

In Massachusetts, Pilgrims signed the Mayflower Compact in 1620. This agreement set up a government for the colony of Plymouth. The Mayflower Compact was the first written plan for self-government in North America.

The representative governments in the colonies were not fair to everyone. Only men who owned property could vote. Even so, colonists had more control over their governments than most people in Europe.

The idea of self-government is one of the essential characteristics of American democracy. Choosing representatives is still a part of local and national government in the United States.

REVIEW What was the Mayflower Compact?

Lesson Summary

English colonists in North America lived in three regions: New England, the Middle Colonies, and the Southern Colonies. The climate and natural resources of each region helped to determine the way of life for colonists living there. Many colonists had some form of self-government.

Why It Matters ...

Self-government in the English colonies led to democratic government in the United States.

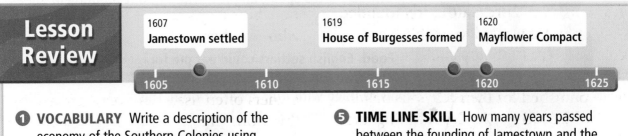

Lesson Review

1607 Jamestown settled	1619 House of Burgesses formed	1620 Mayflower Compact

1605   1610   1615   1620   1625

① **VOCABULARY** Write a description of the economy of the Southern Colonies using the words **cash crop** and **plantation.**

② **READING SKILL** Using information from your chart, write a paragraph that **contrasts** the three colonial regions.

③ **MAIN IDEA: Geography** Which region was better for farming, New England or the Middle Colonies? Why?

④ **MAIN IDEA: Economics** What were the most important cash crops in the South?

⑤ **TIME LINE SKILL** How many years passed between the founding of Jamestown and the signing of the Mayflower Compact?

⑥ **CRITICAL THINKING: Decision Making** What were the short-term effects of the Pilgrims' decision to settle in America? What were the long-term effects?

HANDS ON

MAP ACTIVITY A number of state and city names in the United States came from the names of their founders. Look at a map or book and make a list of state or city names and the people after whom these places were named.

ENGLISH INFLUENCE

Have you ever heard the saying "as American as apple pie"? When English settlers arrived in North America, they brought apples and pies. People in North America have been eating apple pie ever since. The English also influenced the traditions, language, architecture, and other cultural patterns of North America.

English legal traditions are important in North America. Both the United States and Canada use groups of ordinary citizens, known as juries, to decide court cases. This system has been used in England for more than 500 years.

Language in North America may show the strongest English influence. Today, about 92 percent of people in the United States speak English, while about 60 percent speak it in Canada.

Food English settlers could eat pie for breakfast, dinner, and dessert. The pies were filled with fruit, meat, or both. This woman is demonstrating how English settlers made pies in the 1600s at the settlement of Jamestown, Virginia.

Architecture Many college and university buildings in the United States, such as University Hall at the University of Toledo, are built to look like England's old universities.

Traditions Juries of citizens decide court cases in the United States and Canada. English settlers brought this tradition to North America in the 1600s.

Activities

1. **COMPARE IT** Look at the buildings shown on this page and on pages 123 and 129. List ways that they are alike and different.

2. **RESEARCH IT** Use library or Internet resources to learn about children's rhymes and games that came to North America from England. Write a paragraph discussing what you found.

137

Skillbuilder

Make a Line Graph

► **VOCABULARY**
data
line graph

Sometimes information, especially data, is easier to understand when it is presented as a graph or a table. Data are facts or numbers. A line graph shows changes in data over time. Read the steps below to learn how to communicate research findings by making a table or line graph.

Learn the Skill

Step 1: Collect the data you will use. You can arrange the data in a table, such as the one here.

Step 2: Draw and label the axes of your line graph.

Step 3: Create a grid for your line graph. Divide the axes into equal segments and label each grid line with a number.

Step 4: Draw dots on the graph to show the data. For each year, draw a dot where the grid line for that year and the correct value meet. You may have to estimate where to draw a dot.

Step 5: Draw a line to connect the dots.

Step 6: Give the line graph a title.

Year	Value of New England Exports to England (in British pounds)
1728	64,700
1729	52,500
1730	54,700
1731	49,000
1732	64,100
1733	62,000

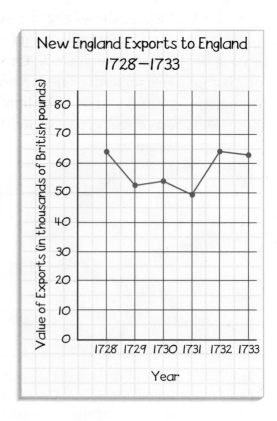

New England Exports to England 1728–1733

Practice the Skill

Make a line graph using the data below. Show how the number of ships built in New England changed between 1700 and 1706. Label the horizontal axis *Year* and the vertical axis *Number of Ships Built.*

Year	Number of Ships
1700	68
1701	47
1702	48
1703	43
1704	63
1705	75
1706	77

Apply the Skill

Collect data that shows change over a period of time. For example, you might collect data showing the change in your height over several years. Or you could research the change in temperature outside every day for a week. Arrange the data in a table, and then show it on a line graph. What does your graph show? State the big idea your graph illustrates.

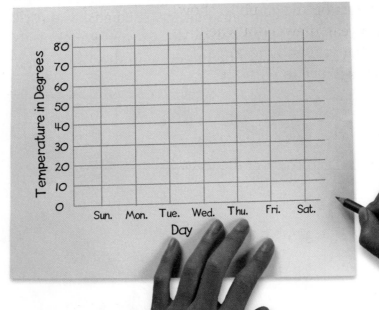

Life Under Slavery

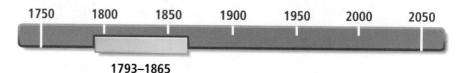

1750   1800   1850   1900   1950   2000   2050

1793–1865

VOCABULARY

abolition
spiritual
free state

Vocabulary Strategy

abolition

Abolition comes from **abolish**. It means the effort to end, or abolish, something.

READING SKILL

Problem and Solution
Look for solutions enslaved people found to the problem of creating a strong culture while living under the cruel system of slavery.

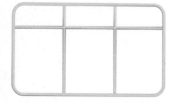

BENCHMARKS
PS B   Interaction

GRADE LEVEL INDICATORS
PS 3   Experiences under slavery

Build on What You Know What does freedom mean to you? Before 1865, millions of people in the United States lived under the institution of slavery. This system did not recognize their right to freedom. People found ways to struggle against slavery.

Slavery in North America

Main Idea People living under the institution of slavery were forced to work without pay.

Beginning in the 1600s, many thousands of Africans were enslaved and brought to the British colonies in North America. They were sold to colonists, who forced them to do hard work without pay. These colonists answered the economic question of how to produce goods by using slave labor. Slavery was legal in all 13 colonies, though it was more common in the Southern Colonies. In the Southern Colonies, the number of large farms grew, and more and more southern planters used enslaved Africans as laborers. The number of Africans brought to North America continued to grow in the 1700s.

The Institution of Slavery

Enslaved Africans were not treated as human beings. They were bought and sold as property. Many worked in the fields of huge farms called plantations. Plantations had houses, barns, fields, and warehouses. Wealthy plantation owners had fine houses, clothing, jewels, and art. The planter's house was surrounded by horse stables, workshops, gardens, fields, and workers' houses. A successful plantation owner needed many workers.

Small farms were much more common in the South than plantations. Most southern colonists lived on small family farms. They might have one or two enslaved workers, or none at all.

After the United States became free from Britain, some people began calling for the abolition of slavery. **Abolition** is the act of ending something. Slavery was already against the law in some areas, such as the lands that became Ohio. In the North, several states passed laws to end slavery right away. Others ended slavery slowly, over time. Southern states chose not to end slavery. Some leaders who helped set up the national government tried to stop slavery in all states. As one said, slavery did not fit with the principles of the country, such as equality for all. **George Mason,** a slaveowner from Virginia, called slavery "a national sin."

REVIEW What did some states do to end slavery?

Plantation Homes Planter families usually lived in grand mansions. Enslaved Africans, on the other hand, lived in small cabins. **SKILL** **Reading Visuals** Compare and contrast the houses shown here.

Slavery Grows

Main Idea Slavery grew and changed in the 1800s.

Many people hoped that slavery in the South would soon die out. Instead, new machines led to more slave labor. In 1793, a machine called the cotton gin made cleaning seeds from cotton plants faster and easier. At the same time, the use of cotton was growing. New textile mills in Britain and New England could make cotton cloth quickly.

Cotton became the South's largest crop. By 1840, southern states grew most of the world's cotton. Plantation owners used their profits to buy more land and slaves. In 1790, there had been about 700,000 enslaved people in the South. By 1860, there were nearly four million.

Enslaved people did most of the work on cotton plantations. They had to work so hard and had such poor food, clothing, and shelter that many died at an early age. Planters also used punishments and harsh laws to stop enslaved workers from fighting back against slaveowners or running away. Workers could be whipped to keep them working hard. Some had to wear heavy iron chains.

Slavery became a source of deep conflict between North and South. Some people in the North argued that it was unfair and wrong. They also believed that it stopped the country's economy from growing faster. Many southerners argued that slavery was an important part of their economy and they could not afford to give it up.

Plantation Work The cotton grown on plantations was made into cloth and shipped around the world. It became so important in the South that it was known as "King Cotton."

Daily Life

The experiences of African Americans under slavery were harsh and painful. Very few or none of the rights of enslaved people were recognized. Workers could do little to get better food, shelter, or clothing for their families. Husbands and wives could be separated. Sometimes parents and children were sold away from each other.

Slaveowners forced men, women, and children to work year round under difficult conditions. Many enslaved people on cotton plantations worked in the fields from dawn to dusk, planting, hoeing, picking, hauling, and cleaning cotton. They repaired tools and buildings, grew food crops, and raised animals. Even small children and elderly people might have to work.

Cotton Fields Picking cotton was hard, exhausting work.

Enslaved people were often given pork, cornmeal, and molasses or sweet potatoes to eat. This diet gave them energy, but not enough nutrition. If they could, they grew vegetables and hunted for meat to improve their diets.

Some enslaved people served in the homes of their owners. Women did laundry, wove cloth, sewed clothing, made meals, and raised children. Men worked as blacksmiths and stable hands. In cities, enslaved men and women who were skilled workers might be hired out for wages. Often the wages were paid to the slaveowner, but some enslaved people earned money of their own. They worked as carpenters, mechanics, mill workers, and tailors.

REVIEW Describe the lives of people under slavery.

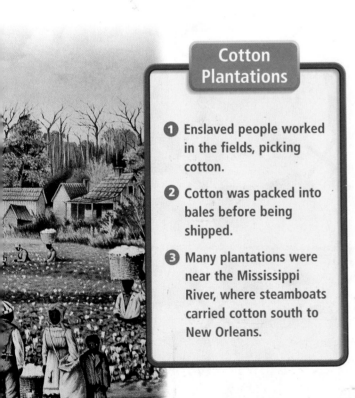

Cotton Plantations

1 Enslaved people worked in the fields, picking cotton.

2 Cotton was packed into bales before being shipped.

3 Many plantations were near the Mississippi River, where steamboats carried cotton south to New Orleans.

A Strong Culture

Main Idea Enslaved people found many ways to survive slavery, including resisting and escaping.

Year after year, enslaved people struggled against hardships. A strong culture grew out of this struggle. It mixed traditions from Africa, Europe, and North America. Baskets, pottery, quilts, and musical instruments showed African influences. People on plantations told folktales about trickster animals, an African tradition. Many enslaved people became Christians, and looked to the Bible and its stories for inspiration. They combined Christian beliefs and musical styles from Africa to create powerful spirituals. A **spiritual** is an African American religious folk song. Others continued the practice of Islam that they brought from Africa. Songs helped all laborers pass the time while working in the fields.

Enslaved people passed cultural practices to their children. Their culture helped them find the strength they needed to survive the hardships of slavery.

Cultural Practices Enslaved Africans made colorful quilts, as well as baskets, bowls, and rugs, that were both useful and beautiful.

Resistance and Escape

Cultural practices offered enslaved people one way to deal with enslavement. They found other ways as well. Enslaved people resisted by working slowly. Some broke tools, faked illnesses, or even burned crops.

Escape was another way to resist. A fugitive, or escaped slave, had to reach free states in the North. A **free state** did not permit slavery. Even in free states, fugitives could be caught and forced back into slavery. To be safe, fugitives needed to reach Canada, Mexico, or another country. Thousands used their courage and intelligence to flee slavery.

In some cases, enslaved people fought against slave owners. In 1831, **Nat Turner** led such a rebellion in Virginia. None of these attempts ended slavery, however.

Free Blacks

As early as the 1600s, small groups of free Africans lived and worked in the British colonies. After the United States became a separate country, the number grew. By 1860, nearly one-half million free blacks lived in the United States, both in the North and South.

Many free blacks lived in cities. Some had jobs requiring special skills. Others lived in the rural South and farmed. Wherever they lived, they faced challenges. Laws in many places limited the rights of free blacks. Still, free blacks were determined to succeed. They educated their children, started churches and other organizations, and worked hard to improve their lives.

REVIEW What problem did free blacks have to try to solve?

Lesson Summary

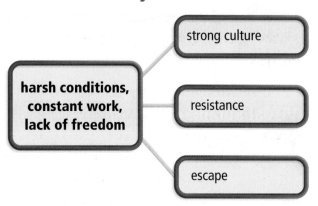

strong culture

harsh conditions, constant work, lack of freedom

resistance

escape

Why It Matters ...

The culture that developed from African American experiences under slavery is part of American culture today.

Lesson Review

| 1793 Cotton gin invented | 1831 Nat Turner's rebellion |

1750 1775 1800 1825 1850

① **VOCABULARY** Write two sentences about **abolition** and **free states** in the United States.

② **READING SKILL** Name one way in which enslaved people found a **solution** to the **problem** of poor nutrition in their diets.

③ **MAIN IDEA: History** In what ways did slavery in the United States change over the years?

④ **MAIN IDEA: Culture** What were some of the things that became part of the culture of enslaved people?

⑤ **TIME LINE SKILL** How many years after the invention of the cotton gin was Nat Turner's rebellion?

⑥ **CRITICAL THINKING: Infer** Tell why you think thousands of enslaved people risked their lives to escape slavery.

HANDS ON **RESEARCH ACTIVITY** Use library or Internet resources to research what slavery was like in the United States. Use the information you find to write a report about the experiences of African Americans under the institution of slavery.

Visual Summary

1. – 3. ✏️ Write a description of each journey named below.

Journeys

Columbus's First Voyage	Hudson's Search for Asia	The Mayflower
_____	_____	_____
_____	_____	_____
_____	_____	_____

Facts and Main Ideas

✅ **TEST PREP** Answer each question with information from the chapter.

4. **Geography** Why did American Indians in the Northwest and Southwest build their homes with different materials?

5. **History** Describe one effect of the Columbian Exchange.

6. **Economics** What helped make Jamestown the first successful English colony?

7. **Citizenship** What were two ways in which English colonists practiced self-government?

8. **History** In what ways did enslaved people resist slavery?

Vocabulary

✅ **TEST PREP** Choose the correct word from the list below to complete each sentence.

agriculture, p. 111
colony, p. 125
tolerance, p. 133

9. After Cortés defeated the Aztecs, the Spanish started a(n) _____ named New Spain.

10. The Quakers practiced religious _____ by respecting different beliefs.

11. Some American Indian groups used _____ instead of hunting to get food.

1535	1607	1620	1664
New Spain founded	Jamestown founded	Plymouth founded	English gain New York

1500   1550   1600   1650   1700

Apply Skills

✓ **TEST PREP** **Chart and Graph Skill**
Read the data below. Then use what you have learned about making a line graph to answer each question.

Year	Population of Massachusetts
1650	14,000
1660	20,000
1670	30,000
1680	40,000
1690	50,000
1700	56,000

12. If you were making a line graph using the data above, what would you label the horizontal axis?

   A. Year

   B. 1650

   C. Massachusetts

   D. 1700

13. If you were making a line graph using the data above, what number would you place at the top of the vertical axis?

   A. 14,000

   B. 40,000

   C. 50,000

   D. 60,000

Short Response

✓ **TEST PREP** Write a short paragraph to answer the question below.

14. Western Great Plains Indians lived in a region with flat, grassy land, while Eastern Woodland Indians lived in a region with mountains, valleys, rivers, and forests. This led to similarities and differences between people in the two regions.

In your **Answer Document,** explain how American Indian life on the Western Great Plains differed from life in the Eastern Woodlands.

Time Line

Use the Chapter Summary Time Line above to answer the question.

15. How long after New Spain was Jamestown founded?

Activities

Draw It Make an illustrated chart to compare the cultural practices and products of European settlers from different countries.

Writing Activity Use library resources to learn more about the experiences of African Americans under slavery. Write an essay about what you found.

Technology
Writing Process Tips
Get help with your essay at
www.eduplace.com/kids/hmss/

Creating a New Nation

Technology

e • glossary
e • word games
www.eduplace.com/kids/hmss/

Vocabulary Preview

revolution

A **revolution** is a complete change of government. In the American Revolution, the colonies overthrew their British rulers and created a new government. **page 152**

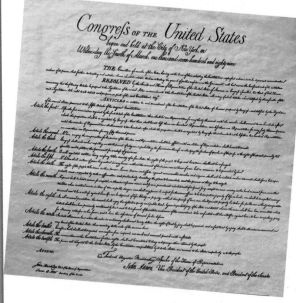

rights

Every person has **rights.** The laws of the United States recognize and protect these freedoms.
page 153

Chapter Time Line

1765
Stamp Act

1773
Boston Tea Party

1776
Declaration of Independence

1765   1770   1775

Reading Strategy

Monitor and Clarify Use this strategy to check your understanding.

 Stop and ask yourself if what you are reading makes sense. Reread, if you need to.

treaty

In 1783, the United States and Britain signed a **treaty** saying that the United States was independent of Britain. This document was called the Treaty of Paris. **page 159**

constitution

During the Revolutionary War, each state government had its own **constitution.** Many of these written plans of government became models for the U.S. Constitution. **page 162**

1783
Treaty of Paris signed

1787
Constitution signed

| 1780 | 1785 | 1790 |

Moving Toward Independence

1750   1755   1760   1765   1770   1775   1780

1754–1776

VOCABULARY

tax
revolution
congress
independence
rights

Vocabulary Strategy

rights

The word **rights** means freedoms that a government should protect. Colonists felt that it was correct, or "right," to have rights.

READING SKILL

Cause and Effect As you read, list causes of the American Revolution.

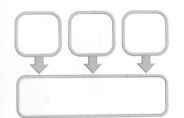

BENCHMARKS
HIS B   Settlement
GOV B   Rules and laws

GRADE LEVEL INDICATORS
HIS 5   United States independence
GOV 3   Founding documents

Build on What You Know You know that the older you get, the more you want to decide things for yourself. In the 1770s, the American colonies had been ruled by Britain for nearly 150 years. Colonists were ready to make their own decisions.

Conflicts Begin

Main Idea Colonists protested when Britain tried to force them to help pay for the French and Indian War.

In the 1750s, Britain and France both wanted to control the Ohio River Valley. In 1754, their conflict turned into a war called the French and Indian War. Most American Indian nations fought on the French side against the British and American colonists.

After almost ten years of fighting, Britain won the war. Now Britain controlled most of the land east of the Mississippi River, but the war had cost a lot of money. Parliament, which made the laws in Britain, wanted American colonists to help pay those costs.

Parliament passed a law called the Stamp Act in 1765. The law made colonists pay a tax. A **tax** is money that citizens pay to their government for services. This tax made colonists pay for a stamp on everything they bought that was printed on paper.

The Stamp Act This act, or law, made colonists pay to have stamps like these put on printed items such as newspapers.

The Boston Tea Party To protest the Tea Act, Boston colonists dressed as Mohawk Indians and dumped 342 crates of tea into the water.

Protesting Taxes

Many colonists objected to the Stamp Act. They were used to running their own governments. They did not want Parliament to tax them because they could not elect representatives to speak for them in Parliament. Across the colonies people cried,

> **66 No taxation without representation! 99**

Groups of colonists called the Sons of Liberty organized protests throughout the colonies. A protest is a public show of dissatisfaction. The Sons of Liberty and other groups attacked tax collectors and broke into their houses.

Colonists also boycotted, or refused to buy, British goods such as cloth. Groups of women called the Daughters of Liberty wove their own cloth instead of buying it from Britain.

British businesses lost money because of these boycotts. Parliament canceled the Stamp Act but taxed other goods instead. Again, colonists protested. These taxes were removed, too.

When Parliament passed a tax on tea, called the Tea Act, protesters in Boston climbed aboard ships and dumped British tea into Boston Harbor. After this event, now called the Boston Tea Party, British leaders sent soldiers to Boston.

To punish Boston, Parliament passed laws that took power away from colonial governments in Boston and Massachusetts. Colonists called these laws the Intolerable Acts. Something that is intolerable cannot be accepted.

REVIEW Why did the colonists protest the taxes that Britain made them pay?

Breaking Away from Britain

Main Idea Conflicts with Britain grew and colonists declared independence.

Colonists became more united against Britain when they learned how Parliament had punished Boston. Many felt that it was time for a revolution. A **revolution** is an overthrow, or a forced change, of a government.

In September 1774, representatives from all the colonies except Georgia met in Philadelphia. This meeting is called the First Continental Congress. A **congress** is an official gathering of people to make decisions.

The congress tried to solve its problems with Britain by sending a letter to protest the taxes and the Intolerable Acts. It also stopped trade between the colonies and Britain. Throughout the colonies, people prepared for war.

The Revolutionary War Begins

In April 1775, British troops marched from Boston to Lexington and Concord to look for weapons. **Paul Revere** and several others rode through the night to warn colonial fighters, called Minutemen.

Minutemen gathered in Lexington. When the British soldiers arrived at dawn, shots were fired and fighting began. The British troops marched on to Concord, where more fighting took place. The Minutemen forced the British back to Boston and kept shooting at them as they marched. Minutemen from all over New England gathered near Boston after they heard about these battles.

In June 1775, Minutemen and British soldiers fought again at the Battle of Bunker Hill. The British won, but nearly half of their soldiers were killed or wounded. Colonists started to believe that they could beat the British.

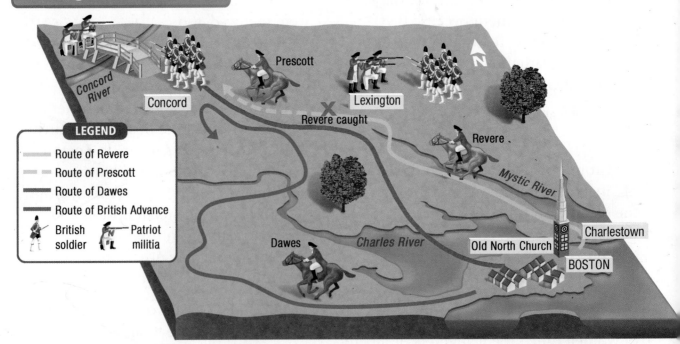

Lexington and Concord

LEGEND
- Route of Revere
- Route of Prescott
- Route of Dawes
- Route of British Advance
- British soldier
- Patriot militia

Concord River, Concord, Prescott, Revere caught, Lexington, Revere, Mystic River, Charles River, Dawes, Old North Church, Charlestown, BOSTON

Lexington and Concord Paul Revere, Samuel Prescott, and William Dawes warned Minutemen that the British troops were coming. **SKILL** **Reading Maps** What appears to be the plan of Revere and Dawes?

The Declaration of Independence

In April of 1776, the colonies sent representatives to the Second Continental Congress. The members agreed that the colonies should separate from Britain. They chose **Thomas Jefferson** to write an official statement called the Declaration of Independence. **Independence** is freedom from being ruled by someone else.

In this declaration, Jefferson wrote what many Americans believed about their rights. **Rights** are freedoms protected by law. Jefferson argued that all people have natural rights that no one can take away. He wrote that all people have rights to "life, liberty, and the pursuit of happiness."

Jefferson argued that a government should protect these rights. If it does not, then the people have the right to start a new government.

Jefferson listed many ways that Britain and its king, **George III**, had abused its power in the colonies. For instance, the government had taken away colonists' rights. It had forced taxes on them and sent soldiers to control them.

The Declaration of Independence explained that the colonists had many reasons to separate from Britain. It said that the colonists were starting a new country because Britain had not protected their rights.

REVIEW What problems with British rule did Jefferson identify?

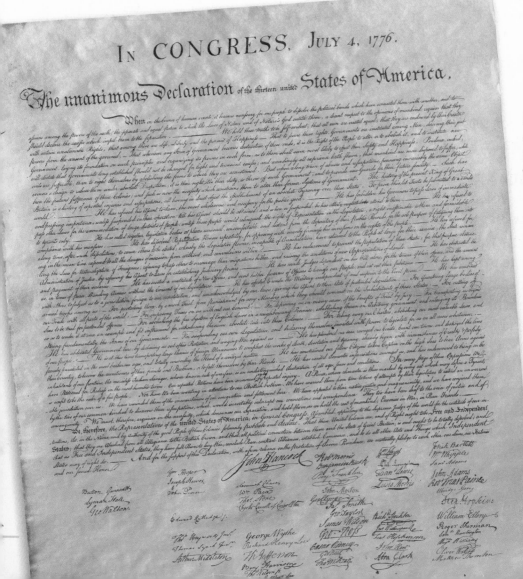

Historic Document The original Declaration of Independence is kept in Washington, D.C.

Signers of the Declaration Thomas Jefferson (1) presents the document to John Hancock (2) and the Continental Congress. Find John Adams (3) and Benjamin Franklin (4).

Significance of the Declaration

Main Idea The Declaration sets forth basic ideas of freedom and equality.

On July 4, 1776, the Second Continental Congress voted to accept the Declaration. The delegates knew that signing the Declaration was dangerous. Britain would call it treason. Treason is the crime of fighting against one's own government. Anyone who signed the Declaration could be charged with treason and hanged. Yet delegates signed.

The Declaration was read aloud to excited crowds across the new nation. People tore down pictures and statues of King George. They celebrated by ringing bells and firing cannons. The Declaration of Independence marked the moment when Americans chose to rule themselves.

Equality Then and Now

The Declaration is important today because it states that the people of the United States believe in equal rights for all. Today we know that Jefferson's words, "all men are created equal," include everyone: women as well as men, every race, every group, every ability. Is that what the words meant when the Declaration was written? Probably not.

In 1776, all Americans could not exercise the same rights. Only white men who owned property could vote. Many believed this was unfair. **Abigail Adams** wanted Congress to recognize the equal rights of women. She wrote to her husband, John Adams,

66 . . . in the new Code of Laws . . . Remember the Ladies . . . **99**

It took many years, but women, African Americans, American Indians, and other groups have gained equal rights. In later lessons, you'll read about important laws that guarantee these rights. The Declaration has inspired people, past and present, to work for liberty and equal rights.

REVIEW Why is the Declaration so important to Americans?

Lesson Summary

> Britain made colonists pay taxes to help with the costs of the French and Indian War.

> Colonists protested the taxes.

> Minutemen and British soldiers fought near Boston in 1775.

> Thomas Jefferson wrote the Declaration of Independence in 1776.

Why It Matters ...

The rights of freedom and equality that Jefferson wrote about are important American values and principles.

Martin Luther King Jr. In the 1960s, Martin Luther King Jr. was a great leader in the struggle for African Americans' equal rights. He and his wife, Coretta Scott King, led many marches to protest unjust treatment.

Lesson Review

1773
Boston Tea Party

1776
Declaration of Independence

| 1773 | 1774 | 1775 | 1776 | 1777 |

1 **VOCABULARY** Write a paragraph about the American colonies using two of the words below.

tax   independence   rights

2 **READING SKILL** For each **cause** you listed, name an **effect** it had on the colonies.

3 **MAIN IDEA: Economics** Why did Parliament want the colonists to pay taxes?

4 **MAIN IDEA: History** Why did the American colonies declare independence from Britain?

5 **TIME LINE SKILL** Where on the time line would you place the battles of Lexington and Concord?

6 **CRITICAL THINKING: Conclude** Why do you think Americans celebrate July 4 as an important day each year?

WRITING ACTIVITY Write a journal entry that a person at the Boston Tea Party might have written describing the event. Do research to find details and facts you can use in your entry.

The War for Independence

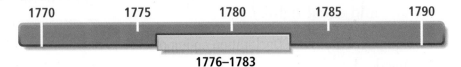

1770   1775   1780   1785   1790

1776–1783

VOCABULARY

Patriot
Loyalist
neutral
treaty

Vocabulary Strategy

| loya**list**

Look for **loyal** in **Loyalist**. During the War for Independence, a Loyalist was faithful to the British government.

READING SKILL

Compare and Contrast Fill out a Venn Diagram to compare and contrast the British army and the Continental Army.

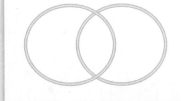

BENCHMARKS
HIS B   Settlement

GRADE LEVEL INDICATORS
HIS 5   United States independence

Build on What You Know What is it like to make a difficult choice? After the colonies declared independence in 1776, ordinary people had to decide whether to support Britain or the Americans. Some took no side at all.

Patriots and Loyalists

Main Idea Americans had different views about independence.

In 1776, the American colonies were at war against Britain. Colonists disagreed about which side to support. About half were Patriots. **Patriots** wanted independence from Britain. A smaller group, called **Loyalists,** believed Britain should rule the colonies. Many people were neutral. To be **neutral** means not to take sides.

Nearly 5,000 free and enslaved African Americans joined the American army, called the Continental Army. Many enslaved African Americans were Loyalists, however, because the British promised them freedom.

Most American Indian nations were neutral. Many who did fight chose the British side. They believed the British would make settlers stop taking Indian land. American Indians trusted the British because the British had tried to stop colonists from moving west.

Joseph Brant He was a Mohawk leader who urged his people to side with the British.

Phillis Wheatley This poet, who was among the women who supported the Patriots wrote poems, letters, and plays.

Many women were Patriots. Some cooked and carried water for the army. Some even fought or served as spies. Women also ran family farms and businesses during the war. **Abigail Adams,** wife of future President **John Adams,** managed their farm while he was at the Second Continental Congress.

The Continental Army

The British army was one of the strongest in the world. The Continental Army was smaller than the British army. The colonies had little money for soldiers or equipment. British soldiers had better training and weapons.

The Continental Army did have some strengths. Its commander was General **George Washington,** a strong, respected leader. Many of its soldiers knew the land they would be fighting on. British soldiers were unfamiliar with the land. Many Patriots fought hard because they believed in their cause. For many in the British army, fighting was just a job.

Fighting the War

Main Idea Americans won their independence after a long and difficult war.

In the spring of 1776, the Continental Army drove the British out of Boston. After that success, however, colonists faced many problems. The British defeated Washington's army in a series of battles near New York City. The American army had to retreat, or move back, all the way to Pennsylvania.

Washington needed to solve the problem of his defeats. On December 26, 1776, Washington and his soldiers crossed the icy Delaware River. They surprised and defeated British soldiers camped at Trenton, New Jersey. That victory lifted the spirits of Washington's army and the nation.

REVIEW What solution did Washington choose for the problem of his defeats?

Surprise Attack Washington caught British forces off guard by crossing the Delaware River.

Victory at Yorktown United States officers accept the British surrender at Yorktown, Virginia. American soldiers were overjoyed by this victory.

Help from Europe

Americans won another important victory near Saratoga, New York, in June of 1777. This victory helped to convince France that the United States could win the war. The French decided to send money, soldiers, and a navy.

People from other countries came on their own to fight for the American side, too. A French soldier, the **Marquis de Lafayette** (mahr KEE duh laf ee ET), wanted to help the American struggle for freedom. He led Americans in many battles. A German officer named **Baron von Steuben** (SHTOY ben) trained American soldiers to fight better.

Marquis de Lafayette

Winning the War

By 1779, neither side was winning the war. The British invaded the South. They hoped the many Loyalists there would help them. By 1780, they controlled Georgia and South Carolina. Led by General **Charles Cornwallis** (korn WAHL iss), they won more battles.

It seemed Americans might lose the war. Southern Patriots looked for ways to solve this problem. They began using new ways of fighting. **Francis Marion** was a commander called the Swamp Fox because he was so good at attacking the enemy and escaping through swamps.

Nathanael Greene, commander of the Continental Army in the South, also frustrated the British. He made Cornwallis's forces chase his army until the British soldiers were worn out and had used up all their supplies. In the spring of 1781, Cornwallis moved his weary troops to Virginia.

Led by **George Rogers Clark,** the Americans also won victories in present-day Indiana and Illinois. In 1779, the Patriots were helped when the Spanish General **Bernardo de Gálvez** captured British forts near the Gulf of Mexico.

In late 1781, Washington's army surrounded General Cornwallis's troops, who were camped at Yorktown, Virginia. The French navy blocked the harbor so the British could not retreat. Cornwallis was trapped. After a week of fighting, he surrendered. The Americans had defeated Cornwallis's entire army and won the last major battle of the war.

Bernardo de Gálvez

In 1783, the United States and Britain signed the Treaty of Paris, ending the war. A **treaty** is an agreement between countries. The treaty stated that the United States was independent. It now stretched north to British Canada, west to the Mississippi River, and south to Spanish Florida. America was its own country at last.

REVIEW What led to Cornwallis's defeat?

Lesson Summary

Colonists were divided into Patriots and Loyalists. After its victory at Saratoga, the Continental Army received valuable help from France. By 1779, most fighting had shifted to the South. Americans won the war after the Battle of Yorktown. In 1783, the Treaty of Paris ended the war.

Why It Matters...

The United States became a new, independent country when it won the Revolutionary War.

Lesson Review

1777 **Battle of Saratoga**	1781 **Battle of Yorktown**	1783 **Treaty of Paris**

1776 1778 1780 1782 1784

1 **VOCABULARY** Write two sentences about Patriot and Loyalist viewpoints in the American Revolution.

2 **READING SKILL** List two advantages the British army had over the Continental Army.

3 **MAIN IDEA: History** Why did many enslaved African Americans support the British in the war?

4 **MAIN IDEA: Geography** How did Francis Marion use the land to help him beat the British in the South?

5 **TIME LINE SKILL** Which event happened first, the Battle of Yorktown or the Treaty of Paris?

6 **CRITICAL THINKING: Cause and Effect** What effect did the Battle of Saratoga have on the war? Why was this important?

HANDS ON **RESEARCH** Examine a written passage from the American Revolution. Write a report explaining whether the author was a Patriot or Loyalist and what the purpose of the passage is.

Valley Forge

Valley Forge stands for an army's courage. Why? The story of Valley Forge tells of terrible hardships. During the winter of 1777–1778, Washington's army suffered from cold and hunger. Supplies had run out. Soldiers should have had coats and warm uniforms, but some had only a shirt or a blanket, not enough against the fierce cold. They had little to eat. Instead of milk, meat, or vegetables, they ate "firecake," which was flour and water cooked over a campfire. Many soldiers got sick and died.

Finally in spring, food arrived. Baron von Steuben came to teach the army how to be better soldiers. In 1778, a well-trained army marched out of Valley Forge.

Those soldiers had not given up. They stayed loyal to Washington, and were ready for victory over the British.

This painting shows Washington and his troops on the way to Valley Forge. The artist who painted it many years after the event knew the story of their trial. The faces show courage. What else do you notice?

Canteens

Soldiers needed canteens for water. For meals at camp, soldiers had simple utensils like the ones below.

"**...Three or four days' bad weather would prove our destruction.**" —George Washington

Uniforms

Notice how ragged many uniforms are. Some soldiers are not even wearing boots. Hats were made of felt, but were not warm enough.

Equipment

Knapsacks held soldiers' belongings. Soldiers also carried up to 60 pounds of equipment. A musket could weigh nearly 10 pounds.

Activities

1. **TALK ABOUT IT** Look at the painting and discuss what it shows about Washington's army.

2. **WRITE ABOUT IT** A motto is a statement to express a goal or a belief. Create a motto for the Continental Army after Valley Forge. Explain why you chose it.

 Technology Learn about other primary sources for this unit at Education Place. www.eduplace.com/kids/hmss/

161

The Constitution

Build on What You Know Builders make a plan before they build a house. The founders of the United States made the Constitution as a plan for the nation's government.

A Plan for Government

Main Idea The Constitution describes how the United States government works.

After the United States became independent, many people thought it needed a strong government. In 1787, delegates from 12 of the states met in Philadelphia to discuss ways to strengthen the government. They created the United States Constitution. A **constitution** is a written plan for government.

The first words of the Constitution are "We the People of the United States." These words tell us that our country is a democracy. A **democracy** is a government in which the people have the power to make political decisions.

An essential characteristic of American democracy is that the people are the source of the government's authority. They take part in making laws and choosing leaders. In the United States, citizens run the government by electing representatives.

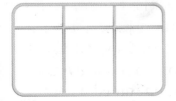

BENCHMARKS
GOV A   Role of government
GOV B   Rules and laws

GRADE LEVEL INDICATORS
GOV 1   Branches of the United States government
GOV 2   Characteristics of American democracy
GOV 3   Founding documents

The Constitution
This important document is on display at the National Archives in Washington, D.C.

State of the Union
Once a year, the President gives a speech called the State of the Union Address. The seal above is the symbol of the President.

Branches of Government

The Constitution divides the national government into three parts, or branches: the legislative branch, the executive branch, and the judicial branch. Each branch does a different job. No single person or branch can govern alone.

The legislative branch makes laws for the country. This branch is called Congress. Congress has two parts: the Senate and the House of Representatives. Each state elects two senators to the Senate. Each state also elects a certain number of representatives to the House. The number of representatives from each state depends on its population.

Congress has the power to raise money through taxes or by borrowing. It uses this money to pay for goods and services such as an army, roads, and national parks.

The executive branch's main job is to carry out the laws of Congress. The head of this branch is the President. United States citizens elect a President every four years. The President can suggest laws, and is the commander of the United States military.

The judicial branch interprets laws, or decides their meaning and whether they have been followed. Many courts across the nation make up the judicial branch. The highest court is the Supreme Court.

The Constitution does not give the federal government unlimited power. It is a plan for a limited government. This means the powers of the government are limited by law. Everyone must follow the law, including those who run the government.

REVIEW What are the major jobs of each branch of the national government?

Limits on Government

Main Idea The Constitution puts limits on the power of the government.

To stop any branch of government from becoming too powerful, the Constitution has checks and balances. **Checks and balances** let each branch limit the power of the other two.

The chart below shows checks and balances. The President can **veto,** or reject, laws. Congress can overrule the President's veto. The Supreme Court decides whether laws follow the rules in the Constitution. If a law does not follow those rules, it is no longer in effect.

The Constitution also limits the powers of the federal government by only giving it control of specific functions. The federal government's jobs include defending the country, running the Post Office, and controlling trade between states and with other countries. However, the law does not let the federal government have control in other areas. For example, states have more power over local issues. Public education and elections are two state responsibilities.

The federal and state governments share certain powers as well. Both federal and state governments collect taxes and set up court systems.

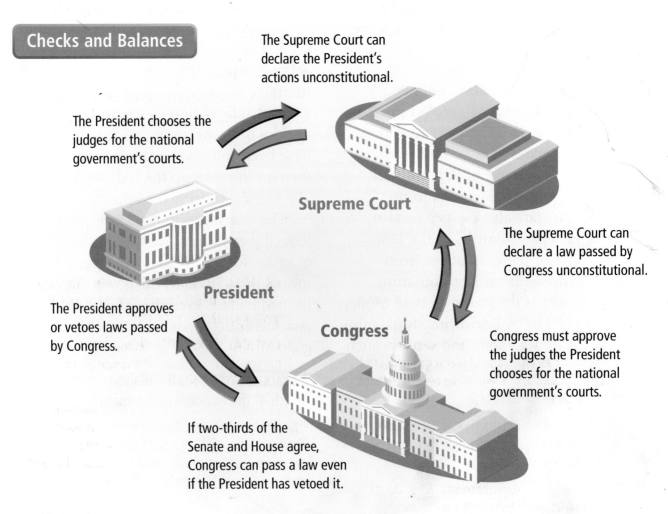

Checks and Balances

The Supreme Court can declare the President's actions unconstitutional.

The President chooses the judges for the national government's courts.

Supreme Court

The Supreme Court can declare a law passed by Congress unconstitutional.

President

The President approves or vetoes laws passed by Congress.

Congress

Congress must approve the judges the President chooses for the national government's courts.

If two-thirds of the Senate and House agree, Congress can pass a law even if the President has vetoed it.

Checks and Balances This diagram shows some of the ways that each branch of the national government can check the power of the other two branches.

Changing the Constitution

The authors of the Constitution knew that the nation would grow and change. They included a way to add amendments to the Constitution. An **amendment** is a change to the Constitution.

When the Constitution was written, many people in the United States wanted it to be amended right away. They did not feel that it clearly protect the rights of individuals. In 1791, a list of 10 amendments known as the Bill of Rights was added to the Constitution. The First Amendment is the most famous of these amendments. It guarantees many of the basic rights of individuals, such as freedom of speech, the freedom of religion, freedom of the press, and the right to assemble peacefully and ask the government to make changes.

The Bill of Rights also says that the federal government only has the powers given to it by the Constitution. All other powers belong to the states or to the people.

REVIEW What problem did the Bill of Rights solve for Americans?

Lesson Summary

- The federal government is divided into the legislative, executive, and judicial branches.
- Checks and balances keep any one branch from becoming too powerful.
- The Constitution divides power between the federal government and the states.
- The Constitution can be changed by amendments.

Why It Matters ...

The Constitution desribes the rules for the government under which you live today.

Lesson Review

1 **VOCABULARY** Use **democracy** and **checks and balances** in a paragraph about the Constitution.

2 **READING SKILL** Think about the **categories** of jobs the federal government does. What jobs can the legislative branch do that other branches cannot?

3 **MAIN IDEA: Government** What does the Constitution say about where the government's authority comes from?

4 **MAIN IDEA: Government** What does the Constitution do to limit the powers of the government?

5 **CRITICAL THINKING: Conclude** Why might the authors of the Constitution want a limited government?

6 **CRITICAL THINKING: Summarize** How do the judicial and executive branches limit the power of the legislative branch?

RESEARCH ACTIVITY Find out who represents you in the Senate and the House of Representatives. The President is also your representative. List these people. Explain what each person's job is and how he or she represents you.

Skillbuilder

Understand Perspective

▶ **VOCABULARY**

point of view

perspective

Information can come from many different sources, including newspapers, books, and television. Each source of information has one perspective or more. A **perspective** is the way someone thinks about an issue, an event, or a person. The phrase **point of view** is another way of saying perspective. A person's perspective is affected by his or her experience and beliefs.

By reading critically, you can identify an author's perspective and purpose for writing the source. The two sources below discuss whether or not to approve the Constitution.

"Who authorized them [the people who wrote the Constitution] to speak the language of We, the People, instead of We, the States? . . . National Government . . . will destroy the state governments and swallow the liberties of the people without giving previous notice [warning]."

— Patrick Henry

"We have seen the necessity of the Union, as our bulwark [protection] against foreign danger, as the conservator of peace among ourselves, as the guardian of our commerce [trade]."

— James Madison

Learn the Skill

Step 1: Identify the perspective. What is the subject, and what does the author think about it?

_____

Step 2: Identify the author. What is the author's purpose for writing this passage?

_____

Step 3: Summarize the author's perspective in your own words. If you know about the person's experiences, explain how they might have influenced his or her perspective.

Practice the Skill

Read the passages on page 166 about the debate over whether the national government should have more power than the states. Then answer these questions.

1 What is Patrick Henry's perspective?

2 What is James Madison's perspective?

3 What do you think was Henry's purpose in writing this passage?

Apply the Skill

Choose a topic below or one of your own. Write a paragraph expressing your perspective on the subject. Describe any personal experiences that affect your perspective.

- Some towns have decided to start and end school later in the day. They are trying to give young people more time to sleep.

- A national helmet law has been suggested. Everyone who uses skates, bikes, and skateboards would need to wear a helmet.

Visual Summary

1. – 4. Write a description of each item below.

Boston Tea Party, 1773	Declaration of Independence, 1776	Victory at Yorktown, 1781	Constitution, 1787
_____	_____	_____	_____
_____	_____	_____	_____
_____	_____	_____	_____
_____	_____	_____	_____
_____	_____	_____	_____

Facts and Main Ideas

TEST PREP Answer each question with information from the chapter.

5. **Citizenship** Name two ways that the Sons of Liberty and the Daughters of Liberty protested British taxes.

6. **History** What happened at the First Continental Congress?

7. **Geography** Where was the first battle of the American Revolution fought?

8. **History** What strengths did the Continental Army have that the British army did not?

9. **Citizenship** Name two rights guaranteed by the Bill of Rights.

Vocabulary

TEST PREP Choose the correct word to complete each sentence.

tax, p. 150
rights, p. 153
constitution, p. 162

10. The new _____ written in 1787 created a government with three branches.

11. The Declaration of Independence states that all people have _____, including "life, liberty, and the pursuit of happiness."

12. The Stamp Act placed a _____ on anything that was printed on paper.

CHAPTER SUMMARY TIME LINE

1765	1773	1776
Stamp Act	**Boston Tea Party**	**Declaration of Independence**

| 1765 | 1770 | 1775 | 1780 |

Apply Skills

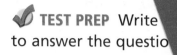 **TEST PREP** **Citizenship Skill** Read the quotations below and use what you have learned about point of view to answer each question.

> "The local interests of a state ought, in every case, to give way to the interests of the Union."
> — Alexander Hamilton

> "…Some have weakly imagined that it is necessary to annihilate [destroy] the several states, and [give] Congress… government of the continent…. This however, would be impractical."
> — *Freeman's Journal* of Philadelphia

13. What was Hamilton's point of view?

  A. States' interests are more important than the interests of the federal government.

  B. The interests of the federal government are more important than states' interests.

  C. The federal government is not important.

  D. States are not important.

14. In your **Answer Document,** describe the point of view expressed by the *Freeman's Journal* in your own words.

Short Response

TEST PREP Write to answer the questio

15. The French and Indian War cost Britain a lot of money. Britain wanted to tax the American colonists to help pay for the cost.

  In your **Answer Document,** explain how the British taxes led American colonists to protest.

Time Line

Use the Chapter Summary Time Line above to answer the question.

16. Which came first, the Declaration of Independence or the Constitution?

Activities

 Time Line Activity Use library resources to learn more about the Revolution. Create a time line of events from the war.

 Writing Activity Write a report explaining the responsibilities of the three branches of United States government.

 Technology
Writing Process Tips
Get help with your report at
www.eduplace.com/kids/hmss/

Characteristics of DEMOCRACY

★ ★ ★

All nations have governments. A government is a group of people who make and enforce the laws of a political region, such as a country. Just as your school has rules, the nation has laws to govern its citizens.

Life in the United States would be difficult without government. The government sets up ways to choose leaders and makes laws to protect people at home and in the community. Governments run public schools and libraries and print stamps and money. When governments work well, they protect freedom and keep order.

American Democracy

Governments take many forms. The United States is a democracy. A democracy is a government in which people govern themselves. In a democracy, citizens have the power to make political decisions.

The United States has a form of democracy called representative democracy. That means citizens elect representatives who speak or act for them in making laws.

Majority and Minority

In the United States, the majority of voters usually decides who will win an election. Majority means more than half. Many important decisions are made by majority rule. For example, the majority of lawmakers in Congress must agree on a law before it is passed.

Even though most decisions are made by majority rule, the rights of the minority are protected. Minority means fewer than half. The majority cannot take away the rights of small groups of people to express unpopular views or take part in the government. This limit on majority rule is sometimes called minority rights.

The Rule of Law

The Constitution is the plan for the United States government. It is also the supreme, or highest, law of the United States. The powers of the government are limited by law. This means that everyone, even the President, must obey the country's laws. This is known as the rule of law. The rule of law promises that laws will protect everyone equally.

Two Hundred Years Thousands of balloons were released to celebrate the 200th anniversary of the U.S. Constitution in 1987.

REVIEW What does the rule of law promise to everyone?

Three Branches
of
GOVERNMENT

★ ★ ★

The federal government is our national government. The Constitution created a federal government with three branches. These branches, or parts, are the legislative, executive, and judicial branches.

The three branches of government work together, but each branch has its own powers. A system of checks and balances prevents any one branch from having too much power. In this system, each branch limits the power of the other two branches.

For example, the President can veto, or reject, laws passed by Congress. Congress can refuse to approve treaties made by the President. The courts of the judicial branch can rule that laws made by Congress or actions taken by the President are unconstitutional.

All three branches are supposed to work toward the common good of the country's citizens. The common good means what is best for the whole country, not just for a few individuals.

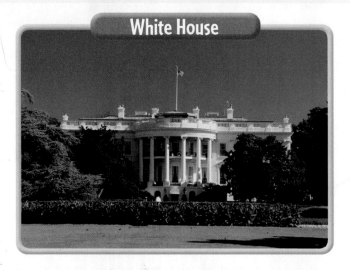

White House

Executive Branch The head of the executive branch is the President. The Vice President and the heads of government departments give advice to the President.

★ proposes, approves, and enforces laws made by Congress

★ makes treaties with other countries

★ leads the military

Capitol

Legislative Branch The legislative branch is called Congress. Congress has two parts: the Senate and the House of Representatives.

★ makes laws

★ raises money by collecting taxes or borrowing money

★ approves the printing of money

★ can declare war

Supreme Court

Judicial Branch The Supreme Court and other courts make up the judicial branch. One Chief Justice and eight Associate Justices serve on the Supreme Court.

★ decides whether laws follow the guidelines of the Constitution

★ decides what laws mean

★ decides whether laws have been followed

REVIEW Why is it important that a balance of power exist among the three branches of government?

Levels *of* Government

The federal government is not the only government in the United States. Every state has a government, which is led by a governor. Some decisions are made by the federal government, while others are made by a state government.

Each state is broken into smaller units that have local governments. These units may include counties (parts of states made up of several towns), townships (small parts of counties), cities, and school districts. Local governments take many forms. Some are headed by a mayor. Others are run by a city manager or by a group of people such as a town council.

Federal, state, and local governments have their own powers, but they also share some powers. For example, both the federal and state governments collect taxes, set up courts, and make and enforce laws.

Federal Government

Main Powers

★ prints money

★ declares war

★ runs the postal system

★ makes treaties with other countries

★ collects income taxes

State Government

⭐

Main Powers

★ issues licenses, such as marriage licenses and driver's licenses

★ runs elections

★ sets up local governments

★ collects income and sales taxes

Local Government

⭐

Main Powers

★ provides police and fire protection

★ runs public schools and public libraries (with help from the state)

★ provides public transportation, such as buses and subways

★ collects sales and property taxes

REVIEW Which level of government has the power to run elections?

The Bill of Rights

The first 10 amendments to the Constitution are called the Bill of Rights. An amendment is an official change or addition to a law. The Bill of Rights lists many of the individual rights the United States government promises to protect. This chart explains each amendment.

> The First Amendment says we have the right to speak our minds.

1 First Amendment The government cannot support any religion above another. It may not prevent people from practicing whichever religion they wish. People have the right to say and write their opinions, and the press has the right to publish them. People can also meet together and ask the government to make changes.

2 Second Amendment Because people may have to fight to protect their country, they may own weapons.

3 Third Amendment People do not have to allow soldiers to live in their homes.

4 Fourth Amendment The police cannot search people or their homes without a good reason.

5 Fifth Amendment People accused of a crime have the right to a fair trial. They cannot be tried more than once for the same crime. Accused people do not have to speak against themselves at a trial.

6 Sixth Amendment People accused of a crime have the right to a speedy, public trial by a jury. A jury is a group of people who hear evidence and make a decision. Accused people also have the right to a lawyer, to be told what crime they are accused of, and to question witnesses.

7 Seventh Amendment People who have a disagreement about something worth more than $20 have the right to a trial by a jury.

8 Eighth Amendment In most cases, accused people can remain out of jail until their trial if they pay bail. Bail is a sum of money they will lose if they don't appear for their trial. Courts cannot demand bail that is too high or punish people in cruel ways.

9 Ninth Amendment People have other rights besides those stated in the Constitution.

10 Tenth Amendment Any powers the Constitution does not give to the federal government belong to the states or the people.

REVIEW List three rights that are protected by the First Amendment.

Review

★ ★ ★

Complete two of the following activities.

Art Activity Work with a group to create a poster titled, *What Democracy Means to Me.* Cut out pictures from newspapers and magazines that illustrate some part of government or something government does.

Writing Activity Choose one of the branches of government and write a short report about it. Give an example of how the branch provides for the common good of the American people.

Research Activity A state capital is a city in which a state's government is located. Make a list of every state's capital. Write a fact card for one capital on your list, including its population and the year it was founded.

Writing Activity Find out who your leaders are at each level of government. Write the names of the President and your senators, representatives, and local leaders. Write to a local leader. Ask questions about that person's job.

Speaking Activity The Bill of Rights still matters today. Prepare an oral report on the First Amendment, explaining how it has affected a current event.

Vocabulary and Main Ideas

✓ **TEST PREP** Write a sentence to answer each question.

1. In what ways was the bison important to the **culture** of Plains Indians?

2. Why did explorers make **expeditions** to the Americas?

3. Explain the reasons that Catholic priests built **missions** throughout New Spain.

4. Why did many people in the colonies want **independence** from Britain?

5. What is the role of citizens in the United States' **democracy?**

6. What basic rights are protected by the **Constitution?**

Critical Thinking

✓ **TEST PREP** Write a short paragraph to answer each question.

7. **Cause and Effect** What effect did new navigational tools have on European exploration and colonization of North America?

8. **Analyze** Why do you think the Constitution, which was written in 1787, has lasted so many years? What does it do to support self-government and democracy? Use details from the unit to support your answer.

Unit Activity

The Big Idea

Create Independence Trading Cards

- Make a list of people and events from the unit that were important in the struggle for independence.

- Research a topic from your list.

- On one side of a blank index card draw a picture of the person or event. On the other side write facts you found.

- Trade cards with your classmates or display the cards in your class.

Independence Card

Declaration of Independence
When: July 4, 1776
Where: Philadelphia
Who: Thomas Jefferson
What: Declared the United States independent of Great Britain
Why: Because of unfair treatment from Great Britain

At the Library

Go to your school or public library to find this book.

Come All You Brave Soldiers: Blacks in the Revolutionary War by Clinton Cox
African American soldiers fought at Lexington, Concord, Yorktown, and elsewhere.

TEST PREP Use the unfinished line graph below and what you know about making a line graph to answer each question.

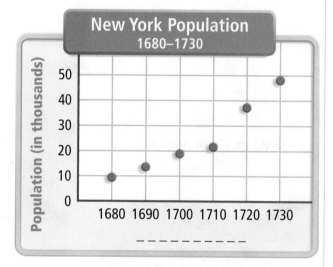

New York Population
1680–1730

9. Which is the best label for the horizontal axis of this line graph?

A. Number of People
B. Time
C. Year
D. Population Growth

10. What should you do after you draw dots to show the data on the line graph?

A. Connect the dots with a line.
B. Draw a bar from the bottom of the graph to where the dot is.
C. Choose a color for the dot.
D. Connect each dot to the correct year.

TEST PREP Answer each question below.

11. What did explorers from Spain, France, and England do when they reached North America?

A. They invented new navigational tools.
B. They set up democratic governments.
C. They sailed on to Asia.
D. They started colonies.

12. Where was the last battle of the American Revolution?

A. Trenton
B. Yorktown
C. Saratoga
D. Boston

13. When Europeans arrived in the Americas, they came in contact with American Indians for the first time. This brought changes for the Europeans and American Indians.

In your **Answer Document,** describe the lasting effects of colonization on culture in North America.

UNIT 4

Growth and Immigration

The Big Idea

What new developments led to the growth of the United States?

 Unit 4 Benchmarks

As you study this unit, you will cover these Ohio Social Studies benchmarks:

History C Explain how new developments led to the growth of the United States.

People in Societies A Compare practices and products of North American cultural groups.

Economics B Explain why entrepreneurship, capital goods, technology, specialization and division of labor are important in the production of goods and services.

Skills and Methods B Use a variety of sources to organize information and draw inferences.

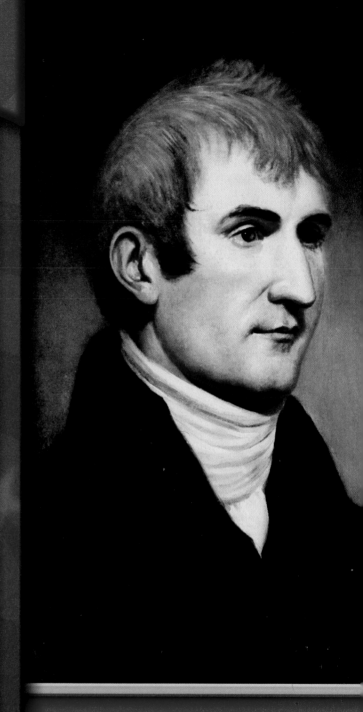

Meriwether Lewis
1774–1809

Thomas Jefferson chose this man to lead the Corps of Discovery across North America. The information that he gathered helped people learn about the West.

page 188

History Makers

Eli Whitney
1765–1825

Can one person change the way goods are made? An American inventor did. Whitney developed ways to produce many goods quickly and at a low cost.
page 199

Wilma Mankiller
1945–

Wilma Mankiller worked to improve health care, education, and government for the Cherokee. She also encouraged young Cherokee girls to get involved in government.
page 209

Almanac

Westward Expansion

L. Superior

Columbia R.

Portland

RED RIVER CESSION–1818
Treaty of 1818
with Great Britain

OREGON TERRITORY–1846
Ceded (given up) by Great Britain

Missouri R.

L. Michigan

Milwaukee

Chicago

Indianapolis

Salt
Lake
City

**LOUISIANA
PURCHASE–1803**
Bought from France

San Francisco

Colorado R.

MEXICAN CESSION–1848
Treaty of Guadalupe Hildago

Kansas City

St. Louis

Nashville

Memphis

Mississippi R.

TEXAS ANNEXATION–1845

Rio Grande

GADSDEN PURCHASE–1853
Bought from Mexico

PACIFIC
OCEAN

San Antonio

Mobile

**WEST FLORIDA
ANNEXATION–
1810, 1813**

Gulf of Mexico

Unit Preview

1790   1800   1810   1820

**1793
Cotton Gin**
Invention changes
agriculture
**Chapter 7,
page 199**

**1803
Louisiana
Purchase**
Jefferson buys
French territory
**Chapter 7,
page 188**

**1804
The 17th State**
Ohio becomes
a state
**Chapter 7,
page 197**

WEBSTER ASHBURTON
TREATY–1842
Border adjustment
with Great Britain

Portland

Boston

L. Huron

L. Ontario

Buffalo

Detroit

L. Erie

Cleveland

Philadelphia

Pittsburgh

New York

Ohio R.

Baltimore

Washington, D.C.

Ohio

UNITED STATES–1783

Norfolk

Lexington

Louisville

Wilmington

Atlanta

Charleston

ATLANTIC

Savannah

OCEAN

Jacksonville

EAST FLORIDA –1819
ceded (given up)
by Spain

N
NE
NW
E
W
SE
SW
S

km 0   150   300

mi 0   150   300

LEGEND
• Major city, 1850

30   1840   1850

1849
Gold Rush
Forty-niners seek
fortune in California
**Chapter 7,
page 206**

Chapter 7,
page 206

Connect to... Today

Population Growth, 1800s

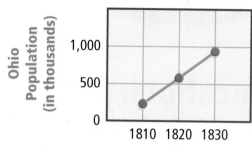

Ohio Population (in thousands)

1,000

500

0

1810 1820 1830

Year

In the early 1800s, people from the
eastern states moved to Ohio, which
had recently become a state.

Population Growth Today

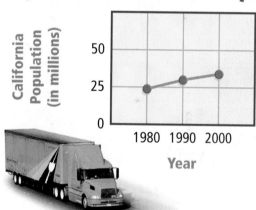

California Population (in millions)

50

25

0

1980 1990 2000

Year

Today people from all over the world
move to California because it offers
economic opportunities.

CURRENT   EVENTS
WEEKLY (WR) READER

Current events on the web!

For a selection of social studies
articles about current events,
go to Education Place:
www.eduplace.com/kids/hmss/

A Growing Nation

Technology

e • glossary
e • word games
www.eduplace.com/kids/hmss/

Vocabulary Preview

suffrage

When territories became new states, all white men in those states were allowed to vote. Even those who did not own land were given **suffrage.** page 190

productivity

With the use of machines, goods could be produced more quickly. Factories increased the **productivity** of the United States. page 199

Chapter Time Line

1803
Louisiana Purchase

1812
Columbus, Ohio founded

1800   1810   1820

Reading Strategy

Question As you read, ask yourself questions to check your understanding.

quick Tip Write down a question you have and answer it when you finish reading.

wagon train

By traveling in a **wagon train,** people moving west could help each other. These lines of covered wagons that moved together could include 1,000 people. **page 205**

forty-niner

Most of those who were part of the California Gold Rush arrived in 1849. They were known as **forty-niners.** page 206

1825
Erie Canal built

1833
National Road completed

1838
Trail of Tears

1830

1840

People on the Move

1750	1770	1790	1810	1830	1850

1763–1838

Build on What You Know Today you can fly across a mountain range in less than an hour. In the late 1700s and early 1800s, it took weeks to make that trip.

Pioneers Cross the Appalachians

Main Idea Pioneers settled land west of the Appalachian Mountains in the late 1700s.

The first settlers who came to the British colonies from Europe settled east of the Appalachian Mountains. This 2,000-mile-long mountain range was difficult to cross. A British law in 1763 also made it illegal for colonists to settle on American Indian lands west of the mountains. But this did not stop people from trying to go there. As more of the East filled in with farms and towns, the pull of economic opportunity caused settlers to find ways to cross the Appalachians in search of land.

The Cumberland Gap This opening, or gap, in the rugged Appalachian Mountains made it easier for colonists to move into the Ohio River Valley.

VOCABULARY

pioneer
frontier
interpreter
doctrine
suffrage

Vocabulary Strategy

interpreter

The prefix **inter-** means between or among. An interpreter goes between people who don't speak the same language to explain what they are saying to each other.

READING SKILL

Sequence As you read, note the order in which events leading to the growth of the nation took place.

1	
2	
3	
4	

BENCHMARKS
HIS C   Growth
GOV A   Role of government

GRADE LEVEL INDICATORS
HIS 6   Impacts on expansion of United States
GOV 2   Characterisitcs of American democracy

The Cumberland Gap

Daniel Boone was a hunter and pioneer who was curious about the land west of the Appalachians. A **pioneer** is one of the first of a certain group to enter or settle a region. In 1769, Boone and five other hunters followed an American Indian trail through a narrow opening, or gap, in the mountains. This opening, called the Cumberland Gap, led from Virginia to thickly forested land in present-day Kentucky. In 1775, Boone helped build a road called the Wilderness Road through the Cumberland Gap.

Thousands of people crossed the Appalachians on the Wilderness Road. Pioneers traveled by wagon and on foot. The Wilderness Road was just a rocky dirt path barely wide enough for a wagon to pass. The road was so bumpy that many wagons broke apart.

After crossing the mountains, settlers journeyed farther west on rivers. Most traveled on the Ohio River. Flatboats carried families, their animals, and their belongings down the river. A flatboat was a large, rectangular boat partly covered by a roof.

Early settlers in Ohio founded towns including Marietta and Cincinnati. The people who built new settlements in the fertile Ohio River Valley thought of the land farther west as a frontier. A **frontier** is the edge of a country or a settled area.

The land beyond the frontier was not empty, however. It was already settled by American Indians. The Shawnee, Choctaw, Cherokee, and other people lived between the Appalachians and the Mississippi River. They didn't want settlers moving onto their lands. On the frontier, American Indians and settlers fought over land, but they also borrowed ideas and customs from one another.

REVIEW What solution did the Cumberland Gap provide for settlers wanting to cross the Appalachians?

Daniel Boone Settlers saw Boone as a hero. Below, Boone leads his team of explorers through the Cumberland Gap.

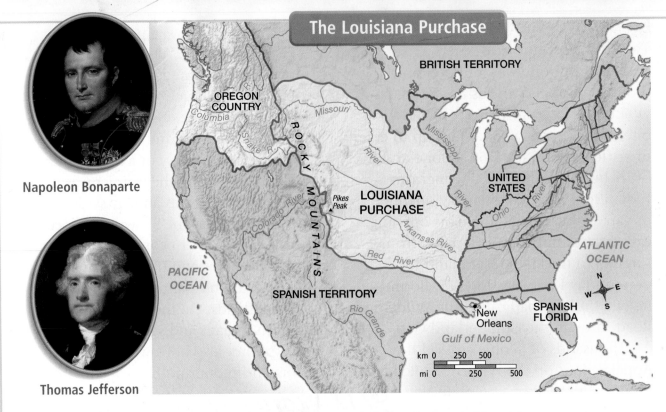

Napoleon Bonaparte

Thomas Jefferson

Louisiana Purchase Napoleon Bonaparte of France sold Louisiana to the United States for $15,000,000. President Thomas Jefferson bought this land to increase the size the United States.

The Louisiana Purchase

Main Idea President Jefferson added territory to the United States and sent explorers there.

When **Thomas Jefferson** was elected President in 1800, the French claimed a large area of land west of the Mississippi River. They called this land Louisiana. France also controlled the port city of New Orleans.

Jefferson sent representatives to France. He wanted the French to let American ships use the port of New Orleans. To his surprise, the French ruler, **Napoleon Bonaparte,** offered to sell all of Louisiana to the United States.

Jefferson quickly accepted the offer. The purchase of this land in 1803 added about 828,000 square miles to the United States. The Louisiana Purchase doubled the size of the country.

Lewis and Clark

President Jefferson wanted to know about the land west of the Mississippi River. He sent a group of soldiers led by **Meriwether Lewis** and **William Clark** to explore it. Jefferson asked them to explore the Missouri and Columbia rivers to find a water route to the Pacific Ocean. He also told them to gather information about the geography, plants, animals, climate, and peoples of the West.

In May of 1804, Lewis and Clark set out from St. Louis, Missouri. Their group was called the Corps (kor) of Discovery. A corps is a team of people working together. A Shoshone (Shoh SHOH nee) woman named **Sacagawea** (sah KAH guh WEE uh) later joined the team and became an interpreter. An **interpreter** explains what is said in one language to people who speak a different language.

Corps of Discovery Sacagawea guided Lewis and Clark west through the Rocky Mountains. The United States Mint honored the 200th anniversary of the Lewis and Clark expedition with a new nickel (right).

American Indians along the way suggested travel routes and traded for supplies and horses. They trusted and helped Lewis and Clark partly because Sacagawea was with them.

The Corps traveled up the Missouri River, over the Rocky Mountains, and down the Columbia River to the Pacific Ocean. It then returned to St. Louis in September 1806 after traveling about 8,000 miles. The explorers had survived hunger, bear attacks, and dangerous, rushing rivers.

Lewis and Clark described the people, wildlife, and land in their journals. Clark made a map of the West that showed mountains and rivers that had never been shown on a map.

Lewis and Clark had learned that there was no water route across the country to the Pacific Ocean. They had shown, however, that it was possible to cross the continent over the Rocky Mountains. The corps had also made friendly contact with western Indians. These discoveries created interest in the West and would help future pioneers and traders for years to come.

REVIEW What did Lewis and Clark learn about the West?

War of 1812

Main Idea As the United States grew, so did conflicts with Britain and American Indians.

People from the United States continued to move west. Fighting increased between settlers and American Indians trying to protect their land. Some people believed that British colonists in Canada were giving weapons to American Indians.

At this time, France and Britain were at war. The United States was neutral, but the British navy seized American ships to stop them from trading with France. The British captured American sailors and forced them to join the British navy. Forcing sailors to serve in the British navy was called impressment.

The United States declared war against Britain in 1812. The two countries fought along the Canadian border and in cities on the East Coast.

Late in the war, British soldiers attacked Washington, D.C. They burned the White House and the Capitol.

By 1814, neither country was winning, so both sides agreed to end the war. Although neither side won any land, Americans were proud that their country had not lost to powerful Britain.

The War of 1812 gave the leaders of the United States confidence. In 1823, President **James Monroe** issued a warning called the Monroe Doctrine. A **doctrine** is an official statement or position. Monroe warned European nations not to start new colonies in the Americas. This warning showed that the United States saw itself as a major power.

After the War of 1812, many new states were added to the United States. All adult white men in these new states were given suffrage. **Suffrage** is the right to vote. For the first time, men who did not own land could legally vote.

War of 1812 In this painting, an American ship captures a British ship in one of the many sea battles of the War of 1812.

President Andrew Jackson

These new voters helped elect President **Andrew Jackson** in 1828. Jackson grew up on the frontier. He was seen as a hero of the War of 1812 and was admired by many as a tough fighter.

Jackson wanted more settlers to own frontier land. To get the land, he signed the Indian Removal Act in 1830. This law ordered American Indian nations east of the Mississippi River to move west to present-day Oklahoma. The U.S. Army forced thousands of American Indians to leave their homes.

People of the Cherokee nation argued that the Indian Removal Act was illegal. Chief **John Ross** took this case to the Supreme Court. The Court agreed that it was against the law to force the Cherokee to move, but President Jackson ignored the ruling. In 1838, the U.S. Army forced the Cherokee to make the nearly 1,000-mile trip west.

Thousands of Cherokee died from the terrible conditions along the way. This heartbreaking journey became known as the Trail of Tears.

REVIEW What was the result of the War of 1812?

Lesson Summary

In the late 1700s, pioneers crossed the Appalachians. President Jefferson arranged to buy the Louisiana Territory in 1803, and the next year, Lewis and Clark set off to explore the West. The United States and Britain fought each other in the War of 1812, but neither side won or lost any land. President Jackson forced American Indians east of the Mississippi to move west in 1830.

Why It Matters ...

In the early 1800s, the United States grew larger and more powerful. Conflicts with American Indians over land, however, would continue throughout the 1800s.

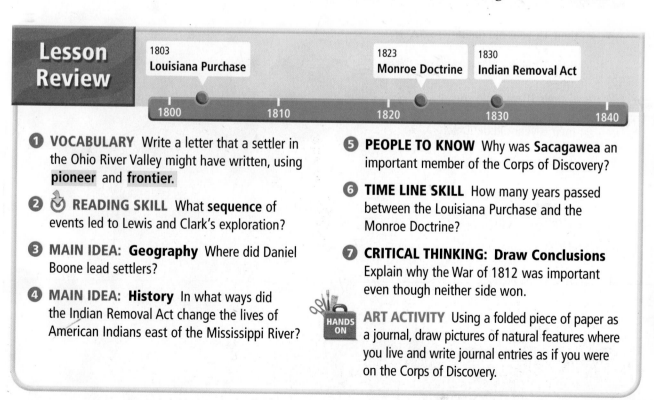

Lesson Review

1803 **Louisiana Purchase**

1823 **Monroe Doctrine**

1830 **Indian Removal Act**

1800 — 1810 — 1820 — 1830 — 1840

❶ **VOCABULARY** Write a letter that a settler in the Ohio River Valley might have written, using **pioneer** and **frontier.**

❷ **READING SKILL** What **sequence** of events led to Lewis and Clark's exploration?

❸ **MAIN IDEA: Geography** Where did Daniel Boone lead settlers?

❹ **MAIN IDEA: History** In what ways did the Indian Removal Act change the lives of American Indians east of the Mississippi River?

❺ **PEOPLE TO KNOW** Why was **Sacagawea** an important member of the Corps of Discovery?

❻ **TIME LINE SKILL** How many years passed between the Louisiana Purchase and the Monroe Doctrine?

❼ **CRITICAL THINKING: Draw Conclusions** Explain why the War of 1812 was important even though neither side won.

HANDS ON **ART ACTIVITY** Using a folded piece of paper as a journal, draw pictures of natural features where you live and write journal entries as if you were on the Corps of Discovery.

Flatboat on the Ohio

What was it like to travel on a flatboat? Imagine that it is spring in the year 1816. A pioneer family is traveling down the Ohio River on a flatboat along with their animals, furniture, food, and supplies. On the twelfth day of the journey, the children raise an excited shout—Cincinnati is up ahead!

Anne

Tom

Characters

Jonah Rees: farmer

Margaret Rees: farmer

Anne: their 15-year-old daughter

Abby: their 12-year-old daughter

Martin: their 10-year-old son

Susie: their 6-year-old daughter

William Rees: Jonah Rees's brother

Tom: William's 16-year-old son

Granny Rees: mother of Jonah and William Rees

Keelboat pilot

Tom: Look, cousins! A big town!

Anne: It must be Cincinnati! Mother, please may I go see? I hear it has five thousand people. People call it "The Queen of the West."

Margaret Rees: Be quick about it, Anne. I want to have a look, too. And check if the hens have laid any eggs while you're at it. Granny! It's Cincinnati!

Granny Rees: Yes—I hear all the noise. I'll take a look from one of those crates. Help me up, Martin.

Martin: There you go, Granny. Just look at all those houses!

Abby: What are those buildings near the river?

Tom: Father says there are lots of cotton mills in Cincinnati. I wonder if we'll go ashore. I'd like to see the town.

Anne: I wish we could live here. It looks so busy and settled.

Abby: Crowded, you mean! I hate to have people breathing down my neck. I can't wait to get to Indiana.

Granny Rees: You sound like your Pa.

Martin: I just hope we're near a settlement with a school and children my age.

Susie: Where are we going to live in Indiana?

Tom: Don't worry. We're buying land from the government.

Anne: Why do we have to move, anyway? Our farm in Pennsylvania was so close to town, so comfortable, wasn't it?

Abby: That's exactly why.

Granny Rees: She means it was getting too crowded for your Pa. Land is cheap in Indiana, and he got a good price for the farm.

Tom: And my father says he needs a change, too. He says he likes a new challenge. Oh, here's your father.

Jonah Rees: Martin! Have you milked Sally yet? She doesn't sound too happy!

Martin: I'll do it right now.

Margaret Rees: And what about the chickens, Anne?

Anne: I got six eggs. Look.

Margaret Rees: Good. I'll go have a look at Cincinnati. Don't let the fire get too big, and watch for sparks. Are we stopping here, Jonah?

Jonah Rees: No reason to. We don't need anything. The children won't want to leave if we do.

Margaret Rees: The children are a touch homesick. Wouldn't you like to see Cincinnati?

Jonah Rees: I can see it from here. I'd rather get to the land office in Jeffersonville so we can make a claim.

Martin: Look! A keelboat is coming up the river. They're signaling.

Keelboat pilot (shouting): Where are you bound?

William Rees: To Jeffersonville, from Pittsburgh!

Keelboat pilot: Watch for a sandbar below Cincinnati, just past Mill Creek.

William Rees: Much obliged, thank you!

Margaret Rees: Anne, oh no! Check that fire! Get some water! Good—that was close. It was sparking, wasn't it?

Anne: I'm sorry, Mother. We were watching the keelboat and the city, and—

Margaret Rees: Don't fret. We're all getting distracted. Be more careful next time.

William Rees: Jonah, if we're going ashore, we need to bring the boat around now.

Jonah Rees: All right. It seems I'm out-voted. Tom, Anne! Help out, now. Take an oar. We're heading in.

Tom: Cousins, did you hear? We're landing in Cincinnati!

Anne, Abby, Martin, Susie: Hooray!

William Rees: Don't get too worked up, now. We're not staying long.

Jonah Rees: That's right. There's land waiting for us in Indiana!

Activities

1. **TALK ABOUT IT** What were three problems that flatboat pioneers had to solve on their journey?

2. **WRITE ABOUT IT** Use a map to locate the route the family is taking. Write another scene about something that could happen before they arrive at their destination.

Skillbuilder

Make an Outline

▶ VOCABULARY
outline

In the last lesson, you read about people moving west across the Appalachian Mountains. You can better understand what you read by taking notes and creating an outline. An **outline** identifies the main ideas and supporting details of a piece of writing. Making an outline can also help you organize your ideas before writing a report.

Learn the Skill

Step 1: Identify the topic of the piece of writing in a title at the top of your outline.

Step 2: Take notes listing each main idea with a Roman numeral. Use your own words to express the ideas.

Step 3: List supporting details under each main idea. Indent each detail and place a capital letter in front of it. Use your own words.

Step 4: Repeat Steps 2 and 3 for the other main ideas in the piece of writing.

Title

I. Main Idea
   A. Supporting detail
   B. Supporting detail

II. Main Idea
   A. Supporting detail
   B. Supporting detail

Practice the Skill

Here is an outline of two paragraphs from Lesson 1. Answer the following questions about the outline.

1 What are the two main ideas in the outline?

2 How many supporting details does the first main idea have?

3 What title would you give this outline?

I.   Land travel was difficult
  A. By wagon or foot
  B. Poor roads
  C. Wagons often needed repairs

II.   Water travel was easier
  A. Families, belongings, animals floated downriver in flatboats
  B. Flatboats had roofs

Apply the Skill

Make an outline of this passage.

Settlers began to arrive in the Ohio Territory soon after Congress passed the Northwest Ordinance in 1787. The first town founded by settlers was Marietta, in 1788. Soon the population of the territory was large enough that Congress gave settlers the power to elect a state legislature. William Henry Harrison represented the Ohio Territory in Congress. In 1803, Ohio became the 17th state.

Ohio's capital moved between Chillicothe and Zanesville for several years. Finally, in 1812, the state government founded a permanent state capital, Columbus. In four years, the government was able to move to its new home, where it has been ever since.

The Industrial Revolution

VOCABULARY

entrepreneur
interchangeable parts
mass production
division of labor
productivity

Vocabulary Strategy

inter**change**able

The word **interchangeable** includes the word **change**. When an interchangeable part breaks, it's easy to change it with a new one.

READING SKILL

Categorize List inventions of the Industrial Revolution in two categories on a chart.

FACTORIES	TRANSPORTATION

BENCHMARKS

HIS C   Growth
ECON B   Production, distribution, and consumption

GRADE LEVEL INDICATORS

HIS 6   Impacts on expansion of United States
ECON 3   Effects on productive capacity

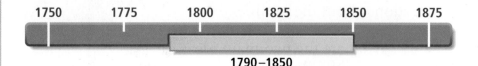

1750	1775	1800	1825	1850	1875

1790–1850

Build on What You Know Most of the things you use are made by machines. People first used machines to make cloth and tools in the late 1700s.

The Industrial Revolution Begins

Main Idea New inventions and ways of working changed how goods were made.

In the early 1700s, people made cloth, tools, and furniture by hand in homes or small shops. That changed in the late 1700s. People found new ways to answer the economic question of how to produce goods. They began to use machines, which could make goods quickly. Also, new forms of transportation moved people and goods faster than ever before. These changes in manufacturing and transportation are known as the Industrial Revolution.

Some machines spun cotton into yarn. Machines could spin cotton much faster than people could do it by hand. In 1790, a British mechanic named **Samuel Slater** opened the first cotton-spinning textile mill, or factory, in the United States. Textile means cloth or fabric.

In 1813, an entrepreneur (AWN trah PAH noor) named **Francis Cabot Lowell** built a mill near Boston. An **entrepreneur** takes risks to start new businesses. Lowell's mill had both cotton-spinning machines and power looms that wove yarn into cloth. It was the first mill in the world to turn raw cotton into finished cloth. Entrepreneurs opened more textile factories, and New England became the center of a growing textile industry.

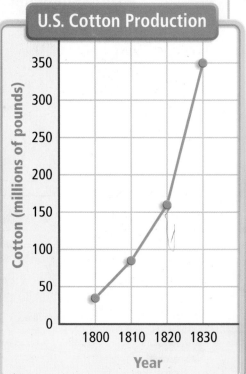

U.S. Cotton Production

Cotton (millions of pounds) vs Year

Textiles Some mills could produce 30 miles of cloth a day. After cloth was woven, designs were printed on it.

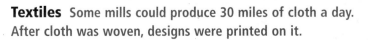

SKILL **Reading Graphs** In which decade did the largest jump in cotton production occur?

Division of Labor

New mills turned cotton into yarn very quickly, but getting cotton ready for these mills took a lot of work. The seeds in the cotton had to be removed before the cotton could be spun into yarn.

In 1793, **Eli Whitney** invented a cotton engine, or gin, that used wire teeth to remove seeds. The gin could do work in minutes that once took a full day for people to do.

The United States hired Whitney to make 10,000 guns for the army. At that time, guns were made one at a time by hand. To make the guns quickly and cheaply, Whitney used interchangeable parts. **Interchangeable parts** are parts made by a machine to be exactly the same so that any of them can fit into another product with the same design.

Whitney used mass production to make the guns. **Mass production** means making many products at once. Instead of making a complete gun, each worker added a certain part to many guns. These parts were always the same. This method of working is known as **division of labor.** Fitting the same parts over and over was faster than making a single gun from start to finish. Other factories used the same methods.

Workers using new machines, interchangeable parts, mass production, and division of labor produced goods more quickly. The productivity of the whole country increased. **Productivity** is the amount of goods produced in a certain amount of time by a person, machine, or group.

REVIEW Why was Whitney able to manufacture guns quickly and cheaply?

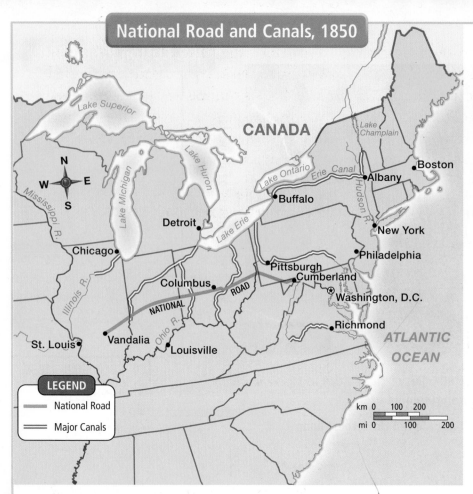

CANADA

Lake Superior

Lake Huron

Lake Michigan

Lake Ontario

Lake Erie

Erie Canal

Lake Champlain

Mississippi R.

Illinois R.

Ohio R.

Hudson R.

Boston

Albany

Buffalo

Detroit

New York

Chicago

Philadelphia

Pittsburgh

Columbus

Cumberland

NATIONAL

ROAD

Washington, D.C.

Richmond

St. Louis

Vandalia

Louisville

ATLANTIC
OCEAN

N W E S

LEGEND
National Road
Major Canals

km 0   100   200
mi 0   100   200

Better Travel Routes

New roads and canals improved travel. By 1840, more than 3,000 miles of canals crossed the eastern United States.

SKILL **Reading Maps** Which land and water routes could a farmer in Columbus, Ohio, take to move goods to New York City?

Changes in Transportation

Main Idea Roads, canals, and railroads improved travel in the 1800s.

Travel was slow and expensive in the early 1800s. Most roads were narrow dirt paths. Snow and rain made roads icy and muddy. Because travel over these roads was difficult, it took a long time and cost a lot of money for farmers to move their goods to cities to be sold.

In 1815, the United States began building a road to connect Ohio with the East. The first section of the road followed an American Indian trail. By 1833, this road, the National Road, went from Maryland to Ohio and was paved with stone. It became the most heavily traveled road in the country. People built towns and businesses all along it.

Steam Power

In the 1700s and early 1800s, shipping goods by water was easier than using roads. However, travel by water was slow, too. Boats could move only by wind or water currents. Then, in 1807, **Robert Fulton** built a successful steamboat, which solved this problem because it could travel against currents. Steam power gave boats more speed. Steamboats soon became common on rivers.

Canals made water travel possible to more cities. Canals are waterways built by people to link bodies of water. In 1825, the Erie Canal opened, connecting the Hudson River to Lake Erie. In Ohio, two major canals connected the Ohio River to Lake Erie. Some towns, such as Akron, began as encampments for workers building the canals.

Travel over land also improved. Trains pulled by steam locomotives were fast. They could run in snow and ice, and travel up and down hills easily. A trip from New York City to Albany, New York, took only 10 hours by railroad instead of 32 hours by steamboat.

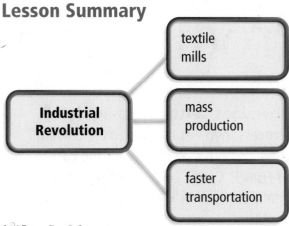

By 1850, the nation had 9,000 miles of railroad track. New tracks were added every day. As more cities were connected by railroads, factories and farmers could ship their goods to almost any city or town in the country.

REVIEW Why were steam locomotives a good solution to transportation problems?

Lesson Summary

Industrial Revolution
- textile mills
- mass production
- faster transportation

Why It Matters ...

New machines and ways of working that were invented during the Industrial Revolution affect the way products are made today.

Locomotives Railroads connected Ohio to the East Coast.

Lesson Review

1793 Eli Whitney invents cotton gin
1813 Lowell builds textile mill
1825 Erie Canal opens

1780 1790 1800 1810 1820 1830

❶ **VOCABULARY** Write a description of Lowell's mill using **division of labor** and **productivity.**

❷ **READING SKILL** Did you **categorize** the cotton gin under factories or transportation? Explain your choice.

❸ **MAIN IDEA: Technology** Why was mass production useful?

❹ **MAIN IDEA: Geography** What bodies of water were connected by the Erie Canal?

❺ **PEOPLE TO KNOW** What did **Eli Whitney** contribute to the Industrial Revolution?

❻ **TIME LINE SKILL** How many years after Lowell opened his mill did the Erie Canal open?

❼ **CRITICAL THINKING: Evaluate** Do you think using interchangeable parts is always the best way to make something? Why or why not?

➤ **WRITING ACTIVITY** Write a news article telling people about the opening of Lowell's textile mill. Tell *Who?*, *What?*, *Where?*, *Why?*, and *When?* in your article.

Mills and Productivity

How does cotton become cloth?
The process involves many steps, including cleaning, spinning, and weaving the cotton. When Francis Cabot Lowell put power looms in his Massachusetts textile factory, he made it possible to do all of the steps of making cloth in one building.

The cloth-making process began on the bottom floor of the mill. After the raw cotton was cleaned, cotton fibers were combed into loose ropes. These ropes were spun into thread on the second floor of the mill. Next, the thread was prepared for weaving on the third floor. Finally, the thread was woven into finished cloth. Dividing the work this way is called division of labor.

Because the labor was divided up, each mill worker specialized in one task. This specialization allowed the workers to become very skilled. They could work faster than someone who had to do all four tasks. By working faster, they increased the mill's productive capacity, or how much cloth it could make.

Bales of Cotton
Workers rip open huge bales of cotton weighing about 500 pounds. The raw cotton is run through machines that clean and sort the cotton fibers.

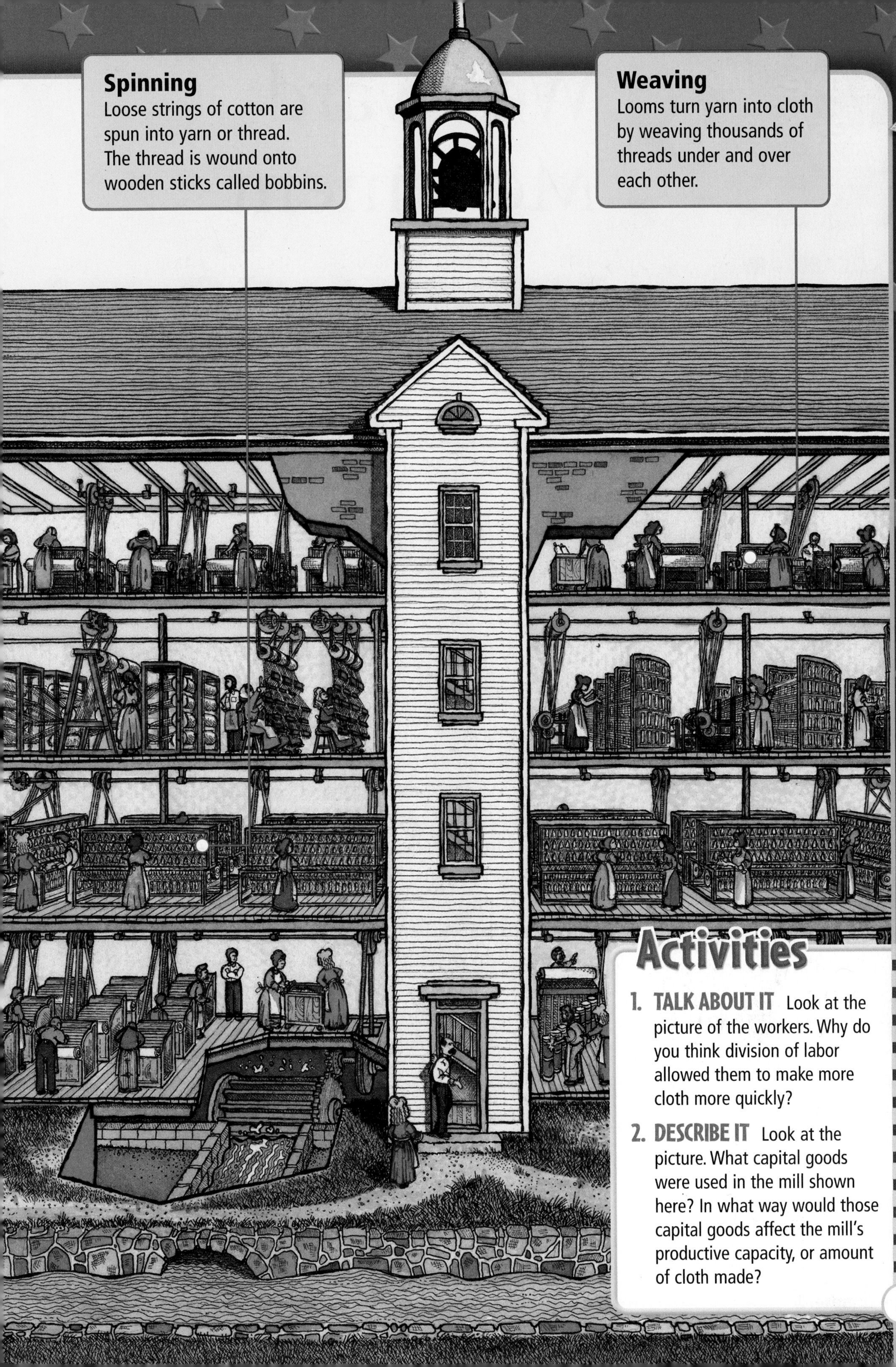

Spinning

Loose strings of cotton are spun into yarn or thread. The thread is wound onto wooden sticks called bobbins.

Weaving

Looms turn yarn into cloth by weaving thousands of threads under and over each other.

Activities

1. **TALK ABOUT IT** Look at the picture of the workers. Why do you think division of labor allowed them to make more cloth more quickly?

2. **DESCRIBE IT** Look at the picture. What capital goods were used in the mill shown here? In what way would those capital goods affect the mill's productive capacity, or amount of cloth made?

Westward Movement

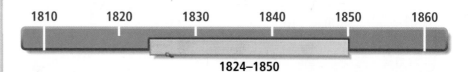

1810　　1820　　1830　　1840　　1850　　1860

1824–1850

VOCABULARY ·

wagon train
forty-niner
gold rush
boomtown

Vocabulary Strategy

> forty-niner

Many people went to California in 1849. They were called **forty-niners.**

READING SKILL

Cause and Effect Note reasons pioneers moved west and what happened as a result.

CAUSES	EFFECTS

BENCHMARKS
HIS C　Growth
PS B　Interaction

GRADE LEVEL INDICATORS
HIS 6　Impacts of settlement, industrialization, and transportation on expansion
PS 2　Cultural traditions of the past and today.

Build on What You Know What made you choose the last book you read? Maybe you heard about it from a friend. Settlers in the 1840s heard exciting things about the West and decided to move there.

Trails West

Main Idea Pioneers made difficult journeys to settle in the West.

In 1824, Crow Indians showed a trapper a way through the Rocky Mountains that was wide enough for wagons. The route was called the South Pass. By the end of the 1850s, thousands of people had traveled through the South Pass on a route known as the Oregon Trail.

The Oregon Trail was about 2,000 miles long. It started in Missouri and stretched west across the Rocky Mountains to present-day Oregon. In some places, the trail was wide and open. When it crossed rivers and mountains, the path became very narrow.

Marcus and **Narcissa Whitman** were two of the first pioneers to travel the Oregon Trail. They were missionaries who settled in eastern Oregon in 1836. They wanted to teach American Indians about Christianity. The Whitman mission became a place where travelers could rest.

Narcissa Whitman She was the first woman from the United States to travel through the South Pass.

Traveling West Settlers traveled in wagon trains for safety and
to keep each other company on the long trip.

Wagon Trains

The first large group of about 1,000
people set out on the Oregon Trail in
1843. They came from Ohio, Indiana,
Illinois, Kentucky, and Tennessee. They
were looking for good, inexpensive land.

Pioneers on the Oregon Trail traveled
by wagon train. A **wagon train** was a line
of covered wagons that moved together.
Oxen, mules, or horses pulled each wagon.

Travelers on the Oregon Trail faced
injuries, diseases, and bad weather. Lack
of food and water were problems, too.
One woman described the trail in her
journal:

66 **Not a drop of water, nor a
spear of grass to be seen,
nothing but barren hills, bare
and broken rock, sand and dust.** 99

Despite the hardships, many people used
the trail to settle in Oregon.

President **James Polk** believed in
manifest destiny. He wanted Oregon to
belong to the United States. At the time,
Oregon was claimed by both the United
States and Britain. In 1846, Polk signed a
treaty with Britain to set the border
between the western United States and
Canada. The land south of this border
became the Oregon Territory in 1848.

Pioneers also took other trails to the
West. People who traveled on the Mormon
Trail were members of the Church of Jesus
Christ of Latter-Day Saints. Members of
this church, which was founded in 1830
in New York, were called Mormons.

Some people would not allow
Mormons to practice their religion. In
1847, **Brigham Young** led the Mormons
west to settle in present-day Utah.

REVIEW What problems did travelers on the
Oregon Trail need to solve?

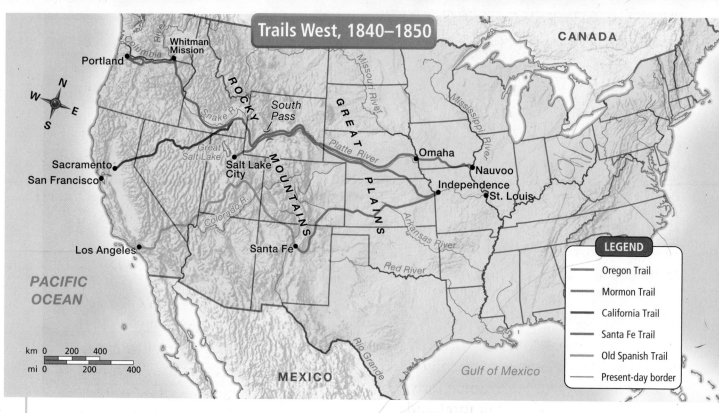

Trails West, 1840–1850

CANADA

Portland
Whitman Mission
Columbia River
ROCKY
South Pass
Snake R.
Great Salt Lake
Sacramento
San Francisco
Salt Lake City
MOUNTAINS
Colorado R.
Missouri River
GREAT PLAINS
Platte River
Omaha
Nauvoo
Independence
St. Louis
Mississippi River
Los Angeles
Santa Fe
Arkansas River
Red River

PACIFIC OCEAN

km 0   200   400
mi 0   200   400

Rio Grande

MEXICO

Gulf of Mexico

LEGEND
Oregon Trail
Mormon Trail
California Trail
Santa Fe Trail
Old Spanish Trail
Present-day border

Overland Trails This map shows the trails most settlers traveled to get to the West. The trails led pioneers along rivers and through mountain passes.

SKILL **Reading Maps** Which trail ends in Sacramento?

The California Gold Rush

Main Idea Thousands rushed to California to dig for gold in the mid-1800s.

Before the 1700s, California Indians lived in villages where they hunted, gathered plants, and fished. When California became part of New Spain, many American Indians were forced to live and work on Spanish missions.

When Mexico gained independence in 1821, California became part of it. Californios, as Mexican citizens in California were called, built large ranches on old mission lands. American Indians were forced to work on the ranches. In 1848, when California joined the United States, Californios could become U.S. citizens. However, very little changed for the American Indians living there.

That same year, gold was discovered in California. Thousands of people from the United States, Mexico, China, Europe, and South America rushed to California to dig for gold. These people became known as forty-niners. A **forty-niner** was a miner who went to California around 1849.

During the California Gold Rush, economic opportunity pulled more than 250,000 people into California. In a **gold rush,** many people hurry to the same area to look for gold. Boomtowns sprang up near the gold mines. A **boomtown** is a town whose population booms, or grows very quickly. Merchants in boomtowns sold food and clothing to the miners. People in boomtowns published newspapers and opened banks and inns. Lawyers found work settling arguments.

Forty-Niners Miners dug for gold with picks and shovels.

After the Gold Rush

The California Gold Rush lasted only about five years. Though a few miners found gold, most did not. Some forty-niners went back home, but thousands stayed and settled in California.

The gold rush changed California. Miners and farmers killed California Indians and took over their land. Newcomers also forced many Californio property owners off their land.

Cities such as San Francisco grew. By 1850, only two years after becoming a U.S. territory, California had enough people to become a state. The new state included American Indians and people from Mexico, China, South America, Europe, and other parts of the United States.

REVIEW Who lived in the boomtowns around the gold mines?

Lesson Summary

- Missionaries, farmers, and other settlers traveled west in wagon trains.
- The discovery of gold in 1848 brought thousands of people to California.
- Growth in California led to conflicts with American Indians and Californios.

Why It Matters ...

In their search for land, religious freedom, and gold, pioneers started new towns in many present-day western states.

Lesson Review

1843	1847	1848
First wagon train to Oregon	Mormons arrived in Utah	Gold discovered in California

1840   1842   1844   1846   1848   1850   1852

❶ **VOCABULARY** Choose the vocabulary word that correctly completes the sentence below.

boomtowns   forty-niners   wagon trains

In 1849, _____ rushed to California for gold.

❷ **READING SKILL** Choose one reason why settlers moved west, and write a summary of what **effect** these settlers had on the country.

❸ **MAIN IDEA: History** Why did the Whitmans settle in eastern Oregon?

❹ **MAIN IDEA: History** Describe two changes in California after the gold rush ended.

❺ **PEOPLE TO KNOW** How did **Marcus** and **Narcissa Whitman** help settlers traveling west?

❻ **TIME LINE SKILL** How many years after the first group of settlers traveled to Oregon did the Mormons arrive in Utah?

❼ **CRITICAL THINKING: Evaluate** Explain an economic reason why a banker, innkeeper, or shopkeeper would have moved to a California boomtown during the gold rush.

WRITING ACTIVITY Write a journal entry that a person traveling in a wagon train might have written. Describe the hardships he or she might have faced.

CULTURAL TRADITIONS TODAY

When settlers moved west, they took over lands where American Indians lived. As the United States and other North American nations grew larger, American Indians lost their lands. Many were forced to move to reservations. A reservation is land that the government set aside for American Indians.

Life on reservations led to many changes in American Indian ways of life and cultural traditions. New technologies and new customs brought more changes. The effects were not the same for all groups. Three groups whose cultural traditions have changed over time are the Cherokee, Diné, and Inuit.

Cherokee Leader Wilma Mankiller was the first woman to be elected Principal Chief of the Cherokee Nation, from 1985 to 1995.

CHEROKEE

Long ago, the Cherokee lived in many towns in what today is the southeastern United States. Each town had two leaders, known as the White Chief and the Red Chief. The White Chief led during times of peace. The Red Chief took over during wartime.

In the 1800s, most Cherokee were forced to move to a large reservation in Oklahoma. There, they rebuilt their government. Like the United States government, the Cherokee have a written constitution and a government with three branches: executive, legislative, and judicial. The Principal Chief, who is elected by Cherokee voters, leads the executive branch. The legislative branch is made up of an elected Tribal Council. The Judicial Appeals Tribunal is the highest court of the Cherokee nation.

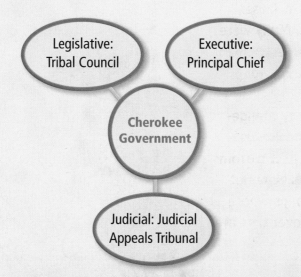

Legislative: Tribal Council

Executive: Principal Chief

Cherokee Government

Judicial: Judicial Appeals Tribunal

DINÉ

For hundreds of years, the Diné (DIN eh), also known as the Navajo (NAHV uh hoh), have lived in the Southwest. In the 1600s, the Diné grew crops and raised sheep for wool. These traditions continued until the Diné were moved onto a reservation where the land was too dry for farming and herding. There, they found new ways to meet their needs.

Mining is now the largest part of the Diné economy. Oil was discovered on the reservation in the 1920s, and coal and natural gas are mined there as well. The Diné also opened their reservation to tourists. Thousands of visitors come every year to see the natural beauty of the area. In the 1990s, the Diné returned to their tradition of farming by using modern methods of planting crops and irrigation.

Diné Economy

Business 32%
Mining 51%
Tourism 17%

Dry Land Into Farms Thelma Yazzie checks the water level on an irrigated field. The Navajo Indian Irrigation Project provides water to more than 60,000 acres of Diné land.

Cultural Products Traditional kayaks and modern motorboats are both part of Inuit life today.

INUIT

The Inuit have lived in the far north for thousands of years. The Canadian territory of Nunavut, where most Inuit live today, is in North America's arctic region. Long ago, the Inuit built homes out of snow and earth. They traveled rivers and lakes in light boats called kayaks to trade cultural products such as furs, stone lamps, cooking pots, and ivory or wood figures.

Today, the Inuit build wooden homes and use motorboats. Inuit groups pass on and share their traditions and history through education, arts and crafts, and even television and radio shows.

Activities

1. **DRAW IT** Make two drawings that compare everyday life for the Diné today and before the reservation system.

2. **RESEARCH IT** Using library or Internet resources, find out about how the government, economy, or culture of two American Indian nations have changed under the reservation system. Create a display comparing the cultures of the nations and how they have changed.

Visual Summary

1. – 3. ✏️ Write a description of each item named below.

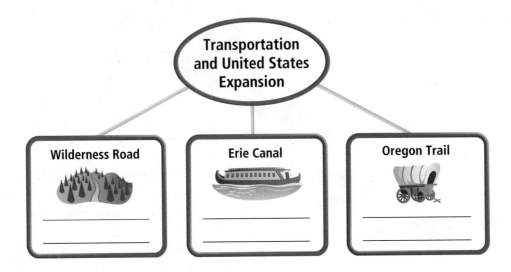

Transportation and United States Expansion

Wilderness Road

Erie Canal

Oregon Trail

Facts and Main Ideas

✓ TEST PREP Answer each question with information from the chapter.

4. **Geography** How did the Cumberland Gap help western settlement?

5. **Government** What was the Indian Removal Act, and why did President Jackson sign it?

6. **Economics** What was the advantage of using division of labor to make goods?

7. **History** Describe the effect of new forms of transportation, such as steamboats and railroads, on the expansion of the United States.

8. **History** Why did many people move to California in 1849?

Vocabulary

✓ TEST PREP Choose the correct word from the list below to complete each sentence.

doctrine, p. 190
entrepreneur, p. 198
boomtown, p. 206

9. When people discovered gold, a(n) _____ might grow up near the mine.

10. Francis Cabot Lowell was a(n) _____ who built a mill near Boston.

11. The Monroe _____ warned European nations not to start new colonies in the Americas.

| 1803 Louisiana Purchase | 1812 War of 1812 begins | 1825 Erie Canal built | 1833 National Road completed | 1838 Trail of Tears |

1800   1810   1820   1830   1840

Apply Skills

☑ TEST PREP **Study Skill** Read the outline below. Use what you have learned about making an outline to answer each question.

> Industrial Revolution
> I. How goods were produced
>   A. New machines
>   B. Interchangeable parts
>   C. Mass production
>   D.
>
>   Changes in transportation
>   A. Better roads
>   B. Canals dug
>   C. Railroads

12. Which supporting details fits best for "D" under the first main idea?

  A. Cars

  B. The Internet

  C. Division of labor

  D. The cotton engine

13. What should be placed in front of "Changes in transportation"?

  A. A.

  B. b.

  C. 2.

  D. II.

Short Response

☑ TEST PREP Write a short paragraph to answer the question below.

14. Before the American Revolution, most settlers lived in the eastern part of North America. During the 1800s, people moved west, building towns on land that is now part of the United States.

In your **Answer Document,** identify and explain causes and effects of the growth of the United States.

Time Line

Use the Chapter Summary Time Line above to answer the question.

15. Which was completed first, the Erie Canal or the National Road?

Activities

Drama Activity Write a scene in which workers at a textile mill discuss division of labor. They might compare the jobs they do, or discuss how mill work is different from farm work.

Writing Activity Using library or Internet resources, write a research report about one development you have read about that contributed to the growth of the United States.

Technology

Writing Process Tip
Get help with your report at
www.eduplace.com/kids/hmss/

Chapter 8

Immigration

Technology

e • **glossary**
e • **word games**
www.eduplace.com/kids/hmss/

Vocabulary Preview

ethnic group

In the United States, people come from many different **ethnic groups.** Their different languages and customs mix to become part of the culture of the whole country. **page 220**

tenement

Immigrants came to the United States with little money to pay for food and a place to live. Most lived in crowded and unsafe buildings called **tenements.** **page 220**

Chapter Time Line

1882
Chinese Exclusion Act

1921
Immigration quotas passed

1880   1900   1920

Reading Strategy

Monitor and Clarify As you read, check your understanding of the text.

Ask yourself if what you are reading makes sense. Reread if you need to.

quota

In the 1920s, the United States put a **quota** on immigrants from different countries. These numbers were set to limit immigration.
page 222

bracero

In the 1940s, Mexican workers were invited to work on United States farms. Hundreds of thousands of **braceros** crossed the border every year. **page 223**

1965
Immigration and Nationality Act

40   1960   1980

Coming to North America

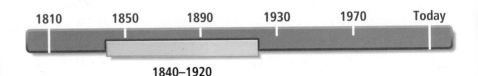

1810   1850   1890   1930   1970   Today

1840–1920

VOCABULARY

immigrant
famine
persecution
ethnic group
tenement

Vocabulary Strategy

ethnic group

Ethnic comes from a word that means nation. An **ethnic group** is a group of people from the same nation or culture.

 READING SKILL

Compare and Contrast
As you read, show how European immigration and Asian immigration were alike and different.

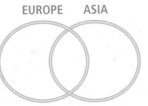

EUROPE   ASIA

BENCHMARKS
PS B   Interaction

GRADE LEVEL INDICATORS
PS 4   North American immigration
PS 5   Experiences of immigrants

Build on What You Know You may have celebrated St. Patrick's Day by wearing green. Irish immigrants brought this holiday to the United States.

German and Irish Immigration

Main Idea Millions of German and Irish immigrants came to the United States in the mid-1800s.

People had been moving to North America from European countries since the 1500s. They were immigrants. An **immigrant** is a person who moves to another country to live. Between 1840 and 1860, the number of immigrants rose sharply. About four million Europeans came to the United States during this time. Almost half of these immigrants were Irish. About one-third were German. The rest came from other parts of Europe.

European Immigration
1840–1860

Other European Countries 24%

Germany 34%

Ireland 42%

SKILL Reading Graphs
What percentage of immigrants coming to the United States between 1840 and 1860 were German?

Why They Came

Irish and German people learned about what to expect in the United States from relatives who lived there. They were told of the land and job opportunities that could be found across the Atlantic Ocean.

Thousands of Germans left Europe because of war and crop failures. When they arrived in the United States, many Germans settled in the Midwest where land was plentiful. Those who had the money, education, and skills bought land and started farms. Some found work in midwestern cities such as Chicago, St. Louis, Cincinnati, and Milwaukee.

Members of a religious group known as the Amish arrived from Germany in large numbers. The first had come to North America in the 1600s, settling in Pennsylvania. About 3,000 more came in the 1800s. Many of them settled in Ohio. Today, Holmes County, Ohio, has the largest Amish population in the world.

Finding Work

The problem of the Irish Potato Famine caused many people to leave Ireland. **Famine** is a widespread shortage of food. Potatoes were the main source of food for the poor in Ireland. When disease destroyed Ireland's potato crop in 1846, more than one million people died.

Over the next ten years, over one million Irish people solved the problem of hunger by coming to the United States. Most didn't have money to buy land. They settled in northeastern port cities to work in factories, as household servants, or as builders.

Immigrants were not the only people who wanted jobs. Blacksmiths, weavers, and other craftspeople were losing work. Goods they had made by hand, such as tools and cloth, were now produced at lower cost in factories. Rural people left farms and workshops to find jobs in cities.

REVIEW What problems led Germans and Irish to immigrate?

Amish Culture Traditions such as not using much modern technology are still practiced by the Amish in Ohio.

New Arrivals
Most ships arriving at Angel Island were from Asia. Some immigrants, however, came from Europe.

New Immigrants Arrive

Main Idea Immigrants came from more countries in the late 1800s and early 1900s.

Between 1880 and 1920, about 25 million immigrants moved to the United States. These new immigrants came mainly from countries in southern or eastern Europe, such as Italy, Russia, Hungary, Greece, and Poland.

Poverty pushed immigrants to leave their countries, and the hope of finding work pulled them to the United States. Persecution also pushed some to leave. **Persecution** is unfair treatment that causes suffering. In the 1880s, thousands of Jews moved from Russia to the United States to escape religious persecution. Freedom in the United States also pulled them.

The most famous immigration station for Europeans was Ellis Island in New York Harbor. Doctors made sure immigrants were healthy. Almost all European immigrants were allowed to stay.

Immigrants from Asia

The first large group of Asian immigrants came to the United States in the early 1850s. At that time, thousands of immigrants traveled from China to California to find gold during the Gold Rush. Chinese continued to arrive in large numbers until 1882. In that year, Congress passed a law called the Chinese Exclusion Act. The law stopped Chinese immigration for 10 years. It did not end immigration from other parts of Asia. Japanese immigrants to California filled many of the jobs that Chinese immigrants had been doing.

The largest California immigration station was Angel Island in San Francisco Bay. Prejudice against Asians made it harder for them to enter America than for Europeans. Some stayed there for months. Many were never let into the country.

Cultural Interaction

Immigrants started organizations to help others in their cultural groups. For example, Chinese immigrants set up community organizations to support each other. These groups included people who came from the same area of China or who did the same kind of work.

Some organizations were based on religion. Many German, Irish, and Polish immigrants were members of the Roman Catholic religion. Cultural pull drew them to live near each other. Immigrants worked with their churches to help more people from their country immigrate. These organizations also helped people find housing and jobs, and gave them a place to celebrate the holidays and carry on their cultural traditions.

Some cultural groups started newspapers. Like other cities with large German populations, Cincinnati had several newspapers written in German.

As immigrants arrived, they interacted with people of other cultures. Over time, people from different cultural groups married and blended their cultures. Today, many Americans have ancestors and relatives from several different countries.

Some traditions brought by certain cultural groups became part of the common culture. For example, people across the country eat Italian or Chinese food. St. Patrick's Day, an important holiday in Ireland, is celebrated in many towns and cities where Irish immigrants settled.

REVIEW What was one consequence of different cultural groups interacting?

Sharing Traditions Groups such as the Marysville, Ohio, German Band let immigrants share their culture with other people.

Immigrants in U.S. Cities, 1920

LEGEND
- • 50,000-99,000 immigrants
- ● 100,000-499,000 immigrants
- ○ 500,000-999,000 immigrants
- ● Over 1,000,000 immigrants

Settling in the United States New York City was the most popular place for immigrants to settle. **SKILL** **Reading Maps** What pattern is indicated by the cities shown on the map?

Living in a New Country

Main Idea Immigrants usually lived in large cities and worked in factories.

After entering the United States, many immigrants moved to large cities such as New York and San Francisco. Immigrant communities in big cities grew quickly as people settled near friends or family. In some cities, whole neighborhoods were made up of a single religious or ethnic group. An **ethnic group** is a group of people who share a culture or language. In an ethnic neighborhood, people spoke their own language, ate the foods of their homeland, and kept many homeland customs and traditions.

Tenements were the first homes for many immigrants living in large cities. A **tenement** was a rundown, poorly maintained apartment building.

Tenements were crowded, dirty, and unsafe. Some tenements had no running water or windows. Often, several families squeezed into one small apartment.

Immigrants had little trouble finding jobs, but their lives were not easy. Many worked in dangerous steel mills or coal mines. Others worked in unsafe factories where they sewed clothing or made thread. In the West, Asian immigrants usually worked in small businesses such as restaurants, or on farms. Nearly all immigrants worked long hours for very low pay. They often made so little money they could barely buy food and clothing for their families.

Immigrants supplied much of the labor that made businesses grow in the early 1900s. With the help of immigrants' hard work, the United States became one of the richest and fastest-growing countries in the world.

Tenements Many immigrants lived in crowded tenement buildings like the ones shown here.

Challenges for Immigrants

In spite of immigrants' contributions, a growing number of Americans feared and disliked these new arrivals. Some people worried about losing their jobs to immigrants because they worked for so little pay. Others distrusted immigrants because they had different customs, languages, and religions.

There were consequences as more and more immigrants came to the United States. Negative feelings against them grew stronger. By the 1920s, many people wanted to limit or stop new immigration.

REVIEW What kinds of jobs did new immigrants take?

Lesson Summary

Millions of immigrants moved to the United States from Europe and Asia. Many of them lived in large cities and worked in factories. The large number of immigrants made some people want to limit immigration.

Why It Matters...

The hard work of immigrants helped to make businesses and the economy strong.

Lesson Review

1846 **Irish Potato Famine**

1882 **Chinese Exclusion Act**

1830 — 1850 — 1870 — 1890 — 1910 — 1930

1 **VOCABULARY** Choose the correct word to complete the sentence.

  persecution   ethnic group   tenement

Many immigrants lived in crowded _____s in large cities.

2 **READING SKILL** Which reasons did European and Asian immigrants share for coming to the United States?

3 **MAIN IDEA: History** Why did so many people want to move to the United States in the late 1800s and early 1900s?

4 **MAIN IDEA: Geography** Where did most immigrants come from between 1840 and 1860?

5 **PLACES TO KNOW** What were Ellis Island and Angel Island?

6 **TIME LINE SKILL** In what year did Congress pass the Chinese Exclusion Act?

7 **CRITICAL THINKING: Decision Making** What were some of the costs and benefits an immigrant had to consider in making the decision to come to the United States?

HANDS ON **INTERVIEW ACTIVITY** Write a list of questions that you would like to ask an immigrant arriving in the United States today. Try your questions out on a partner.

Twentieth-Century Immigration

1910   1930   1950   1970   1990   Today

1920–Today

Build on What You Know You know that the United States has welcomed millions of immigrants from all over the world. In the 1920s, however, the country closed its doors to many immigrants.

Limiting Immigration

Main Idea In the 1920s, the United States government passed laws that limited immigration for over 40 years.

In 1921 and 1924, Congress passed laws to control immigration. These laws had two goals. The first was to limit which countries immigrants came from. The second was to limit the total number of immigrants. The government decided to use quotas to reach these goals. A **quota** is the maximum number of people allowed to enter a country.

VOCABULARY

quota
bracero
refugee

Vocabulary Strategy

> refugee

Find the word **refuge** in **refugee**. A refugee is someone who looks for refuge, or place of safety.

READING SKILL

Cause and Effect Note the effects that new laws had on immigration to the United States.

CAUSE	EFFECT

BENCHMARKS
PS B   Interaction
GEO B   Places and regions

GRADE LEVEL INDICATORS
PS 4   North American immigrants
PS 5   Experiences of immigrants
GEO 7   Regional conflicts and cooperation

New York City Immigrant neighborhoods, such as New York City's Lower East Side, grew quickly in the early 1900s.

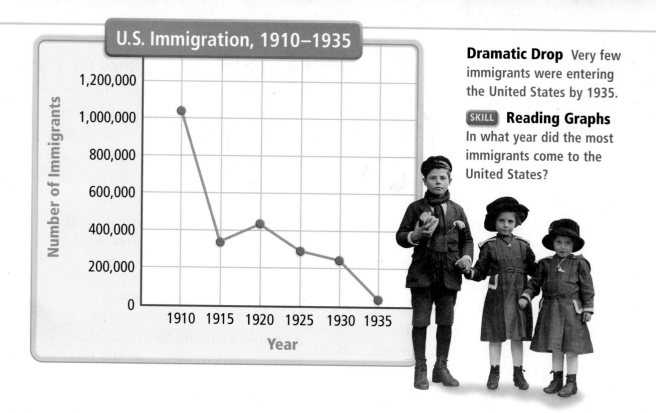

U.S. Immigration, 1910–1935

Number of Immigrants (vertical axis): 0, 200,000, 400,000, 600,000, 800,000, 1,000,000, 1,200,000

Year (horizontal axis): 1910, 1915, 1920, 1925, 1930, 1935

Dramatic Drop Very few immigrants were entering the United States by 1935.

SKILL **Reading Graphs** In what year did the most immigrants come to the United States?

New Immigration Laws

With these new laws, each country was given a quota. Only the number of immigrants allowed by the quota could come to the United States. The new quotas did not treat all countries the same. They favored some countries, such as Great Britain and Germany. Other countries, such as Italy and Spain, had much lower quotas. Few immigrants from Asia or Africa were allowed in.

The quotas also lowered the total number of immigrants that came each year. By 1930, the total had dropped from over 400,000 to about 240,000 per year. The United States used these quotas until 1965.

The quotas did not apply to Canada or Latin America. The United States did not want to harm its neighbors. Also, workers from Latin America, and especially Mexico, had become very important to the United States economy.

Mexican Immigration

Since the late 1800s, thousands of Mexican immigrants had worked on railroads, mines, and large farms, mainly in the western United States. Between 1910 and 1920, about one million Mexicans came to the United States to work.

In the 1940s, the country faced a shortage of farm workers. To help solve the problem, many Mexicans were invited to work in the United States as temporary workers. They were called **braceros,** a Spanish word for laborer. By the 1950s, more than 200,000 braceros came to the United States almost every year.

Thousands of other Mexicans crossed the border to work without permission. They risked being arrested to earn more money in the United States. Employers hired them because they worked hard and would accept low pay. Many people, however, felt jobs were being taken from United States citizens.

REVIEW What effect did quotas have on immigration?

A New Era of Immigration

Main Idea After 1965, immigrants could come to the United States from all over the world.

Feelings about immigration changed during the 1950s and 1960s. The economy was doing well. Businesses needed more workers. Many government leaders did not like the old quota laws. They wanted people from every country to have the same chance to immigrate.

In 1965, the government passed the Immigration and Nationality Act. This law changed the old quotas and allowed many more people to immigrate. Under the new rules, relatives of people who had already immigrated to the United States were allowed to enter the country. People who had certain skills were also let in. The 1965 law increased immigration from Asia, Latin America, and southern Europe.

Refugees Come to America

Another change in immigration laws allowed more refugees to enter the country. A **refugee** is a person who has left his or her home country to escape danger. Since 1965, millions of people have had to flee their home countries to escape war, persecution, or hunger. President **Jimmy Carter** expressed the feelings of many when he said:

> 66 To help [them] is a simple human duty. As Americans, as a people made up largely of the descendants of refugees, we feel that duty with a special keenness. 99

In the 1960s, thousands of refugees left the island of Cuba. During a civil war in the 1980s, people also fled the Central American country of El Salvador.

Americans felt a special responsibility to help refugees from the Asian country of South Vietnam (VEE eht nahm). Soldiers from the United States and South Vietnam had fought together in a long war. The government allowed thousands of Vietnamese refugees to come to the country.

As in the 1800s, each ethnic group brought its own foods, art, language, and religion. Over time, these cultural practices and products began to blend with each other and with those of earlier immigrant groups.

New Immigrants Mexican immigrants living in Texas hold up their new citizenship papers.

Vietnamese Celebration
The Los Angeles area has the largest Vietnamese community outside of Vietnam. Here, a Vietnamese American celebrates the Vietnamese New Year.

Many immigrants have settled in Ohio. Today, cities such as Cleveland, Toledo, and Columbus are home to large Asian and Hispanic populations.

The lives of immigrants in the United States have often been hard. Even so, immigrants have used their skills and values to contribute to the economy and culture of the United States.

REVIEW What are two ways in which immigration changed after 1965?

Lesson Summary
- Between 1921 and 1965, immigration was limited by a system of quotas.
- Since 1965, the United States has accepted immigrants who have family members already in the United States, have special skills, or are refugees.

Why It Matters ...
After 1965, laws made it possible for immigrants from all over the world to bring new ideas, values, and skills to the United States.

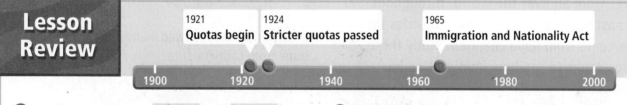

Lesson Review

	1921 **Quotas begin**	1924 **Stricter quotas passed**		1965 **Immigration and Nationality Act**		
1900	1920	1940		1960	1980	2000

❶ **VOCABULARY** Use **refugee** and **bracero** in a paragraph explaining why each group has come to the United States.

❷ 🕑 **READING SKILL** What were the **effects** on immigration of the 1965 law?

❸ **MAIN IDEA: Government** Why did the government change immigration laws in 1965?

❹ **MAIN IDEA: History** Why did the United States give special help to refugees from Vietnam?

❺ **PEOPLE TO KNOW** Who were the braceros and what was their role in the U.S. economy?

❻ **TIME LINE SKILL** When did the United States start using a quota system for immigration?

❼ **CRITICAL THINKING: Infer** Why do you think refugees would want to come to the United States? In your response, discuss jobs and other opportunities.

✏ **WRITING ACTIVITY** Write a personal essay telling how you think the United States' history of immigration affects the country today.

CHANGES IN IMMIGRATION

In the last century, immigrants have come to the United States from many different countries by ship, train, car, and airplane. Before steamships became widely used in the late 1800s, it took most immigrants almost two weeks to sail from Europe by ship and almost two months from Asia. Travel by train could take several days from parts of Canada and Mexico. Now, most people can come to the United States by airplane in a day.

Immigrants have come to the United States from all over the world. Throughout the past century, however, the countries they have come from have changed. Study these circle graphs to see how immigration has changed.

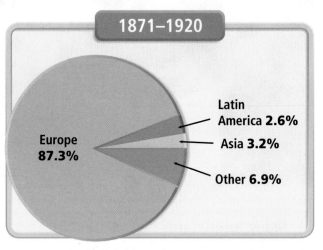

1871–1920

Europe 87.3%
Latin America 2.6%
Asia 3.2%
Other 6.9%

During this period, large numbers of immigrants came from Germany, Italy, and Russia.

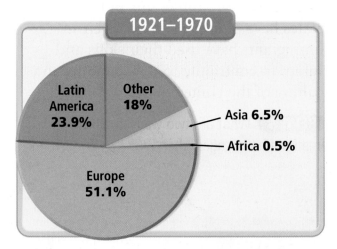

1921–1970

Latin America 23.9%
Other 18%
Asia 6.5%
Africa 0.5%
Europe 51.1%

Immigration laws allowed many more immigrants to come from Latin America.

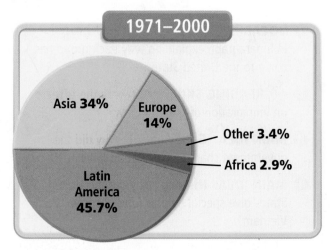

1971–2000

Asia 34%
Europe 14%
Other 3.4%
Africa 2.9%
Latin America 45.7%

How much has the percentage of immigrants from Latin America and Asia increased since 1970?

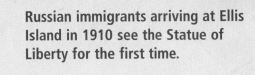

Russian immigrants arriving at Ellis Island in 1910 see the Statue of Liberty for the first time.

Activities

1. **THINK ABOUT IT** Look at the photo on this page. Why might this family have come to the United States? What might they be thinking?

2. **WRITE ABOUT IT** Interview someone you know whose parents or grandparents came to the United States after 1900. Ask when and how they came. Summarize what you find out.

Skillbuilder

Draw Inferences

> **VOCABULARY**
>
> **inference**

When you read about immigration, you can draw the inference that groups of immigrants brought cultural practices and products with them when they came to the United States. An **inference** is an idea that is not directly stated. The text does not say this directly, but if you combine what you know with the information in the text, you can make a reasonable inference that this was the case.

Learn the Skill

In the 1960s, thousands of refugees from Cuba settled in Florida. Today, shops and restaurants in many Florida cities sell plantain chips and empanadas, which are pastries stuffed with meat or vegetables.

Step 1: What information do you read or see?

In the 1960s, thousands of people left Cuba and settled in Florida.

Step 2: What information do you already know?

Immigrants brought their cultural practices and products with them to the United States.

Step 3: Make an inference based on the new information and the things you already know.

Empanadas and plantain chips are foods from Cuba.

Practice the Skill

> Findlay Market in Cincinnati was a log cabin store owned by James Findlay in 1793. The market grew, and immigrants from Germany settled around it in the 1830s and 1840s. Today, the market still has stores founded by German immigrants. It also includes shops owned by Italian, Irish, African-American, Latino, Lebanese, and Vietnamese families. The market offers fruits and vegetables, baked goods, and homemade food products.

1 What information did you learn about who owns shops in Findlay Market?

2 Do you think the ethnic groups who live around Findlay Market have changed since the 1840s? Explain your answer.

3 What inference can you draw about the types of things you can buy in Findlay Market today?

Apply the Skill

Go back and re-read Lesson 2, *Coming to North America.* Study two of the groups of people discussed in this lesson. Find out information about the cultural practices of these groups. What inference can you draw about how these groups are alike and different?

Visual Summary

1. – 4. ✏️➤ Write a description of each period of immigration named below.

🧳 Immigration to the United States	
1840 to 1860	
1880 to 1920	
1920 to 1965	
1965 to Today	

Facts and Main Ideas

✔️ **TEST PREP** Answer each question with information from the chapter.

5. History What effects did problems such as wars and crop failures in Europe have on immigration to the United States?

6. History Where did most immigrants settle in the late 1800s and early 1900s?

7. Government What was a consequence of laws limiting immigration in the 1920s?

8. Geography Name one country from which many refugees have come to the United States.

Vocabulary

✔️ **TEST PREP** Choose the correct word from the list below to complete each sentence.

persecution, p. 218
ethnic group, p. 220
quota, p. 222

9. Laws in the 1920s set a(n) _____ for how many immigrants could enter the country.

10. Thousands of Russian immigrants came to the United States to escape _____.

11. Each _____ has brought its culture and traditions to the United States.

Apply Skills

✔ **TEST PREP** **Reading and Thinking Skill** Read the passage below. Then use what you have learned about drawing inferences to answer each question.

> After 1840, the number of Irish immigrants to Ohio grew rapidly. Many of them worked at difficult jobs, such as building canals and railroads. Some people did not want the immigrants to come to Ohio. They tried to stop more immigration from Ireland.

12. What do you already know about Irish immigration to the United States?
   A. The voyage was easy.
   B. They had no trouble finding jobs.
   C. They immigrated to escape a famine.
   D. Everyone in Ohio welcomed them.

13. In your **Answer Document,** use the information in the paragraph and what you already know to draw an inference about Irish immigration to Ohio.

Extended Response

✔ **TEST PREP** Write a paragraph to answer the question below.

14. Some of the earliest cultural groups to immigrate to the United States in large numbers included the Irish and Germans. Today, many come from Latin America and Asia.

   In your **Answer Document,** explain the reasons people from various groups came to North America. Then explain one consequence of the interactions of these groups in the United States.

Time Line

Use the Chapter Summary Time Line above to answer the question.

15. In which decade was the Immigration and Nationality Act passed?

Activities

Map Activity Make a map to show which countries different waves of immigrants to the United States have come from.

Writing Activity Find out more about the art, food, and religion of different cultural groups that have immigrated to the United States. Write a report comparing these cultural practices.

Technology
Writing Process Tips
Get help with your report at
www.eduplace.com/kids/hmss/

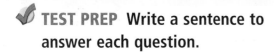

Vocabulary and Main Ideas

TEST PREP Write a sentence to answer each question.

1. Why might a **pioneer** have wanted to cross the Appalachian Mountains in the late 1700s?

2. How did **mass production** change **productivity** in the early 1800s?

3. What effects did flatboats and **wagon trains** have on the growth of the United States?

4. What changes did **forty-niners** bring to California?

5. Why did new immigrants to the United States often live with other members of their **ethnic groups?**

6. What type of **quotas** did Congress pass in the 1920s?

Critical Thinking

TEST PREP Write a short paragraph to answer each question.

7. **Cause and Effect** Explain ways in which changes in transportation affected United States expansion.

8. **Evaluate** Describe the reasons people immigrated to the United States. Compare their reasons with their experiences when they arrived in the United States.

Unit Activity

Create a Web about Expansion

- Choose an event from this unit that affected the growth of the United States.

- Research other events or changes that were caused by the event you chose.

- Write a phrase for that event in an oval. Draw lines from the central event to the effects it caused.

- Post your United States Growth Web in your class.

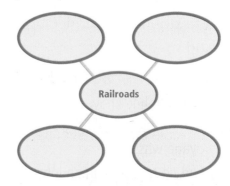

Railroads

At the Library

You may find these books at your school or public library.

Animals on the Trail with Lewis and Clark by Dorothy Henshaw Patent
Lewis and Clark identified dozens of animals on their 1804–1806 expedition.

Rodzina by Karen Cushman
Twelve-year-old Polish immigrant Rodzina traveled on an orphan train bound for California.

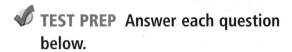

Apply Skills

✔ **TEST PREP** Use the paragraph below and what you have learned about drawing inferences to answer each question.

> In the early 1800s, people in Ohio wanted to find ways to make travel easier. Two major canals built in the 1830s and 1840s connected the Ohio River to Lake Erie. The canals made shipping goods faster and less expensive. By the 1840s, though, many railroads were also being built in Ohio.

9. What information do you already know about the topic?

   A. Most people thought railroads were a bad idea.
   B. People in the early 1800s traveled for fun.
   C. People in Ohio still use canals today.
   D. Trains could travel faster than boats on canals.

10. In your **Answer Document,** use the information in the paragraph and what you already know to make an inference about travel in Ohio in the 1800s.

Multiple Choice and Short Response

✔ **TEST PREP** Answer each question below.

11. In New England textile mills, workers could produce large amounts of cloth much faster that an individual could. Eli Whitney was able to make 10,000 guns for the United States government much more quickly than other manufacturers. What was one reason for this increase in productivity?

    A. division of labor
    B. immigration quotas
    C. steamboats and railroads
    D. the growth of the United States

12. The Immigration and Nationality Act allowed increased immigration from which region?

    A. Northern Europe
    B. Latin America
    C. Canada
    D. Australia

13. Over the past 200 years, people from many different cultural groups have moved to Ohio.

    In your **Answer Document,** compare the practices and products of some of these groups and describe how they affect life in Ohio.

UNIT 5

Citizenship and Government

The Big Idea

How have citizens of the United States promoted the common good and preserved democratic government?

 Unit 5 Benchmarks

As you study this unit, you will cover these Ohio Social Studies benchmarks:

Citizenship A Explain how citizens take part in civic life in order to promote the common good.

Citizenship B Identify rights and responsibilities of citizenship in the United States that are important for preserving democratic government.

Skills and Methods A Obtain information from a variety of primary and secondary sources using the component parts of the source.

Frederick Douglass
1818–1895

Because he was enslaved for many years, Douglass knew the horror of slavery. He escaped, gave speeches about his experience, and started an anti-slavery newspaper. **page 241**

History Makers

Rosa Parks
1913–2005

When she refused to give up her seat on a bus, Parks challenged Alabama's laws. Her arrest and the boycott that followed it inspired people to protest unfair laws.
page 255

Madeleine Albright
1937–

Can a refugee achieve success in the United States? Albright fled Eastern Europe after World War II. She became U.S. Ambassador to the United Nations and then Secretary of State. **page 287**

Members of the U.S. House of Representatives

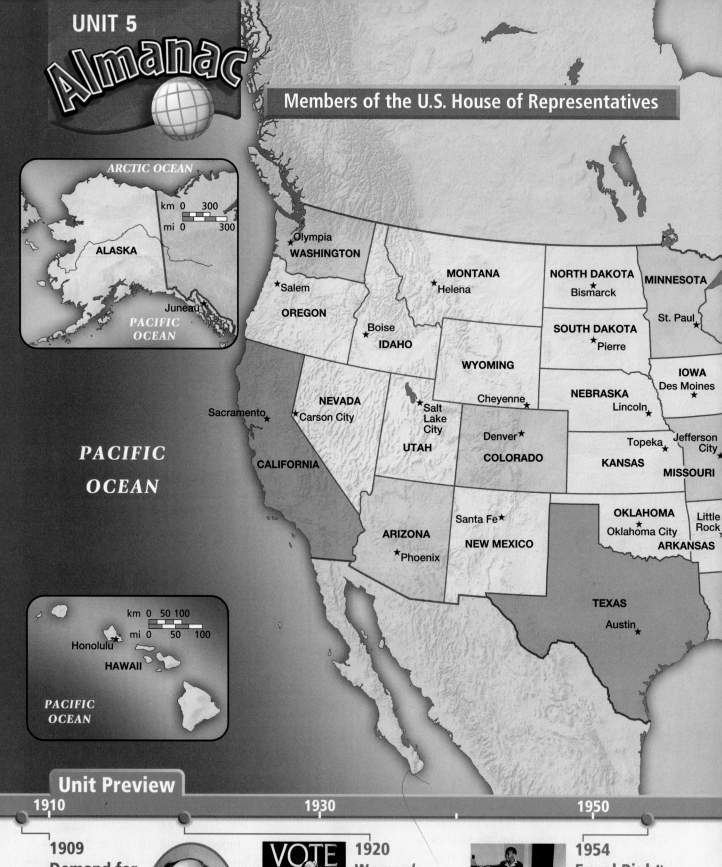

ARCTIC OCEAN

km 0   300
mi 0   300

ALASKA

Juneau ★

PACIFIC OCEAN

★ Olympia
WASHINGTON

★ Salem

OREGON

MONTANA
Helena ★

★ Boise
IDAHO

WYOMING

Cheyenne ★

NORTH DAKOTA
Bismarck ★

MINNESOTA

St. Paul ★

SOUTH DAKOTA
Pierre ★

IOWA
Des Moines ★

PACIFIC OCEAN

Sacramento ★

NEVADA
★ Carson City

Salt Lake City ★

UTAH

Denver ★
COLORADO

NEBRASKA
Lincoln ★

CALIFORNIA

Topeka ★
KANSAS

Jefferson City ★

MISSOURI

ARIZONA

★ Phoenix

Santa Fe ★

NEW MEXICO

OKLAHOMA
Oklahoma City ★

Little Rock ★

ARKANSAS

TEXAS
Austin ★

km 0 50 100
mi 0   50 100

Honolulu ★

HAWAII

PACIFIC OCEAN

Unit Preview

1910 — 1930 — 1950

1909
Demand for Basic Rights
W.E.B. Du Bois founds NAACP
Chapter 9, page 250

1920
Women's Right to Vote
Constitution changed to protect this right
Chapter 9, page 250

VOTE
BALLOT BOX
League of Women Voters

1954
Equal Rights
Supreme Court rules school segregation unconstitutional
Chapter 9, page 254

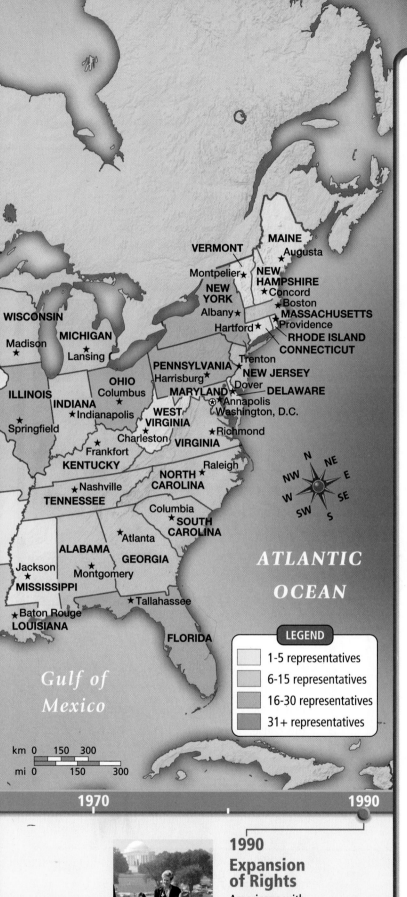

WISCONSIN
Madison ★

MICHIGAN
Lansing ★

★ Madison

MINNESOTA

ILLINOIS
Springfield ★

INDIANA
★ Indianapolis

OHIO
Columbus ★

KENTUCKY
Frankfort ★

TENNESSEE
★ Nashville

MISSISSIPPI
Jackson ★

ALABAMA
Montgomery ★

GEORGIA
Atlanta ★

LOUISIANA
★ Baton Rouge

FLORIDA
★ Tallahassee

SOUTH
CAROLINA
Columbia ★

NORTH
CAROLINA
Raleigh ★

VIRGINIA
★ Richmond

WEST
VIRGINIA
Charleston ★

PENNSYLVANIA
Harrisburg ★

MARYLAND
Annapolis ⊛
Washington, D.C.

DELAWARE
Dover ★

NEW JERSEY
Trenton ★

NEW
YORK
Albany ★

CONNECTICUT
Hartford ★

RHODE ISLAND
Providence ★

MASSACHUSETTS
★ Boston

NEW
HAMPSHIRE
★ Concord

VERMONT
Montpelier ★

MAINE
★ Augusta

ATLANTIC
OCEAN

Gulf of
Mexico

LEGEND
☐ 1-5 representatives
☐ 6-15 representatives
☐ 16-30 representatives
☐ 31+ representatives

km 0   150   300
mi 0   150   300

1970

1990

**1990
Expansion
of Rights**
Americans with
Disabilities Act passes
**Chapter 9,
page 259**

Chapter 9,
page 259

Connect to Today

Election of 1920

PRESIDENT WILSON SAYS:
This is the time to support Woman Suffrage

1920
Estimated number
of women voters in
1920 election:
10 million

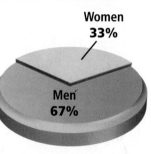

Women
33%

Men
67%

Election of 2000

Today
Estimated number
of women voters
in 2000 election:
59 million

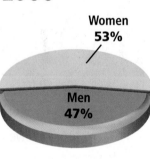

Women
53%

Men
47%

About how many more women voted in
2000 than in 1920?

**CURRENT   EVENTS
WEEKLY (WR) READER**

Current events on the web!

Read social studies articles about current
events at
www.eduplace.com/kids/hmss/

Vocabulary Preview

abolitionist

Harriet Beecher Stowe was an **abolitionist** who wrote a book called *Uncle Tom's Cabin.* It convinced many people that slavery was wrong. **page 240**

activist

A woman who fought for her right to vote was an **activist.** She might exercise her rights to march, carry a banner, and sign petitions for this cause. **page 250**

Chapter Time Line

1865
Slavery ends

1920
Women gain the vote

| 1860 | 1880 | 1900 | 1920 | 194 |

Reading Strategy

Summarize As you read, use this strategy to focus on important ideas.

Quick Tip Reread sections and put them in your own words.

civil rights

Dr. Martin Luther King Jr. was a leader in the fight for the **civil rights** of African Americans. These rights are guaranteed to all citizens and protected by the Constitution. **page 254**

responsibility

People in the United States have many rights. They also have **responsibilities** to their country. One of these duties is to vote in elections. **page 269**

1964
Civil Rights Act

1990
Americans With Disabilities Act

1960   1980   Today

Winning Freedom

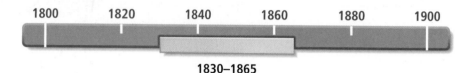

| 1800 | 1820 | 1840 | 1860 | 1880 | 1900 |

1830–1865

Build on What You Know Think about different ways people can fight injustice today. They can use television, telephones, and the Internet to gather support. In the 1800s, thousands of people took action against slavery. They gave speeches, wrote newspapers, and helped enslaved people escape.

The Antislavery Movement

Main Idea People who wanted to end slavery formed groups in the 1800s.

In the 1800s, many people in the United States knew that slavery was wrong. Some who opposed slavery became abolitionists. An **abolitionist** is a person who joined the movement to abolish, or end, slavery. Abolitionists believed that slavery went against the teachings of Christianity and the Declaration of Independence, which says that everyone has rights.

Abolitionists included people in the North and South, free African Americans, whites, men, women, and children. They wrote pamphlets and traveled across the country, speaking against slavery. The First Amendment protected their rights to do this.

Peter Clark He published an abolitionist newspaper, the *Herald of Freedom*, in Cincinnati.

VOCABULARY

abolitionist
convention
Underground Railroad

Vocabulary Strategy

abolitionist

Abolitionist comes from the word **abolish**. Abolitionists were people who wanted to abolish, or end, slavery.

READING SKILL

Main Idea and Details
As you read, note details that support the first main idea.

BENCHMARKS
PS B   Interaction
GOV B   Rules and laws
CRR B   Rights and responsibilities

GRADE LEVEL INDICATORS
PS 3   Experiences under slavery
GEO 7   Regional conflicts and cooperation
GOV 3   Founding documents
CRR 3   The First Amendment

Cincinnati Museum At the National Underground Railroad Freedom Center, museum head Spencer Crew stands by a display about abolitionist Sojourner Truth.

Abolitionists Speak Out

By 1860, about 500,000 free African Americans lived in the United States. Those in the North could use the freedoms of speech, assembly, and the press to organize groups and publish newspapers. Many took part in the abolitionist movement. African American leaders helped to start the American Anti-Slavery Society in 1833.

Frederick Douglass, a well-known abolitionist, had escaped from slavery. He spoke about his experiences, saying,

> 66 I can tell you what I have seen with my own eyes . . . 99

Sojourner Truth was also born into slavery. After she won her freedom, she spoke often of the need for abolition and women's rights. Truth spoke at events across the country. She gave her most famous speech at a women's rights convention in Akron. A **convention** is a formal meeting of a group.

Ohio Abolitionists

Many people from Ohio became involved in the abolitionist movement. **Peter Clark,** a writer and speaker from Cincinnati, published an antislavery newspaper there. He also worked on Frederick Douglass's newspaper.

Some abolitionists came to Ohio because so many people there were working against slavery. Teachers at Oberlin College were abolitionists who wanted equal opportunities for African Americans. The college was one of the first to admit African Americans.

Harriet Beecher Stowe, a writer from New England, became an abolitionist while living in Cincinnati. There, she met escaped slaves who told her about their experiences. The book she wrote about the horrors of slavery, *Uncle Tom's Cabin*, sold 300,000 copies in one year.

REVIEW Why were First Amendment rights important for abolitionists?

The Underground Railroad

Main Idea The Underground Railroad helped people escape from slavery.

Abolitionists tried to influence the decisions of the government, but too many other people supported slavery. Congress refused to pass laws or amend the Constitution to end slavery.

Some abolitionists worked in secret to help slaves escape to freedom. They set up what is known today as the Underground Railroad. The **Underground Railroad** was a series of guides, escape routes, and hiding places that helped slaves escape from the South.

Hiding places on the Underground Railroad were called "stations." These were homes and barns where escaped slaves could rest on their journey north. "Conductors," or guides, led fugitive slaves to freedom.

One conductor, **John Parker,** bought his own freedom. He settled in Ripley, Ohio, on the Ohio River. He crossed the river again and again to help fugitive slaves escape from Kentucky. Parker took many to the home of **John Rankin,** a minister and abolitionist. So many escaping slaves reached Ohio that a church started Wilberforce University near Xenia to educate former slaves.

The Oberlin Rescuers This group of Ohio abolitionists freed a fugitive slave from jail and took him to safety in Canada.

Slavery Ends

In the 1850s, people in the North and South argued more and more about slavery. A terrible war broke out between the two sides in 1861. Known as the Civil War, it ended in 1865 when the North won. During the war, President **Abraham Lincoln** signed a document called the Emancipation Proclamation. This order freed every slave in the states that were fighting the North. After the war, the national government finally changed the Constitution to end slavery throughout the United States.

Emancipation Proclamation This copy was made so that people could read it at home and in school.

Enslaved people were free at last. Under slavery, most had been denied an education. The United States government started the Freedman's Bureau. This agency set up schools and colleges throughout the South for former slaves. Eager students filled them, in the hope that education would give them a chance for a better life.

REVIEW Why were abolitionists unable to solve the problem of slavery?

Lesson Summary

In the 1830s and 1840s, abolitionists worked hard to end slavery. Some were part of the Underground Railroad and helped enslaved people escape. After slavery ended, many enslaved people were eager to go to school.

Why It Matters ...

By ending slavery, the nation took a large step toward the fulfillment of its ideal that "all [people] are created equal."

Lesson Review

1833
American-Anti Slavery Society Founded

1865
Slavery ends

1830 — 1840 — 1850 — 1860 — 1870

1 **VOCABULARY** Use **abolitionist** in a sentence about the struggle against slavery.

2 **READING SKILL** Use the **details** in your chart to explain the significance of the Declaration of Independence and the Constitution to abolitionists.

3 **MAIN IDEA: History** In what ways did free African Americans work to end slavery?

4 **MAIN IDEA: History** What did the people who took part in the Underground Railroad do?

5 **TIME LINE SKILL** In what year did slavery end in the United States?

6 **CRITICAL THINKING: Analyze** What was the point of view of abolitionists? How might it have been different from that of slaveowners in the South?

RESEARCH ACTIVITY Using library or Internet resources, learn about an abolitionist who came from or worked in Ohio. Write a short report about his or her life.

African American Education

The Freedmen's Bureau closed, but African Americans kept their schools open. After the Civil War, the Freedmen's Bureau gave money to set up schools and colleges for African Americans in the South. The head of the bureau said that they helped start 4,239 schools. More than 240,000 students attended these schools.

When the Freedmen's Bureau closed in 1872, African Americans raised money to keep schools open. Their efforts increased the number of African American colleges to 34 by the year 1900. Many of these schools are still open today.

Tuskegee One of the most famous schools for African Americans was the Tuskegee Institute, shown above. It specialized in practical education. Students learned skills such as shoemaking, carpentry, and cabinetmaking.

A Freedmen's Bureau School

On the chalkboard: BLACK SMITHING. TOP FULLER. MACHINE WRENCH. CARPENTRY MORTISE & TEN JOINT

The Institute Grows
The Institute started in a small building with 30 students. By 1915, it had 100 buildings and 1500 students.

Activities

1. **MAKE YOUR OWN** Create a poster that might have appeared in the 1870s to raise money for a new African American college.

2. **WRITE ABOUT IT** What courses do you think would have been important for elementary school students to learn in the 1870s? Write a brief description of a typical school day.

245

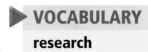
Study Skills

Find and Evaluate Sources

▶ **VOCABULARY**
research

In Lesson 1, you read about ways enslaved people gained protection of their rights. To learn more about that topic, you can do research. **Research** is the search for facts. These steps will help you to use encyclopedias and websites to research a topic.

Learn the Skill

Step 1: Form a question about what you want to research.

Step 2: Identify a key word or phrase in your question. Key words are the most important words.

- **Encyclopedias** — Look in the volume that includes the first letter of your key word. If there is no information on that topic, look for a list of related topics and articles, or try another key word.

- **The Internet** — Use a search engine. When you type your key word into a search engine, it will show you a list of websites related to the word. If those websites aren't helpful, try another key word or phrase.

Step 3: Evaluate your sources to see if they are reliable and accurate. Use these questions to evaluate them:

- What is the purpose of the source? Is it designed to teach, to entertain, or to sell?

- Is the source written by an expert or an average person?

- Is the information correct? Check it in another source.

Step 4: Make sure the information is relevant to your original question. If it is not, look for new sources. If it is, take notes.

Practice the Skill

Think of a question about abolitionism that you would like to research. Find an encyclopedia article and a website that provide the information you want. Then answer the questions.

1 What related articles listed after the encyclopedia entry might also be helpful?

2 What information about the author and the website lead you to believe that they are reliable?

3 How are the two articles similar? How are they different?

Apply the Skill

Using the two sources you found, write a paragraph that answers your research question about abolitionism.

The Struggle for Equality

VOCABULARY

suffragist
prejudice
activist

Vocabulary Strategy

| prejudice |

The prefix **pre-** means "before." A **prejudice** is a prejudgment, or a judgment made before you know all the facts.

READING SKILL

Sequence As you read, list important events of the women's rights movement.

1	
2	
3	
4	

BENCHMARKS
GOV A   Role of government
GOV B   Rules and laws
CRR B   Rights and responsibilities

GRADE LEVEL INDICATORS
GOV 1   Branches of the United States government
GOV 2   Characteristics of American democracy
GOV 3   Founding documents
CRR 3   The First Amendment

1880	1890	1900	1910	1920	1930

1890–1919

Build on What You Know The Constitution and the Bill of Rights promise democracy and freedom to all. In the early 1900s, women, African Americans, and others worked hard to make that promise a reality.

The Fight for Women's Rights

Main Idea Susan B. Anthony led a national women's rights movement.

In the 1800s, women in the United States were not guaranteed all of the same rights that men had. Women could not vote in most state or national elections. Often they could not own property, go to college, or hold certain jobs. Women began joining together to fix these inequalities. People working to influence the government is an essential characteristic of American democracy.

One of the leaders of this movement was **Susan B. Anthony.** She and other women worked to convince Congress to improve laws that affected women across the country.

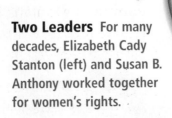

Two Leaders For many decades, Elizabeth Cady Stanton (left) and Susan B. Anthony worked together for women's rights.

Suffrage Demonstration Supporters of women's suffrage came from different Ohio counties to demonstrate at the Statehouse in 1914. **SKILL** **Reading Visuals** Is a banner from your county in this photo?

Influencing Government

One of the most important rights women worked for was suffrage, or the right to vote. Delegates at an early suffrage meeting wrote a Declaration of Sentiments, which used the language of the Declaration of Independence: "We hold these truths to be self-evident, that all men and women are created equal . . ."

In 1890, several groups joined together to form the National American Woman Suffrage Association (NAWSA). **Elizabeth Cady Stanton,** a friend of Anthony, was its first president. NAWSA members held meetings and made speeches in Congress. By 1900, NAWSA was a powerful organization with members from all over the country.

Many people at the time did not like the idea of women voting. Sometimes angry mobs attacked the suffragists. A **suffragist** was a person who worked for the right to vote. The suffragists did not give up. They continued to spread their message.

By the early 1900s, a few states recognized women's right to vote in state elections. Some women were elected to state legislatures. They represented those who voted for them by supporting women's suffrage. In 1917, **Jeannette Rankin** of Montana became the first female member of the United States House of Representatives.

REVIEW What were some of the inequalities the women's movement wanted to correct?

The Nineteenth Amendment

The events of World War I helped the women's movement. When the United States entered World War I, women filled the jobs of men who went to fight in the war. Women proved that they could do the jobs as well as men. Their work, combined with the NAWSA's marches and speeches, convinced many people that women's right to vote should be guaranteed by the Constitution.

Because the government is run by the people through its representatives, pressure increased in Congress for a national law on women's suffrage. In 1919, Congress passed the Nineteenth Amendment to the Constitution. The states approved it in 1920, which meant that women could finally vote throughout the United States.

W.E.B. Du Bois He believed that a college education was important for African Americans. He wrote many books and articles about African American politics.

African American Rights

Main Idea W.E.B. Du Bois helped create the first national civil rights movement for African Americans.

The Fifteenth Amendment was supposed to protect the right of African American men to vote. Most southern states, however, had laws that prevented them from voting. These laws were passed because of prejudice against African Americans. **Prejudice** is an unjust negative opinion about a group of people. Prejudice against African Americans prevented them from using some of the rights they were guaranteed under the Constitution.

One leader who worked for the protection of basic rights for African Americans was **W.E.B. Du Bois** (doo BOYS). He was an African American scholar, writer, and activist. An **activist** takes action to change social conditions or laws. Du Bois believed there should be

> 66 **ceaseless agitation and insistent demand for equality.** 99

The NAACP

In 1909, Du Bois and other black activists founded the National Association for the Advancement of Colored People, or NAACP. The NAACP's main goal was to get equal opportunity for African Americans. The members of the NAACP wanted to change laws that discriminated against African Americans in voting, education, and the legal system.

Cleveland Meeting The NAACP held a meeting in Cleveland to celebrate its 20th anniversary.

NAACP leaders used the rights protected by the First Amendment to win justice. They spoke with members of Congress. They wrote articles about the unjust treatment of African Americans. They made speeches and called supporters to large meetings and marches. These early steps advanced the equal rights movement for African Americans.

REVIEW What did the NAACP do to solve the problem of inequalities?

Lesson Summary

- Susan B. Anthony was a leader of the women's suffrage movement.
- The Nineteenth Amendment guaranteed women's right to vote.
- W.E.B. Du Bois and others created the NAACP to fight prejudice toward African Americans.

Why It Matters ...

At the end of the 1800s and the beginning of the 1900s, women and African Americans organized to fight for their rights.

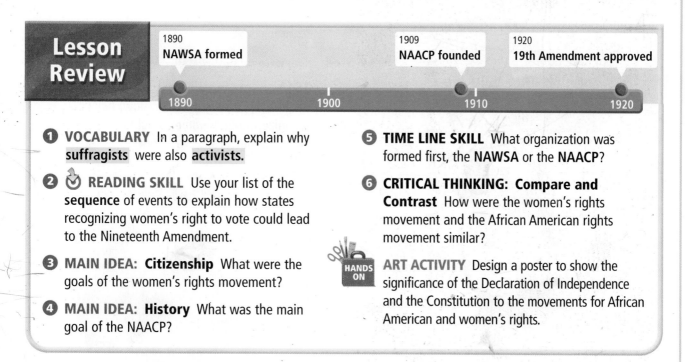

Lesson Review

1890 — **NAWSA formed**
1909 — **NAACP founded**
1920 — **19th Amendment approved**

1890 · 1900 · 1910 · 1920

1. **VOCABULARY** In a paragraph, explain why **suffragists** were also **activists.**

2. **READING SKILL** Use your list of the **sequence** of events to explain how states recognizing women's right to vote could lead to the Nineteenth Amendment.

3. **MAIN IDEA: Citizenship** What were the goals of the women's rights movement?

4. **MAIN IDEA: History** What was the main goal of the NAACP?

5. **TIME LINE SKILL** What organization was formed first, the **NAWSA** or the **NAACP**?

6. **CRITICAL THINKING: Compare and Contrast** How were the women's rights movement and the African American rights movement similar?

HANDS ON **ART ACTIVITY** Design a poster to show the significance of the Declaration of Independence and the Constitution to the movements for African American and women's rights.

251

Women's Rights Movement

Women are citizens, but their rights have not always been protected. In the early 1800s, they were prevented from voting or holding political office. They had far fewer chances than men to get an education. If a woman owned property, it became her husband's when she married.

People's views of women's rights have changed a great deal in the past two hundred years. Congress has passed many laws that protect suffrage and other rights. Today, women vote and hold political offices. They attend college as often as men and work as carpenters, forest rangers, and business leaders. Look at this time line to see some of the most important steps in the march toward women's equality in American life.

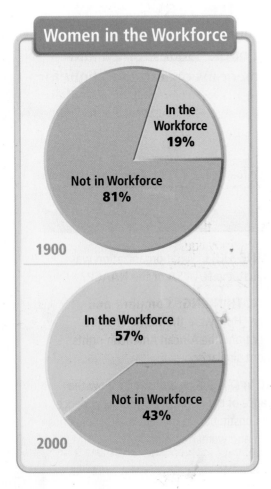

Women in the Workforce

In the Workforce 19%

Not in Workforce 81%

1900

In the Workforce 57%

Not in Workforce 43%

2000

1878
Lawmakers defeat an amendment giving women the vote. The amendment is reintroduced in every session of Congress until 1919, when it passes.

1890
33 states have laws that allow married women some control over their property.

1840 | 1880

1848
Elizabeth Cady Stanton (below) helps organize the first women's rights convention held in Seneca Falls, New York.

◀ How much did the percentage of women in the workforce grow in the 20th Century?

League of Women Voters

1972
Gloria Steinem (above) of Toledo, Ohio, becomes editor of *Ms.,* a new magazine about women's rights.

1981
Sandra Day O'Connor (above) becomes the first woman appointed to the U.S. Supreme Court.

1920
The 19th Amendment guarantees equal voting rights for women.

1920   1960   2000

1917
Jeanette Rankin (below) of Montana becomes the first woman elected to the U.S. Congress.

1963
Congress passes the Equal Pay Act, requiring equal pay for men and women doing the same jobs.

Activities

1. **TALK ABOUT IT** If you were helping to pass the 19th Amendment, what would you say to influence leaders in Congress?

2. **LIST IT** Find out about a woman who is a leader in the federal, state, or local government. Make a list of laws she has worked for.

Protecting Rights

1940	1950	1960	1970	1980	1990	2000

1954–1990

Build on What You Know Sometimes, when you
want to reach a goal, it helps to work with others. In the
1950s, 1960s, and 1970s, groups of people worked together
to protect their rights.

The Civil Rights Movement

Main Idea Using court cases and protests, African Americans
won greater recognition of their rights.

Throughout the first half of the 1900s, the U.S.
government did not protect many of the civil rights of
African Americans. **Civil rights** are rights and freedoms
people have because they are citizens of a country. In the
1950s, African Americans and other ethnic groups made
more progress. They began going to court to change laws
that did not treat them the same as other citizens. The
judicial branch has the power to interpret the law and
say whether a law is allowed by the Constitution.
Trying to change laws is one way citizens take part
in government.

In 1954, the NAACP won a case in the Supreme Court
called *Brown* v. *Board of Education of Topeka*. The Supreme
Court said that laws allowing separate public schools for
blacks and whites were unconstitutional. The court case
made segregation of public schools illegal. Segregation is
the separation of people by racial or ethnic group. *Brown*
v. *Board of Education* was the first of many important civil
rights victories for African Americans and other groups
in the 1950s.

March on Washington
On August 28, 1963, King (second from right) and others led this march. They protested job discrimination and prejudice toward African Americans.

Martin Luther King Jr.

In Montgomery, Alabama, buses were segregated. City law said that African Americans had to sit in their own section, usually at the back of the bus. In 1955, an African American woman named **Rosa Parks** refused to give up her seat at the front of a crowded bus and go to the back. The police arrested Parks.

Members of Parks's church organized a protest. They asked everyone in the city of Montgomery to boycott the buses. A young minister named **Martin Luther King Jr.** helped lead the boycott.

King believed in nonviolent protest. **Nonviolent protest** is a way of bringing change without using violence. In late 1956, the Supreme Court ruled that segregation on buses was illegal.

In 1963, Martin Luther King Jr. and other black leaders organized a march in Washington, D.C., to protest unequal protection of civil rights. Over 200,000 people marched on the nation's capital. The right to assemble and call for change is protected by the First Amendment.

King gave his most famous speech at the march. He said,

> 66 **I have a dream that my four little children will one day live in a nation where they will not be judged by the color of their skin, but by the content of their character.** 99

Martin Luther King Jr.'s "I Have a Dream" speech and the March on Washington caused more Americans to pay attention to the civil rights movement.

As more people began supporting civil rights, their views influenced the legislative branch, which passes laws. In 1964, Congress passed the Civil Rights Act. This law banned segregation in schools, work places, and public places such as restaurants and theaters. A year later, Congress passed the Voting Rights Act of 1965 to prevent discrimination in voting. The struggle for equal rights would continue, however, and include many other groups of people.

REVIEW What rights helped civil rights protesters win change?

CIVIL RIGHTS FOR ALL

The ERA Supporters used marches, fundraisers, posters, petitions, and nonviolent protest to fight for the amendment.

Ellen Ochoa Ochoa grew up near Los Angeles, California. In 1991, she became the first Hispanic female astronaut.

The Growth of Civil Rights

Main Idea The advances of African Americans inspired other groups to fight for their rights.

Women had won the right to vote in 1920. In the 1960s, however, women were still not treated as equal to men. For example, men were usually paid more than women for doing the same kind of work. Some businesses gave jobs to men instead of women, even though women were as skilled as the men.

The First Amendment to the Constitution protected women's freedom of speech and freedom to write books and articles. A writer named **Betty Friedan** became a leader of a new women's rights movement.

Friedan and other women started the National Organization for Women (NOW) in 1966 to fight for women's rights. The members of NOW tried to convince states to pass an amendment to the Constitution. The amendment would guarantee equal rights for women. It was called the Equal Rights Amendment (ERA).

Although the ERA failed to pass, the women's movement changed the United States. The number of women serving in state legislatures doubled between 1975 and 1988. Today, four of the seven judges on the Supreme Court of Ohio are women. By the late 1980s, 40 out of 50 states had laws that said that men and women doing the same kind of work had to receive the same pay.

The Longest Walk In 1978, supporters of American Indian rights marched from California to Washington, D.C.

Ben Nighthorse Campbell A U.S. Senator from Colorado, Campbell is also a chief of the Northern Cheyenne Tribe.

Rights for American Indians

American Indians also had a difficult time having their civil rights recognized. They could not live on many of the lands that their ancestors had lived on. In the 1960s, American Indian groups began to organize and speak out. One group, called the American Indian Movement, asked that the United States government return lands taken from American Indians in the past.

Just as African Americans and women had done, American Indians held protests. Sometimes they took over the land they wanted back and refused to leave, even though they risked going to jail.

In 1969, almost 100 American Indians took over the Island of Alcatraz in San Francisco Bay. They stayed for almost 18 months, demanding that land be given back to American Indian nations.

Eventually, these protests influenced the decisions of the government. The United States government returned land in New Mexico to the Taos Pueblo Indians. They also returned land in Alaska to native Alaskans and land in Washington State to the Yakima Indians.

In 1968, Congress passed the Indian Civil Rights Act. This law stated that the governments of American Indian nations must guarantee most of the civil rights that the United States Constitution guarantees to all citizens. The Act created an Indian Bill of Rights to protect freedom of speech, of the press, and of religion.

REVIEW What did citizens do to take part in government in the women's rights and American Indian rights movements?

Rights for Migrant Workers

Migrant workers were another group trying to improve their lives in the 1960s and 1970s. A **migrant worker** is a person who moves from place to place to find work. In California and Texas, large numbers of Mexican migrant workers worked on farms that grew crops such as vegetables and fruits. When they finished harvesting a crop in one area, migrant workers had to move to another area to find new work. Most migrant workers did not have enough money to take care of themselves and their families. The large farms they worked for paid very little and did not provide health care.

Because migrant workers moved so much, it was difficult for their children to go to school. Lack of education made it hard for workers to get any jobs other than migrant work.

In the 1960s, migrant workers in California began challenging the big farm companies. The workers wanted higher wages, better education for their children, and health care for their families. **Cesar Chavez** helped workers organize and speak out about their cause. Like Martin Luther King Jr., Chavez was an inspiring leader. His speeches attracted college students, religious leaders, and civil rights organizations to the migrant workers' cause.

In 1962, Chavez and a woman named **Dolores Huerta** organized the workers into the National Farm Workers Association (NFWA). In 1966, the NFWA joined with other unions to form the United Farm Workers (UFW).

The protests of the UFW taught people about the hard conditions that farm workers and their families faced. The public began to pressure big farm companies to make changes. Finally, this pressure forced some companies to give their workers better pay and health care.

Cesar Chavez He and the United Farm Workers encouraged people to boycott products as a way to force big farm companies to change.

Rights for People with Disabilities

People with disabilities have also worked hard for equal treatment. People who use wheelchairs, visually impaired people, and people who have other physical or mental challenges often face discrimination. Many people fought for a law to change this, and in 1990, the Americans with Disabilities Act (ADA) was passed.

A New Law George H.W. Bush was President when the ADA was signed into law.

The ADA protects the civil rights of people with disabilities. It makes it illegal to refuse to hire people because they have a disability. The ADA also says that government buildings, buses, trains, restaurants, and stores have to be built so that people can more easily enter them with wheelchairs or crutches.

REVIEW What did migrant workers fight for?

Lesson Summary

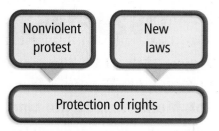

Why It Matters ...

The United States is a more democratic country because of the work and successes of civil rights groups over the last 50 years.

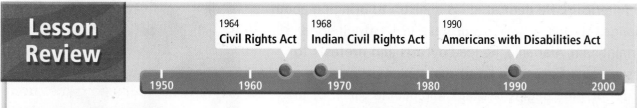

Lesson Review

| 1964 Civil Rights Act | 1968 Indian Civil Rights Act | 1990 Americans with Disabilities Act |

| 1950 | 1960 | 1970 | 1980 | 1990 | 2000 |

❶ **VOCABULARY** Choose the correct words to complete the sentence.

civil rights nonviolent protest
migrant worker

Cesar Chavez used _____ to help protect the _____ of farm workers.

❷ 🕐 **READING SKILL** What **outcome** did you **predict** for the farm workers' protests? What was the actual outcome?

❸ **MAIN IDEA: Government** What did the judicial and legislative branches do in the civil rights movement?

❹ **FACTS TO KNOW** What is the Americans with Disabilities Act?

❺ **TIME LINE SKILL** What relationship can you see between the 1964 Civil Rights Act and the other events on the time line?

❻ **CRITICAL THINKING: Compare and Contrast** How were the goals of Martin Luther King Jr. and Cesar Chavez similar? How were they different?

✏️ ▸ **WRITING ACTIVITY** Write a paragraph on the importance of citizens taking part in government. Give reasons to support your position.

Dr. Martin Luther King Jr.

(1929–1968)

It is August 28th, 1963. Thousands of demonstrators have marched from the Washington Monument to the Lincoln Memorial. Folk singers have performed and civil rights leaders have spoken to the crowd. Now Dr. Martin Luther King Jr. steps forward to the podium.

Dr. King has written part of the speech only hours ago. He has given other parts before. He looks out at the crowd. So many people have joined together in one place in the cause of equality and justice.

Throughout his life, Dr. King worked for civil rights for all Americans. He dedicated his ministry to bringing about change through nonviolent protest. In Montgomery and Birmingham, Alabama, he led boycotts and protests to desegregate buses and lunch counters.

As Dr. King begins to speak, the people cheer. Of the many speeches given on this day, this is the one that most will remember. People join hands as they listen to his message of freedom.

Major Achievements

1957
Travels thousands of miles and gives over 200 speeches

1963
Leads March on Washington and gives "I Have a Dream" speech

1963
Meets with President Kennedy about civil rights

"When we allow freedom to ring, when we let it ring from every village and every hamlet, from every state and every city, we will be able to speed up that day when all God's children, black men and white men, Jews and Gentiles, Protestants and Catholics, will be able to join hands and sing in the words of the old Negro spiritual: "Free at last! Free at last! Thank God Almighty, we are free at last!"

From the speech "I Have a Dream" given by Dr. Martin Luther King Jr., August 28, 1963

1964
Wins Nobel Peace Prize

1965
Leads voting rights march from Selma, Alabama, to Montgomery, Alabama

Activities

1. **THINK ABOUT IT** Why do you think Dr. Martin Luther King Jr. decided to speak at the March on Washington?

2. **WRITE ABOUT IT** Read Dr. Martin Luther King Jr.'s "I Have a Dream" speech on page R31. Choose a favorite passage from the speech and write about why it inspires you.

TECHNOLOGY Find out about other important people in this unit at Education Place.

Freedom's Legacy

READING SKILL

Draw Conclusions Use details from the lesson to draw a conclusion about how the lives of African Americans have changed since the end of slavery.

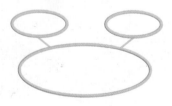

BENCHMARKS
PS A   Cultures
GOV A   Role of government

GRADE LEVEL INDICATORS
PS 1   Cultural practices and products
GOV 1   Role of government
GOV 2   Characteristics of American democracy

1760	1810	1860	1910	1960	Today

1865–Today

Build on What You Know People move for many reasons. Many African Americans left the South to get jobs.

The Great Migration

Main Idea In the late 1800s and early 1900s, thousands of African Americans moved north to find jobs.

As people around the country struggled for their rights, African Americans in Ohio did the same. Some fought discrimination by working in government. **Discrimination** is the unfair treatment of particular groups. In 1880, **George Washington Williams** became the first African American member of the Ohio state legislature. **Harry C. Smith,** another Ohio lawmaker, worked to pass laws to protect the rights of African Americans.

George Washington Williams This historian, journalist, and minister is honored in a mural at the Ohio Statehouse.

Moving North

Between 1910 and 1920, manufacturers in the Midwest needed more workers in their factories. A **manufacturer** owns a company that uses machines to make goods. These companies advertised jobs in southern newspapers and sent people south to find African American workers. Northern manufacturers offered higher wages than African Americans could earn in the South. A wage is pay earned by a worker. Many companies paid to move workers north.

By the 1940s, more than one million African Americans had moved. More than 150,000 moved to Ohio. This movement north is called the Great Migration.

Entrepreneurs Ella Stewart's Toledo pharmacy was one of many African American businesses to open in Ohio.

African Americans in Ohio

Some African Americans in Ohio found work in coal mines, but most worked in cities with large factories. The steel industry in Cleveland and rubber factories in Akron employed many people. Some African Americans started businesses. In 1922, **Ella Stewart** opened the first black-owned pharmacy in Toledo. A pharmacy sells medicine and health care products.

Others found success in technology or sports. A business owner and inventor from Cleveland named **Garrett Augustus Morgan** invented the stop light in 1923. **Jesse Owens,** who moved from Alabama to Ohio as a boy, won four gold medals at the 1936 Olympics.

REVIEW In what ways did moving to Ohio in the early 1900s solve a problem for many African Americans?

The Civil Rights Movement

Main Idea African Americans in Ohio and the nation fought for recognition of their rights.

Although some African Americans found success, discrimination was still a problem. While people in Alabama and other southern states worked to change unfair laws, Ohioans also took part in the civil rights movement.

In the 1950s and 1960s, some Ohioans traveled to the South to protest against discrimination. They saw it as their duty as citizens to influence the government. People protested by marching, carrying signs, helping African Americans sign up to vote, and refusing to leave businesses that did not serve African Americans. Many learned these methods of nonviolent protest at the Western College for Women in Oxford, Ohio.

African Americans in Government

In Ohio, African Americans influenced the government by voting for representatives who would work for laws they wanted. **Carl Burton Stokes** became mayor of Cleveland in 1968. He was the first black mayor of a major American city. Stokes hired African Americans for jobs in the city's government. His brother, **Louis Stokes,** was elected to the United States Congress as a representative from Cleveland.

In 1970, Louis Stokes became one of the founding members of the Congressional Black Caucus (CBC). A caucus is a group of people who join together to make political decisions. The CBC includes members of Congress who work to pass laws that will improve conditions for African Americans and other groups that face discrimination.

Active Citizens Students who have trained at Western College for Women sing together before leaving to take part in the civil rights movement.

Writers and Entertainers

Ohio is home to many famous African American writers, artists, and actors. **Sharon Draper** of Cleveland is an award-winning writer of children's books. A teacher in Cincinnati for more than 30 years, she won the National Teacher of the Year award in 1997. Grammy Award winner **Kathleen Battle** is a world-famous opera singer from Portsmouth. **Halle Berry,** who was born in Cleveland, won the Academy Award for Best Actress in 2002. In 1993, **Toni Morrison** of Lorain became the first African American woman to win the Nobel Prize for Literature, one of the world's top honors for a writer.

REVIEW What did people do to end discrimination in the 1960s?

Lesson Summary

- During the Great Migration, thousands of African Americans moved to Ohio and other northern states for jobs.
- Though they faced discrimination, many African Americans succeeded in government and business.
- Nonviolent protest led to laws that made discrimination illegal.

Why It Matters ...

The struggle of African Americans for justice has inspired others to work for fairness and equality.

Kathleen Battle

Lesson Review

1880 George Washington Williams elected			1968 Carl Burton Stokes elected	
1850	1900		1950	2000

1 **VOCABULARY** Use **manufacturer** in a sentence about African Americans in Ohio.

2 **READING SKILL** Review your **conclusion.** Explain what effect you think the Great Migration had on African Americans coming to Ohio from the South.

3 **MAIN IDEA: Economics** Why did African Americans move to Ohio between 1910 and 1950?

4 **MAIN IDEA: Citizenship** What did civil rights protesters see as their duty?

5 **TIME LINE SKILL** Draw a time line like the one above. Add Toni Morrison's Nobel Prize to your time line. Where did you put it?

6 **CRITICAL THINKING: Making Decisions** What might some of the consequences have been for African Americans who made the decision to move north during the Great Migration?

ART ACTIVITY Make a display of African American leaders and heroes. Use photographs, drawings, and captions to explain their contributions and achievements.

Ohio Winners

For more than one hundred years, African Americans from Ohio have influenced United States history and culture. From government to literature to science, they have helped shape our country. Two of the most famous are the athlete Jesse Owens and the writer Toni Morrison.

JESSE OWENS

Jesse Owens not only broke world records, he also broke down barriers. When Owens was growing up, African Americans throughout the United States faced injustice and unfair treatment. Owens overcame these challenges to go to Ohio State University and become a champion runner.

Running for the United States Olympic team in 1936, Owens came in first in four events and won four gold medals. Owens's success filled people throughout the United States with pride, but his achievements had special meaning for African Americans. Owens led the way for other African Americans who wanted to compete in sports events.

College Student At Ohio State University, Owens set three track world records and tied a fourth at one meet.

TONI MORRISON

What is your favorite way to spend time? When Toni Morrison was growing up in Lorain, Ohio, she spent hours reading at the local library. Young Toni loved reading. She also enjoyed hearing her parents tell traditional African legends, tales about African American life in the past, and thrilling ghost stories.

A few years after college, Morrison began writing stories. Her first book, *The Bluest Eye,* was published in 1970. Since then, she has written more than 15 novels and children's books. Some of her books are about the experiences of African Americans under slavery. Others talk about the way people live today. Morrison has won many awards, including the Pulitzer Prize and the Nobel Prize for Literature.

Activities

1. **THINK ABOUT IT** Compare how Owens and Morrison helped shape the history and culture of our country.

2. **RESEARCH IT** Use the Internet and library resources to learn about other African Americans who have made important contributions to the United States and the world. Write a report summarizing what you find.

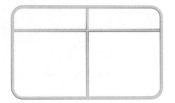

Core Lesson 5

Responsibilities of Citizenship

VOCABULARY

naturalization
responsibility
selective service
volunteer

Vocabulary Strategy

| responsibility |

Responsibility, meaning duty, is related to **respond.** Citizens in a democracy must respond to their duties.

READING SKILL

Classify Put information into these two categories: Rights and Responsibilities.

Build on What You Know You know that a car needs an engine to run. Democracy is the engine that keeps the United States running. For this engine to run smoothly, citizens need to exercise their rights and fulfill their responsibilities.

Citizenship

Main Idea Citizens in a democracy have rights.

Every person born in the United States is a citizen of the United States. Immigrants can become United States citizens through naturalization. **Naturalization** is the legal process of learning the laws, rights, and duties of being a citizen and passing a citizenship test. This process often takes two years. The last step of naturalization is a public pledge to obey the Constitution.

Being a citizen of a democracy like the United States is special. Citizens are the source of the government's authority. The choices they make help shape and influence their government.

BENCHMARKS

GOV A	Role of government
CRR A	Participation
CRR B	Rights and responsibilities

GRADE LEVEL INDICATORS

GOV 2	Characteristics of American democracy
CRR 1	Becoming a citizen
CRR 2	Upholding the Constitution

The Citizenship Pledge
Here, members of the U.S. armed forces say the pledge and become citizens.

Rights of Citizens

Vote
Join groups of your choice
Express opinions freely
Practice religion of choice
Have a fair trial
Own property and businesses
Not be discriminated against in jobs and housing

Freedom of Speech All citizens should know the rights protected by the Constitution. Here, students hold a mock debate at the Ohio Statehouse.

Upholding the Constitution

An essential characteristic of democracy in the United States is that citizens have rights. Many of these rights are guaranteed by the Constitution. One of the rights American citizens have is the right to vote. Voting lets citizens choose leaders and make decisions in their communities. At age 18, a citizen can register, or sign up, to vote. Citizens also have the right to run for political office.

Although citizens have many freedoms, that doesn't mean people can do whatever they want. Citizens also have responsibilities to the country. A **responsibility** is a duty that someone is expected to fulfill. All citizens have a responsibility to uphold the United States Constitution. The Constitution is the highest law in the nation. Citizens uphold it in many ways, such as by accepting the results of elections and following the government's decisions.

Obeying the law is another way citizens uphold the Constitution. In a democracy, it is the responsibility of citizens to create a safe and orderly society. When people obey laws, they help make a safer community.

Paying taxes is another responsibility. The government uses taxes to pay for eduction, fire and police departments, and good roads. By paying taxes, citizens ensure that the government will be able to fullfill its tasks.

Citizens also have a responsibility to serve on juries. A jury is a group of ordinary citizens who decide in court whether a person has committed a crime. Without people serving on juries, the justice system could not work.

Men who are 18 and over must register for the military draft, or **selective service.** If the nation is at war, the government can call on them to fight.

REVIEW Why is it a responsibility of citizens to uphold the Constitution?

269

Citizen Participation

Main Idea Citizens have a responsibility to help out in their community.

There is more to being a responsible citizen than just following the rules. Being a good citizen also means getting involved in issues that affect the community and the country. It can mean speaking out against injustice or other problems. Or it can mean taking action and influencing government to change things for the better.

Young people, like adults, have responsibilities as citizens. They are expected to go to school. What they learn in school helps prepare them to contribute to society and take a part in a democracy. Being informed about important issues can help young people make good choices when they become old enough to vote.

Young people can take part in government even before they can vote. When they find issues that they care about, such as protecting the environment or changing an unfair law, young people can do many things. They can send letters to lawmakers and newspapers. They can sign petitions asking for change. They can even help a political candidate get elected.

Finding Ways to Help

Another way young people can help their communities is by becoming volunteers. A **volunteer** helps other people without being paid. Volunteers give their time and use their talents for the common good of their communities.

After Hurricane Katrina struck New Orleans, students in Ohio volunteered to help. A Bedford school raised more than $10,000. One girl in Bolivar asked people to donate money to Katrina victims instead of buying her birthday presents. She raised more than $400.

Volunteer efforts can help people all over the world. In December 2004, a tsunami, which is a giant wave, reached land in Indonesia, Sri Lanka, Thailand, and other nations. Thousands of people were killed and many coastal communities were destroyed. Schoolchildren all over the world responded by raising money for survivors. Young people held bake sales, donated their own money, and held other fundraisers to help people rebuild.

Volunteers Children in Rockford, Ohio, volunteer to fill sandbags that will prevent their town from flooding.

Responsibilities of Citizens

Personal	Civic
These actions improve your life and the lives of others.	These actions help make a democratic system work.
Educate yourself	Vote
Respect others	Obey laws
Help in your community	Pay taxes
Set a good example	Serve on juries

Citizens' Responsibilities
As citizens, young people need to know their responsibilities, just as adults do.

The future of the United States depends on the strength of its democracy. All citizens have a responsibility to keep democracy strong and preserve the Constitution. This means protecting and respecting the rights of all Americans. It can also mean obeying laws, becoming active in politics, or working to improve your community. In big and small ways, each citizen can contribute to democracy and make the United States a better country.

REVIEW What are the responsibilities of United States citizens?

Lesson Summary

Being a citizen of a democracy means having rights, such as freedom of speech. Citizens also have a responsibility to help create an orderly society. Young people can fulfill their responsibilities by going to school and helping others in their communities.

Why It Matters ...

Good citizenship is necessary for a better country and safer communities.

Lesson Review

1. **VOCABULARY** Choose the correct word to complete the sentence.

   responsibility   **volunteer**

   Many citizens believe it is their _____ to help others in their community.

2. **READING SKILL** What did you **classify** as responsibilities? Explain why you did so.

3. **MAIN IDEA: Citizenship** What are four ways citizens uphold the Constitution?

4. **MAIN IDEA: Citizenship** What are some ways that students can be good citizens?

5. **FACTS TO REMEMBER** What is the process immigrants go through to become citizens?

6. **CRITICAL THINKING: Decision Making** What might be the costs and benefits of a student's decision to spend one afternoon each week volunteering at a local library?

SPEAKING ACTIVITY Make a list of projects your class could do to help the school or community. Pick one project, and prepare a speech telling why you think students should volunteer to help.

HANDS ON

Visual Summary

1. – 4. 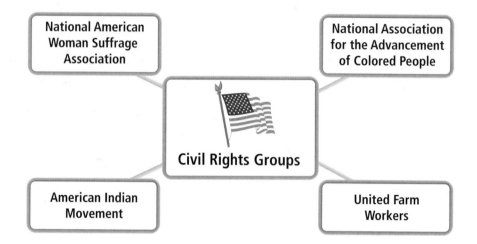 Write a description of each group named below.

National American Woman Suffrage Association

National Association for the Advancement of Colored People

Civil Rights Groups

American Indian Movement

United Farm Workers

Facts and Main Ideas

✓ TEST PREP Answer each question with information from the chapter.

5. **History** What did John Parker and John Rankin do as members of the Underground Railroad?

6. **Citizenship** What did women do to gain the recognition of their right to vote?

7. **History** What was the Great Migration?

8. **Government** What is the source of the United States government's authority?

9. **Citizenship** Why is obeying laws a part of upholding the Constitution?

Vocabulary

✓ TEST PREP Choose the correct word from the list below to complete each sentence.

abolitionist, p. 240
discrimination, p. 262
responsibility, p. 269

10. Frederick Douglass was a(n) _____ who had escaped from slavery.

11. Voting is a(n) _____ of all United States citizens.

12. After the Civil War ended, many African Americans faced _____.

1865 Slavery ends	1920 Women gain the vote	1964 Civil Rights Act

| 1860 | 1880 | 1900 | 1920 | 1940 | 1960 | 1980 | Today |

Apply Skills

☑ **TEST PREP** **Study Skill** Read the paragraph below. Then evaluate the source to answer each question.

> In the early 1900s, many African American farmers in the South struggled to make a living. They owed money to the people who owned their land, and could not make enough to pay their debts. Laws also limited their rights. Many thought about moving north, where there were factory jobs and no limits on their rights.

13. What key words would be best used to find this source?

　A. 1900s

　B. pay their debts

　C. struggled to make a living

　D. African American farmers

14. What is the purpose of this source?

　A. to entertain readers

　B. to sell readers plane tickets to northern cities

　C. to explain why many African Americans moved north

　D. to persuade readers that farming is harder than factory work

Extended Response

☑ **TEST PREP** Write a short paragraph to answer the question below.

15. In the 1950s and 1960s, African Americans succeeded in gaining protection for their rights.

In your **Answer Document,** identify ways African Americans were able to influence laws. Explain the significance of First Amendment rights to these efforts.

Time Line

Use the Chapter Summary Time Line above to answer the question.

16. How many years after the end of slavery was the Civil Rights Act passed?

Activities

Art Activity Create an illustrated time line that shows the events in the struggle for equal rights. Include the end of slavery and the Civil Rights Act.

Writing Activity Write an essay about your rights and responsibilities as a citizen of the United States.

Technology
Writing Process Tips
Get help with your essay at
www.eduplace.com/kids/hmss/

Vocabulary Preview

province

The United States has 50 states. Canada has political regions called **provinces** and territories. Each province has a capital and a government. **page 276**

tariff

North American countries removed **tariffs** on products such as lumber. Once people didn't have to pay taxes on imported goods, trade between the countries grew. **page 278**

Chapter Time Line

1821
Mexican independence

1867
Canadian independence

1800   1850   1900

Reading Strategy

Monitor and Clarify As you read, check your understanding of the text.

Ask yourself if what you are reading makes sense. Reread, if you need to.

heritage

The ideals of democracy and human rights are part of the history of the United States. The Liberty Bell is a symbol of this **heritage.**
page 288

motto

The short statement on the U.S. dollar means "out of many, one." This **motto** expresses one of the ideals of the United States.
page 289

1992
NAFTA signed

1950   2000

Nations of North America

| 1500 | 1600 | 1700 | 1800 | 1900 | Today |

1521–Today

Build on What You Know You and your neighbors share the same street. The United States and its neighbors, Canada and Mexico, share the same continent. Some parts of the histories of each country are similar as well.

Canada

Main Idea The United States and Canada have similar histories and are important trading partners.

Canada is the United States' neighbor to the north. Canada covers a large area of land, but it has only about 33 million people. In contrast, the United States is smaller than Canada in land area, but it has over 300 million people. Canada's capital is Ottawa. The country has three territories and ten provinces. A **province** is a political region of a country. Like a state, a province has its own government.

Canada and the United States share a 5,500-mile border that stretches from the Atlantic Ocean to the Pacific Ocean and along the eastern edge of Alaska. Thousands of cars and trucks cross the border every day.

Canadian Flag The maple leaf symbolizes the land and people of Canada. Red and white are Canada's official colors.

VOCABULARY

province
tariff
plaza
maquiladora

Vocabulary Strategy

tariff

Tariff and **tax** start with the same two letters. A **tariff** is a **tax** on imported goods.

READING SKILL

Compare and Contrast
As you read, take notes on the similarities and differences between Canada and Mexico.

Alike	Different

BENCHMARKS
PS B   Interaction
GEO B   Places and regions
ECON C Markets

GRADE LEVEL INDICATORS
PS 4   North American immigration
GEO 7   Regional conflicts and cooperation
ECON 4 Interdependence and specialization

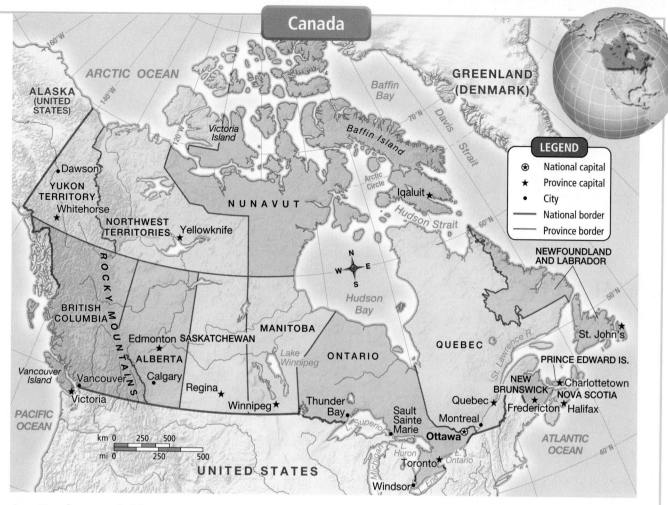

Our Northern Neighbor Canada is the second largest country in area in the world.

Canada's History and Culture

The history of Canada is similar to the history of the United States. The first people to live in Canada were native peoples, such as the Cree, Huron, and the Inuit, who are also known as Eskimos. Like the United States, Canada was colonized by Europeans. At first, the colonists were mainly French. In 1754, France and Britain fought for control of North America. France lost, and the British gained control of Canada.

In 1867, Canada became a self-governing country. It has a representative democracy, with powers divided between the provinces and a federal government. From 1867 through the mid-1900s, millions of immigrants came to Canada from Europe.

Immigration to Canada

In the second half of the 20th century, large numbers of immigrants arrived from Asia, Latin America, the Caribbean, and Africa. Many settled in cities. Today, one in six people in Canada is an immigrant. With so many immigrants, Canada is a very diverse society.

Although immigration has changed Canada, native peoples are still an important part of society. The Inuit have their own territory called Nunavut.

French influences also remain strong. In Quebec, for example, most people speak French or both French and English. French and English are the two official languages of Canada.

REVIEW How did immigration to Canada change in the second half of the 1900s?

277

Ottawa Canada's leaders meet in the Parliament building in Ottawa.

Canada and the United States

In 1992, Canada signed the North American Free Trade Agreement (NAFTA) with the United States and Mexico. The agreement says that the countries will remove tariffs and taxes on the products they sell to each other. A **tariff** is a tax on imported goods. Today, the United States and Canada trade more with each other than with any other countries.

The United States buys oil, electricity, lumber, car parts, and paper from Canada. In return, the United States sells cars, machines, chemicals, and other products to Canada. The two nations also cooperate to solve problems that affect both countries.

One example of cooperation is the effort to improve the environment in the two countries. In 1991, they signed a treaty that reduced air pollution produced by power plants in both countries.

Canada's Exports

Fish/shellfish	
Oil	
Natural gas	
Lumber/wood products	
Farm animals and products	

SKILL **Readings Charts** Which of Canada's exports are taken from the ground?

Mexico

Main Idea Mexico was colonized by the Spanish, but it has been an independent country since 1821.

Mexico is the United States' neighbor to the south. The 2,000-mile border between the United States and Mexico stretches from California to Texas. About 108 million people live in Mexico. Mexico City is the capital of Mexico and is one of the largest cities in the world.

The country has 31 states and one federal district. Northern Mexico has a central plateau with basins and ranges. This area is warm and dry. The south has mountains and tropical rain forests that cross Mexico's southern border and continue into Belize and Guatemala.

Settlement and Immigration

The Mayas and Aztecs lived in Mexico before Spanish explorers conquered and settled the region in the 1520s. In 1821, Mexico won a war for independence against Spain. Today, Mexico has a representative government.

Most Mexicans are descended from native people and early Spanish settlers. Since Mexico became independent, Spanish, Syrian, Lebanese, and Jewish people from Europe have moved to Mexico. In addition, immigrants from Guatemala, El Salvador, and other Central American countries have settled in Mexico.

REVIEW How and when did Mexico gain its independence?

Our Southern Neighbor Mexico has the largest population of any Spanish-speaking country in the world. **SKILL** **Reading Maps** Which Mexican states border the United States?

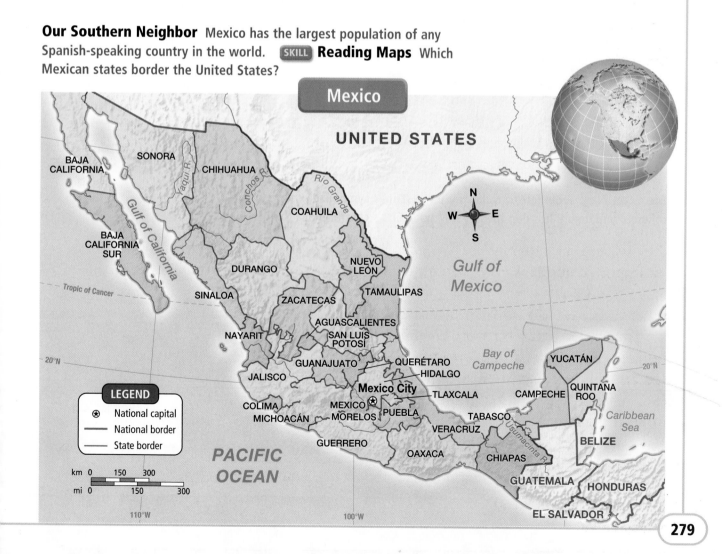

Mexico

UNITED STATES

BAJA CALIFORNIA
SONORA
CHIHUAHUA
Yaqui R.
Conchos R.
Rio Grande
COAHUILA
BAJA CALIFORNIA SUR
Gulf of California
DURANGO
NUEVO LEÓN
Tropic of Cancer
SINALOA
ZACATECAS
TAMAULIPAS
Gulf of Mexico
AGUASCALIENTES
NAYARIT
SAN LUIS POTOSÍ
20°N
GUANAJUATO
QUERÉTARO
Bay of Campeche
YUCATÁN
20°N
JALISCO
HIDALGO
LEGEND
Mexico City
TLAXCALA
CAMPECHE
QUINTANA ROO
National capital
MEXICO
National border
COLIMA
MORELOS
PUEBLA
TABASCO
Caribbean Sea
State border
MICHOACÁN
VERACRUZ
BELIZE
GUERRERO
Usumacinta R.
PACIFIC OCEAN
OAXACA
CHIAPAS
km 0   150   300
mi 0   150   300
GUATEMALA
HONDURAS
110°W
100°W
EL SALVADOR

279

Mexican Culture

Mexico's people have a Spanish and Indian heritage. Most Mexicans are mestizo (meh STEE zoh), which means people of both Spanish and Mexican Indian ancestry. Spanish is the official language, but many Indian languages are also spoken. Most Mexicans are Catholics, and the Catholic Church has shaped Mexico's culture in many ways.

Many Mexicans live in small villages in the countryside, where farming is an important part of life. Even more Mexicans live in busy modern cities. Most Mexican cities have a Spanish-style central plaza. A **plaza** is an open square. Art inspired by the country's Mayan heritage decorates many public places.

Mexico and the United States

Mexico and the United States have had close contact for more than 150 years. Because much of the southwestern United States was once part of Mexico, Mexican arts, food, and building styles are common in California, Texas, Arizona, and New Mexico.

Many Mexicans immigrate to the United States. Immigration provides workers for the United States economy and gives jobs to Mexicans. Many Mexicans immigrate illegally, however, which has caused conflicts between Mexico and the United States. The two nations disagree about how to control immigration across their shared border.

Mexico and the United States have important economic ties. Since the 1970s, businesses in the United States and other countries have built factories in Mexico near the border. This kind of factory is called a **maquiladora** (mah kee lah DOH rah). Thousands of Mexicans work in maquiladoras. They put together cars, televisions, computers, and other products that are sold all over the world.

Mexican Flag From left to right, the three stripes symbolize independence, religion, and union. The flag flies over Mexico City's central plaza (below).

NAFTA

Although trade has created some conflicts between the United States and Mexico, the countries have cooperated to solve them. In the 1980s, some people opposed paying tariffs on goods imported and exported between these nations. They believed that removing tariffs would allow the countries to sell more goods to each other, and also to Canada.

Mexico's Exports

Farm crops	
Oil	
Farm animals and products	
Precious metals	
Iron	

SKILL **Reading Charts** Which of Mexico's exports are the same as Canada's exports?

After NAFTA was signed, Mexico's trade with the United States and Canada greatly increased. Today, Mexico's most important trading partner is the United States. Mexico is the United States' second most important trading partner after Canada.

REVIEW What are some of Mexico's connections with the United States?

Lesson Summary

- Britain and France have a lasting influence in Canada.
- Spanish and Mexican Indian cultures have a lasting influence in Mexico.
- Canada, Mexico, and the United States signed NAFTA to increase trade among the three countries.

Why It Matters...

The United States, Canada, and Mexico are neighbors in North America. They all gain from trade and cultural sharing across the borders.

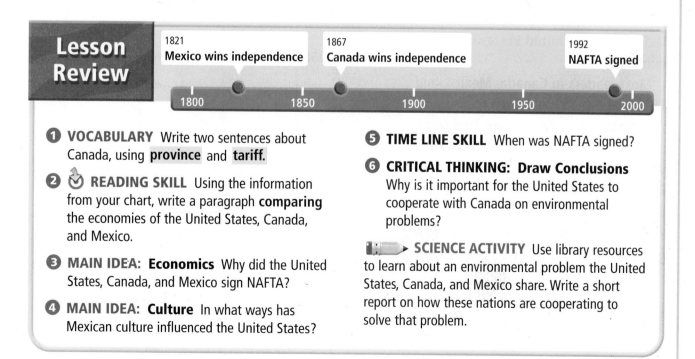

Lesson Review

1821 **Mexico wins independence**

1867 **Canada wins independence**

1992 **NAFTA signed**

1800 — 1850 — 1900 — 1950 — 2000

❶ **VOCABULARY** Write two sentences about Canada, using **province** and **tariff.**

❷ 📖 **READING SKILL** Using the information from your chart, write a paragraph **comparing** the economies of the United States, Canada, and Mexico.

❸ **MAIN IDEA: Economics** Why did the United States, Canada, and Mexico sign NAFTA?

❹ **MAIN IDEA: Culture** In what ways has Mexican culture influenced the United States?

❺ **TIME LINE SKILL** When was NAFTA signed?

❻ **CRITICAL THINKING: Draw Conclusions** Why is it important for the United States to cooperate with Canada on environmental problems?

✏️ **SCIENCE ACTIVITY** Use library resources to learn about an environmental problem the United States, Canada, and Mexico share. Write a short report on how these nations are cooperating to solve that problem.

TRADE AMONG NATIONS

Before NAFTA was signed into law, no one knew how free trade would affect the U.S. economy. People had opinions, though. Some warned that Americans would lose jobs if trade became more free. They predicted that companies would move their factories to Mexico.

Most economists believed NAFTA would be good for each country. They argued that cooperating to create free trade would help businesses and keep prices low.

Years after NAFTA passed, it is clear that North American trade has grown. Between 1993 and 2005, total trade between Canada, Mexico, and the United States more than doubled.

Most leaders in Canada, Mexico, and the United States have been pleased by the increase in trade that resulted from cooperation. However, some report that NAFTA has not helped to create enough jobs. Other nations will watch NAFTA's effects carefully. If free trade works in North America, they may want similar agreements with the United States.

LUMBER Canada's forests are the largest in North America. Wood and wood products from those forests are important exports.

Trade Between U.S. and Canada 1993–2005

Dollars (in Billions) vs. Year

- Exports to Canada
- Imports from Canada

Canada is our nation's biggest trading partner. By about how much did exports grow between 1993 and 2005?

AUTOMOBILES Cars and car parts are important to North American trade. Car parts from the United States are put together in this Mexican factory.

OIL In recent years, Mexico has become a leading oil exporter. Most of its oil exports go to its NAFTA trading partners.

Trade Between U.S. and Mexico 1993–2005

- Exports to Mexico
- Imports from Mexico

Dollars (in Billions) / *Year*

After NAFTA, Mexican imports to the United States more than quadrupled between 1993 and 2005.

Activities

1. **LIST IT** List three questions to ask other students about the information in the charts.

2. **GRAPH IT** Create a bar graph from the line graphs, comparing Canadian and Mexican trade with the United States.

Skillbuilder

Analyze the News

You just read about the history, culture, and politics of Canada and Mexico. To learn about other places or current events, you can use the radio, television, newspapers, or the Internet. As you listen to or read these different news sources, you need to evaluate the information carefully. The steps below will help you to analyze news sources.

▶ **VOCABULARY**

news article

editorial

Learn the Skill

Step 1: Identify the kind of article you are listening to or reading.

- A **news article** describes a recent event. It answers the questions *Who, What, Where, When,* and *Why.* Its purpose is to inform people.

- An **editorial** presents an opinion about an issue or an event. It can present facts, but an editorial's main purpose is to persuade its audience.

Step 2: Decide whether the article has an opinion or perspective. Although news articles are mostly factual, writers sometimes present a perspective. Editorials always have a perspective.

Step 3: If possible, double-check the article's facts in another source.

Practice the Skill

Read the following article, then answer the questions.

Canadian Leader Visits Washington

The Prime Minister of Canada arrived in Washington, D.C. today. His first stop was at the White House, where he discussed trade with the President. Visits such as these are important. The United States trades with Canada more than any other nation. This trade creates jobs for workers in the United States, and we should do everything we can to support it, including removing tariffs.

1 What kind of article is it?

2 What facts are given? What perspectives or opinions are given?

3 How would you describe the writer's point of view?

Apply the Skill

Choose a current event that interests you. Find an article about it. You might select something from a newspaper, magazine, television program, or website. Then answer the questions below.

1 What type of article did you find? How do you know what type it is?

2 What facts are given? How can you double-check them?

3 Are there any opinions or perspectives? What are they? How do you know they are opinions?

Core Lesson 2

The United States Today

VOCABULARY

heritage
motto

Vocabulary Strategy

heritage

The words **heritage** and **inherit** are related in meaning. A heritage is something you inherit, or receive, from your family or culture.

READING SKILL

Draw Conclusions As you read, note details that support the conclusion that immigrants have strengthened the United States.

BENCHMARKS

PS A   Cultures
GOV A   Role of government
GOV B   Rules and laws
CRR B   Rights and responsibilities

GRADE LEVEL INDICATORS

PS 1   Cultural practices and products
GOV 2   Characteristics of American
             democracy
GOV 3   Founding documents
CRR 2   Upholding the Constitution

Build on What You Know Think about how each of your classmates contributes special skills and talents to your class. In a similar way, each of the over 300 million people in the United States contributes to the country.

Many People, One Nation

Main Idea The United States is made up of people from many different backgrounds and cultures.

The people of the United States come from a great number of countries and cultures. About one in every ten citizens was born in another country. Millions more are the descendents of immigrants.

Each generation has contributed something new to the story of immigration. Today, almost one-third of immigrants to the United States are from Latin America. One-half of those immigrants come from Mexico. Another third of all immigrants today come from countries in Asia such as India, China, and South Korea.

Generations Some families, such as the one shown here, have many generations.

Roberto Goizueta He led an international company with branches in over 200 countries.

Madeleine Albright She was the first woman to hold the job of Secretary of State.

Pitambar Somani He was the first person from India to run a department in a state government in the United States.

Many Ethnic Groups

Diversity of backgrounds is one of the United States' greatest strengths. Each ethnic and religious group adds a new language, new foods, and new customs to the culture of the United States. For example, many words we use come from different languages. The word *kindergarten* is originally a German word. *Mosquito* is Spanish. The word *skunk* comes from an American Indian language.

The culture of the United States is a mixture of traditions from around the world. Some ethnic traditions change when immigrants come to the United States. New traditions are also created. The first St. Patrick's Day parade was held in Boston, not in Ireland. The first Chinese New Year's parade with marching bands and floats was held in San Francisco. These holidays came from other countries, but the way people celebrated them in the United States was new.

Individual immigrants have also brought their knowledge and talents to the United States, making the country stronger. **Roberto Goizueta** was a refugee from Cuba who became the president of The Coca-Cola Company. **Pitambar Somani** is an immigrant from India. He became head of Ohio's Department of Health and worked to improve health care for Ohioans.

Immigrants and their children have also made important contributions to the national government. **Madeleine Albright** immigrated to the United States from eastern Europe. In 1996, President Bill Clinton chose her to be the Secretary of State. **Daniel Inouye,** the son of Japanese immigrants, is a senator from Hawaii. He is one of the longest-serving members of the Senate.

REVIEW What are two contributions that immigrants have made to the United States?

The White House Many citizens go to Washington, D.C. to learn about their democratic heritage. The White House has been the home of the President, who leads the executive branch, since 1800.

Our Shared Values

Main Idea Americans share the belief that the government should protect citizens' rights.

All Americans share a democratic heritage. A **heritage** is something that is handed down from past generations. The values of democracy and equal rights have been an important part of the history of the United States. This democratic heritage is expressed in the Constitution and the Bill of Rights. These documents explain the government, the rights, and the duties that all Americans share.

Although the Constitution did not originally protect the rights of every American, it established a democratic form of government. The Constitution keeps any single person or group from taking power away from the people. This system has worked, and our democracy has lasted for more than 200 years.

During that time, Americans have amended the Constitution and created laws that have made the nation even more democratic and just. The Bill of Rights guarantees all citizens the freedoms of speech, religion, and assembly, or the right to gather together.

The rights protected by the Bill of Rights are significant because they mean people in the United States can hold their own opinions and discuss them. Citizens can disagree with each other and even with the government.

Not every group in the United States has always enjoyed these rights. Some ethnic groups, such as African Americans and American Indians, have faced discrimination. Their rights to equal schools, housing, and jobs were not recognized or defended. Each ethnic group coming to the United States has struggled for protection of their rights.

E Pluribus Unum

Just as there have always been people who have faced unfair treatment, there have always been people who have worked for justice. The history of the United States is a story of brave people who have fought to expand the democratic principles and ideas upon which the nation was founded.

One motto of the United States is "E Pluribus Unum" (EE PLUR ih buhs OON uhm). A **motto** is a short statement that explains an ideal or goal. "E Pluribus Unum" is a Latin phrase that means "out of many, one."

"E Pluribus Unum" This motto can be found on all U.S. coins.

"E pluribus unum" is written on coins and government buildings throughout the country. The motto is a reminder that the original thirteen colonies formed one country. Today, fifty states form one democratic nation with a culture that is as diverse as the people who live in it.

REVIEW What rights does the Bill of Rights guarantee?

Lesson Summary

```
                The American People
       ┌─────────────────┼─────────────────┐
  Come             Share a            Share a rich
  from many        culture that       democratic
  different        is a mix of        heritage of
  ethnic           old and new        rights and
  backgrounds      traditions         freedoms
```

Why It Matters...

The shared values and democratic heritage of the United States help people from many different backgrounds to live with and learn from each other.

Lesson Review

1. **VOCABULARY** Use the word **heritage** in a paragraph describing the background that all United States citizens share.

2. **READING SKILL** What immigrant contributions in this lesson support the **conclusion** that immigrants have strengthened the United States?

3. **MAIN IDEA: History** What caused the United States' population to become so diverse?

4. **MAIN IDEA: Government** What is the significance of the Constitution in the democratic system of the United States?

5. **PEOPLE TO KNOW** Who is **Madeleine Albright** and what job did she hold in the government?

6. **CRITICAL THINKING: Synthesize** Why do you think the United States could be called one of the first international nations?

7. **CRITICAL THINKING: Analyze** Why is it important for the government to protect the rights of all its citizens?

HANDS ON **CITIZENSHIP ACTIVITY** Make a poster that shows what the motto "E Pluribus Unum" means to you. Use pictures from magazines and headlines from articles and newspapers.

Visual Summary

1. – 3. ✏️ Write a description of each aspect of life in the United States.

Life in the United States	
Trade with Canada and Mexico	
Diverse Population	
Heritage	

Facts and Main Ideas

✅ **TEST PREP** Answer each question with information from the chapter.

4. **Citizenship** Explain two ways in which the United States cooperates with other countries.

5. **Geography** Which country borders the United States to the south?

6. **Economics** What effect did the North American Free Trade Agreement have on nations in North America?

7. **Citizenship** From what two regions do most immigrants come to the United States today?

8. **Citizenship** Why are the rights guaranteed by the Bill of Rights significant?

Vocabulary

✅ **TEST PREP** Choose the correct word from the list below to complete each sentence.

province, p. 276
tariff, p. 278
heritage, p. 288

9. A tax on imported goods is called a _____.

10. Quebec is a _____ of Canada where most people speak French.

11. The democractic _____ of the United States is expressed in the Constitution and Bill of Rights.

1821
Mexico's independence

1867
Canada's independence

1992
NAFTA passed

1800   1850   1900   1950   Present

Apply Skills

✔ TEST PREP **Study Skill** Read the article below and use what you have learned about analyzing the news to answer each question.

Working With Mexico

Floods and pollution affect cities along the border of the United States and Mexico. Unless we deal with these problems, they will get worse. The United States government needs to cooperate with Mexico to solve this problem. We must stop pollution. It is our responsibility to protect the environment.

12. Which of the following statements describes the type of article above?

A. It is an editorial because it tries to convince readers to agree with it.

B. It is an editorial because it contains no facts.

C. It is a news article because it contains only facts.

D. It is a news article because it answers *Who, Want, When, Where,* and *Why.*

13. Which of the following summarizes the writer's perspective?

A. The United States should not work with Mexico to keep rivers clean.

B. Cleaning up rivers that form the border is Mexico's responsibility.

C. The United States should work with Mexico to keep rivers clean.

D. A perspective is not stated.

Extended Response

✔ TEST PREP Write a short paragraph to answer the question below.

14. People from many cultural groups have come to the United States. In the United States, they interact with each other and contribute to the nation's diversity.

In your **Answer Document,** explain the consequences of the interactions of various cultural groups on the culture of the United States.

Time Line

Use the Chapter Summary Time Line above to answer the question.

15. Which country gained independence first, Canada or Mexico?

Activities

 Research Activity Use a dictionary to find the origins of the words below.
giraffe   walrus   kayak
kimono   shampoo   llama

 Writing Activity Write a personal essay that explains how the democratic heritage of the United States has affected you. You may wish to describe a time you went to a religious service or expressed an opinion.

 Technology
Writing Process Tips
Get help with your essay at
www.eduplace.com/kids/hmss/

Review and Test Prep

Vocabulary and Main Ideas

✓ **TEST PREP** Write a sentence to answer each question.

1. What effect did **abolitionists** such as Harriet Beecher Stowe have?

2. What rights helped **suffragists** work for changes to laws?

3. Why were the Declaration of Independence and Constitution important to the **civil rights** movement?

4. What rights and **responsibilities** do all United States citizens have?

5. What did North American countries do to cooperate on **tariffs?**

6. What is the **heritage** that all United States citizens share, and why is it significant?

Critical Thinking

✓ **TEST PREP** Write a short paragraph to answer each question.

7. **Analyze** Explain what citizens in a democracy can do to influence their government. Use examples from history in your answer.

8. **Cause and Effect** What has been the influence of immigrants from different cultural groups on the culture of the United States?

Unit Activity

Create a Diagram of Cultural Interaction

- List ways you interact with various cultural groups in the United States.

- Your interactions could include celebrating holidays, eating foods, listening to music, or using words from different cultural groups.

- Create a poster illustrating your list.

- Write captions to go with your poster.

- Display your poster in your classroom.

At the Library

You may find these books at your school or public library.

Remember: A Pictorial Tribute to the Brown v. Board of Eduction Supreme Court Decision by Toni Morrison
Photographs and storytelling bring the history of school desegregation to life.

In Defense of Liberty: The Story of America's Bill of Rights
by Russell Freedman
This history of the Bill of Rights gives examples of how it applies to today's world.

✔ **TEST PREP** Read the paragraph below. Then use what you know about finding and evaluating sources to answer each question.

Immigration is an important part of United States history. People from all over the world have come to this country and become citizens. In the 1800s, most immigrants came from Europe. Today, many come from Latin America. They can become citizens by being naturalized. To do this, they have to learn the laws, rights, and duties of being a citizen, and pass a test as well. Then they promise to obey the Constitution.

9. What key term might someone use to find this source?

   A. laws
   B. Europe
   C. immigration
   D. history

10. What could you do to better analyze the reliability of the source?

   A. Check the information in another source.
   B. Ask a friend if the information sounds correct.
   C. Read the passage several times.
   D. Find out how many copies of the source have been sold.

✔ **TEST PREP** Answer each question below.

11. What are two rights that women, African Americans, and American Indians used in their struggles for equality?

   A. freedom of speech and the right of petition
   B. freedom of speech and freedom of religion
   C. freedom of religion and the right to petition
   D. freedom of the press and freedom of religion

12. The United States Constitution explains the structure of the national government. Ohio's constitution explains the structure of the state government. Both documents also guarantee certain rights for citizens.

   In your **Answer Document,** name some of the rights protected by the United States Constitution or Ohio's constitution. Then explain how these documents foster self-government in a democracy.

References

Citizenship Handbook

Resources

Pledge of Allegiance

I pledge allegiance to the flag of the United States of America and to the Republic for which it stands, one Nation under God, indivisible, with liberty and justice for all.

Spanish

Prometo lealtad a la bandera
de los Estados Unidos de América,
y a la república que representa,
una nación bajo Diós, indivisible,
con libertad y justicia para todos.

Russian

Я даю клятву верности флагу
Соединённых Штатов Америки
и стране, символом которой
он является, народу, единому
перед Богом, свободному
и равноправному.

Tagalog

Ako ay nanunumpa ng katapatan
sa bandila ng Estados Unidos
ng Amerika, at sa Republikang
kanyang kinakatawan, isang
Bansang pumapailalim sa isang
Maykapal hindi nahahati, may
kalayaan at katarungan para
sa lahat.

Arabic

ادين بالولاء لعلم الولايات المتحده الامريكيه والى
الجمهوريه التي تمثلها دولة واحدة تؤمن باللة
متحدة تمنح الحرية والعدالة للجميع

Chinese

言 誓 忠 誠 旗 國 我 發 誓 忠 于 美 利 屬 帝 和 國 旗 所 征 的 共 生 眾 下 之 一 國 不 可 分 國 眾，所 享。 有 自 由 正 義象，與 上 有

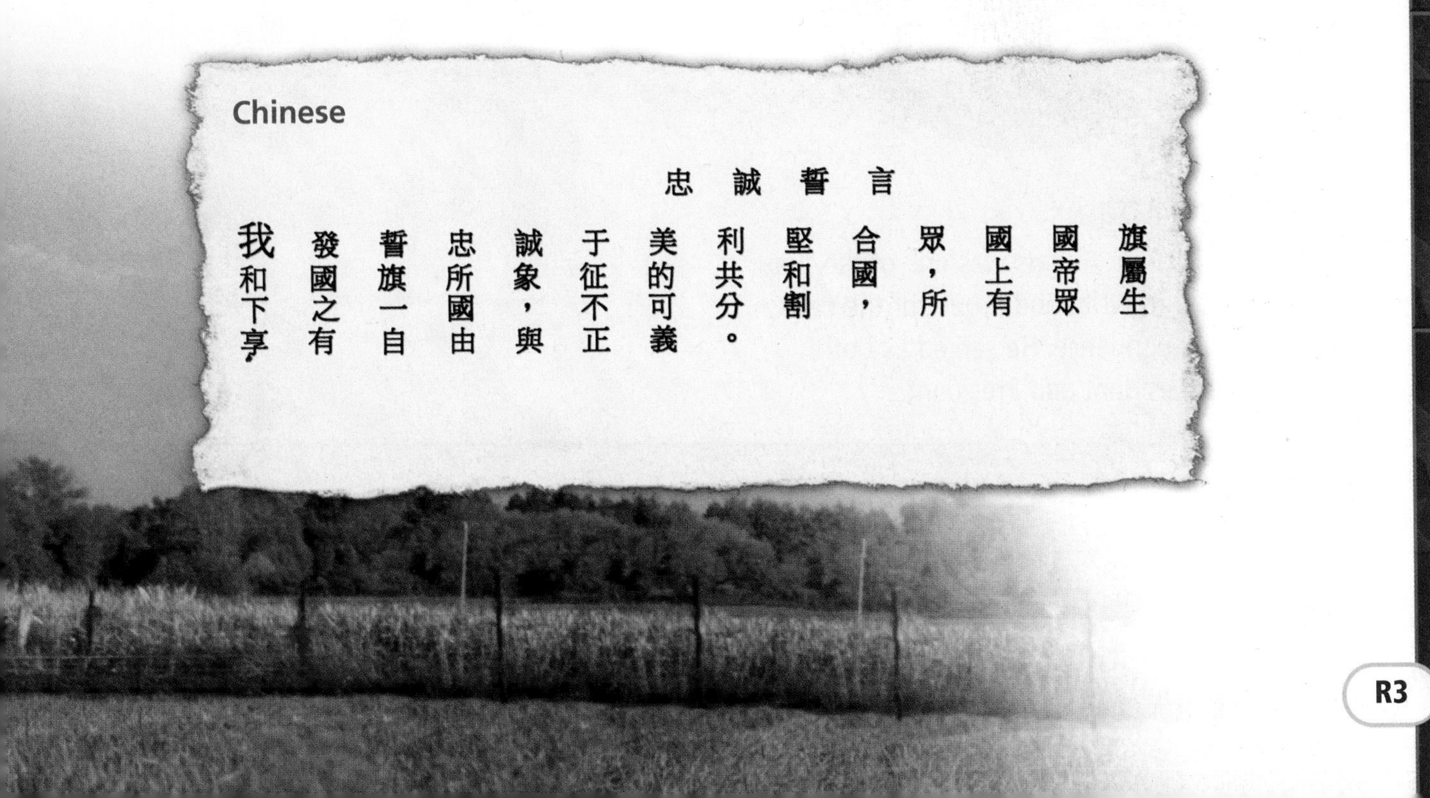

Character Traits

Character includes feelings, thoughts, and behaviors. A character trait is something people show by the way they act. To act bravely shows courage, and courage is one of several character traits.

Positive character traits, such as honesty, caring, and courage, lead to positive actions. Character traits are also called "life skills." Life skills can help you do your best, and doing your best leads to reaching your goals.

Coretta Scott King

Responsibility King spoke out for the rights of African Americans. Her sense of responsibility toward many people of this nation set an example.

John Adams

Patriotism Adams was one of the first people to write and argue for the cause of independence. He served as both Vice President and President.

Courage means acting bravely. Doing what you believe to be good and right, and telling the truth, requires courage.

Patriotism means working for the goals of your country. When you show national pride, you are being patriotic.

Responsibility is taking care of work that needs to be done. Responsible people are reliable and trustworthy, which means they can be counted on.

Respect means paying attention to what other people want and believe. The "golden rule," or treating others as you would like to be treated, shows thoughtfulness and respect.

Fairness means working to make things fair, or right, for everyone. Often one needs to try again and again to achieve fairness. This requires diligence, or not giving up.

Civic virtue is good citizenship. It means doing things, such as cooperating and solving problems, to help communities live and work well together.

Caring means noticing what others need and helping them get what they need. Feeling concern or compassion is another way to define caring.

Historical Documents

Pilgrims are shown writing the Mayflower Compact while still aboard the ship.

The Mayflower Compact (1620)

". . . We whose names are underwritten, . . . Having undertaken, for the Glory of God, and Advancement of the Christian Faith, and Honor of our King and Country, a Voyage to plant the first Colony in the northern Parts of Virginia; Do by these Presents, solemnly and mutually, in the Presence of God and one of another, covenant and combine ourselves together into a civil Body Politick, for our better Ordering and Preservation, and Furtherance of the Ends aforesaid: And by Virtue hereof do enact, constitute, and frame such just and equal Laws, Ordinances, Acts, Constitutions, and Officers, from time to time, as shall be thought most meet and convenient for the general Good of the Colony; unto which we promise all due Submission and Obedience. . . ."

Mr. John Carver	Mr. Samuel Fuller	Edward Tilly
Mr. William Bradford	Mr. Christopher Martin	John Tilly
Mr. Edward Winslow	Mr. William Mullins	Francis Cooke
Mr. William Brewster	Mr. William White	Thomas Rogers
Isaac Allerton	Mr. Richard Warren	Thomas Tinker
Myles Standish	John Howland	John Ridgdale
John Alden	Mr. Steven Hopkins	Edward Fuller
John Turner	Digery Priest	Richard Clark
Francis Eaton	Thomas Williams	Richard Gardiner
James Chilton	Gilbert Winslow	Mr. John Allerton
John Craxton	Edmund Margesson	Thomas English
John Billington	Peter Brown	Edward Doten
Joses Fletcher	Richard Britteridge	Edward Liester
John Goodman	George Soule	

Pitt's Speech to Parliament on the Stamp Act (1766)

"The Americans have not acted in all things with prudence and temper. They have been wronged. They have been driven to madness by injustice. Will you punish them for the madness you have occasioned? Rather let prudence and temper come first from this side. I will undertake for America, that she will follow the example. . . .

Upon the whole, I will beg leave to tell the House what is really my opinion. It is, that the Stamp-Act be repealed absolutely, totally, and immediately; that the reason for the repeal should be assigned, because it was founded on an erroneous principle."

William Pitt

Burke's Speech to Parliament on Conciliation with America (1775)

"The proposition is peace. Not peace through the medium of war; not peace to be hunted through the labyrinth of intricate and endless negotiations . . . It is simple peace, sought in its natural course and in its ordinary haunts. . . .

Let the colonies always keep the idea of their civil rights associated with your government — they will cling and grapple to you, and no force under heaven will be of power to tear them from their allegiance. But let it be once understood that your government may be one thing and their privileges another, that these two things may exist without any mutual relation — the cement is gone, the cohesion is loosened, and everything hastens to decay and dissolution. . . .

Magnanimity in politics is not seldom the truest wisdom; and a great empire and little minds go ill together."

Edmund Burke

Members of the Continental Congress are shown signing the Declaration of Independence.

The Declaration of Independence

In Congress, July 4, 1776

The unanimous declaration of the thirteen United States of America

Introduction*

When, in the course of human events, it becomes necessary for one people to dissolve the political bonds which have connected them with another, and to assume, among the powers of the earth, the separate and equal station to which the laws of nature and of nature's God entitle them, a decent respect to the opinions of mankind requires that they should declare the causes which impel them to the separation.

Basic Rights

WE hold these truths to be self-evident: That all men are created equal, that they are endowed by their Creator with certain unalienable rights; that among these are life, liberty, and the pursuit of happiness; that, to secure these rights, governments are instituted among men, deriving their just powers from the consent of the governed; that whenever any form of government becomes destructive of these ends, it is the right of the people to alter or to abolish it, and to institute new government, laying its foundation on such principles, and organizing its powers in such form, as to them shall seem most likely to effect their safety and happiness. Prudence, indeed, will dictate that governments long established should not be changed for light and transient causes; and accordingly all experience hath shown that mankind are more disposed to suffer, while evils are sufferable, than to right themselves by abolishing the forms to which they are accustomed. But when a long train of abuses and usurpations, pursuing invariably the same object, evinces a design to reduce them under absolute despotism, it is their right, it is their duty, to throw off such government, and to provide new guards for their future security. Such has been the patient sufferance of these colonies; and such is now the necessity which constrains them to alter their former systems of government. The history of the present King of Great Britain is a history of repeated injuries and usurpations, all having in direct object the establishment of an absolute tyranny over these states. To prove this, let facts be submitted to a candid world.

Charges Against the King

HE has refused his assent to laws, the most wholesome and necessary for the public good.

HE has forbidden his governors to pass laws of immediate and pressing importance, unless suspended in their operation till his assent should be obtained; and, when so suspended, he has utterly neglected to attend to them.

HE has refused to pass other laws for the accommodation of large districts of people, unless those people would relinquish the right of representation in the legislature, a right inestimable to them, and formidable to tyrants only.

HE has called together legislative bodies at places unusual, uncomfortable, and distant from the depository of their public records, for the sole purpose of fatiguing them into compliance with his measures.

HE has dissolved representative houses repeatedly, for opposing, with manly firmness his invasions on the rights of the people.

*Titles have been added to the Declaration to make it easier to read. These titles are not in the original document.

HE has refused for a long time, after such dissolutions, to cause others to be elected; whereby the legislative powers, incapable of annihilation, have returned to the people at large for their exercise; the state remaining in the mean time, exposed to all the dangers of invasions from without and convulsions within.

HE has endeavored to prevent the population of these states; for that purpose obstructing the laws for the naturalization of foreigners; refusing to pass others to encourage their migration hither, and raising the conditions of new appropriations of lands.

HE has obstructed the administration of justice, by refusing his assent to laws for establishing judiciary powers.

HE has made judges dependent on his will alone, for the tenure of their offices, and the amount of payment of their salaries.

HE has erected a multitude of new offices, and sent hither swarms of officers to harass our people and eat out their substance.

HE has kept among us, in times of peace, standing armies, without the consent of our legislatures.

HE has affected to render the military independent of, and superior to, the civil power.

HE has combined with others to subject us to a Jurisdiction foreign to our constitution and unacknowledged by our laws, giving his assent to their acts of pretended legislation:

FOR quartering large bodies of armed troops among us;

FOR protecting them, by a mock trial, from punishment for any murders which they should commit on the inhabitants of these states;

FOR cutting off our trade with all parts of the world;

FOR imposing taxes on us without our consent;

FOR depriving us, in many cases, of the benefits of trial by jury;

FOR transporting us beyond seas, to be tried for pretended offenses;

FOR abolishing the free system of English laws in a neighboring province, establishing therein an arbitrary government, and enlarging its boundaries, so as to render it at once an example and fit instrument for introducing the same absolute rule into these colonies;

FOR taking away our charters, abolishing our most valuable laws, and altering fundamentally the forms of our governments;

FOR suspending our own legislatures, and declaring themselves invested with power to legislate for us in all cases whatsoever.

HE has abdicated Government here, by declaring us out of his protection and waging war against us.

HE has plundered our seas, ravaged our coasts, burned our towns, and destroyed the lives of our people.

HE is at this time transporting large armies of foreign mercenaries to complete the works of death, desolation, and tyranny, already begun with circumstances of cruelty and perfidy scarcely paralleled in the most barbarous ages, and totally unworthy the head of a civilized nation.

HE has constrained our fellow-citizens, taken captive on the high seas, to bear arms against their country, to become the executioners of their friends and brethren, or to fall themselves by their hands.

The king had made colonial assemblies meet at unusual times and places. This made going to assembly meetings hard for colonial representatives.

In some cases the king stopped the assembly from meeting at all.

The king tried to stop people from moving to the colonies and into new western lands.

The king prevented the colonies from choosing their own judges. Instead, he sent over judges who depended on him for their jobs and pay.

The king kept British soldiers in the colonies, even though the colonists had not asked for them.

King George III

The king and Parliament had taxed the colonists without their consent. This was one of the most important reasons the colonists were angry at Britain.

The colonists felt that the king had waged war on them.

The king had hired German soldiers and sent them to the colonies to keep order.

British soldiers became a symbol of British misrule to many colonists.

The colonists said that they had asked the king to change his policies, but he had not listened to them.

The writers declared that the colonies were free and independent states, equal to the world's other states. They had the powers to make war and peace and to trade with other countries.

The signers pledged their lives to the support of this Declaration. The Continental Congress ordered copies of the Declaration of Independence to be sent to all the states and to the army.

HE has excited domestic insurrections amongst us, and has endeavored to bring on the inhabitants of our frontiers, the merciless Indian savages, whose known rule of warfare is an undistinguished destruction of all ages, sexes, and conditions.

Response to the King

IN every stage of these oppressions we have petitioned for redress in the most humble terms; Our repeated petitions have been answered only by repeated injury. A prince, whose character is thus marked by every act which may define a tyrant, is unfit to be the ruler of a free people.

NOR have we been wanting in our attentions to our British brethren. We have warned them from time to time, of attempts by their legislature to extend an unwarrantable jurisdiction over us. We have reminded them of the circumstances of our emigration and settlement here. We have appealed to their native justice and magnanimity; and we have conjured them, by the ties of our common kindred, to disavow these usurpations, which, would inevitably interrupt our connections and correspondence. They, too, have been deaf to the voice of justice and of consanguinity. We must, therefore, acquiesce in the necessity which denounces our separation, and hold them, as we hold the rest of mankind, enemies in war, in peace, friends.

Independence

WE, therefore, the representatives of the United States of America, in General Congress Assembled, appealing to the Supreme Judge of the world for the rectitude of our intentions, do, in the name and by authority of the good people of these colonies, solemnly publish and declare, that these United Colonies are, and of right ought to be, FREE AND INDEPENDENT STATES; that they are absolved from all allegiance to the British crown, and that all political connection between them and the state of Great Britain is, and ought to be, totally dissolved; and that, as free and independent states, they have full power to levy war, conclude peace, contract alliances, establish commerce, and do all other acts and things which independent states may of right do. And for the support of this declaration, with a firm reliance on the protection of Divine Providence, we mutually pledge to each other our lives, our fortunes, and our sacred honor.

NEW HAMPSHIRE
Josiah Bartlett
William Whipple
Matthew Thornton

MASSACHUSETTS
John Hancock
John Adams
Samuel Adams
Robert Treat Paine
Elbridge Gerry

NEW YORK
William Floyd
Philip Livingston
Francis Lewis
Lewis Morris

RHODE ISLAND
Stephen Hopkins
William Ellery

NEW JERSEY
Richard Stockton
John Witherspoon
Francis Hopkinson
John Hart
Abraham Clark

PENNSYLVANIA
Robert Morris
Benjamin Rush
Benjamin Franklin
John Morton
George Clymer
James Smith
George Taylor
James Wilson
George Ross

DELAWARE
Caesar Rodney
George Read
Thomas McKean

MARYLAND
Samuel Chase
William Paca
Thomas Stone
Charles Carroll
  of Carrollton

NORTH CAROLINA
Willam Hooper
Joseph Hewes
John Penn

VIRGINIA
George Wythe
Richard Henry Lee
Thomas Jefferson
Benjamin Harrison
Thomas Nelson, Jr.
Francis Lightfoot Lee
Carter Braxton

SOUTH CAROLINA
Edward Rutledge
Thomas Heyward, Jr.
Thomas Lynch, Jr.
Arthur Middleton

CONNECTICUT
Roger Sherman
Samuel Huntington
William Williams
Oliver Wolcott

GEORGIA
Button Gwinnett
Lyman Hall
George Walton

The Constitution of the United States

Preamble*

W̲e the people of the United States, in order to form a more perfect Union, establish justice, insure domestic tranquility, provide for the common defense, promote the general welfare, and secure the blessings of liberty to ourselves and our posterity, do ordain and establish this Constitution for the United States of America.

ARTICLE I
Legislative Branch

SECTION 1. CONGRESS

All legislative powers herein granted shall be vested in a Congress of the United States, which shall consist of a Senate and House of Representatives.

SECTION 2. HOUSE OF REPRESENTATIVES

1. **Election and Term of Members** The House of Representatives shall be composed of members chosen every second year by the people of the several States, and the electors in each State shall have the qualifications requisite for electors of the most numerous branch of the State Legislature.

2. **Qualifications** No person shall be a representative who shall not have attained to the age of twenty-five years, and been seven years a citizen of the United States, and who shall not, when elected, be an inhabitant of that State in which he shall be chosen.

3. **Number of Representatives per State** Representatives ~~and direct taxes~~** shall be apportioned among the several States which may be included within this Union, according to their respective numbers, ~~which shall be determined by adding to the whole number of free persons, including those bound to service for a term of years, and excluding Indians not taxed, three fifths of all other persons.~~ The actual enumeration shall be made within three years after the first meeting of the Congress of the United States, and within every subsequent term of ten years, in such manner as they shall by law direct. The number of representatives shall not exceed one for every thirty thousand, but each State shall have at least one representative; ~~and until such enumeration shall be made, the State of New Hampshire shall be entitled to choose three, Massachusetts eight, Rhode Island and Providence Plantations one, Connecticut five, New York six, New Jersey four, Pennsylvania eight, Delaware one, Maryland six, Virginia ten, North Carolina five, South Carolina five, and Georgia three.~~

4. **Vacancies** When vacancies happen in the representation from any State, the executive authority thereof shall issue writs of election to fill such vacancies.

5. **Special Powers** The House of Representatives shall choose their speaker and other officers; and shall have the sole power of impeachment.

*The titles of the Preamble, and of each article, section, clause, and amendment have been added to make the Constitution easier to read. These titles are not in the original document.

**Parts of the Constitution have been crossed out to show that they are not in force any more. They have been changed by amendments or they no longer apply.

Historical Documents

Preamble The Preamble, or introduction, states the purposes of the Constitution. The writers wanted to strengthen the national government and give the nation a more solid foundation. The Preamble makes it clear that it is the people of the United States who have the power to establish or change a government.

Congress Section 1 gives Congress the power to make laws. Congress has two parts, the House of Representatives and the Senate.

Election and Terms of Members Citizens elect the members of the House of Representatives every two years.

Qualifications Representatives must be at least 25 years old. They must have been United States citizens for at least seven years. They also must live in the state they represent.

Number of Representatives per State The number of representatives each state has is based on its population. The biggest states have the most representatives. Each state must have at least one representative. An enumeration, or census, must be taken every 10 years to find out a state's population. The number of representatives in the House is now fixed at 435.

George Washington watches delegates sign the Constitution.

Americans often use voting machines on election day.

Number, Term, and Selection of Members In each state, citizens elect two members of the Senate. This gives all states, whether big or small, equal power in the Senate. Senators serve six year terms. Originally, state legislatures chose the senators for their states. Today, however, people elect their senators directly. The Seventeenth Amendment made this change in 1913.

Qualifications Senators must be at least 30 years old and United States citizens for at least nine years. Like representatives, they must live in the state they represent.

President of the Senate The Vice President of the United States acts as the President, or chief officer, of the Senate. The Vice President votes only in cases of a tie.

Impeachment Trials If the House of Representatives impeaches, or charges, an official with a crime, the Senate holds a trial. If two-thirds of the senators find the official guilty, then the person is removed from office. The only Presidents ever impeached were Andrew Johnson in 1868 and Bill Clinton in 1998. Both were found not guilty.

Election of Congress Each state decides where and when to hold elections. Today congressional elections are held in even-numbered years, on the Tuesday after the first Monday in November.

Annual Sessions The Constitution requires Congress to meet at least once a year. In 1933, the 20th Amendment made January 3rd the day for beginning a regular session of Congress.

Organization A quorum is the smallest number of members that must be present for an organization to hold a meeting. For each house of Congress, this number is the majority, or more than one-half, of its members.

SECTION 3. SENATE

1. ***Number, Term, and Selection of Members*** *The Senate of the United States shall be composed of two senators from each State, chosen by the Legislature thereof, for six years; and each Senator shall have one vote.*

2. ***Overlapping Terms and Filling Vacancies*** *Immediately after they shall be assembled in consequence of the first election, they shall be divided as equally as may be into three classes. ~~The seats of the senators of the first class shall be vacated at the expiration of the second year, of the second class at the expiration of the fourth year, and of the third class at the expiration of the sixth year, so~~ that one-third may be chosen every second year; ~~and if vacancies happen by resignation, or otherwise, during the recess of the legislature of any State, the executive thereof may make temporary appointments until the next meeting of the legislature, which shall then fill such vacancies.~~*

3. ***Qualifications*** *No person shall be a senator who shall not have attained to the age of thirty years, and been nine years a citizen of the United States, and who shall not, when elected, be an inhabitant of that State for which he shall be chosen.*

4. ***President of the Senate*** *The Vice President of the United States shall be President of the Senate, but shall have no vote, unless they be equally divided.*

5. ***Other Officers*** *The Senate shall choose their other officers, and also a President pro tempore, in the absence of the Vice President, or when he shall exercise the office of the President of the United States.*

6. ***Impeachment Trials*** *The Senate shall have the sole power to try all impeachments. When sitting for that purpose, they shall be on oath or affirmation. When the President of the United States is tried, the Chief Justice shall preside: and no person shall be convicted without the concurrence of two-thirds of the members present.*

7. ***Penalties*** *Judgment in cases of impeachment shall not extend further than to removal from office, and disqualification to hold and enjoy any office of honor, trust, or profit under the United States: but the party convicted shall nevertheless be liable and subject to indictment, trial, judgement and punishment, according to law.*

SECTION 4. ELECTIONS AND MEETINGS

1. ***Election of Congress*** *The times, places and manner of holding elections for senators and representatives, shall be prescribed in each State by the legislature thereof; but the Congress may at any time by law make or alter such regulations, except as to the places of choosing Senators.*

2. ***Annual Sessions*** *The Congress shall assemble at least once in every year, ~~and such meeting shall be on the first Monday in December,~~ unless they shall by law appoint a different day.*

SECTION 5. RULES OF PROCEDURE

1. ***Organization*** *Each house shall be the judge of the elections, returns and qualifications of its own members, and a majority of each shall constitute a quorum to do business; but a smaller number may adjourn from day to day, and may be authorized to compel the attendance of absent members, in such manner, and under such penalties as each house may provide.*

2. **Rules** *Each house may determine the rules of its proceedings, punish its members for disorderly behavior, and, with the concurrence of two-thirds, expel a member.*

3. **Journal** *Each house shall keep a journal of its proceedings, and from time to time publish the same, excepting such parts as may in their judgement require secrecy; and the yeas and nays of the members of either house on any question shall, at the desire of one-fifth of those present, be entered on the journal.*

4. **Adjournment** *Neither house, during the session of Congress, shall, without the consent of the other, adjourn for more than three days, nor to any other place than that in which the two houses shall be sitting.*

SECTION 6. PRIVILEGES AND RESTRICTIONS

1. **Pay and Protection** *The senators and representatives shall receive a compensation for their services, to be ascertained by law, and paid out of the treasury of the United States. They shall in all cases, except treason, felony and breach of the peace, be privileged from arrest during their attendance at the session of their respective houses, and in going to and returning from the same; and for any speech or debate in either house, they shall not be questioned in any other place.*

2. **Restrictions** *No senator or representative shall, during the time for which he was elected, be appointed to any civil office under the authority of the United States, which shall have been created, or the emoluments whereof shall have been increased during such time; and no person holding any office under the United States, shall be a member of either house during his continuance in office.*

SECTION 7. MAKING LAWS

1. **Tax Bills** *All bills for raising revenue shall originate in the House of Representatives; but the Senate may propose or concur with amendments as on other bills.*

2. **Passing a Law** *Every bill which shall have passed the House of Representatives and the Senate, shall, before it became a law, be presented to the President of the United States; if he approve, he shall sign it, but if not, he shall return it, with his objections, to that house in which it shall have originated, who shall enter the objections at large on their journal, and proceed to reconsider it. If after such reconsideration two-thirds of that house shall agree to pass the bill, it shall be sent, together with the objections, to the other house, by which it shall likewise be reconsidered, and if approved by two-thirds of that house, it shall become a law. But in all such cases the votes of both houses shall be determined by yeas and nays, and the names of the persons voting for and against the bill shall be entered on the journal of each house respectively. If any bill shall not be returned by the president within ten days (Sundays excepted) after it shall have been presented to him, the same shall be a law, in like manner as if he had signed it, unless the Congress by their adjournment prevent its return, in which case it shall not be a law.*

3. **Orders and Resolutions** *Every order, resolution, or vote to which the concurrence of the Senate and House of Representatives may be necessary (except on a question of adjournment) shall be presented to the President of the United States; and before the same shall take effect, shall be approved by him, or, being disapproved by him, shall be repassed by two-thirds of the Senate and House of Representatives, according to the rules and limitations prescribed in the case of a bill.*

Rules Each house can make rules for its members and expel a member by a two-thirds vote.

Journal The Constitution requires each house to keep a record of its proceedings. *The Congressional Record* is published every day. It includes parts of speeches made in each house and allows any person to look up the votes of his or her representative.

Pay and Protection Congress sets the salaries of its members, and they are paid by the federal government. No member can be arrested for anything he or she says while in office. This protection allows members to speak freely in Congress.

Restrictions Members of Congress cannot hold other federal offices during their terms. This rule strengthens the separation of powers and protects the checks and balances system set up by the Constitution.

Tax Bills A bill is a proposed law. Only the House of Representatives can introduce bills that tax the people.

Passing a Law A bill must be passed by the majority of members in each house of Congress. Then it is sent to the President. If the President signs it, the bill becomes a law. If the President refuses to sign a bill, and Congress is in session, the bill becomes law ten days after the President receives it.

The President can also veto, or reject, a bill. However, if each house of Congress repasses the bill by a two-thirds vote, it becomes a law. Passing a law after the President vetoed it is called overriding a veto. This process is an important part of the checks and balances system set up by the Constitution.

Orders and Resolutions Congress can also pass resolutions that have the same power as laws. Such acts are also subject to the President's veto.

Taxation Only Congress has the power to collect taxes. Federal taxes must be the same in all parts of the country.

Commerce Congress controls both trade with foreign countries and trade among states.

Naturalization and Bankruptcy Naturalization is the process by which a person from another country becomes a United States citizen. Congress decides the requirements for this procedure.

Coins and Measures Congress has the power to coin money and set its value.

Copyrights and Patents Copyrights protect authors. Patents allow inventors to profit from their work by keeping control over it for a certain number of years. Congress grants patents to encourage scientific research.

Declaring War Only Congress can declare war on another country.

Militia Today the Militia is called the National Guard. The National Guard often helps people after floods, tornadoes, and other disasters.

National Capital Congress makes the laws for the District of Columbia, the area where the nation's capital is located.

Necessary Laws This clause allows Congress to make laws on issues, such as television and radio, that are not mentioned in the Constitution.

SECTION 8. POWERS DELEGATED TO CONGRESS

1. **Taxation** The Congress shall have the power to lay and collect taxes, duties, imposts, and excises, to pay the debts and provide for the common defense and general welfare of the United States; but all duties, imposts and excises shall be uniform throughout the United States;

2. **Borrowing** To borrow money on the credit of the United States;

3. **Commerce** To regulate commerce with foreign nations, and among the several States, and with the Indian tribes;

4. **Naturalization and Bankruptcy** To establish an uniform rule of naturalization, and uniform laws on the subject of bankruptcies throughout the United States;

5. **Coins and Measures** To coin money, regulate the value thereof, and of foreign coin, and fix the standard of weights and measures;

6. **Counterfeiting** To provide for the punishment of counterfeiting the securities and current coin of the United States;

7. **Post Offices** To establish post offices and post roads;

8. **Copyrights and Patents** To promote the progress of science and useful arts by securing for limited times to authors and inventors the exclusive right to their respective writings and discoveries;

9. **Courts** To constitute tribunals inferior to the Supreme Court;

10. **Piracy** To define and punish piracies and felonies committed on the high seas, and offenses against the law of nations;

11. **Declaring War** To declare war, ~~grant letters of marque and reprisal,~~ and make rules concerning captures on land and water;

12. **Army** To raise and support armies, but no appropriation of money to that use shall be for a longer term than two years;

13. **Navy** To provide and maintain a navy;

14. **Military Regulations** To make rules for the government and regulation of the land and naval forces;

15. **Militia** To provide for calling forth the militia to execute the laws of the Union, suppress insurrections and repel invasions;

16. **Militia Regulations** To provide for organizing, arming and disciplining the militia, and for governing such part of them as may be employed in the service of the United States, reserving to the States respectively the appointment of the officers, and the authority of training the militia according to the discipline prescribed by Congress;

17. **National Capital** To exercise exclusive legislation in all cases whatsoever, over such district (not exceeding ten miles square) as may, by cession of particular states, and the acceptance of Congress, become the seat of the government of the United States, and to exercise like authority over all places purchased by the consent of the legislature of the State in which the same shall be, for the erection of forts, magazines, arsenals, dock-yards, and other needful buildings;—and

18. **Necessary Laws** To make all laws which shall be necessary and proper for carrying into execution the foregoing powers, and all other powers vested by this Constitution in the government of the United States, or in any department or officer thereof.

SECTION 9. POWERS DENIED TO CONGRESS

1. **Slave Trade** ~~The migration or importation of such persons as any of the States now existing shall think proper to admit, shall not be prohibited by the Congress prior to the year 1808, but a tax or duty may be imposed on such importation, not exceeding ten dollars for each person.~~

2. **Habeas Corpus** *The privilege of the writ of habeas corpus shall not be suspended, unless when in cases of rebellion or invasion the public safety may require it.*

3. **Special Laws** *No bill of attainder or ex post facto law shall be passed.*

4. **Direct Taxes** ~~No capitation or other direct tax shall be laid, unless in proportion to the census or enumeration herein before directed to be taken.~~

5. **Export Taxes** *No tax or duty shall be laid on articles exported from any State.*

6. **Ports** *No preference shall be given by any regulation of commerce or revenue to the ports of one State over those of another; nor shall vessels bound to, or from, one State, be obliged to enter, clear, or pay duties in another.*

7. **Regulations on Spending** *No money shall be drawn from the treasury, but in consequence of appropriations made by law; and a regular statement and account of the receipts and expenditures of all public money shall be published from time to time.*

8. **Titles of Nobility and Gifts** *No title of nobility shall be granted by the United States: and no person holding any office or profit or trust under them, shall, without the consent of the Congress, accept of any present, emolument, office, or title, of any kind whatever, from any king, prince, or foreign state.*

SECTION 10. POWERS DENIED TO THE STATES

1. **Complete Restrictions** *No State shall enter into any treaty, alliance, or confederation; grant letters of marque and reprisal; coin money; emit bills of credit; make anything but gold and silver coin a tender in payment of debts; pass any bill of attainder, ex post facto law, or law impairing the obligation of contracts, or grant any title of nobility.*

2. **Partial Restrictions** *No State shall, without the consent of the Congress, lay any imposts or duties on imports or exports, except what may be absolutely necessary for executing its inspection laws; and the net produce of all duties and imposts, laid by any State on imports or exports, shall be for the use of the treasury of the United States; and all such laws shall be subject to the revision and control of the Congress.*

3. **Other Restrictions** *No State shall, without the consent of Congress, lay any duty of tonnage, keep troops, or ships of war in time of peace, enter into any agreement or compact with another State, or with a foreign power, or engage in war, unless actually invaded, or in such imminent danger as will not admit of delay.*

ARTICLE II
Executive Branch

SECTION 1. PRESIDENT AND VICE PRESIDENT

1. **Term of Office** *The executive power shall be vested in a President of the United States of America. He shall hold his office during the term of four years, and together with the Vice President, chosen for the same term, be elected as follows:*

2. **Electoral College** *Each State shall appoint, in such manner as the legislature thereof may direct, a number of electors, equal to the whole number of senators and representatives to which the State may be entitled in the Congress; but no*

Slave Trade This clause was another compromise between the North and the South. It prevented Congress from regulating the slave trade for 20 years. Congress outlawed the slave trade in 1808.

Habeas Corpus A writ of habeas corpus requires the government either to charge a person in jail with a particular crime or let the person go free. Except in emergencies, Congress cannot deny the right of a person to a writ.

Ports When regulating trade, Congress must treat all states equally. Also, states cannot tax goods traveling between states.

Regulations on Spending Congress controls the spending of public money. This clause checks the President's power.

Complete Restrictions The Constitution prevents the states from acting like individual countries. States cannot make treaties with foreign nations. They cannot issue their own money.

Partial Restrictions States cannot tax imports and exports without approval from Congress.

Other Restrictions States cannot declare war. They cannot keep their own armies.

Term of Office The President has the power to carry out the laws passed by Congress. The President and the Vice President serve four-year terms.

Electoral College A group of people called the Electoral College actually elects the President. The number of electors each state receives equals the total number of its representatives and senators.

senator or representative, or person holding an office of trust or profit under the United States, shall be appointed an elector.

3. *Election Process* ~~The electors shall meet in their respective States, and vote by ballot for two persons, of whom one at least shall not be an inhabitant of the same State with themselves. And they shall make a list of all the persons voted for, and of the number of votes for each; which list they shall sign and certify, and transmit sealed to the seat of the government of the United States, directed to the President of the Senate. The President of the Senate shall, in the presence of the Senate and House of Representatives, open all the certificates, and the votes shall then be counted. The person having the greatest number of votes shall be the President, if such number be a majority of the whole number of electors appointed, and if there be more than one who have such majority, and have an equal number of votes, then the House of Representatives shall immediately choose by ballot one of them for President; and if no person have a majority, then from the five highest on the list the said house shall in like manner choose the President. But in choosing the President, the votes shall be taken by States, the representation from each State having one vote; a quorum for this purpose shall consist of a member or members from two-thirds of the States, and a majority of all the States shall be necessary to a choice. In every case, after the choice of the President, the person having the greatest number of votes of the electors shall be the Vice President. But if there should remain two or more who have equal votes, the Senate shall choose from them by ballot the Vice President.~~

4. *Time of Elections* The Congress may determine the time of choosing the electors, and the day on which they shall give their votes; which day shall be the same throughout the United States.

5. *Qualifications* No person except a natural-born citizen, ~~or a citizen of the United States at the time of the adoption of this Constitution,~~ shall be eligible to the office of President; neither shall any person be eligible to that office who shall not have attained to the age of thirty-five years, and been fourteen years a resident within the United States.

6. *Vacancies* ~~In case of the removal of the President from office, or of his death, resignation, or inability to discharge the powers and duties of the said office, the same shall devolve on the Vice President, and the Congress may by law provide for the case of removal, death, resignation, or inability, both of the President and Vice President, declaring what officer shall then act as President, and such officer shall act accordingly, until the disability be removed, or a President shall be elected.~~

7. *Salary* The President shall, at stated times, receive for his services a compensation, which shall neither be increased nor diminished during the period for which he shall have been elected, and he shall not receive within that period any other emolument from the United States, or any of them.

8. *Oath of Office* Before he enter on the execution of his office, he shall take the following oath or affirmation:—"I do solemnly swear (or affirm) that I will faithfully execute the office of President of the United States, and will to the best of my ability, preserve, protect and defend the Constitution of the United States."

SECTION 2. POWERS OF THE PRESIDENT

1. *Military Powers* The President shall be commander in chief of the army and navy of the United States, and of the militia of the several States, when called into the actual service of the United States; he may require the opinion, in writing, of the principal officer in each of the executive departments, upon any subject relating to the duties of their respective offices, and he shall have power to

---

Election Process Originally, electors voted for two people. The candidate who received the majority of votes became President. The runner-up became Vice President. Problems with this system led to the 12th Amendment, which changed the electoral college system.

Today electors almost always vote for the candidate who won the popular vote in their states. In other words, the candidate who wins the popular vote in a state also wins its electoral votes.

Time of Elections Today we elect our President on the Tuesday after the first Monday in November.

Qualifications A President must be at least 35 years old, a United States citizen by birth, and a resident of the United States for at least 14 years.

Vacancies If the President resigns, dies, or is impeached and found guilty, the Vice President becomes President. The 25th Amendment replaced this clause in 1967.

Salary The President receives a yearly salary that cannot be increased or decreased during his or her term. The President cannot hold any other paid government positions while in office.

Oath of Office Every President must promise to uphold the Constitution. The Chief Justice of the Supreme Court usually administers this oath.

Military Powers The President is the leader of the country's military forces.

grant reprieves and pardons for offenses against the United States, except in cases of impeachment.

2. Treaties and Appointments He shall have power, by and with the advice and consent of the Senate, to make treaties, provided two-thirds of the Senators present concur; and he shall nominate, and by and with the advice and consent of the Senate, shall appoint ambassadors, other public ministers and consuls, judges of the Supreme Court, and all other officers of the United States, whose appointments are not herein otherwise provided for, and which shall be established by law: but the Congress may by law vest the appointment of such inferior officers, as they think proper, in the President alone, in the courts of law, or in the heads of departments.

3. Temporary Appointments The President shall have power to fill up all vacancies that may happen during the recess of the Senate, by granting commissions which shall expire at the end of their next session.

SECTION 3. DUTIES

He shall from time to time give to the Congress information of the State of the Union, and recommend to their consideration such measures as he shall judge necessary and expedient; he may on extraordinary occasions, convene both houses, or either of them, and in case of disagreement between them with respect to the time of adjournment, he may adjourn them to such time as he shall think proper; he shall receive ambassadors and other public ministers; he shall take care that the laws be faithfully executed, and shall commission all the officers of the United States.

SECTION 4. IMPEACHMENT

The President, Vice President, and all civil officers of the United States, shall be removed from office on impeachment for, and conviction of, treason, bribery, or other high crimes and misdemeanors.

ARTICLE III
Judicial Branch

SECTION 1. FEDERAL COURTS

The judicial power of the United States shall be vested in one Supreme Court, and in such inferior courts as the Congress may from time to time ordain and establish. The judges, both of the Supreme and inferior courts, shall hold their offices during good behaviour, and shall, at stated times, receive for their services, a compensation, which shall not be diminished during their continuance in office.

SECTION 2. AUTHORITY OF THE FEDERAL COURTS

1. General Jurisdiction The judicial power shall extend to all cases, in law and equity, arising under this Constitution, the laws of the United States, and treaties made, or which shall be made, under their authority; to all cases affecting ambassadors, other public ministers and consuls; to all cases of admiralty and maritime jurisdiction; to controversies to which the United States shall be a party; to controversies between two or more States; between a State and citizens of another State; between citizens of different States; between citizens of the same State claiming lands under grants of different States, and between a State, or the citizens thereof, and foreign states, citizens or subjects.

Treaties and Appointments The President can make treaties with other nations. However, treaties must be approved by a two-thirds vote of the Senate. The President also appoints Supreme Court Justices and ambassadors to foreign countries. The Senate must approve these appointments.

Duties The President must report to Congress at least once a year and make recommendations for laws. This report is known as the State of the Union address. The President delivers it each January.

Impeachment The President and other officials can be forced out of office only if found guilty of particular crimes. This clause protects government officials from being impeached for unimportant reasons.

Federal Courts The Supreme Court is the highest court in the nation. It makes the final decisions in all of the cases it hears. Congress decides the size of the Supreme Court. Today it contains nine judges. Congress also has the power to set up a system of lower federal courts. All federal judges may hold their offices for as long as they live.

General Jurisdiction Jurisdiction means the right of a court to hear a case. Federal courts have jurisdiction over such cases as those involving the Constitution, federal laws, treaties, and disagreements between states.

The President delivers the State of the Union address each year.

The Supreme Court One of the Supreme Court's most important jobs is to decide whether laws that pass are constitutional. This power is another example of the checks and balances system in the federal government.

Trial by Jury The Constitution guarantees everyone the right to a trial by jury. The only exception is in impeachment cases, which are tried in the Senate.

Definition People cannot be convicted of treason in the United States for what they think or say. To be guilty of treason, a person must rebel against the government by using violence or helping enemies of the country.

Official Records Each state must accept the laws, acts, and legal decisions made by other states.

Privileges States must give the same rights to citizens of other states that they give to ther own citizens.

Return of a Person Accused of a Crime If a person charged with a crime escapes to another state, he or she must be returned to the original state to go on trial. This act of returning someone from one state to another is called extradition.

Every American has a right to a trial by jury. Jurors' chairs are shown below.

2. *The Supreme Court* *In all cases affecting ambassadors, other public ministers and consuls, and those in which a State shall be party, the Supreme Court shall have original jurisdiction. In all the other cases before mentioned, the Supreme Court shall have appellate jurisdiction, both as to law and fact, with such exceptions, and under such regulations as the Congress shall make.*

3. *Trial by Jury* *The trial of all crimes, except in cases of impeachment, shall be by jury; and such trial shall be held in the State where the said crimes shall have been committed; but when not committed within any state, the trial shall be at such place or places as the Congress may by law have directed.*

SECTION 3. TREASON

1. *Definition* *Treason against the United States shall consist only in levying war against them, or in adhering to their enemies, giving them aid and comfort. No person shall be convicted of treason unless on the testimony of two witnesses to the same overt act, or on confession in open court.*

2. *Punishment* *The Congress shall have power to declare the punishment of treason, but no attainder of treason shall work corruption of blood, or forfeiture except during the life of the person attainted.*

ARTICLE IV
Relations Among the States

SECTION 1. OFFICIAL RECORDS

Full faith and credit shall be given in each state to the public acts, records and judicial proceedings of every other State. And the Congress may by general laws prescribe the manner in which such acts, records, and proceedings shall be proved, and the effect thereof.

SECTION 2. PRIVILEGES OF THE CITIZENS

1. *Privileges* *The citizens of each State shall be entitled to all privileges and immunities of citizens in the several states.*

2. *Return of a Person Accused of a Crime* *A person charged in any State with treason, felony, or other crime, who shall flee from justice, and be found in another State, shall on demand of the executive authority of the State from which he fled, be delivered up, to be removed to the State having jurisdiction of the crime.*

3. *Return of Fugitive Slaves* ~~*No person held to service or labor in one State, under the laws thereof, escaping into another, shall, in consequence of any law or regulation therein, be discharged from such service or labor, but shall be delivered up on claim of the party to whom such service or labor may be due.*~~

SECTION 3. NEW STATES AND TERRITORIES

1. **New States** *New states may be admitted by the Congress into this Union; but no new State shall be formed or erected within the jurisdiction of any other State, nor any State be formed by the junction of two or more States, or parts of States, without the consent of the legislatures of the States concerned, as well as of the Congress.*

2. **Federal Lands** *The Congress shall have power to dispose of and make all needful rules and regulations respecting the territory or other property belonging to the United States; and nothing in this Constitution shall be so construed as to prejudice any claims of the United States, or of any particular State.*

SECTION 4. GUARANTEES TO THE STATES

The United States shall guarantee to every State in this Union a republican form of government, and shall protect each of them against invasion; and on application of the legislature, or of the executive (when the legislature cannot be convened) against domestic violence.

ARTICLE V
Amending the Constitution

The Congress, whenever two-thirds of both houses shall deem it necessary, shall propose amendments to this Constitution, or, on the application of the legislatures of two-thirds of the several States, shall call a convention for proposing amendments, which, in either case, shall be valid to all intents and purposes, as part of this Constitution, when ratified by the legislatures of three-fourths of the several States, or by conventions in three-fourths thereof, as the one or the other mode of ratification may be proposed by the Congress; provided, that no amendment which may be made prior to the year 1808, shall in any manner affect the first and fourth clauses in the ninth section of the first article; *and that no State, without its consent, shall be deprived of its equal suffrage in the Senate.*

ARTICLE VI
General Provisions

1. **Public Debt** *All debts contracted and engagements entered into, before the adoption of this Constitution, shall be as valid against the United States under this Constitution, as under the Confederation.*

2. **Federal Supremacy** *This Constitution, and the laws of the United States which shall be made in pursuance thereof; and all treaties made, or which shall be made, under the authority of the United States, shall be the supreme law of the land; and the judges in every State shall be bound thereby, anything in the Constitution or laws of any State to the contrary notwithstanding.*

3. **Oaths of Office** *The senators and representatives before mentioned, and the members of the several State legislatures, and all executive and judicial officers, both of the United States, and of the several States, shall be bound by oath or affirmation to support this Constitution; but no religious test shall ever be required as a qualification to any office or public trust under the United States.*

New States Congress has the power to create new states out of the nation's territories. All new states have the same rights as the old states. This clause made it clear that the United States would not make colonies out of its new lands.

Guarantees to the State The federal government must defend the states from rebellions and from attacks by other countries.

Amending the Constitution An amendment to the Constitution may be proposed either by a two-thirds vote of each house of Congress or by a national convention called by Congress at the request of two-thirds of the state legislatures. To be ratified, or approved, an amendment must be supported by three-fourths of the state legislatures or by three-fourths of special conventions held in each state.

Once an amendment is ratified, it becomes part of the Constitution. Only a new amendment can change it. Amendments have allowed people to change the Constitution to meet the changing needs of the nation.

Federal Supremacy The Constitution is the highest law in the nation. Whenever a state law and a federal law are different, the federal law must be obeyed.

Oaths of Office All state and federal officials must take an oath promising to obey the Constitution.

ARTICLE VII
Ratification

Ratification The Constitution went into effect as soon as nine of the 13 states approved it.

Each state held a special convention to debate the Constitution. The ninth state to approve the Constitution, New Hampshire, voted for ratification on June 21, 1788.

The ratification of the conventions of nine States shall be sufficient for the establishment of this Constitution between the States so ratifying the same.

Done in Convention by the unanimous consent of the States present the seventeenth day of September in the year of our Lord one thousand seven hundred and eighty-seven and of the independence of the United States of America the twelfth. In witness whereof we have hereunto subscribed our names.

George Washington, President and deputy from Virginia

DELAWARE
George Read
Gunning Bedford, Junior
John Dickinson
Richard Bassett
Jacob Broom

MARYLAND
James McHenry
Daniel of St. Thomas Jenifer
Daniel Carroll

VIRGINIA
John Blair
James Madison, Junior

NORTH CAROLINA
William Blount
Richard Dobbs Spaight
Hugh Williamson

SOUTH CAROLINA
John Rutledge
Charles Cotesworth
  Pinckney
Charles Pinckney
Pierce Butler

GEORGIA
William Few
Abraham Baldwin

NEW HAMPSHIRE
John Langdon
Nicholas Gilman

MASSACHUSETTS
Nathaniel Gorham
Rufus King

CONNECTICUT
William Samuel Johnson
Roger Sherman

NEW YORK
Alexander Hamilton

NEW JERSEY
William Livingston
David Brearley
William Paterson
Jonathan Dayton

PENNSYLVANIA
Benjamin Franklin
Thomas Mifflin
Robert Morris
George Clymer
Thomas FitzSimons
Jared Ingersoll
James Wilson
Gouverneur Morris

Delegates wait for their turn to sign the new Constitution.

AMENDMENTS TO THE CONSTITUTION

AMENDMENT I (1791)*
Basic Freedoms

Congress shall make no law respecting an establishment of religion, or prohibiting the free exercise thereof; or abridging the freedom of speech, or of the press; or the right of the people peaceably to assemble, and to petition the government for a redress of grievances.

AMENDMENT II (1791)
Weapons and the Militia

A well-regulated militia, being necessary to the security of a free State, the right of the people to keep and bear arms, shall not be infringed.

AMENDMENT III (1791)
Housing Soldiers

No soldier shall, in time of peace, be quartered in any house, without the consent of the owner, nor in time of war, but in a manner to be prescribed by law.

AMENDMENT IV (1791)
Search and Seizure

The right of the people to be secure in their persons, houses, papers, and effects, against unreasonable searches and seizures, shall not be violated, and no warrants shall issue, but upon probable cause, supported by oath or affirmation, and particularly describing the place to be searched, and the persons or things to be seized.

AMENDMENT V (1791)
Rights of the Accused

No person shall be held to answer for a capital, or otherwise infamous crime, unless on a presentment or indictment of a grand jury, except in cases arising in the land or naval forces, or in the militia, when in actual service in time of war or public danger; nor shall any person be subject for the same offense to be twice put in jeopardy of life or limb; nor shall be compelled in any criminal case to be a witness against himself, nor be deprived of life, liberty, or property, without due process of law; nor shall private property be taken for public use without just compensation.

AMENDMENT VI (1791)
Right to a Fair Trial

In all criminal prosecutions, the accused shall enjoy the right to a speedy and public trial, by an impartial jury of the State and district wherein the crime shall have been committed, which district shall have been previously ascertained by law, and to be informed of the nature and cause of the accusation; to be confronted with the witnesses against him; to have compulsory process for obtaining witnesses in his favor, and to have the assistance of counsel for his defense.

AMENDMENT VII (1791)
Jury Trial in Civil Cases

In suits at common law, where the value in controversy shall exceed twenty dollars, the right of trial by jury shall be preserved, and no fact tried by a jury shall be otherwise reexamined in any court of the United States, than according to the rules of the common law.

Amendments to the Constitution

Basic Freedoms The government cannot pass laws that favor one religion over another. Nor can it stop people from saying or writing whatever they want. The people have the right to gather openly and discuss problems they have with the government.

Weapons and the Militia This amendment was included to prevent the federal government from taking away guns used by members of state militias.

Housing Soldiers The army cannot use people's homes to house soldiers unless it is approved by law. Before the American Revolution, the British housed soldiers in private homes without permission of the owners.

Search and Seizure This amendment protects people's privacy in their homes. The government cannot search or seize anyone's property without a warrant, or a written order, from a court. A warrant must list the people and the property to be searched and give reasons for the search.

Rights of the Accused A person accused of a crime has the right to a fair trial. A person cannot be tried twice for the same crime. This amendment also protects a person from self-incrimination, or having to testify against himself or herself.

Right to a Fair Trial Anyone accused of a crime is entitled to a quick and fair trial by jury. This right protects people from being kept in jail without being convicted of a crime. Also, the government must provide a lawyer for anyone accused of a crime who cannot afford to hire a lawyer.

Jury Trial in Civil Cases Civil cases usually involve two or more people suing each other over money, property, or personal injury. A jury trial is guaranteed in large lawsuits.

*The date after each amendment indicates the year the amendment was ratified.

Bail and Punishment Courts cannot treat people accused of crimes in ways that are unusually harsh.

Powers Reserved to the People The people keep all rights not listed in the Constitution.

Powers Reserved to the States Any rights not clearly given to the federal government by the Constitution belong to the states or the people.

Suits Against the States A citizen from one state cannot sue the government of another state in a federal court. Such cases are decided in state courts.

Election of the President and Vice President Under the original Constitution, each member of the Electoral College voted for two candidates for President. The candidate with the most votes became President. The one with the second highest total became Vice President.

The 12th Amendment changed this system. Members of the electoral college distinguish between their votes for the President and Vice President. This change was an important step in the development of the two party system. It allows each party to nominate its own team of candidates.

The Twelfth Amendment allowed parties to nominate teams of candidates, as this campaign poster shows.

AMENDMENT VIII (1791)
Bail and Punishment

Excessive bail shall not be required, nor excessive fines imposed, nor cruel and unusual punishments inflicted.

AMENDMENT IX (1791)
Powers Reserved to the People

The enumeration in the Constitution, of certain rights, shall not be construed to deny or disparage others retained by the people.

AMENDMENT X (1791)
Powers Reserved to the States

The powers not delegated to the United States by the Constitution, nor prohibited by it to the States, are reserved to the States respectively, or to the people.

AMENDMENT XI (1795)
Suits Against States

The judicial power of the United States shall not be construed to extend to any suit in law or equity, commenced or prosecuted against one of the United States by citizens of another State, or by citizens or subjects of any foreign State.

AMENDMENT XII (1804)
Election of the President and Vice President

The electors shall meet in their respective States and vote by ballot for President and Vice President, one of whom, at least, shall not be an inhabitant of the same State with themselves; they shall name in their ballots the person voted for as President, and in distinct ballots the person voted for as Vice President, and they shall make distinct lists of all persons voted for as President, and of all persons voted for as Vice President, and of the number of votes for each, which lists they shall sign and certify, and transmit sealed to the seat of the government of the United States, directed to the President of the Senate; the President of the Senate shall, in the presence of the Senate and House of Representatives, open all the certificates and the votes shall then be counted; the person having the greatest number of votes for President, shall be the President, if such number be a majority of the whole number of electors appointed; and if no person have such majority, then from the persons having the highest numbers not exceeding three on the list of those voted for as President, the House of Representatives shall choose immediately, by ballot, the President. But in choosing the President, the votes shall be taken by States, the representation from each State having one vote; a quorum for this purpose shall consist of a member or members from two-thirds of the States, and a majority of all the States shall be necessary to a choice. And if the House of Representatives shall not choose a President whenever the right of choice shall devolve upon them, before the fourth day of March next following, then the Vice President shall act as President, as in case of the death or other constitutional disability of the President. The person having the greatest number of votes as Vice President, shall be the Vice President, if such number be a majority of the whole number of electors appointed, and if no person have a majority, then from the two highest numbers on the list, the Senate shall choose the Vice President; a quorum for the purpose shall consist of two-thirds of the whole number of senators, and a majority of the whole number shall be necessary to a choice. But no person constitutionally ineligible to the office of President shall be eligible to that of Vice President of the United States.

This etching shows a group of former slaves celebrating their emancipation.

AMENDMENT XIII (1865)
End of Slavery

SECTION 1. ABOLITION

Neither slavery nor involuntary servitude, except as a punishment for crime whereof the party shall have been duly convicted, shall exist within the United States, or any place subject to their jurisdiction.

SECTION 2. ENFORCEMENT

Congress shall have power to enforce this article by appropriate legislation.

AMENDMENT XIV (1868)
Rights of Citizens

SECTION 1. CITIZENSHIP

All persons born or naturalized in the United States, and subject to the jurisdiction thereof, are citizens of the United States and of the State wherein they reside. No State shall make or enforce any law which shall abridge the privileges or immunities of citizens of the United States; nor shall any State deprive any person of life, liberty, or property, without due process of law; nor deny to any person within its jurisdiction the equal protection of the laws.

SECTION 2. NUMBER OF REPRESENTATIVES

Representatives shall be apportioned among the several States according to their respective numbers, counting the whole number of persons in each State, excluding Indians not taxed. But when the right to vote at any election for the choice of electors for President and Vice President of the United States, representatives in Congress, the executive and judicial officers of a State, or the members of the legislature thereof, is denied to any of the male inhabitants of such State, being twenty-one years of age, and citizens of the United States, or in any way abridged, except for participation in rebellion, or other crime, the basis of representation therein shall be reduced in the proportion which the number of such male citizens shall bear to the whole number of male citizens twenty-one years of age in such State.

SECTION 3. PENALTY FOR REBELLION

No person shall be a senator or representative in Congress, or elector of President and Vice President, or hold any office, civil or military, under the United States, or under any State, who, having previously taken an oath, as a member of Congress, or as an officer of the United States, or as a member of any State legislature, or as an executive or judicial officer of any State, to support the Constitution of the United States, shall have engaged in insurrection or rebellion against the same, or given aid or comfort to the enemies thereof. But Congress may by a vote of two-thirds of each house, remove such disability.

SECTION 4. GOVERNMENT DEBT

The validity of the public debt of the United States, authorized by law, including debts incurred for payment of pensions and bounties for services in suppressing insurrection or rebellion, shall not be questioned. But neither the United States nor any State shall assume or pay any debt or obligation incurred in aid of insurrection or rebellion against the United States, or any claim for the loss or emancipation of any slave; but all such debts, obligations and claims shall be held illegal and void.

Abolition This amendment ended slavery in the United States. It was ratified after the Civil War.

Citizenship This amendment defined citizenship in the United States. "Due process of law" means that no state can deny its citizens the rights and privileges they enjoy as United States citizens. The goal of this amendment was to protect the rights of the recently freed African Americans.

Number of Representatives This clause replaced the Three-Fifths Clause in Article 1. Each state's representation is based on its total population. Any state denying its male citizens over the age of 21 the right to vote will have its representation in Congress decreased.

Penalty of Rebellion Officials who fought against the Union in the Civil War could not hold public office in the United States. This clause tried to keep Confederate leaders out of power. In 1872, Congress removed this limit.

Government Debt The United States paid all of the Union's debts from the Civil War. However, it did not pay any of the Confederacy's debts. This clause prevented the southern states from using public money to pay for the rebellion or from compensating citizens who lost their enslaved persons.

SECTION 5. ENFORCEMENT

The Congress shall have power to enforce, by appropriate legislation, the provisions of this article.

AMENDMENT XV (1870)
Voting Rights

SECTION 1. RIGHT TO VOTE

The right of citizens of the United States to vote shall not be denied or abridged by the United States or by any State on account of race, color, or previous condition of servitude.

SECTION 2. ENFORCEMENT

The Congress shall have power to enforce this article by appropriate legislation.

AMENDMENT XVI (1913)
Income Tax

The Congress shall have power to lay and collect taxes on incomes, from whatever sources derived, without apportionment among the several States, and without regard to any census or enumeration.

AMENDMENT XVII (1913)
Direct Election of Senators

SECTION 1. METHOD OF ELECTION

The Senate of the United States shall be composed of two senators from each State, elected by the people thereof, for six years; and each senator shall have one vote. The electors in each State shall have the qualifications requisite for electors of the most numerous branch of the State legislatures.

SECTION 2. VACANCIES

When vacancies happen in the representation of any State in the Senate, the executive authority of such State shall issue writs of election to fill such vacancies: Provided, that the legislature of any State may empower the executive thereof to make temporary appointments until the people fill the vacancies by election as the legislature may direct.

SECTION 3. EXCEPTION

This amendment shall not be so construed as to affect the election or term of any Senator chosen before it becomes valid as part of the Constitution.

AMENDMENT XVIII (1919)
Ban on Alcoholic Drinks

SECTION 1. PROHIBITION

After one year from the ratification of this article the manufacture, sale, or transportation of intoxicating liquors within, the importation thereof into, or the exportation thereof from the United States and all territory subject to the jurisdiction thereof for beverage purposes is hereby prohibited.

SECTION 2. ENFORCEMENT

The Congress and the several States shall have concurrent power to enforce this article by appropriate legislation.

Right to Vote No state can deny its citizens the right to vote because of their race. This amendment was designed to protect the voting rights of African Americans.

Income Tax Congress has the power to tax personal incomes.

Direct Election of Senators In the original Constitution, the state legislatures elected senators. This amendment gave citizens the power to elect their senators directly. It made senators more responsible to the people they represented.

The Prohibition movement used posters like this to reach the public.

Prohibition This amendment made it against the law to make or sell alcoholic beverages in the United States. This law was called prohibition. Fourteen years later, the 21st Amendment ended Prohibition.

SECTION 3. RATIFICATION

~~This article shall be inoperative unless it shall have been ratified as an amendment to the Constitution by the legislatures of the several States, as provided in the Constitution, within seven years from the date of the submission hereof to the States by Congress.~~

AMENDMENT XIX (1920)
Women's Suffrage

SECTION 1. RIGHT TO VOTE

The right of citizens of the United States to vote shall not be denied or abridged by the United States or by any State on account of sex.

SECTION 2. ENFORCEMENT

The Congress shall have power to enforce this article by appropriate legislation.

AMENDMENT XX (1933)
Terms of Office

SECTION 1. BEGINNING OF TERMS

The terms of the President and Vice-President shall end at noon on the 20th day of January, and the terms of senators and representatives at noon on the 3rd day of January, of the years in which such terms would have ended if this article had not been ratified; and the terms of their successors shall then begin.

SECTION 2. SESSIONS OF CONGRESS

The Congress shall assemble at least once in every year, and such meeting shall begin at noon on the 3rd day of January, unless they shall by law appoint a different day.

SECTION 3. PRESIDENTIAL SUCCESSION

If, at the time fixed for the beginning of the term of the President, the President-elect shall have died, the Vice President-elect shall become President. If a President shall not have been chosen before the time fixed for the beginning of his term, or if the President-elect shall have failed to qualify, then the Vice President-elect shall act as President until a President shall have qualified; and the Congress may by law provide for the case wherein neither a President-elect nor a Vice President-elect shall have qualified, declaring who shall then act as President, or the manner in which one who is to act shall be selected, and such person shall act accordingly until a President or Vice President shall have qualified.

SECTION 4. ELECTIONS DECIDED BY CONGRESS

The Congress may by law provide for the case of the death of any of the persons from whom the House of Representatives may choose a President whenever the right of choice shall have devolved upon them, and for the case of the death of any of the persons from whom the Senate may choose a Vice President whenever the right of choice shall have devolved upon them.

SECTION 5. EFFECTIVE DATE

~~Sections 1 and 2 shall take effect on the 15th day of October following the ratification of this article.~~

Ratification The amendment for Prohibition was the first one to include a time limit for ratification. To go into effect, the amendment had to be approved by three-fourths of the states within seven years.

Women's Suffrage This amendment gave the right to vote to all women 21 years of age and older.

This 1915 banner pushed the cause of women's suffrage.

Beginning of Terms The President and Vice President's terms begin on January 20th of the year after their election. The terms for senators and representatives begin on January 3rd. Before this amendment, an official defeated in November stayed in office until March.

Presidential Succession A President who has been elected but has not yet taken office is called the President-elect. If the President-elect dies, then the Vice President-elect becomes President. If neither the President-elect nor the Vice President-elect can take office, then Congress decides who will act as President.

President Kennedy delivers his inaugural address in 1961.

SECTION 6. RATIFICATION

This article shall be inoperative unless it shall have been ratified as an amendment to the Constitution by the legislatures of three fourths of the several States within seven years from the date of its submission.

AMENDMENT XXI (1933)
End of Prohibition

SECTION 1. REPEAL OF EIGHTEENTH AMENDMENT

The eighteenth article of amendment to the Constitution of the United States is hereby repealed.

SECTION 2. STATE LAWS

The transportation or importation into any State, territory, or possession of the United States for delivery or use therein of intoxicating liquors, in violation of the laws thereof, is hereby prohibited.

SECTION 3. RATIFICATION

This article shall be inoperative unless it shall have been ratified as an amendment to the Constitution by conventions in the several States, as provided in the Constitution, within seven years from the date of the submission hereof to the States by the Congress.

AMENDMENT XXII (1951)
Limit on Presidential Terms

SECTION 1. TWO-TERM LIMIT

No person shall be elected to the office of the President more than twice, and no person who has held the office of President, or acted as President, for more that two years of a term to which some other person was elected President shall be elected to the office of the President more than once. But this article shall not apply to any person holding the office of President when this article was proposed by the Congress, and shall not prevent any person who may be holding the office of President, or acting as President, during the term within which this article becomes operative from holding the office of President or acting as President during the remainder of such term.

SECTION 2. RATIFICATION

This article shall be inoperative unless it shall have been ratified as an amendment to the Constitution by the legislatures of three fourths of the several States within seven years from the date of its submission to the States by the Congress.

AMENDMENT XXIII (1961)
Presidential Votes for Washington, D.C.

SECTION 1. NUMBER OF ELECTORS

The District constituting the seat of government of the United States shall appoint in such manner as the Congress may direct:

A number of electors of President and Vice President equal to the whole number of senators and representatives in Congress to which the District would be entitled if it were a State, but in no event more than the least populous State; they shall be in addition to those appointed by the States, but they shall be considered, for the purposes of the election of President and Vice President, to be elec-

End of Prohibition This amendment repealed, or ended, the 18th Amendment. It made alcoholic beverages legal once again in the United States. However, states can still control or stop the sale of alcohol within their borders.

Two-Term Limit George Washington set a precedent that Presidents should not serve more than two terms in office. However, Franklin D. Roosevelt broke the precedent. He was elected President four times between 1932 and 1944. Some people feared that a President holding office for this long could become too powerful. This amendment limits Presidents to two terms in office.

Presidential Votes for Washington, D.C. This amendment gives people who live in the nation's capital a vote for President. The electoral votes in Washington D.C., are based on its population. However, it cannot have more votes than the state with the smallest population. Today, Washington, D.C. has three electoral votes.

tors appointed by a State; and they shall meet in the District and perform such duties as provided by the twelfth article of amendment.

SECTION 2. ENFORCEMENT

The Congress shall have power to enforce this article by appropriate legislation.

AMENDMENT XXIV (1964)
Ban on Poll Taxes

SECTION 1. POLL TAXES ILLEGAL

The right of citizens of the United States to vote in any primary or other election for President or Vice President, for electors for President or Vice President, or for senator or representative in Congress, shall not be denied or abridged by the United States or any State by reason of failure to pay any poll tax or other tax.

SECTION 2. ENFORCEMENT

The Congress shall have power to enforce this article by appropriate legislation.

AMENDMENT XXV (1967)
Presidential Succession

SECTION 1. VACANCY IN THE PRESIDENCY

In case of the removal of the President from office or of his death or resignation, the Vice President shall become President.

SECTION 2. VACANCY IN THE VICE PRESIDENCY

Whenever there is a vacancy in the office of the Vice President, the President shall nominate a Vice President who shall take office upon confirmation by a majority vote of both houses of Congress.

SECTION 3. DISABILITY OF THE PRESIDENT

Whenever the President transmits to the President pro tempore of the Senate and the Speaker of the House of Representatives his written declaration that he is unable to discharge the powers and duties of his office, and until he transmits to them a written declaration to the contrary, such powers and duties shall be discharged by the Vice President as Acting President.

SECTION 4. DETERMINING PRESIDENTIAL DISABILITY

Whenever the Vice President and a majority of either the principal officers of the executive departments or of such other body as Congress may by law provide, transmit to the President pro tempore of the Senate and the Speaker of the House of Representatives their written declaration that the President is unable to discharge the powers and duties of his office, the Vice President shall immediately assume the powers and duties of the office as Acting President.

Thereafter, when the President transmits to the President pro tempore of the Senate and the Speaker of the House of Representatives his written declaration that no inability exists, he shall resume the powers and duties of his office unless the Vice President and a majority of either the principal officers of the executive departments or of such other body as Congress may by law provide, transmit within four days to the President pro tempore of the Senate and the Speaker of the House of Representatives their written declaration that the President is unable to discharge the powers and duties of his office. Thereupon Congress shall decide

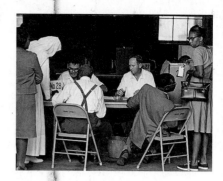

African Americans vote in Selma, Alabama, in 1966.

Ban on Poll Taxes A poll tax requires a person to pay a certain amount of money to register to vote. These taxes were used to stop poor African Americans from voting. This amendment made any such taxes illegal in federal elections.

Vacancy in the Vice Presidency If the Vice President becomes President, he or she may nominate a new Vice President. This nomination must be approved by both houses of Congress.

Disability of the President This section tells what happens if the President suddenly becomes ill or is seriously injured. The Vice President takes over as Acting President. When the President is ready to take office again, he or she must tell Congress.

the issue, assembling within 48 hours for that purpose if not in session. If the Congress, within 21 days after receipt of the latter written declaration, or, if Congress is not in session, within 21 days after Congress is required to assemble, determines by two-thirds vote of both houses that the President is unable to discharge the powers and duties of his office, the Vice President shall continue to discharge the same as Acting President; otherwise, the President shall resume the powers and duties of his office.

AMENDMENT XXVI (1971)
Voting Age

SECTION 1. RIGHT TO VOTE

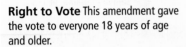

Right to Vote This amendment gave the vote to everyone 18 years of age and older.

The right of citizens of the United States, who are 18 years of age or older, to vote shall not be denied or abridged by the United States or by any state on account of age.

SECTION 2. ENFORCEMENT

The Congress shall have power to enforce this article by appropriate legislation.

AMENDMENT XXVII (1992)
Congressional Pay

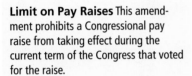

Limit on Pay Raises This amendment prohibits a Congressional pay raise from taking effect during the current term of the Congress that voted for the raise.

No law, varying the compensation for the services of the senators and representatives, shall take effect, until an election of representatives shall have intervened.

The voting age was lowered to 18 in 1971.

from *The Federalist* (No. 10) (1787)

The two great points of difference between a democracy and a republic are: first, the delegation of the government, in the latter, to a small number of citizens selected by the rest; secondly, the greater number of citizens and greater sphere of country, over which the latter may be extended.

The effect of the first difference is, on the one hand, to refine and enlarge the public views, by passing them through the medium of a chosen body of citizens, whose wisdom may best discern the true interest of their country and whose patriotism and love of justice will be least likely to sacrifice it to temporary or partial considerations. . . .

By enlarging too much the number of electors, you render the representative too little acquainted with all their local circumstances and lesser interests; as by reducing it too much, you render him unduly attached to these, and too little fit to comprehend and pursue great and national objects. . . .

Extend the sphere and you take in a greater variety of parties and interests; you make it less probable that a majority of the whole will have a common motive to invade the rights of other citizens.

The Star-Spangled Banner (1814)

O say, can you see, by the dawn's early light,
What so proudly we hailed at the twilight's last gleaming,
Whose broad stripes and bright stars, through the perilous fight,
O'er the ramparts we watched were so gallantly streaming?
And the rockets' red glare, the bombs bursting in air,
Gave proof through the night that our flag was still there.
O say, does that Star-Spangled Banner yet wave
O'er the land of the free and the home of the brave?

On the shore, dimly seen through the mists of the deep,
Where the foe's haughty host in dread silence reposes,
What is that which the breeze, o'er the towering steep,
As it fitfully blows, half conceals, half discloses?
Now it catches the gleam of the morning's first beam,
In full glory reflected now shines on the stream;
'Tis the Star-Spangled Banner, O long may it wave
O'er the land of the free and the home of the brave!

O thus be it ever when free men shall stand
Between their loved homes and the war's desolation!
Blest with vict'ry and peace, may the heav'n-rescued land
Praise the Power that hath made and preserved us a nation.
then conquer we must, for our cause it is just,
And this be our motto: 'In God is our trust.'
And the Star-Spangled Banner in triumph shall wave
O'er the land of the free and the home of the brave.

Francis Scott Key wrote "The Star-Spangled Banner" in 1814 while aboard ship during the battle of Fort McHenry. The gallantry and courage displayed by his fellow countrymen that night inspired Key to pen the lyrics to the song that officially became our national anthem in 1931.

from President John F. Kennedy's Inaugural Address (1961)

John F. Kennedy was the 35th President of the United States.

"*In your hands, my fellow citizens, more than mine, will rest the final success or failure of our course. Since this country was founded, each generation of Americans has been summoned to give testimony to its national loyalty. The graves of young Americans who answered the call to service surround the globe.*

Now the trumpet summons us again—not as a call to bear arms, though arms we need—not as a call to battle, though embattled we are—but a call to bear the burden of a long twilight struggle, year in and year out, 'rejoicing in hope, patient in tribulation'—a struggle against the common enemies of man: tyranny, poverty, disease, and war itself.

Can we forge against these enemies a grand and global alliance, North and South, East and West, that can assure a more fruitful life for all mankind? Will you join in that historic effort? . . .

And so, my fellow Americans: ask not what your country can do for you—ask what you can do for your country.

My fellow citizens of the world: ask not what America will do for you, but what together we can do for the freedom of man."

President Kennedy gives a speech. Jackie Kennedy is at his left.

from Martin Luther King Jr.'s "I Have a Dream" Speech (1963)

"I say to you today, my friends, that in spite of the difficulties and frustrations of the moment I still have a dream. It is a dream deeply rooted in the American dream.

I have a dream that one day this nation will rise up and live out the true meaning of its creed: 'We hold these truths to be self-evident; that all men are created equal.'

I have a dream that one day on the red hills of Georgia the sons of former slaves and the sons of former slaveowners will be able to sit down together at the table of brotherhood. . . .

I have a dream that my four little children will one day live in a nation where they will not be judged by the color of their skin but by the content of their character.

I have a dream today. . . .

. . . From every mountainside, let freedom ring.

When we let freedom ring, when we let it ring from every village and every hamlet, from every state and every city, we will be able to speed up that day when all of God's children, black men and white men, Jews and Gentiles, Protestants and Catholics, will be able to join hands and sing in the words of the old Negro spiritual, 'Free at last! Free at last! Thank God Almighty, we are free at last!'"

In August 1963, while Congress debated civil rights legislation, Martin Luther King Jr. led a quarter of a million demonstrators on a march on Washington. On the steps of the Lincoln Memorial he gave a stirring speech in which he told of his dream for America.

Historical Documents

Presidents of the United States

George Washington   ①

(1732–1799)
President from: 1789–1797
Party: Federalist
Home state: Virginia
First Lady: Martha Dandridge Custis Washington

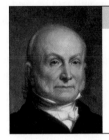

John Quincy Adams   ⑥

(1767–1848)
President from: 1825–1829
Party: Democratic-Republican
Home state: Massachusetts
First Lady: Louisa Catherine Johnson Adams

John Adams   ②

(1735–1826)
President from: 1797–1801
Party: Federalist
Home state: Massachusetts
First Lady: Abigail Smith Adams

Andrew Jackson   ⑦

(1767–1845)
President from: 1829–1837
Party: Democratic
Home state: Tennessee
First Lady: Emily Donelson (late wife's niece)

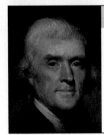

Thomas Jefferson   ③

(1743–1826)
President from: 1801–1809
Party: Democratic-Republican
Home state: Virginia
First Lady: Martha Jefferson Randolph (daughter)

Martin Van Buren   ⑧

(1782–1862)
President from: 1837–1841
Party: Democratic
Home state: New York
First Lady: Angelica Singleton Van Buren (daughter-in-law)

James Madison   ④

(1751–1836)
President from: 1809–1817
Party: Democratic-Republican
Home state: Virginia
First Lady: Dolley Payne Todd Madison

William Henry Harrison   ⑨

(1773–1841)
President: 1841
Party: Whig
Home state: Ohio
First Lady: Jane Irwin Harrison (daughter-in-law)

James Monroe   ⑤

(1758–1831)
President from: 1817–1825
Party: Democratic-Republican
Home state: Virginia
First Lady: Elizabeth Kortright Monroe

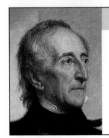

John Tyler   ⑩

(1790–1862)
President from: 1841–1845
Party: Whig
Home state: Virginia
First Lady: Letitia Christian Tyler

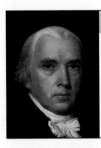

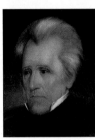

5 pres from virginia

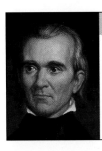

James K. Polk 11

(1795–1849)
President from: 1845–1849
Party: Democratic
Home state: Tennessee
First Lady: Sarah Childress Polk

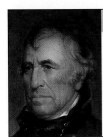

Zachary Taylor 12

(1784–1850)
President from: 1849–1850
Party: Whig
Home state: Louisiana
First Lady: Margaret Mackall Smith
Taylor

Millard Fillmore 13

(1800–1874)
President from: 1850–1853
Party: Whig
Home state: New York
First Lady: Abigail Powers Fillmore

Franklin Pierce 14

(1804–1869)
President from: 1853–1857
Party: Democratic
Home state: New Hampshire
First Lady: Jane Means Appleton
Pierce

James Buchanan 15

(1791–1868)
President from: 1857–1861
Party: Democratic
Home state: Pennsylvania
First Lady: Harriet Lane (niece)

Abraham Lincoln 16

(1809–1865)
President from: 1861–1865
Party: Republican
Home state: Illinois
First Lady: Mary Todd Lincoln

Andrew Johnson 17

(1808–1875)
President from: 1865–1869
Party: Democratic
Home state: Tennessee
First Lady: Eliza McCardle Johnson

Ulysses S. Grant 18

(1822–1885)
President from: 1869–1877
Party: Republican
Home state: Illinois
First Lady: Julia Dent Grant

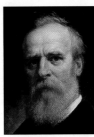

Rutherford B. Hayes 19

(1822–1893)
President from: 1877–1881
Party: Republican
Home state: Ohio
First Lady: Lucy Ware Webb Hayes

James A. Garfield 20

(1831–1881)
President: 1881
Party: Republican
Home state: Ohio
First Lady: Lucretia Rudolph Garfield

Chester A. Arthur 21

(1830–1886)
President from: 1881–1885
Party: Republican
Home state: New York
First Lady: Mary Arthur McElroy
(sister)

Grover Cleveland 22 24

(1837–1908)
President from: 1885–1889 and
1893–1897
Party: Democratic
Home state: New York
First Lady: Frances Folsom Cleveland

5 pres from Ohio

Benjamin Harrison  **23**

(1833–1901)
President from: 1889–1893
Party: Republican
Home state: Indiana
First Lady: Caroline Lavina Scott
Harrison

William McKinley  **25**

(1843–1901)
President from: 1897–1901
Party: Republican
Home state: Ohio
First Lady: Ida Saxton McKinley

Theodore Roosevelt  **26**

(1858–1919)
President from: 1901–1909
Party: Republican
Home state: New York
First Lady: Edith Kermit Carow
Roosevelt

William Howard Taft  **27**

(1857–1930)
President from: 1909–1913
Party: Republican
Home state: Ohio
First Lady: Helen Herron Taft

Woodrow Wilson  **28**

(1856–1924)
President from: 1913–1921
Party: Democratic
Home state: New Jersey
First Lady: Edith Bolling Galt Wilson

Warren G. Harding  **29**

(1865–1923)
President from: 1921–1923
Party: Republican
Home state: Ohio
First Lady: Florence Kling Harding

Calvin Coolidge  **30**

(1872–1933)
President from: 1923–1929
Party: Republican
Home state: Massachusetts
First Lady: Grace Anna Goodhue
Coolidge

Herbert Hoover  **31**

(1874–1964)
President from: 1929–1933
Party: Republican
Home state: California
First Lady: Lou Henry Hoover

Franklin Delano Roosevelt  **32**

(1882–1945)
President from: 1933–1945
Party: Democratic
Home state: New York
First Lady: Anna Eleanor Roosevelt
Roosevelt

Harry S. Truman  **33**

(1884–1972)
President from: 1945–1953
Party: Democratic
Home state: Missouri
First Lady: Elizabeth Virginia Wallace
Truman

Dwight D. Eisenhower  **34**

(1890–1969)
President from: 1953–1961
Party: Republican
Home state: New York
First Lady: Mamie Geneva Doud
Eisenhower

John F. Kennedy  **35**

(1917–1963)
President from: 1961–1963
Party: Democratic
Home state: Massachusetts
First Lady: Jacqueline Lee Bouvier
Kennedy

U.S. Presidents

Lyndon Baines Johnson 36

(1908–1973)
President from: 1963–1969
Party: Democratic
Home state: Texas
First Lady: Claudia Alta (Lady Bird)
Taylor Johnson

Ronald Reagan 40

(1911–2004)
President from: 1981–1989
Party: Republican
Home state: California
First Lady: Nancy Davis Reagan

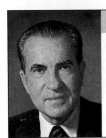

Richard M. Nixon 37

(1913–1994)
President from: 1969–1974
Party: Republican
Home state: California
First Lady: Thelma Catherine (Pat)
Ryan Nixon

George Bush 41

(1924–)
President from: 1989–1993
Party: Republican
Home state: Texas
First Lady: Barbara Pierce Bush

Gerald R. Ford 38

(1913–2006)
President from: 1974–1977
Party: Republican
Home state: Michigan
First Lady: Elizabeth Bloomer Ford

William Clinton 42

(1946–)
President from: 1993–2001
Party: Democratic
Home state: Arkansas
First Lady: Hillary Rodham Clinton

Jimmy Carter 39

(1924–)
President from: 1977–1981
Party: Democratic
Home state: Georgia
First Lady: Rosalynn Smith Carter

George W. Bush 43

(1946–)
President from: 2001–
Party: Republican
Home state: Texas
First Lady: Laura Welch Bush

U.S. Presidents

Biographical Dictionary

The page number after each entry refers to the place where the person is first mentioned. For more complete references to people, see the Index.

Adams, Abigail 1744–1818, Patriot in the American Revolution (p. 154).

Adams, John 1735–1826, 2nd President of the United States, 1797–1801 (p. 154).

Albright, Madeleine K. 1937–, first female Secretary of State for the United States (p. 287).

Anthony, Susan B. 1820–1906, reformer who fought for women's rights (p. 248).

Abigail Adams

B

Battle, Kathleen 1948–, Grammy Award-winning opera singer from Ohio (p. 265).

Begay, Fred 1932–, Diné nuclear physicist (p. 115).

Berry, Halle 1966–, Academy Award-winning actress from Ohio (p. 265).

Kathleen Battle

Bonaparte, Napoleon 1769–1821, French ruler who agreed to the Louisiana Purchase (p. 188).

Boone, Daniel 1734–1820, frontiersman who cut a trail into Kentucky (p. 187).

Brant, Joseph 1742–1807, Mohawk chief who fought for the British (p. 156).

Bush, George H. W. 1924–, 41st President of the United States, 1989–1993 (p. 259).

C

Cabot, John 1450–1499, English explorer; reached Newfoundland (p. 120).

Cabral, Pedro Álvarez 1467–1520, explorer who claimed Brazil for Portugal (p. 120).

Calvert, Cecilius 1605–1675, Catholic leader of the Maryland colony; also called Lord Baltimore (p. 134).

Campbell, Ben Nighthorse 1933–, Northern Cheyenne chief and U.S. Senator (p. 257).

Carter, Jimmy 1924–, 39th President of the United States, 1977–1981 (p. 224).

Cartier, Jacques 1491–1557, French explorer; sailed up St. Lawrence River (p. 120).

Ben Nighthorse Campbell

Champlain, Samuel de 1567–1635, French explorer; founded Quebec in 1608 (p. 126).

Charles II 1630–1685, king of England, 1660–1685; son of King Charles I who formed Carolina and New Hampshire colonies (p. 134).

Chavez, Cesar 1927–1993, labor leader; founded the United Farm Workers with Dolores Huerta (p. 258).

Cesar Chavez

Clark, George Rogers 1752–1818, captured three British forts during American Revolution (p. 159).

Clark, Peter 1829–1925, speaker and writer; published an abolitionist newspaper in Cincinnati, Ohio (p. 241).

Clark, William 1770–1838, explored Louisiana Purchase with Meriwether Lewis (p. 188).

Columbus, Christopher 1451–1506, Italian navigator; reached the Americas (p. 119).

Cornwallis, Charles 1738–1805, English general in American Revolution; surrendered to Americans at Yorktown in 1781 (p. 158).

Coronado, Francisco Vázquez de 1510–1554, Spanish conquistador (p. 125).

Cortés, Hernán 1485–1547, Spanish conquistador (p. 124).

Crew, Spencer 1949–, historian and president of the National Underground Railroad Freedom Center in Cincinnati, Ohio (p. 241).

D

Dawes, William 1745–1799, Patriot who rode with Paul Revere to warn that British soldiers were marching from Boston (p. 152).

Douglass, Frederick 1817–1895, abolitionist and writer; escaped from slavery (p. 241).

Draper, Sharon 1952–, award-winning writer and teacher from Cleveland, Ohio (p. 265).

Du Bois, W.E.B. 1868–1963, educator who helped create the NAACP (p. 250).

W.E.B. Du Bois

E

Eisenhower, Dwight D. 1890–1969, general in U.S. Army; 34th President of the United States, 1953–1961 (p. 15).

Elizabeth II 1926–, Queen of England, 1952– (p. 15).

F

Ferdinand 1452–1516, king of Spain who paid for Columbus's voyage to find a westward route to Asia (p. 119).

Franklin, Benjamin 1706–1790, printer, writer, publisher, scientist, and inventor; started the *Pennsylvania Gazette* (p. 59).

Franklin, James 1697–1735, brother of Benjamin Franklin; published *New England Courant* (p. 59).

Benjamin Franklin

Friedan, Betty 1921–2006, author of *The Feminine Mystique* and a leader of the women's rights movement (p. 256).

Fulton, Robert 1765–1815, civil engineer; built first profitable steamboat (p. 200).

G

Gálvez, Bernardo de 1746–1786, Spanish colonial administrator (p. 159).

Gama, Vasco da 1460–1524, Portuguese navigator (p. 119).

George III 1738–1820, king of England, 1760–1820; supported British policies that led to American Revolution (p. 153).

Goizueta, Roberto 1931–1997, Cuban immigrant who became president of The Coca-Cola Company (p. 287).

Greene, Nathanael 1742–1786, colonist and Patriot general in South during American Revolution (p. 158).

H

Hamilton, Alexander 1755–1804, contributor to *The Federalist*; first Secretary of the Treasury (p. 169).

Harrison, William Henry 1773–1841, Ohio member of U.S. House of Representatives, 1816–1819; 9th President of the United States, 1841 (p. 197).

Henry 1394–1460, Portuguese prince who started a school for navigation (p. 119).

Henry, Patrick 1736–1799, Revolutionary leader and orator (p. 166).

Hudson, Henry ?–1611, English navigator; the Hudson River is named for him (p. 120).

Huerta, Dolores 1930–, labor leader; founded United Farm Workers with Cesar Chavez (p. 258).

Dolores Huerta

I

Inouye, Daniel 1924–, U.S. senator from Hawaii; son of Japanese immigrants (p. 287).

Isabella 1451–1504, queen of Spain, 1474–1504; supported and financed Columbus (p. 119).

J

Jackson, Andrew 1767–1845, 7th President of the United States, 1829–1837; encouraged Western expansion (p. 191).

Jefferson, Thomas 1743–1826, 3rd President of the United States, 1801–1809; wrote Declaration of Independence (p. 153).

Thomas Jefferson

K

King, Martin Luther, Jr. 1929–1968, civil rights leader (p. 255).

L

Lafayette, Marquis de 1757–1834, French; fought in American Revolution (p. 158).

Lewis, Meriwether 1774–1809, explored Louisiana Purchase with William Clark (p. 188).

Lincoln, Abraham 1809–1865, 16th President of the United States; issued Emancipation Proclamation (p. 243).

Lowell, Francis Cabot 1775–1817, built first complete cotton spinning and weaving mill in the United States (p. 198).

Marquis de Lafayette

M

Madison, James 1751–1836, 4th President of the United States, 1809–1817; helped create the Constitution (p. 166).

Mankiller, Wilma 1945–, Cherokee chief; first woman chief of a major American Indian nation (p. 208).

Marion, Francis 1732?–1795, commander in the American Revolution (p. 158).

Masayesva, Victor, Jr. 1951–, Hopi filmmaker and artist (p. 114).

Mason, George 1725–1792, Virginia delegate at the Constitutional Convention and slave owner (p. 141).

Moctezuma 1480?–1520, Aztec emperor during Spanish conquest of Mexico (p. 124).

Monroe, James 1758–1831, 5th President of the United States, 1817–1825; issued the Monroe Doctrine (p. 190).

Morgan, Garrett Augustus 1877–1963, Ohio inventor of the stop light (p. 263).

Morrison, Toni 1931–, Ohio author and winner of Nobel Prize for Literature (p. 265).

James Madison

O

Ochoa, Ellen 1958–, first Hispanic woman to fly in space (p. 256).

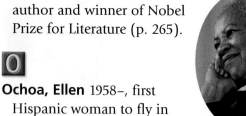
Toni Morrison

O'Connor, Sandra Day 1930–, first woman appointed to U.S. Supreme Court (p. 253).

Oglethorpe, James 1696–1785, founder of Georgia (p. 134).

Owens, Jesse 1913–1980, Ohio athlete; winner of four gold medals at 1936 Olympic games (p. 263).

P

Parker, John 1827–1900, former slave who bought his own freedom and became a conductor on the Underground Railroad in Ohio (p. 242).

Parks, Rosa 1913–2005, African American who refused to obey segregation laws in Alabama (p. 255).

Penn, William 1644–1718, founder of Pennsylvania (p. 133).

Pocahontas 1595?–1617, Powhatan who married colonist John Rolfe.

Polk, James 1795–1849, 11th President of the United States, 1845–1849 (p. 205).

Polo, Marco 1254–1324, Italian merchant who worked in China and published a book about his travels (p. 118).

Prescott, Samuel 1751–1777, Patriot who rode with Paul Revere to warn that British soldiers were marching from Boston (p. 152).

Rosa Parks

R

Rankin, Jeanette 1880–1973, first woman elected to U.S. Congress (p. 249).

Rankin, John 1793–1886, Ohio abolitionist whose home was a station on the Underground Railroad (p. 242).

Revere, Paul 1735–1818, warned Patriots that British soldiers were marching from Boston (p. 152).

Rolfe, John 1585–1622, English colonist; married Pocahontas (p. 131).

Ross, John 1790–1866, Cherokee chief who led the fight against American Indian removal (p. 191).

Biographical Dictionary

S

Sacagawea 1787?–1812, Shoshone interpreter for Lewis and Clark (p. 188).

Silko, Leslie Marmon 1948–, Laguna Pueblo writer and teacher (p. 115).

Slater, Samuel 1768–1835, set up cotton mill in Rhode Island (p. 198).

Smith, Harry C. 1863–1941, Ohio lawmaker; worked to protect rights of African Americans (p. 262).

Smith, John 1580–1631, leader of Jamestown colony (p. 130).

Somani, Pitambar 1937–, doctor and former head of Ohio's Department of Health (p. 287).

Soto, Hernando de 1500?–1542, Spanish explorer (p. 125).

John Smith

Sprague, William 18th c., opened the first carpet mill in the United States (p. 58).

Squanto ?–1622?, Wampanoag who taught the Pilgrims to farm, hunt, and fish (p. 131).

Stanton, Elizabeth Cady 1815–1902, organized first women's rights conference in Seneca Falls (p. 249).

Pitambar Somani

Steinem, Gloria 1934–, Ohio-born leader of women's rights movement (p. 253).

Steuben, Baron Friedrich von 1730–1794, German soldier; trained American soldiers during American Revolution (p. 158).

Stewart, Ella 1893–1987, first African American owner of a pharmacy in Toledo, Ohio (p. 263).

Stokes, Carl Burton 1927–1996, mayor of Cleveland, Ohio, 1968–1972; first African American mayor of a major U.S. city (p. 264).

Stokes, Louis 1925–, Ohio member of U.S. House of Representatives, 1969–1999 (p. 264).

Stowe, Harriet Beecher 1811–1896, author of *Uncle Tom's Cabin* (p. 241).

 T

Truth, Sojourner 1797?–1883, abolitionist and supporter of women's rights (p. 241).

Turner, Nat 1800–1831, led rebellion of enslaved people (p. 144).

 W

Washington, George 1732–1799, commanded Continental armies during American Revolution; first President of the United States, 1789–1797 (p. 157).

George Washington

Whitman, Marcus 1802–1847, missionary and pioneer in Oregon territory (p. 204).

Whitman, Narcissa 1808–1847, missionary and pioneer in Oregon territory (p. 204).

Whitney, Eli 1765–1825, inventor of the cotton gin (p. 199).

Williams, George Washington 1849–1891, first African American member of Ohio state legislature (p. 262).

Williams, Roger 1603?–1683, founder of Rhode Island in 1636 (p. 132).

George Washington Williams

Y

Young, Brigham 1801–1877, Mormon leader; settled in Utah (p. 205).

Alabama

STATE FLAG:

FULL NAME:
State of Alabama

ADMITTED TO THE UNION (RANK):
December 14, 1819 (22nd)

POPULATION 2006 (RANK):
4,599,030 (23rd)

LAND AREA (RANK):
50,744 square miles;
131,426 square kilometers (28th)

CAPITAL: Montgomery

POSTAL ABBREVIATION: AL

STATE NICKNAMES:
Yellowhammer State,
The Heart of Dixie,
The Cotton State

MOTTO:
Audemus jura nostra defendere
(We dare defend our rights)

LOCATION:

SONG:
"Alabama"
(music by Edna Glockel-Gussen,
words by Julia Tutwiler)

STATE SYMBOLS:
Flower: Camellia
Tree: Southern longleaf pine
Bird: Yellowhammer
Gem: Star blue quartz
Stone: Marble
Nut: Pecan
Dance: Square dance

ECONOMY:
Agriculture: Poultry, soybeans, milk, vegetables, wheat, cattle, cotton, peanuts, fruit, hogs, corn

Industry: Paper, lumber and wood products, mining, rubber and plastic products, transportation equipment, apparel

State Databank

Alaska

STATE FLAG:

FULL NAME:
State of Alaska

ADMITTED TO THE UNION (RANK):
January 3, 1959 (49th)

POPULATION 2006 (RANK):
670,053 (47th)

LAND AREA (RANK):
571,951 square miles;
1,481,347 square kilometers (1st)

CAPITAL: Juneau

POSTAL ABBREVIATION: AK

STATE NICKNAMES:
The Last Frontier,
Land of the Midnight Sun

MOTTO:
North to the Future

LOCATION:

SONG:
"Alaska's Flag"
(music by Elinor Dusenbury,
words by Marie Drake)

STATE SYMBOLS:
Flower: Forget-me-not
Tree: Sitka spruce
Bird: Willow ptarmigan
Gem: Jade
Mineral: Gold
Sport: Dog mushing
Fossil: Woolly mammoth

ECONOMY:
Agriculture: Seafood, nursery stock, dairy products, vegetables, livestock

Industry: Petroleum and natural gas, gold and other mining, food processing, lumber and wood products, tourism

Arizona

STATE FLAG:

LOCATION:

ARIZONA

FULL NAME:
State of Arizona

ADMITTED TO THE UNION (RANK):
February 14, 1912 (48th)

POPULATION 2006 (RANK):
6,166,318 (16th)

LAND AREA (RANK):
113,635 square miles;
294,312 square kilometers (6th)

CAPITAL: Phoenix

POSTAL ABBREVIATION: AZ

STATE NICKNAME:
Grand Canyon State

MOTTO:
Ditat deus
(God endures)

SONG:
"Arizona March Song"
(music by Margaret Rowe Clifford)

STATE SYMBOLS:
Flower: Saguaro cactus blossom
Tree: Palo verde
Bird: Cactus wren
Gem: Turquoise
Stone: Petrified wood
Reptile: Arizona ridgenose rattlesnake
Amphibian: Arizona tree frog

ECONOMY:
Agriculture: Cattle, cotton, dairy products, lettuce, nursery stock, hay

Industry: Petroleum and natural gas, gold and other mining, food processing, lumber and wood products, tourism

State Databank

Arkansas

STATE FLAG:

FULL NAME:
State of Arkansas

ADMITTED TO THE UNION (RANK):
June 15, 1836 (25th)

POPULATION 2006 (RANK):
2,810,872 (33rd)

LAND AREA (RANK):
52,068 square miles;
134,856 square kilometers (27th)

CAPITAL: Little Rock

POSTAL ABBREVIATION: AR

STATE NICKNAME:
The Natural State

MOTTO:
Regnat populus
(The people rule)

LOCATION:

SONG:
"The Arkansas Traveller"
(music by Colonel Sanford Faulkner)

STATE SYMBOLS:
Flower: Apple blossom
Tree: Pine tree
Bird: Mockingbird
Gem: Diamond
Insect: Honeybee

ECONOMY:

Agriculture: Poultry and eggs, soybeans, sorghum, cattle, cotton, rice, hogs, milk

Industry: Food processing, electric equipment, fabricated metal products, machinery, paper products, bromine, vanadium

California

STATE FLAG:

LOCATION:

CALIFORNIA

FULL NAME:
State of California

ADMITTED TO THE UNION (RANK):
September 9, 1850 (31st)

POPULATION 2006 (RANK):
36,457,549 (1st)

LAND AREA (RANK):
155,959 square miles;
403,933 square kilometers (3rd)

CAPITAL: Sacramento

POSTAL ABBREVIATION: CA

STATE NICKNAME:
The Golden State

MOTTO:
Eureka
(I have found it)

SONG:
"I Love You California"
(music by A. F. Frankenstein,
words by F. B. Silverwood)

STATE SYMBOLS:
Flower: Golden poppy
Tree: California redwood
Bird: California valley quail
Gem: Bentonite (blue diamond)
Animal: California grizzly bear
Fish: California golden trout

ECONOMY:

Agriculture: Vegetables, fruits and nuts, dairy products, cattle, nursery stock, grapes

Industry: Electronic components and equipment, aerospace, film production, food processing, petroleum, computers and computer software, tourism

State Databank

Colorado

STATE FLAG:

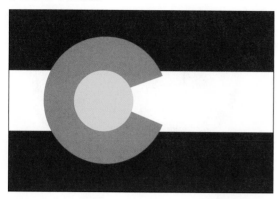

FULL NAME:
State of Colorado

ADMITTED TO THE UNION (RANK):
August 1, 1876 (38th)

POPULATION 2006 (RANK):
4,753,377 (22nd)

LAND AREA (RANK):
103,718 square miles;
268,627 square kilometers (8th)

CAPITAL: Denver

POSTAL ABBREVIATION: CO

STATE NICKNAME:
Centennial State

MOTTO:
Nil sine Numine
(Nothing without Providence)

LOCATION:

SONG:
"Where the Columbines Grow"
(music by A. J. Fynn)

STATE SYMBOLS:
Flower: Rocky Mountain columbine
Tree: Colorado blue spruce
Bird: Lark bunting
Gem: Aquamarine
Animal: Rocky Mountain bighorn sheep
Fossil: Stegosaurus

ECONOMY:
Agriculture: Cattle, wheat, dairy products, corn, hay

Industry: Scientific instruments, food processing, transportation equipment, machinery, chemical products, gold and other mining, tourism

Connecticut

STATE FLAG:

LOCATION:

CONNECTICUT

FULL NAME:
State of Connecticut

ADMITTED TO THE UNION (RANK):
January 9, 1788 (5th)

POPULATION 2006 (RANK):
3,504,809 (29th)

LAND AREA (RANK):
4,845 square miles;
12,548 square kilometers (48th)

CAPITAL: Hartford

POSTAL ABBREVIATION: CT

STATE NICKNAMES:
Constitution State,
Nutmeg State,
Provisions State,
Land of Steady Habits

MOTTO:
Qui transtulit sustinet
(He who transplanted still sustains)

SONG:
"Yankee Doodle"
(music by George M. Cohan)

STATE SYMBOLS:
Flower: Mountain laurel
Tree: Charter oak
Bird: American robin
Mineral: Garnet
Animal: Sperm whale
Insect: Praying mantis

ECONOMY:
Agriculture: Nursery stock, eggs, dairy products, cattle

Industry: Transportation equipment, machinery, electric equipment, fabricated metal products, chemical products, scientific instruments

Delaware

STATE FLAG:

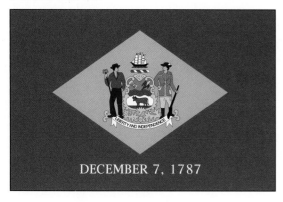

DECEMBER 7, 1787

FULL NAME:
State of Delaware

ADMITTED TO THE UNION (RANK):
December 7, 1787 (1st)

POPULATION 2006 (RANK):
853,476 (45th)

LAND AREA (RANK):
1,954 square miles;
5,060 square kilometers (49th)

CAPITAL: Dover

POSTAL ABBREVIATION: DE

STATE NICKNAMES:
Diamond State,
First State,
Small Wonder,
Blue Hen State

MOTTO:
Liberty and independence

LOCATION:

DELAWARE

SONG:
"Our Delaware"
(music by William M. S. Brown,
words by George B. Hynson)

STATE SYMBOLS:
Flower: Peach blossom
Tree: American holly
Bird: Blue hen chicken
Animal: Horseshoe crab
Insect: Ladybug
Butterfly: Tiger swallowtail
Beverage: Milk

ECONOMY:
Agriculture: Poultry, nursery stock, soybeans, dairy products, corn

Industry: Chemical products, food processing, paper products, rubber and plastic products, scientific instruments, printing and publishing

Florida

STATE FLAG:

FULL NAME:
State of Florida

ADMITTED TO THE UNION (RANK):
March 3, 1845 (27th)

POPULATION 2006 (RANK):
18,089,888 (4th)

LAND AREA (RANK):
53,927 square miles;
139,670 square kilometers (26th)

CAPITAL: Tallahassee

POSTAL ABBREVIATION: FL

STATE NICKNAMES:
Sunshine State,
Orange State,
Everglades State,
Alligator State,
Southernmost State

MOTTO:
In God we trust

LOCATION:

FLORIDA

SONG:
"The Swanee River
(Old Folks at Home)"
(music and words by Stephen Foster)

STATE SYMBOLS:
Flower: Orange blossom
Tree: Sabal palmetto
Bird: Mockingbird
Gem: Moonstone
Stone: Agatized coral
Animal: Florida panther

ECONOMY:
Agriculture: Citrus, vegetables, nursery stock, cattle, sugarcane, dairy products

Industry: Tourism, electric equipment, food processing, printing and publishing, transportation equipment, machinery

Georgia

STATE FLAG:

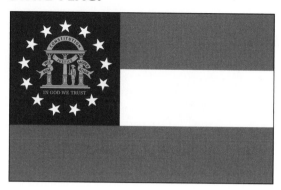

FULL NAME:
State of Georgia

ADMITTED TO THE UNION (RANK):
January 2, 1788 (4th)

POPULATION 2006 (RANK):
9,363,941 (9th)

LAND AREA (RANK):
57,906 square miles;
149,976 square kilometers (21st)

CAPITAL: Atlanta

POSTAL ABBREVIATION: GA

STATE NICKNAMES:
Peach State,
Empire State of the South

MOTTO:
Wisdom, justice, and moderation

LOCATION:

SONG:
"Georgia on My Mind"
(music by Hoagy Carmichael,
words by Stuart Gorrell)

STATE SYMBOLS:
Flower: Cherokee rose
Tree: Live oak
Bird: Brown thrasher
Gem: Quartz

ECONOMY:

Agriculture: Poultry and eggs, peanuts, cattle, hogs, dairy products, vegetables

Industry: Textiles and apparel, transportation equipment, food processing, paper products, chemical products, electric equipment, tourism

Hawaii

STATE FLAG:

LOCATION:

HAWAII

FULL NAME:
State of Hawaii

ADMITTED TO THE UNION (RANK):
August 21, 1959 (50th)

POPULATION 2006 (RANK):
1,285,498 (42nd)

LAND AREA (RANK):
6,423 square miles;
16,635 square kilometers (47th)

CAPITAL: Honolulu

POSTAL ABBREVIATION: HI

STATE NICKNAME:
The Aloha State

MOTTO:
Ua Mau Ke Ea O Ka Aina I Ka Pono
(The life of the land is perpetuated
in righteousness)

SONG:
"Hawaii Panoi"
(music by Capt. Henri Berger,
words by King Kalakaua)

STATE SYMBOLS:
Flower: Yellow hibiscus
Tree: Candlenut
Bird: Hawaiian goose
Gem: Black coral

ECONOMY:
Agriculture: Sugarcane, pineapples,
nursery stock, livestock,
macadamia nuts

Industry: Tourism; food processing;
apparel; fabricated metal
products; stone, clay, and
glass products

State Databank

Idaho

STATE FLAG:

FULL NAME:
State of Idaho

ADMITTED TO THE UNION (RANK):
July 3, 1890 (43rd)

POPULATION 2006 (RANK):
1,466,465 (39th)

LAND AREA (RANK):
82,747 square miles;
214,314 square kilometers (11th)

CAPITAL: Boise

POSTAL ABBREVIATION: ID

STATE NICKNAME:
Gem State

MOTTO:
Esto perpetua
(It is forever)

LOCATION:

SONG:
"Here We Have Idaho"
(music by Sallie Hume-Douglas, words by
Albert J. Tompkins and McKinley Helm)

STATE SYMBOLS:
Flower: Syringa
Tree: Western white pine
Bird: Mountain bluebird
Gem: Star garnet
Horse: Appaloosa
Folk Dance: Square dance

ECONOMY:

Agriculture: Cattle, potatoes, dairy
products, wheat, sugar
beets, barley

Industry: Food processing, lumber
and wood products,
machinery, chemical
products, paper products,
silver and other mining,
tourism

Illinois

STATE FLAG:

LOCATION:

FULL NAME:
State of Illinois

ADMITTED TO THE UNION (RANK):
December 3, 1818 (21st)

POPULATION 2006 (RANK):
12,831,970 (5th)

LAND AREA (RANK):
55,584 square miles;
143,961 square kilometers (24th)

CAPITAL: Springfield

POSTAL ABBREVIATION: IL

STATE NICKNAME:
Prairie State

MOTTO:
State sovereignty, national union

SONG:
"Illinois"
(music by Archibald Johnston,
words by C. H. Chamberlain)

STATE SYMBOLS:
Flower: Native violet
Tree: White oak
Bird: Cardinal
Mineral: Fluorite
Animal: White-tailed deer
Insect: Monarch butterfly
Fish: Bluegill

ECONOMY:
Agriculture: Corn, soybeans, hogs, cattle, dairy products, wheat

Industry: Machinery, food processing, electric equipment, chemical products, printing and publishing, fabricated metal products, transportation equipment, coal, petroleum

Indiana

STATE FLAG:

FULL NAME:
State of Indiana

ADMITTED TO THE UNION (RANK):
December 11, 1816 (19th)

POPULATION 2006 (RANK):
6,313,520 (15th)

LAND AREA (RANK):
35,867 square miles;
92,895 square kilometers (38th)

CAPITAL: Indianapolis

POSTAL ABBREVIATION: IN

STATE NICKNAME:
Hoosier State

MOTTO:
The Crossroads of America

LOCATION:

SONG:
"On the Banks of the Wabash,
Far Away"
(music by Paul Dresser)

STATE SYMBOLS:
Flower: Peony
Tree: Tulip poplar
Bird: Cardinal
Stone: Limestone
River: Wabash

ECONOMY:
Agriculture: Eggs, dairy products, cattle, soybeans, corn, hogs

Industry: Steel, electric equipment, transportation equipment, chemical products, petroleum and coal products, machinery

Iowa

STATE FLAG:

LOCATION:

FULL NAME:
State of Iowa

ADMITTED TO THE UNION (RANK):
December 28, 1846 (29th)

POPULATION 2006 (RANK):
2,982,085 (30th)

LAND AREA (RANK):
55,869 square miles;
144,701 square kilometers (23rd)

CAPITAL: Des Moines

POSTAL ABBREVIATION: IA

STATE NICKNAME:
Hawkeye State

MOTTO:
Our liberties we prize and our rights
we will maintain

SONG:
"Song of Iowa"
(music by S.H.M. Byers)

STATE SYMBOLS:
Flower: Wild rose
Bird: Eastern goldfinch
Colors: Red, white, and blue
(in state flag)

ECONOMY:
Agriculture: Hogs, corn, soybeans,
oats, cattle, dairy
products

Industry: Food processing,
machinery, electric
equipment, chemical
products, printing
and publishing,
primary metals

Kansas

STATE FLAG:

FULL NAME:
State of Kansas

ADMITTED TO THE UNION (RANK):
January 29, 1861 (34th)

POPULATION 2006 (RANK):
2,764,075 (33rd)

LAND AREA (RANK):
81,815 square miles;
211,900 square kilometers (13th)

CAPITAL: Topeka

POSTAL ABBREVIATION: KS

STATE NICKNAMES:
Sunflower State,
Jayhawk State

MOTTO:
Ad astra per aspera
(To the stars through difficulties)

LOCATION:

SONG:
"Home on the Range"
(music and words by Dr. Brewster Higley)

STATE SYMBOLS:
Flower: Sunflower
Tree: Cottonwood
Bird: Western meadowlark
Animal: American buffalo

ECONOMY:
Agriculture: Cattle, wheat, sorghum, soybeans, hogs, corn

Industry: Transportation equipment, food processing, printing and publishing, chemical products, machinery, apparel, petroleum, mining

Kentucky

STATE FLAG:

LOCATION:

FULL NAME:
Commonwealth of Kentucky

ADMITTED TO THE UNION (RANK):
June 1, 1792 (15th)

POPULATION 2006 (RANK):
4,206,074 (26th)

LAND AREA (RANK):
39,728 square miles;
102,896 square kilometers (36th)

CAPITAL: Frankfort

POSTAL ABBREVIATION: KY

STATE NICKNAME:
Bluegrass State

MOTTO:
United we stand, divided we fall

SONG:
"My Old Kentucky Home,
Good Night!"
(music and words by Stephen Foster)

STATE SYMBOLS:
Flower: Goldenrod
Tree: Tulip poplar
Bird: Kentucky cardinal
Gem: Freshwater pearl

ECONOMY:

Agriculture: Horses, cattle, tobacco, dairy products, hogs, soybeans, corn

Industry: Transportation equipment, chemical products, electric equipment, machinery, food processing, tobacco products, coal, tourism

Louisiana

STATE FLAG:

FULL NAME:
State of Louisiana

ADMITTED TO THE UNION (RANK):
April 30, 1812 (18th)

POPULATION 2006 (RANK):
4,287,768 (25th)

LAND AREA (RANK):
43,562 square miles;
112,825 square kilometers (33rd)

CAPITAL: Baton Rouge

POSTAL ABBREVIATION: LA

STATE NICKNAME:
Pelican State

MOTTO:
Union, justice, and confidence

LOCATION:

SONGS:
"Give Me Louisiana"
(music by Dr. John Croom,
words by Doralice Fontane),
"You Are My Sunshine"
(music and words by Jimmy Davis
and Charles Mitchell)

STATE SYMBOLS:
Flower: Magnolia bloom
Tree: Bald cypress
Bird: Eastern brown pelican

ECONOMY:

Agriculture: Seafood, cotton, soybeans, cattle, sugarcane, poultry and eggs, dairy products, rice

Industry: Chemical products, petroleum and coal products, food processing, transportation equipment, paper products, tourism

Maine

STATE FLAG:

LOCATION:

FULL NAME:
State of Maine

ADMITTED TO THE UNION (RANK):
March 15, 1820 (23rd)

POPULATION 2006 (RANK):
1,321,574 (40th)

LAND AREA (RANK):
30,862 square miles;
79,931 square kilometers (39th)

CAPITAL: Augusta

POSTAL ABBREVIATION: ME

STATE NICKNAME:
Pine Tree State

MOTTO:
Dirigo
(I lead)

SONG:
"State of Maine"
(music and words by Roger Vinton Snow)

STATE SYMBOLS:
Flower: White pine cone and tassel
Tree: Eastern white pine
Bird: Chickadee
Gem: Tourmaline
Animal: Moose
Cat: Maine coon cat
Insect: Honeybee

ECONOMY:
Agriculture: Seafood, poultry and eggs, potatoes, dairy products, cattle, blueberries, apples

Industry: Paper, lumber, and wood products, electric equipment, food processing, leather products, textiles, tourism

Maryland

STATE FLAG:

FULL NAME:
State of Maryland

ADMITTED TO THE UNION (RANK):
April 28, 1788 (7th)

POPULATION 2006 (RANK):
5,615,727 (19th)

LAND AREA (RANK):
9,774 square miles;
25,314 square kilometers (42nd)

CAPITAL: Annapolis

POSTAL ABBREVIATION: MD

STATE NICKNAMES:
Free State,
Old Line State

MOTTO:
Fatti maschii, parole femine
(Manly deeds, womanly words)

LOCATION:

SONG:
"Maryland, My Maryland"
(music from an old German carol,
words by Finley Johnson)

STATE SYMBOLS:
Flower: Black-eyed susan
Tree: White oak
Bird: Baltimore oriole
Gem: Tourmaline
Crustacean: Maryland blue crab
Sport: Jousting
Boat: Skipjack

ECONOMY:
Agriculture: Seafood, poultry and eggs, dairy products, nursery stock, cattle, soybeans, corn

Industry: Electric equipment, food processing, chemical products, printing and publishing, transportation equipment, machinery, primary metals, coal, tourism

Massachusetts

STATE FLAG:

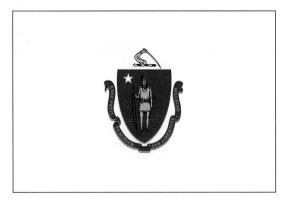

LOCATION:

MASSACHUSETTS

FULL NAME:
Commonwealth of Massachusetts

ADMITTED TO THE UNION (RANK):
February 6, 1788 (6th)

POPULATION 2006 (RANK):
6,437,193 (13th)

LAND AREA (RANK):
7,840 square miles;
20,306 square kilometers (45th)

CAPITAL: Boston

POSTAL ABBREVIATION: MA

STATE NICKNAMES:
Bay State,
Old Colony State

MOTTO:
Ense petit placidam sub libertate quietem (By the sword we seek peace, but peace only under liberty)

SONG:
"All Hail to Massachusetts"
(music by Arthur J. Marsh)

STATE SYMBOLS:
Flower: Mayflower
Tree: American elm
Bird: Black-capped chickadee
Gem: Rhodonite
Beverage: Cranberry juice
Muffin: Corn muffin
Cookie: Chocolate chip
Dessert: Boston cream pie

ECONOMY:
Agriculture: Seafood, nursery stock, dairy products, cranberries, vegetables

Industry: Machinery, electric equipment, scientific instruments, printing and publishing, tourism

Michigan

STATE FLAG:

FULL NAME:
State of Michigan

ADMITTED TO THE UNION (RANK):
January 26, 1837 (26th)

POPULATION 2006 (RANK):
10,095,643 (8th)

LAND AREA (RANK):
56,804 square miles;
147,121 square kilometers (22nd)

CAPITAL: Lansing

POSTAL ABBREVIATION: MI

STATE NICKNAMES:
Wolverine State,
Great Lake State

MOTTO:
Si quaeris peninsulam amoenam circumspice (If you seek a pleasant peninsula, look around you)

LOCATION:

SONG:
"Michigan, My Michigan"
(music by William Otto Miessner and Douglas M. Malloch)

STATE SYMBOLS:
Flower: Apple blossom
Tree: White pine
Bird: Robin
Gem: Isle royal greenstone
Stone: Petoskey stone
Mammal: White-tailed deer
Wildflower: Dwarf lake iris
Reptile: Painted turtle

ECONOMY:

Agriculture: Dairy products, apples, blueberries, cattle, vegetables, hogs, corn, nursery stock, soybeans

Industry: Motor vehicles and parts, machinery, fabricated metal products, food processing, chemical products, mining, tourism

Minnesota

STATE FLAG:

LOCATION:

MINNESOTA

FULL NAME:
State of Minnesota

ADMITTED TO THE UNION (RANK):
May 11, 1858 (32nd)

POPULATION 2006 (RANK):
5,167,101 (21st)

LAND AREA (RANK):
79,610 square miles;
206,189 square kilometers (14th)

CAPITAL: St. Paul

POSTAL ABBREVIATION: MN

STATE NICKNAMES:
North Star State,
Gopher State,
Land of 10,000 Lakes

MOTTO:
L'Etoile du Nord
(The North Star)

SONG:
"Hail, Minnesota"
(music by Truman E. Richard, words by
Truman E. Richard and Arthur E. Upson)

STATE SYMBOLS:
Flower: Lady slipper
Tree: Red (Norway) pine
Bird: Common loon
Fish: Walleye
Mushroom: Morel

ECONOMY:
Agriculture: Dairy products, corn, cattle, soybeans, hogs, wheat, turkeys

Industry: Machinery, food processing, printing and publishing, fabricated metal products, electric equipment, mining, tourism

State Databank

Mississippi

STATE FLAG:

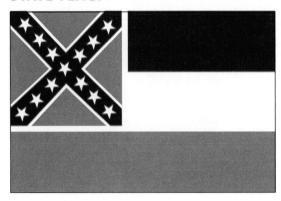

FULL NAME:
State of Mississippi

ADMITTED TO THE UNION (RANK):
December 10, 1817 (20th)

POPULATION 2006 (RANK):
2,910,540 (31st)

LAND AREA (RANK):
46,907 square miles;
121,488 square kilometers (31st)

CAPITAL: Jackson

POSTAL ABBREVIATION: MS

STATE NICKNAME:
Magnolia State

MOTTO:
Virtute et armis
(By valor and arms)

LOCATION:

SONG:
"Go Mississippi"
(music and words by Houston Davis)

STATE SYMBOLS:
Flower: Magnolia bloom
Tree: Magnolia
Bird: Mockingbird
Stone: Petrified wood
Land mammals: White-tailed deer, red fox
Water mammal: Bottlenosed dolphin or porpoise
Shell: Oyster shell

ECONOMY:
Agriculture: Cotton, poultry, cattle, catfish, soybeans, dairy products, rice

Industry: Apparel, furniture, lumber and wood products, food processing, electrical machinery, transportation equipment

Missouri

STATE FLAG:

FULL NAME:
State of Missouri

ADMITTED TO THE UNION (RANK):
August 10, 1821 (24th)

POPULATION 2006 (RANK):
5,842,713 (18th)

LAND AREA (RANK):
68,886 square miles;
178,414 square kilometers (18th)

CAPITAL: Jefferson City

POSTAL ABBREVIATION: MO

STATE NICKNAME:
Show-me State

MOTTO:
Salus populi suprema lex esto
(The welfare of the people shall
be the supreme law)

LOCATION:

SONG:
"Missouri Waltz"
(music by John Valentine Eppel,
words by Jim R. Shannon)

STATE SYMBOLS:
Flower: Hawthorn blossom
Tree: Flowering dogwood
Bird: Eastern bluebird
Mineral: Galena
Stone: Mozarkite
Animal: Mule
Musical Instrument: Fiddle
Fish: Channel catfish

ECONOMY:
Agriculture: Cattle, soybeans, hogs, dairy products, corn, poultry and eggs

Industry: Transportation equipment, food processing, chemical products, electric equipment, fabricated metal products

Montana

STATE FLAG:

LOCATION:

FULL NAME:
State of Montana

ADMITTED TO THE UNION:
November 8, 1889 (41st)

POPULATION 2006 (RANK):
944,632 (44th)

LAND AREA (RANK):
145,552 square miles;
376,979 square kilometers (4th)

CAPITAL: Helena

POSTAL ABBREVIATION: MT

STATE NICKNAMES:
Treasure State,
Big Sky Country

MOTTO:
Oro y plata
(Gold and silver)

SONG:
"Montana"
(music Joseph E. Howard,
words by Charles C. Cohan)

STATE SYMBOLS:
Flower: Bitterroot
Tree: Ponderosa pine
Bird: Western meadowlark
Gems: Montana sapphire and agate
Animal: Grizzly bear

ECONOMY:
Agriculture: Cattle, wheat, barley, sugar beets, hay, hogs

Industry: Mining, lumber and wood products, food processing, tourism

Nebraska

STATE FLAG:

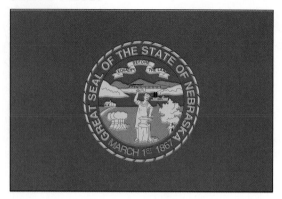

LOCATION:

FULL NAME:
State of Nebraska

ADMITTED TO THE UNION (RANK):
March 1, 1867 (37th)

POPULATION 2006 (RANK):
1,768,331 (38th)

LAND AREA (RANK):
76,872 square miles;
199,099 square kilometers (15th)

CAPITAL: Lincoln

POSTAL ABBREVIATION: NE

STATE NICKNAMES:
Cornhusker State,
Beef State

MOTTO:
Equality before the law

SONG:
"Beautiful Nebraska"
(music by Jim Fras, words by Jim Fras
and Guy G. Miller)

STATE SYMBOLS:
Flower: Goldenrod
Tree: Cottonwood
Bird: Western meadowlark
Gem: Blue agate
Stone: Prairie agate
Mammal: White-tailed deer
Beverage: Milk
Ballad: "A Place Like Nebraska"

ECONOMY:
Agriculture: Cattle, corn, hogs, soybeans, wheat, sorghum

Industry: Food processing, machinery, electric equipment, printing and publishing

Nevada

STATE FLAG:

FULL NAME:
State of Nevada

ADMITTED TO THE UNION (RANK):
October 31, 1864 (36th)

POPULATION 2006 (RANK):
2,495,529 (35th)

LAND AREA (RANK):
109,826 square miles;
284,448 square kilometers (7th)

CAPITAL: Carson City

POSTAL ABBREVIATION: NV

STATE NICKNAMES:
Sagebrush State,
Silver State,
Battle Born State

MOTTO:
All for Our Country

LOCATION:

SONG:
"Home Means Nevada"
(music and words by Bertha Raffetto)

STATE SYMBOLS:
Flower: Sagebrush
Trees: Bristlecone pine,
Single-leaf pinon
Bird: Mountain bluebird
Gem: Black fire opal
Stone: Sandstone
Animal: Desert bighorn sheep
Metal: Silver
Reptile: Desert tortoise

ECONOMY:
Agriculture: Cattle, hay, dairy
products, potatoes

Industry: Tourism, mining,
machinery, printing
and publishing, food
processing, electric
equipment

New Hampshire

STATE FLAG:

LOCATION:

NEW HAMPSHIRE

FULL NAME:
State of New Hampshire

ADMITTED TO THE UNION (RANK):
June 21, 1788 (9th)

POPULATION 2006 (RANK):
1,314,895 (41st)

LAND AREA (RANK):
8,968 square miles;
23,227 square kilometers (44th)

CAPITAL: Concord

POSTAL ABBREVIATION: NH

STATE NICKNAME:
Granite State

MOTTO:
Live free or die

SONG:
"Old New Hampshire"
(music by Maurice Hoffmann,
words by John F. Holmes)

STATE SYMBOLS:
Flower: Purple lilac
Tree: White birch
Bird: Purple finch
Gem: Smoky quartz
Animal: White-tailed deer
Insect: Ladybug
Amphibian: Spotted newt
Butterfly: Karner blue

ECONOMY:

Agriculture: Dairy products, nursery stock, cattle, apples, eggs

Industry: Machinery, electric equipment, rubber and plastic products, tourism

New Jersey

STATE FLAG:

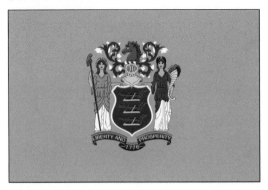

LOCATION:

NEW JERSEY

FULL NAME:
State of New Jersey

ADMITTED TO THE UNION (RANK):
December 18, 1787 (3rd)

POPULATION 2006 (RANK):
8,724,560 (11th)

LAND AREA (RANK):
7,417 square miles;
19,211 square kilometers (46th)

CAPITAL: Trenton

POSTAL ABBREVIATION: NJ

STATE NICKNAME:
Garden State

MOTTO:
Liberty and prosperity

SONG:
"I'm from New Jersey"
(music by Red Mascara)

STATE SYMBOLS:
Flower: Purple violet
Tree: Red oak
Bird: Eastern goldfinch
Animal: Horse
Fish: Brook trout
Folk Dance: Square dance
Shell: Knobbed whelk
Colors: Buff and blue

ECONOMY:
Agriculture: Nursery stock, horses, vegetables, fruits and nuts, seafood, dairy products

Industry: Chemical products, food processing, electric equipment, printing and publishing, tourism

New Mexico

STATE FLAG:

LOCATION:

FULL NAME:
State of New Mexico

ADMITTED TO THE UNION (RANK):
January 6, 1912 (47th)

POPULATION 2006 (RANK):
1,954,599 (36th)

LAND AREA (RANK):
121,356 square miles;
314,309 square kilometers (5th)

CAPITAL: Santa Fe

POSTAL ABBREVIATION: NM

STATE NICKNAME:
Land of Enchantment

MOTTO:
Crescit eundo
(It grows as it goes)

SONG:
"O Fair New Mexico"
(music and words by Elizabeth Garrett)

STATE SYMBOLS:
Flower: Yucca
Tree: Pinon
Bird: Roadrunner
Gem: Turquoise
Animal: Black bear
Cookie: Bizcochito
Vegetables: Chili and frijol

ECONOMY:
Agriculture: Cattle, dairy products, hay, nursery stock, chilies

Industry: Electric equipment; petroleum and coal products; food processing; printing and publishing; stone, glass, and clay products; tourism

New York

STATE FLAG:

LOCATION:

FULL NAME:
State of New York

ADMITTED TO THE UNION (RANK):
July 26, 1788 (11th)

POPULATION 2006 (RANK):
19,306,183 (3rd)

LAND AREA (RANK):
47,214 square miles;
122,283 square kilometers (30th)

CAPITAL: Albany

POSTAL ABBREVIATION: NY

STATE NICKNAME:
Empire State

MOTTO:
Excelsior
(Ever upward)

SONG:
"I Love New York"
(music by Steve Karmen)

STATE SYMBOLS:
Flower: Rose
Tree: Sugar maple
Bird: Bluebird
Gem: Garnet
Animal: Beaver
Insect: Ladybug
Fish: Brook trout

ECONOMY:

Agriculture: Dairy products, cattle and other livestock, vegetables, nursery stock, apples

Industry: Printing and publishing, scientific instruments, electric equipment, machinery, chemical products, tourism

North Carolina

STATE FLAG:

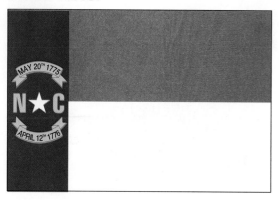

LOCATION:

NORTH CAROLINA

FULL NAME:
State of North Carolina

ADMITTED TO THE UNION (RANK):
November 21, 1789 (12th)

POPULATION 2006 (RANK):
8,856,505 (10th)

LAND AREA (RANK):
48,711 square miles;
126,161 square kilometers (29th)

CAPITAL: Raleigh

POSTAL ABBREVIATION: NC

STATE NICKNAME:
Tar Heel State

MOTTO:
Esse quam videri
(To be rather than to seem)

SONG:
"The Old North State"
(music by E. E. Randolph,
words by William Gaston)

STATE SYMBOLS:
Flower: Dogwood
Tree: Pine
Bird: Cardinal
Gem: Emerald
Stone: Granite
Mammal: Gray squirrel
Reptile: Eastern box turtle
Fruit: Scuppernong grape

ECONOMY:

Agriculture: Poultry and eggs,
tobacco, hogs, milk,
nursery stock, cattle,
soybeans

Industry: Tobacco products, textile
goods, chemical products,
electric equipment,
machinery, tourism

State Databank

North Dakota

STATE FLAG:

LOCATION:

FULL NAME:
State of North Dakota

ADMITTED TO THE UNION (RANK):
November 2, 1889 (39th)

POPULATION 2006 (RANK):
635,867 (48th)

LAND AREA (RANK):
68,976 square miles;
178,647 square kilometers (17th)

CAPITAL: Bismarck

POSTAL ABBREVIATION: ND

STATE NICKNAMES:
Sioux State,
Flickertail State,
Peace Garden State,
Rough Rider State

MOTTO:
Liberty and union, now and forever:
one and inseparable

SONG:
"North Dakota Hymn"
(music by C. S. Putnam,
words by James W. Foley)

STATE SYMBOLS:
Flower: Wild prairie rose
Tree: American elm
Bird: Western meadowlark
Gems: Montana sapphire and agate
Equine: Nokota horse
Fossil: Teredo petrified wood
Beverage: Milk
Dance: Square dance

ECONOMY:

Agriculture: Wheat, cattle, barley, sunflowers, milk, sugar beets

Industry: Food processing, machinery, mining, tourism

Ohio

STATE FLAG:

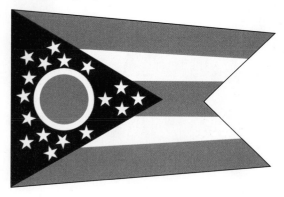

LOCATION:

FULL NAME:
State of Ohio

ADMITTED TO THE UNION (RANK):
March 1, 1803 (17th)

POPULATION 2006 (RANK):
11,478,006 (7th)

LAND AREA (RANK):
40,948 square miles;
106,056 square kilometers (35th)

CAPITAL: Columbus

POSTAL ABBREVIATION: OH

STATE NICKNAME:
Buckeye State

MOTTO:
With God all things are possible

SONG:
"Beautiful Ohio"
(music by Mary Earl)

STATE SYMBOLS:
Flower: Scarlet carnation
Tree: Ohio buckeye
Bird: Cardinal
Gem: Ohio flint
Animal: White-tailed deer
Beverage: Tomato juice
Fossil: Trilobite
Wildflower: Large white trillium

ECONOMY:
Agriculture: Soybeans, dairy products, corn, tomatoes, hogs, cattle, poultry and eggs

Industry: Transportation equipment, fabricated metal products, machinery, food processing, electric equipment

Oklahoma

STATE FLAG:

LOCATION:

FULL NAME:
State of Oklahoma

ADMITTED TO THE UNION (RANK):
November 16, 1907 (46th)

POPULATION 2006 (RANK):
3,579,212 (28th)

LAND AREA (RANK):
68,667 square miles;
177,847 square kilometers (19th)

CAPITAL: Oklahoma City

POSTAL ABBREVIATION: OK

STATE NICKNAME:
Sooner State

MOTTO:
Labor omni vincit
(Labor conquers all things)

SONG:
"Oklahoma"
(music by Richard Rodgers,
words by Oscar Hammerstein II)

STATE SYMBOLS:
Flower: Mistletoe
Tree: Redbud
Bird: Scissor-tailed flycatcher
Stone: Rose rock
Animal: Bison
Colors: Green and white
Poem: "Howdy Folks"
by David Randolph Milsten

ECONOMY:
Agriculture: Cattle, wheat, milk,
poultry, cotton

Industry: Transportation
equipment, machinery,
electric products, rubber
and plastic products,
food processing

Oregon

STATE FLAG:

LOCATION:

FULL NAME:
State of Oregon

ADMITTED TO THE UNION (RANK):
February 14, 1859 (33rd)

POPULATION 2006 (RANK):
3,700,758 (27th)

LAND AREA (RANK):
95,997 square miles;
248,631 square kilometers (10th)

CAPITAL: Salem

POSTAL ABBREVIATION: OR

STATE NICKNAME:
Beaver State

MOTTO:
Alis volat Propriis
(She flies with her own wings)

SONG:
"Oregon, My Oregon"
(music by Henry B. Murtagh,
words by J. A. Buchanan)

STATE SYMBOLS:
Flower: Oregon grape
Tree: Douglas fir
Bird: Western meadowlark
Gem: Sunstone
Stone: Thunderegg
Animal: Beaver
Nut: Hazelnut
Seashell: Oregon hairy triton
Mushroom: Pacific golden chanterelle

ECONOMY:
Agriculture: Cattle, vegetables, nursery stock, fruits and nuts, dairy products, wheat

Industry: Lumber and wood products, tourism, food processing, paper products, machinery, scientific instruments

Pennsylvania

STATE FLAG:

FULL NAME:
Commonwealth of Pennsylvania

ADMITTED TO THE UNION (RANK):
December 12, 1787 (2nd)

POPULATION 2006 (RANK):
12,440,621 (6th)

LAND AREA (RANK):
44,817 square miles;
116,074 square kilometers (32nd)

CAPITAL: Harrisburg

POSTAL ABBREVIATION: PA

STATE NICKNAME:
Keystone State

MOTTO:
Virtue, liberty, and independence

LOCATION:

SONG:
"Pennsylvania"
(music by Eddie Khoury and Ronnie Bonner)

STATE SYMBOLS:
Flower: Mountain laurel
Tree: Hemlock
Bird: Ruffed grouse
Dog: Great Dane
Colors: Blue and gold

ECONOMY:
Agriculture: Dairy products, poultry, cattle, nursery stock, mushrooms, hogs, hay

Industry: Food processing, chemical products, machinery, electric equipment, tourism

Rhode Island

STATE FLAG:

LOCATION:

RHODE ISLAND

FULL NAME:
State of Rhode Island

ADMITTED TO THE UNION (RANK):
May 29, 1790 (13th)

POPULATION 2006 (RANK):
1,067,610 (43rd)

LAND AREA (RANK):
1,045 square miles;
2,607 square kilometers (50th)

CAPITAL: Providence

POSTAL ABBREVIATION: RI

STATE NICKNAME:
The Ocean State

MOTTO:
Hope

SONG:
"Rhode Island It's for Me"
(music by Maria Day, words by Charlie Hall)

STATE SYMBOLS:
Flower: Violet
Tree: Red maple
Bird: Rhode Island red hen
Mineral: Bowenite
Stone: Cumberlandite
Shell: Quahog
Colors: Blue, white and gold
(in state flag)

ECONOMY:
Agriculture: Nursery stock, vegetables, dairy products, eggs

Industry: Fashion jewelry, fabricated metal products, electric equipment, machinery, shipbuilding and boatbuilding, tourism

State Databank

South Carolina

LOCATION:

FULL NAME:
State of South Carolina

ADMITTED TO THE UNION (RANK):
May 23, 1788 (8th)

POPULATION 2006 (RANK):
4,321,249 (24th)

LAND AREA (RANK):
30,109 square miles;
77,893 square kilometers (40th)

CAPITAL: Columbia

POSTAL ABBREVIATION: SC

STATE NICKNAME:
Palmetto State

MOTTOES:
Animis opibusque parati
(Prepared in mind and resources),
Dum spiro spero
(While I breathe, I hope)

SONG:
"Carolina"
(music by Anne Custis Burgess,
words by Henry Timrod)

STATE SYMBOLS:
Flower: Carolina yellow jessamine
Tree: Palmetto tree
Bird: Carolina wren

ECONOMY:
Agriculture: Tobacco, poultry, cattle, hogs, dairy products, soybeans

Industry: Textile goods, chemical products, paper products, machinery, tourism

State Databank

South Dakota

STATE FLAG:

LOCATION:

FULL NAME:
State of South Dakota

ADMITTED TO THE UNION (RANK):
November 2, 1889 (40th)

POPULATION 2006 (RANK):
781,919 (46th)

LAND AREA (RANK):
75,885 square miles;
196,540 square kilometers (16th)

CAPITAL: Pierre

POSTAL ABBREVIATION: SD

STATE NICKNAMES:
Mount Rushmore State,
Coyote State

MOTTO:
Under God the people rule

SONG:
"Hail! South Dakota"
(music and words by DeeCort Hammitt)

STATE SYMBOLS:
Flower: American pasqueflower
Tree: Black Hills spruce
Bird: Chinese ring-necked pheasant
Gem: Fairburn agate
Stone: Rose quartz
Animal: Coyote
Musical Instrument: Fiddle
Dessert: Kuchen

ECONOMY:
Agriculture: Cattle, hogs, wheat, soybeans, milk, corn

Industry: Food processing, machinery, lumber and wood products, tourism

Tennessee

STATE FLAG:

FULL NAME:
State of Tennessee

ADMITTED TO THE UNION:
June 1, 1796 (16th)

POPULATION 2006 (RANK):
6,038,803 (17th)

LAND AREA (RANK):
41,217 square miles;
106,752 square kilometers (24th)

CAPITAL: Nashville

POSTAL ABBREVIATION: TN

STATE NICKNAME:
Volunteer State

MOTTO:
Agriculture and Commerce

LOCATION:

SONGS:
"Tennessee Waltz" (music by Pee Wee King, words by Redd Stewart),
"My Homeland, Tennessee" (music by Roy Lamont Smith, words by Nell Grayson),
"When It's Iris Time in Tennessee" (music and words by Willa Waid Newman),
"My Tennessee" (music and words by Frances Hannah Tranum),
"Rocky Top" (music and words by Boudleaux Bryant and Felice Bryant),
"Tennessee" (music and words by Vivan Rorie)

STATE SYMBOLS:
Flower: Iris
Tree: Tulip poplar
Bird: Mockingbird
Gem: Tennessee pearl
Animal: Raccoon
Horse: Tennessee walking horse
Wildflower: Passion flower

ECONOMY:
Agriculture: Soybeans, cotton, tobacco, livestock and livestock products, dairy products, cattle, hogs

Industry: Chemicals, transportation equipment, rubber, plastics

Texas

STATE FLAG:

FULL NAME:
State of Texas

ADMITTED TO THE UNION (RANK):
December 29, 1845 (28th)

POPULATION 2006 (RANK):
23,507,783 (2nd)

LAND AREA (RANK):
261,797 square miles;
678,051 square kilometers (2nd)

CAPITAL: Austin

POSTAL ABBREVIATION: TX

STATE NICKNAME:
Lone Star State

MOTTO:
Friendship

LOCATION:

SONG:
"Texas, Our Texas"
(music by William J. Marsh
and Gladys Yoakum Wright)

STATE SYMBOLS:
Flower: Bluebonnet
Tree: Pecan
Bird: Mockingbird
Gem: Texas blue topaz
Stone: Petrified palmwood
Small Mammal: Armadillo
Flying Mammal: Mexican free-tailed bat
Dish: Chili
Plant: Prickly pear cactus

ECONOMY:

Agriculture: Cattle, cotton, dairy products, nursery stock, poultry, sorghum, corn, wheat

Industry: Chemical products, petroleum and natural gas, food processing, electric equipment, machinery, mining, tourism

Utah

STATE FLAG:

FULL NAME:
State of Utah

ADMITTED TO THE UNION (RANK):
January 4, 1896 (45th)

POPULATION 2006 (RANK):
2,550,063 (34th)

LAND AREA (RANK):
82,144 square miles;
212,751 square kilometers (12th)

CAPITAL: Salt Lake City

POSTAL ABBREVIATION: UT

STATE NICKNAME:
Beehive State

MOTTO:
Industry

LOCATION:

SONG:
"Utah . . . This Is the Place"
(music by Gary Francis, words by Gary Francis and Sam Francis)

STATE SYMBOLS:
Flower: Sego lily
Tree: Blue spruce
Bird: California seagull
Gem: Topaz
Stone: Coal
Animal: Rocky Mountain elk
Fruit: Cherry
Fossil: Allosaurus
Cooking pot: Dutch oven

ECONOMY:
Agriculture: Cattle, dairy products, hay, turkeys

Industry: Machinery, aerospace, mining, food processing, electric equipment, tourism

Vermont

STATE FLAG:

FULL NAME:
State of Vermont

ADMITTED TO THE UNION (RANK):
March 4, 1791 (14th)

POPULATION 2006 (RANK):
623,908 (49th)

LAND AREA (RANK):
9,250 square miles;
23,956 square kilometers (43rd)

CAPITAL: Montpelier

POSTAL ABBREVIATION: VT

STATE NICKNAME:
Green Mountain State

MOTTO:
Vermont, Freedom, and Unity

LOCATION:

SONG:
"These Green Mountains"
(music and words by Diane Martin)

STATE SYMBOLS:
Flower: Red clover
Tree: Sugar maple
Bird: Hermit thrush
Animal: Morgan horse
Insect: Honeybee

ECONOMY:

Agriculture: Dairy products, cattle, hay, apples, maple products

Industry: Electronic equipment, fabricated metal products, printing and publishing, paper products, tourism

Virginia

STATE FLAG:

LOCATION:

FULL NAME:
Commonwealth of Virginia

ADMITTED TO THE UNION (RANK):
June 25, 1788 (10th)

POPULATION 2006 (RANK):
7,642,884 (12th)

LAND AREA (RANK):
39,594 square miles;
102,548 square kilometers (37th)

CAPITAL: Richmond

POSTAL ABBREVIATION: VA

STATE NICKNAMES:
The Old Dominion,
Mother of Presidents

MOTTO:
Sic semper tyrannis
(Thus always to tyrants)

SONG:
"Carry Me Back to Old Virginny"
(music and words by James A. Bland)

STATE SYMBOLS:
Flower: American dogwood
Tree: Flowering dogwood
Bird: Cardinal
Dog: American foxhound
Shell: Oyster shell

ECONOMY:
Agriculture: Cattle, poultry, dairy products, tobacco, hogs, soybeans

Industry: Transportation equipment, textiles, food processing, printing, electric equipment, chemicals

Washington

STATE FLAG:

LOCATION:

FULL NAME:
State of Washington

ADMITTED TO THE UNION (RANK):
November 11, 1889 (42nd)

POPULATION 2006 (RANK):
6,395,798 (14th)

LAND AREA (RANK):
66,544 square miles;
172,348 square kilometers (20th)

CAPITAL: Olympia

POSTAL ABBREVIATION: WA

STATE NICKNAME:
Evergreen State

MOTTO:
Al-Ki
(American Indian word meaning "by and by")

SONG:
"Washington, My Home"
(music by Helen Davis, arranged by Stuart Churchill)

STATE SYMBOLS:
Flower: Western rhododendron
Tree: Western hemlock
Bird: American goldfinch
Gem: Petrified wood
Fruit: Apple
Insect: Blue darner dragonfly
Fossil: Columbian mammoth

ECONOMY:
Agriculture: Seafood, dairy products, apples, cattle, wheat, potatoes, nursery stock

Industry: Aerospace, software development, food processing, paper products, lumber and wood products, chemical products, tourism

West Virginia

STATE FLAG:

LOCATION:

FULL NAME:
State of West Virginia

ADMITTED TO THE UNION (RANK):
June 20, 1863 (35th)

POPULATION 2006 (RANK):
1,818,470 (37th)

LAND AREA (RANK):
24,078 square miles;
62,361 square kilometers (41st)

CAPITAL: Charleston

POSTAL ABBREVIATION: WV

STATE NICKNAME:
Mountain State

MOTTO:
Montani semper liberi
(Mountaineers are always free)

SONGS:
"West Virginia Hills"
(music by H. E. Engle, words by Ellen King),
"West Virginia, My Home Sweet Home"
(music by Col. Julian G. Hearne, Jr.),
"This Is My West Virginia"
(music by Iris Bell)

STATE SYMBOLS:
Flower: Big rhododendron
Tree: Sugar maple
Bird: Cardinal
Gem: Mississippian fossil coral
Animal: Black bear
Colors: Blue and gold

ECONOMY:
Agriculture: Cattle, dairy products, poultry, apples

Industry: Chemical products, mining, primary metals, stone, clay, glass products, tourism

Wisconsin

STATE FLAG:

LOCATION:

FULL NAME:
State of Wisconsin

ADMITTED TO THE UNION (RANK):
May 29, 1848 (30th)

POPULATION 2006 (RANK):
5,556,506 (20th)

LAND AREA (RANK):
54,310 square miles;
140,663 square kilometers (25th)

CAPITAL: Madison

POSTAL ABBREVIATION: WI

STATE NICKNAME:
Badger State

MOTTO:
Forward

SONG:
"On Wisconsin"
(music by William T. Purdy, words by
J. S. Hubbard and Charles D. Rosa)

STATE SYMBOLS:
Flower: Wood violet
Tree: Sugar maple
Bird: Robin
Mineral: Galena
Stone: Red granite
Animal: Badger
Dance: Polka
Symbol of Peace: Mourning dove
Domestic Animal: Dairy cow

ECONOMY:

Agriculture: Cheese, dairy products, cattle, hogs, vegetables, corn, cranberries

Industry: Machinery, food processing, paper products, electric equipment, fabricated metal products, tourism

Wyoming

STATE FLAG:

FULL NAME:
State of Wyoming

ADMITTED TO THE UNION (RANK):
July 10, 1890 (44th)

POPULATION 2006 (RANK):
515,004 (50th)

LAND AREA (RANK):
97,100 square miles;
251,489 square kilometers (9th)

CAPITAL: Cheyenne

POSTAL ABBREVIATION: WY

STATE NICKNAME:
Equality State

MOTTO:
Equal rights

LOCATION:

SONG:
"Wyoming"
(music by G. E. Knapp, words by C. E. Winter)

STATE SYMBOLS:
Flower: Indian paintbrush
Tree: Plains cottonwood
Bird: Western meadowlark
Gem: Jade
Mammal: Bison
Dinosaur: Triceratops
Reptile: Horned toad

ECONOMY:
Agriculture: Cattle, sugar beets, sheep, hay, wheat

Industry: Mining, chemical products, lumber and wood products, printing and publishing, machinery, tourism

Canada

FLAG:

LOCATION:

POPULATION 2006:
33,098,932

LAND AREA:
3,855,083 square miles;
9,984,670 square kilometers

HIGHEST ELEVATION:
Mount Logan, 19,551 feet;
5,959 meters

CAPITAL:
Ottawa

HEAD OF GOVERNMENT:
Prime Minister

CURRENCY:
Canadian Dollar

MOTTO:
A Mari Usque Ad Mari
(From sea to sea)

NATIONAL ANTHEM:
"O Canada"
(by Calixa Lavallée)

NATIONAL SYMBOLS:
Animal: Beaver
Tree: Maple

NATIONAL HOLIDAY:
Canada Day, July 1

ECONOMY:
Agriculture: wheat, barley, oil seed, tobacco, fruits
Manufacturing: transportation equipment, machinery, chemicals, processed and unprocessed minerals, food products

Mexico

FLAG:

LOCATION:

FULL NAME:
Estados Unidos Mexicanos
(United Mexican States)

POPULATION 2006:
107,449,525

LAND AREA:
756,066 square miles;
1,958,201 square kilometers

HIGHEST ELEVATION:
Pico de Orizaba, 18,410 feet;
5,610 meters

CAPITAL:
Mexico City

HEAD OF GOVERNMENT:
President

CURRENCY:
Peso

NATIONAL ANTHEM:
Himno Nacional de México
(National Anthem of Mexico)
(music by Jaime Nunó, words by Francisco
González Bocanegra)

NATIONAL SYMBOLS:
Flower: Dahlia
Bird: Crested caracara

NATIONAL HOLIDAY:
Independence Day, September 16

ECONOMY:
Agriculture: corn, coffee, cotton,
sugar cane, tomatoes,
bananas, oranges,
wheat, sorghum, barley,
rice, beans, potatoes
Manufacturing: motor vehicles,
processed foods,
beverages, iron
and steel, chemicals,
electrical machinery

Geographic Terms

basin
a round area of land surrounded by higher land

bay
part of a lake or ocean extending into the land

coast
the land next to an ocean

coastal plain
a flat, level area of land near an ocean

delta
a triangular area of land formed by deposits at the mouth of a river

desert
a dry area where few plants grow

▲ **glacier**
a large ice mass that moves slowly down a mountain or over land

gulf
a large body of sea water partly surrounded by land

harbor
a sheltered body of water where ships can safely dock

hill
a raised area of land, smaller than a mountain

island
a body of land surrounded by water

isthmus
a narrow strip of land connecting two larger bodies of land

lake
a body of water surrounded by land

mountain range

valley

river

tributary

lake

hill

wetland

coastal plain

delta

bay

mesa
a wide flat-topped mountain with steep sides, found mostly in dry areas

mountain
a steeply raised mass of land, much higher than the surrounding country

mountain range
a row of mountains

ocean or sea
a salty body of water covering a large area of the earth

plain
a large area of flat or nearly flat land

plateau
a large area of flat land higher than the surrounding land

prairie
a large, level area of grassland with few or no trees

river
a large stream that runs into a lake, ocean, or another river

sea level
the level of the surface of the ocean

strait
a narrow channel of water connecting two larger bodies of water

tree line
the area on a mountain above which no trees grow

tributary
a river or stream that flows into a larger river

valley
low land between hills or mountains

volcano
an opening in the earth, through which lava and gases from the earth's interior escape

wetland
a low area saturated with water

Atlas

The World: Political

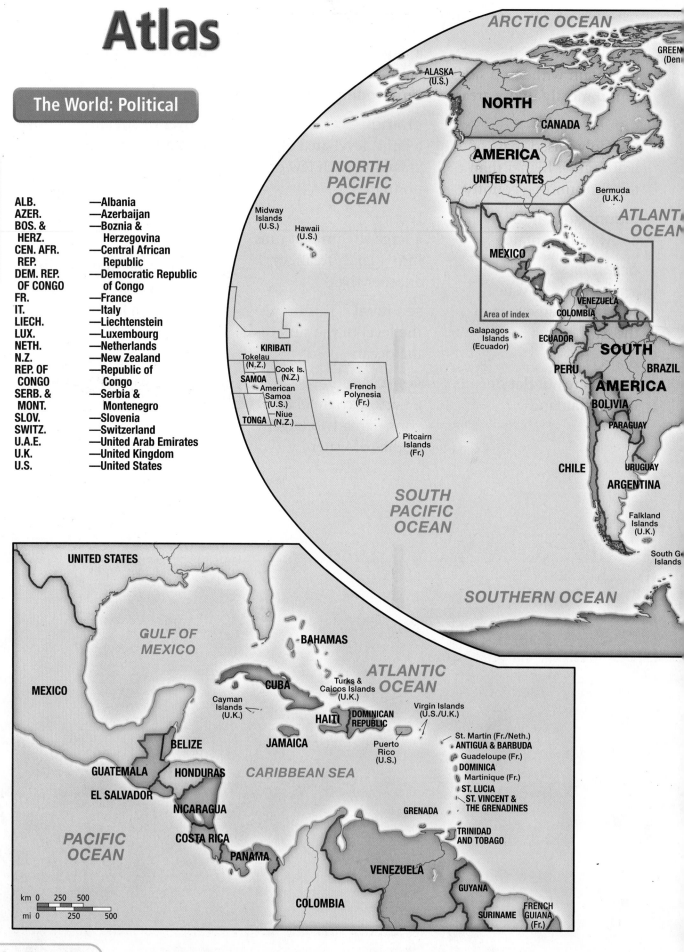

ALB.	—Albania
AZER.	—Azerbaijan
BOS. & HERZ.	—Boznia & Herzegovina
CEN. AFR. REP.	—Central African Republic
DEM. REP. OF CONGO	—Democratic Republic of Congo
FR.	—France
IT.	—Italy
LIECH.	—Liechtenstein
LUX.	—Luxembourg
NETH.	—Netherlands
N.Z.	—New Zealand
REP. OF CONGO	—Republic of Congo
SERB. & MONT.	—Serbia & Montenegro
SLOV.	—Slovenia
SWITZ.	—Switzerland
U.A.E.	—United Arab Emirates
U.K.	—United Kingdom
U.S.	—United States

ARCTIC OCEAN

RUSSIA

ASIA

ICELAND

Area of index

EUROPE

KAZAKHSTAN

MONGOLIA

GEORGIA
ARMENIA
TURKEY
AZER.

UZBEKISTAN
KYRGYZSTAN
TURKMENISTAN
TAJIKISTAN

CHINA

N. KOREA
S. KOREA

JAPAN

PACIFIC
OCEAN

TUNISIA

CYPRUS
LEBANON
ISRAEL

SYRIA
IRAQ
JORDAN

AFGHANISTAN

NEPAL
BHUTAN

TAIWAN

Northern
Mariana
Islands
(U.S.)

MARSHALL
ISLANDS

MOROCCO

IRAN
KUWAIT

PAKISTAN

BANGLADESH

Guam (U.S.)

ALGERIA

LIBYA

EGYPT

QATAR

U. A. E.

INDIA

MYANMAR

FEDERATED STATES
OF MICRONESIA

WESTERN
SAHARA
(Morocco)

SAUDI
ARABIA

LAOS

THAILAND

VIETNAM

PHILIPPINES

PALAU

KIRIBATI

MAURITANIA

MALI

AFRICA

NIGER

CHAD

OMAN

ERITREA

YEMEN

DJIBOUTI

SRI LANKA

CAMBODIA

BRUNEI

NAURU

SENEGAL
GAMBIA
GUINEA BISSAU
GUINEA
SIERRA
LEONE
LIBERIA

BURKINA
FASO

NIGERIA

GHANA
TOGO
BENIN

SUDAN

CEN.AFR.
REP.

ETHIOPIA

SOMALIA

MALDIVES

MALAYSIA

SINGAPORE

PAPUA
NEW
GUINEA

SOLOMON
ISLANDS

TUVALU

IVORY
COAST

CAMEROON

UGANDA

KENYA

EQU.
GUINEA

SAO TOME
AND PRINCIPE

GABON

DEM.
REP.
OF
CONGO

RWANDA
BURUNDI

TANZANIA

INDONESIA

EAST
TIMOR

VANUATU

New
Caledonia
(Fr.)

FIJI

ANGOLA

ZAMBIA

MALAWI

COMOROS

INDIAN
OCEAN

AUSTRALIA

MOZAMBIQUE

ZIMBABWE

MADAGASCAR

MAURITIUS
Reunion
(Fr.)

NAMIBIA

BOTSWANA

SWAZILAND
LESOTHO

SOUTH AFRICA

km 0   1000   2000

mi 0   1000   2000

NEW
ZEALAND

ATLANTIC
OCEAN

SOUTHERN OCEAN

ANTARCTICA

FINLAND

SWEDEN

RUSSIA

NORWAY

ESTONIA

LATVIA
LITHUANIA

km 0   150 300

mi 0   150   300

NORTH
SEA

DENMARK

RUSSIA

BELARUS

IRELAND

UNITED
KINGDOM

NETH.

GERMANY

POLAND

BELGIUM

LUX.

CZECH
REPUBLIC

UKRAINE

ATLANTIC
OCEAN

FRANCE

LIECH.

SWITZ.

AUSTRIA

SLOVAKIA

HUNGARY

MOLDOVA

MONACO

SAN
MARINO

SLOV.
CROATIA
BOS. &
HERZ.

SERB. &
MONT.

ROMANIA

PORTUGAL

ANDORRA

Corsica
(Fr.)

Sardinia
(It.)

ITALY

MACEDONIA
ALB.

BULGARIA

GREECE

SPAIN

Balearic
Islands

TURKEY

GIBRALTAR
(U.K.)

Sicily (It.)

MEDITERRANEAN SEA

MOROCCO

ALGERIA

TUNISIA

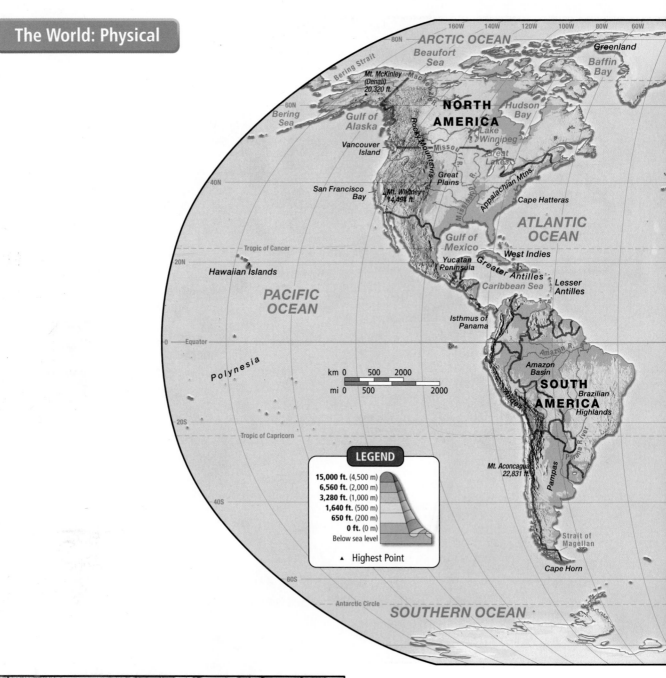

Atlas

LEGEND

15,000 ft. (4,500 m)
6,560 ft. (2,000 m)
3,280 ft. (1,000 m)
1,640 ft. (500 m)
650 ft. (200 m)
0 ft. (0 m)
Below sea level

▲ Highest Point

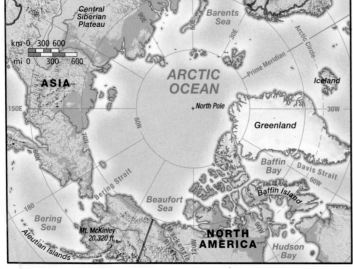

Main Map Labels

ARCTIC OCEAN

Barents Sea

Arctic Circle

EUROPE

North Sea

Northern European Plain

ASIA

Central Siberian Plateau

Ob River

Yenisey River

Volga R.

Danube

Alps

Pyrenees

Atlas Mtns.

Black Sea

Mediterranean Sea

Mt. Elbrus 18,510 ft.

Caucasus Mountains

Aral Sea

Caspian Sea

Gobi Desert

Amur River

Lake Baikal

Sea of Okhotsk

Kamchatka Peninsula

Sea of Japan

PACIFIC OCEAN

40N

Plateau of Tibet

Himalaya Mountains

Mt. Everest 29,035 ft.

Ganges River

East China Sea

Tropic of Cancer

20N

SAHARA

SAHEL

Niger River

Nile River

AFRICA

Arabian Sea

Bay of Bengal

South China Sea

Philippine Islands

Micronesia

Congo River

Lake Victoria

Mt. Kilimanjaro 19,340 ft.

Great Rift Valley

Sumatra

Borneo

New Guinea

Melanesia

Equator 0

Java

Strait of Sunda

INDIAN OCEAN

Madagascar

Great Sandy Desert

Coral Sea

20S

Kalahari Desert

Tropic of Capricorn

AUSTRALIA

Nullarbor Plain

Darling River

Tasman Sea

ATLANTIC OCEAN

Cape of Good Hope

Mt. Kosciusko 7,310 ft.

North Island

South Island

SOUTHERN OCEAN

60S

Antarctic Circle

ANTARCTICA

Inset Map (Antarctica)

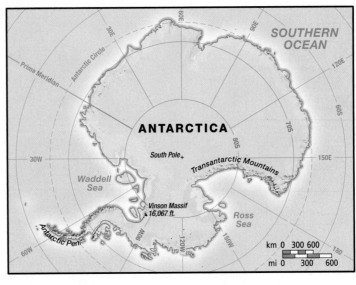

SOUTHERN OCEAN

Prime Meridian

Antarctic Circle

60E

30E

90E

120E

ANTARCTICA

South Pole +

Transantarctic Mountains

70S

80S

60S

150E

30W

Waddell Sea

Vinson Massif 16,067 ft.

Ross Sea

Antarctic Pen.

60W

90W

120W

150W

180

km 0 300 600

mi 0 300 600

Western Hemisphere: Political

ARCTIC
OCEAN

Beaufort
Sea

GREENLAN
(DENMARK

Alaska
(U.S.)

140°W

60°N

Hudson
Bay

Labrador
Sea

CANADA

Great
Lakes

Ottawa

40°N

Great
Salt
Lake

UNITED STATES

Washington, D.C.

ATLANTIC
OCEAN

Gulf of
Mexico

BAHAMAS

Havana

Tropic of Cancer

Hawaii (U.S.)

MEXICO

CUBA

HAITI

DOMINICAN REPUBLIC

PUERTO RICO (U.S.)

Mexico City

Kingston

U.S. VIRGIN ISLANDS

BELIZE

ST. KITTS AND NEVIS

GUATEMALA

Belmopan

Santo
Domingo

JAMAICA

Guatemala City

Tegucigalpa

Port-Au-
Prince

ST. LUCIA

EL SALVADOR

BARBADOS

San Salvador

Managua

San José

GRENADA

HONDURAS

PACIFIC
OCEAN

NICARAGUA

Panama
City

Caracas

COSTA RICA

Georgetown

VENEZUELA

Paramaribo

PANAMA

Cayenne

Bogotá

FRENCH GUIA

COLOMBIA

SURINAME

(FRANCE)

0°

Equator

GUYANA

Galápagos Is.
(Ecuador)

ECUADOR

Quito

Lima

BRAZIL

PERU

La Paz

Brasilia

French Polynesia
(France)

BOLIVIA

Sucre

20°S

Tropic of Capricorn

PARAGUAY

CHILE

Asunción

N

W   E

S

URUGUAY

Santiago

Buenos Aires

Montevideo

ARGENTINA

40°S

Falkland Islands
(U.K.)

LEGEND

⊛   National capital

———   National border

km 0   500   1000

mi 0   500   1000

South Georgi
(U.K.)

60°S

140°W   120°W   100°W   80°W   60°W

Western Hemisphere: Physical

GREENLAND

ARCTIC
OCEAN

Beaufort
Sea

Baffin
Bay

Davis
Strait

Bering
Strait

Yukon R.

Mackenzie R.

Mt. McKinley (Denali)
20,320 ft.
(6,194 m)

Gulf of
Alaska

Hudson
Bay

Labrador
Sea

Bering
Sea

Coast Mountains

ROCKY MOUNTAINS

CANADIAN SHIELD

NORTH AMERICA

Great
Lakes

APPALACHIAN MOUNTAINS

Coast Ranges

Great
Salt Lake

Missouri R.

Mississippi R.

GREAT
PLAINS

Range
and Basin

Death Valley
-282 ft.
(-86 m)

Mt. Whitney
14,495 ft.
(4,418 m)

Rio Grande

Coastal Plain

ATLANTIC
OCEAN

Gulf of
Mexico

Bahamas

Cuba

Hispaniola

Puerto Rico

Tropic of Cancer

Hawaiian
Islands

Caribbean
Sea

PACIFIC
OCEAN

Lake
Nicaragua

Lake
Maracaibo

Line
Islands

Equator

Galápagos
Islands

Amazon R.

AMAZON
BASIN

Marquesas

SOUTH
AMERICA

Society
Islands

Cook
Islands

Tropic of Capricorn

Atacama
Desert

Mt. Aconcagua
22,834 ft.
(6,960 m)

Rio de la Plata

LEGEND

15,000 ft. (4,500 m)
6,560 ft. (2,000 m)
3,280 ft. (1,000 m)
1,640 ft. (500 m)
650 ft. (200 m)
0 ft. (0 m)
Below sea level

▲ Highest Point

Valdés Peninsula
-131 ft.
(-40 m)

Falkland
Islands

km 0   500   1000

mi 0   500   1000

Strait of
Magellan

South
Georgia

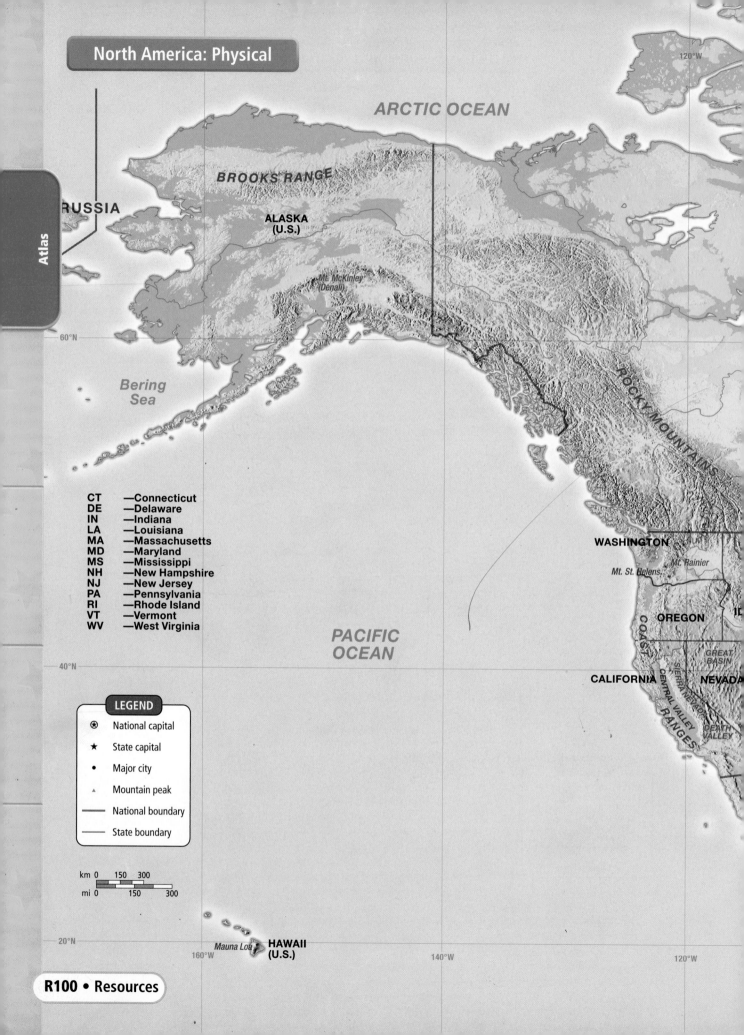

ARCTIC OCEAN

BROOKS RANGE

RUSSIA

ALASKA
(U.S.)

Mt. McKinley
(Denali)

60°N

Bering
Sea

ROCKY MOUNTAINS

CT —Connecticut
DE —Delaware
IN —Indiana
LA —Louisiana
MA —Massachusetts
MD —Maryland
MS —Mississippi
NH —New Hampshire
NJ —New Jersey
PA —Pennsylvania
RI —Rhode Island
VT —Vermont
WV —West Virginia

WASHINGTON

Mt. Rainier

Mt. St. Helens

OREGON

ID

PACIFIC
OCEAN

GREAT
BASIN

40°N

CALIFORNIA

NEVADA

CENTRAL VALLEY

SIERRA NEVADA

COAST RANGES

DEATH
VALLEY

LEGEND

⊗ National capital
★ State capital
• Major city
▲ Mountain peak
— National boundary
— State boundary

km 0   150   300
mi 0   150   300

HAWAII
(U.S.)

Mauna Loa

160°W

140°W

120°W

20°N

GREENLAND
(Denmark)

Baffin
Bay

Labrador
Sea

60°W

60°N

Hudson
Bay

C A N A D A

Lake
Winnipeg

St. Lawrence River

Great
Lakes

MINNESOTA

MONTANA   NORTH DAKOTA

MAINE

MICHIGAN

SOUTH DAKOTA

WISCONSIN

Ottawa

NEW
YORK   VT   Mt. Washington

WYOMING

Missouri River

NEBRASKA   IOWA

NH

MA

CT   RI

ROCKY MOUNTAINS

GREAT PLAINS

Pike's Peak

ILLINOIS   IN

OHIO

PA

NJ

COLORADO   KANSAS

CENTRAL
PLAINS

Ohio River

WV   MD   DE

40°N

Washington, D.C.

GRAND
CANYON

MISSOURI

Arkansas River

KENTUCKY

VIRGINIA

ONA

ARKANSAS   TENNESSEE

NORTH CAROLINA

APPALACHIAN MOUNTAINS

NEW
MEXICO

OKLAHOMA

Mississippi River

SOUTH
CAROLINA

MS

ALABAMA

GEORGIA

TEXAS   LA

GULF COASTAL PLAIN

ATLANTIC
OCEAN

MEXICO

Rio Grande

SIERRA MADRE OCCIDENTAL

SIERRA MADRE ORIENTAL

FLORIDA

Gulf of
Mexico

B A H A M A S

Havana

C U B A

PUERTO RICO
(U.S.)

Mexico City

80°W

60°W

20°N

100°W

80°W

60°W

United States: Political

ALASKA (inset)

ARCTIC OCEAN

RUSSIA

ALASKA

CANADA

Yukon R.

Fairbanks

Anchorage

Juneau ★

PACIFIC OCEAN

Aleutian Islands

km 0 250 500
mi 0 250 500

N
W   E
S

Main Map

WASHINGTON

Seattle
★ Olympia

Portland

Columbia R.

★ Salem

OREGON

IDAHO

Helena ★   MONTANA

Billings

★ Boise

Pocatello

Snake R.

WYOMING

Casper

Reno
★ Carson City

Salt Lake City ★
Provo

Cheyenne

Sacramento ★

NEVADA

UTAH

COLORADO

Denver ★

San Francisco

Colorado Springs

Pueblo

PACIFIC OCEAN

CALIFORNIA

Las Vegas

Colorado R.

Los Angeles

ARIZONA

Santa Fe ★
Albuquerque

San Diego

★ Phoenix

NEW MEXICO

Tucson

El Paso

Rio Grande

LEGEND

⊛ National capital

★ State capital

• Major city

— National boundary

— State boundary

Gulf of California

MEXICO

HAWAII (inset)

Kauai

Niihau

HAWAII

Oahu   Kailua
Molokai
Honolulu   Lanai   Maui
Kahoolawe

PACIFIC OCEAN

Hilo
Hawaii

km 0 50 100
mi 0 50 100

CANADA

St. Lawrence R.

NORTH DAKOTA
Bismarck • • Fargo

MINNESOTA

SOUTH DAKOTA
Pierre ★
Minneapolis • ★ St. Paul

• Sioux Falls

IOWA
Cedar Rapids •

NEBRASKA
• Omaha ★ Des Moines
Lincoln ★

KANSAS
Kansas City
Topeka ★ • Kansas City
★ Jefferson City

MISSOURI

OKLAHOMA
• Tulsa
Oklahoma ★ • City
Fort Smith •

ARKANSAS
Little ★ Rock

TEXAS
• Dallas

Austin ★
Houston •
• San Antonio

Baton Rouge ★

LOUISIANA
New Orleans •

MISSISSIPPI
Jackson ★

Mobile •

L. Superior

WISCONSIN
Madison ★
• Milwaukee

MICHIGAN
Grand Rapids •
Lansing ★
L. Michigan
L. Huron

Chicago •

ILLINOIS
Springfield ★

INDIANA
Indianapolis ★

St. Louis •

Louisville •
Frankfort ★

KENTUCKY

Ohio R.

Nashville ★

TENNESSEE
Memphis •

Birmingham •

Montgomery ★

ALABAMA
Tallahassee ★

Detroit •
L. Erie

Cleveland •

OHIO
Columbus ★

Cincinnati •

WEST VIRGINIA
Charleston ★

L. Ontario

Rochester •

Buffalo •

NEW YORK
Albany ★

PENNSYLVANIA
Harrisburg ★
Pittsburgh •

Baltimore •

Richmond ★

VIRGINIA
Norfolk •

Greensboro •
Raleigh ★

NORTH CAROLINA

Columbia •

SOUTH CAROLINA
Charleston •

GEORGIA
Atlanta ★
Savannah •

NEW HAMPSHIRE
VERMONT
Montpelier ★
Burlington •

Concord ★
• Manchester

MAINE
Augusta ★
• Portland

Boston ★

MASSACHUSETTS
Hartford ★ Providence ★

New Haven • **RHODE ISLAND**
CONNECTICUT

Newark • • New York

Trenton ★
Philadelphia •
Dover ★ **NEW JERSEY**
DELAWARE

Annapolis ★
⊛ Washington, D.C.

MARYLAND

ATLANTIC OCEAN

Jacksonville •

FLORIDA
Tampa •

Gulf of Mexico

Miami •

BAHAMAS

km 0 100 200 300 400 500
mi 0   100   200   300   400   500

CUBA

R103

United States: Physical

ARCTIC OCEAN

RUSSIA

Brooks Range

Bering Strait

Yukon R.

CANADA

Mt. McKinley
(Denali)
20,320 ft. ▲

Alaska Range

Bering
Sea

Gulf of
Alaska

70°N

60°N

170°W

160°W

150°W

140°W

Aleutian
Islands

Kodiak Is.

km 0   250   500
mi 0   250   500

110°W

Mt. Rainier
14,410 ft.

COLUMBIA PLATEAU

Columbia R.

Mt. Hood
11,239 ft.

BITTERROOT RANGE

Missouri

River

Yellowstone River

C O A S T

C A S C A D E   R A N G E

Mt. Shasta
14,162 ft.

Snake River

ROCKY

BIGHORN MTNS.

G R E A T

Black
Hills

Badlands

35°N

Sacramento R.

S I E R R A

N E V A D A

CENTRAL
VALLEY

San Joaquin R.

BASIN
AND
RANGE

WASATCH RANGE

Green

M O U N T A I N S

Pikes Peak
14,110 ft.

San Francisco
Bay

R A N G E S

Mt. Whitney
14,494 ft. ▲

Death Valley
282ft. below sea level

Colorado River

Painted
Desert

Colorado
Plateau

SANGRE DE
CRISTO MTNS.

PACIFIC
OCEAN

Mojave
Desert

Grand
Canyon

Channel Islands

30°N

Gila River

CONTINENTAL DIVIDE

Llano
Estacado

LEGEND

15,000 ft. (4,500 m)
6,560 ft. (2,000 m)
3,280 ft. (1,000 m)
1,640 ft. (500 m)
650 ft. (200 m)
0 ft. (0 m)
Below sea level

▲ Mountain Peak

Sonoran
Desert

Rio Grande

Pecos

25°N

160°W

155°W

Kauai

Niihau

Oahu

Molokai

Lanai

Maui

Kahoolawe

Hawaii

Mauna Kea
13,796 ft.

20°N

PACIFIC OCEAN

Mauna Loa
13,678 ft.

Tropic of Cancer

Gulf of California

MEXICO

km 0   50   100
mi 0   50   100

115°W

110°W

105°W

CANADA

Mesabi Range

Lake Superior

Lake Michigan

Lake Huron

Lake Erie

St. Lawrence River

Mt. Washington 6,288 ft. ▲
White Mtns.

L. Ontario

Adirondack Mountains

Catskill Mtns.

Hudson R.

Connecticut R.

Nantucket
Martha's Vineyard

Long Island

ALLEGHENY PLATEAU

APPALACHIAN MOUNTAINS

Delaware River

Susquehanna River

Delaware Bay

Chesapeake Bay

Sand Hills

Missouri River

Des Moines River

Mississippi River

Platte River

CENTRAL PLAINS

Ohio R.

Wabash River

OZARK PLATEAU

Arkansas River

Mt. Mitchell 6,684 ft.

Cumberland Plateau

Tennessee R.

BLUE RIDGE MOUNTAINS

FALL LINE

ATLANTIC COASTAL PLAIN

35°N

OUACHITA MOUNTAINS

Red River

Mississippi River

Tombigbee R.

Savannah River

Oconee R.

Chattahoochee River

ATLANTIC OCEAN

Sabine River

Pearl

Alabama

Altamaha R.

30°N

Brazos River

Colorado River

COASTAL PLAIN

GULF

Galveston Bay

Mobile Bay

Pensacola Bay

Tampa Bay

Gulf of Mexico

Everglades

BAHAMAS

25°N

Florida Keys

km 0   100 200 300 400 500
mi 0   100   200   300   400   500

Tropic of Cancer

CUBA

95°W   90°W   85°W   75°W

Glossary

Words in red have been selected as important for Ohio fifth graders to learn.
They will help you do well on the Ohio Achievement Test.

abolition (ab uh LIH shuhn) the act of ending something. (p. 141)

abolitionist (ab uh LIH shuhn ist) someone who joined the movement to abolish, or end, slavery. (p. 240)

absolute location (AB suh loot loh KAY shuhn) the location of a point on the Earth's surface as measured by latitude and longitude. (p. 72)

activist (AK tuh vihst) a person who takes action to change social conditions or laws. (p. 250)

adapt (uh DAPT) to change in order to better fit the environment. (p. 63)

agriculture (AG rih kuhl chur) farming, or growing plants. (p. 111)

amendment (uh MEND muhnt) a change to the Constitution. (p. 165)

artifact (AHR tih fakt) an object such as a tool or article of clothing that provides information about a culture.

barter (BAHR tur) the trade of goods and services for other goods and services without the use of money.

bay (bay) a body of water partly surrounded by land but open to the sea. (p. 50)

benefit (BEHN uh fiht) that which is received as an improvement or advantage as the result of a decision.

boomtown (BOOM town) a town whose population booms, or grows very quickly. (p. 206)

braceros (bruh SAIR ohs) laborers invited to work in the United States. (p. 223)

cape (kayp) a point of land that sticks out into the water. (p. 49)

capital good (KAP ih til guhd) a productive resource consisting of human-made materials needed to produce goods and services, including buildings, machinery, equipment, and tools. (p. 56)

capital resources (KAP ih til REE sor sihz) the tools, machines, buildings, and other equipment that a business uses. (p. 56)

cardinal directions (KAR din uhl dih REHK shuhns) the four main points of the compass (north, east, south, and west).

cash crop (kash krahp) a crop that people grow and sell to earn money. (p. 131)

caucus (KAW kuhs) a group of people who join together to make political decisions. (p. 264)

century (SEHN chuh ree) a period of 100 years. (p. 58)

checks and balances (chehks uhnd BAHL uhns ehz) a system that lets each branch of government limit the power of the other two. (p. 164)

civil rights (SIHV uhl ryts) the rights and freedoms people have because they are citizens of a country. (p. 254)

coast (kohst) the land that borders an ocean. (p. 48)

coastal plain (KOHST uhl playn) the flat, level land along a coast. (p. 48)

colony (KAHL uh nee) a territory ruled by another country. (p. 125)

Columbian Exchange (kuh LUHM bee uhn ihks CHAYNJ) the movement of goods between the Western and Eastern hemispheres after Columbus's first trip to the Americas. (p. 121)

command economy (KUH mahnd ih KAHN uh mee) an economic system in which all decisions on production and consumption are made by a central government. (p. 54)

compass rose (KUHM puhs rohz) an element of a map used to show direction, usually cardinal directions and frequently intermediate directions.

competition (kahm puh TIHSH uhn) when businesses that sell similar goods and services try to attract the most consumers. (p. 33)

congress (KAHNG grihs) an official gathering of people to make decisions. (p. 152)

consequence (KAHN sih kwehns) a result of a decision or an action. (p. 36)

conservation (kahn sur VAY shuhn) the protection and wise use of natural resources. (p. 10)

constitution (kahn stih TOO shuhn) a written plan for government. (p. 162)

consumer (kuhn SOO mur) a person who buys and uses goods and services. (p. 67)

consumption (kuhn SUHM shuhn) the purchase and/or use of goods and services.

convention (kahn VEHN shuhn) a formal meeting of members of a group. (p. 241)

convert (kahn VURT) to change a religion or a belief. (p. 125)

coordinate (koh ORD ih niht) one of a set of numbers used to describe a location.

cost (kahst) an alternative given up as the result of a decision.

country (KUHN tree) a unit of political space; the entire land area of a nation or state.

credibility (krehd uh BIL ih tee) the quality or state of offering reasonable grounds for being believed.

criteria (kry TEER ee uh) guidelines to evaluate whether a decision was effective. (p. 36)

cultural institution (KUHL chur uhl ihn stih TOO shuhn) an established custom, practice, or relationship of importance in a society.

cultural practice (KUHL chur uhl PRAK tihs) a pattern of behavior accepted by a society.

cultural product (KUHL chur uhl PRAH duhkt) an object, such as a painting, a cathedral, a mosque, a book, or tool, or something such as an oral tale, a dance, a sacred ritual, or a system of education produced by a cultural group.

culture (KUHL chur) learned behavior of a group of people, which includes their belief systems and languages, their social relationships, their institutions and organizations, and their material goods such as food, clothing, buildings, tools, and machines. (p. 111)

dam (dam) a barrier built across a waterway to control the flow and level of water. (p. 66)

data (DAY tuh) information such as facts or numbers. (p. 138)

decade (DEHK ayd) a period of 10 years. (p. 58)

delta (DEHL tuh) a triangle-shaped area at the mouth of a river. (p. 61)

demand (dih MAHND) the amount of a good or service that consumers are willing and able to buy at various prices. (p. 32)

democracy (dih MAHK ruh see) a system of government in which political control is exercised by the people, either directly or through their elected representatives. (p. 162)

dictatorship (dihk TAY tur shihp) a system of government in which leaders rule by force and are not held responsible to the will of the people.

direction indicator (duh REHK shuhn ihn dih KAY tur) an element of a map used to show direction, usually labeling north and frequently all cardinal directions.

discrimination (dih skrihm uh NAY shuhn) the unfair treatment of particular groups. (p. 262)

division of labor (dih VIHZH uhn uhv LAY bur) the separation of the total work required to produce a good or service into individual interrelated tasks. (p. 199)

doctrine (DAHK trihn) an official statement or position. (p. 190)

Earth-Sun relationship (urth sun ree LAY shuhn shihp) the position of Earth relative to the sun that helps to determine day and night, seasons, climate, and time zones. (p. 20)

economic system (ehk uh NAHM ihk SIHS tuhm) a set of ideas that guides how a country will use its resources and produce its goods. (p. 30)

economy (ih KAHN uh mee) the system people use to produce goods and services. (p. 18)

ecosystem (EE koh sihs tuhm) a community of plants and animals, along with the surrounding soil, air, and water. (p. 29)

editorial (ehd ih TOHR ee uhl) a piece of writing that presents an opinion about an issue or event. (p. 284)

empire (EHM pyr) a group of nations or territories ruled by a single government or leader. (p. 124)

entrepreneur (ahn truh pruh NUR) an individual who uses productive resources and often takes risks to start a business. (p. 198)

entrepreneurship (ahn truh pruh NUR shihp) the organization of productive resources by a person willing to take risks to start a business. (p. 56)

environment (ehn VY ruhn muhnt) the surroundings in which people, plants, and animals live. (p. 27)

erosion (ih ROH zhuhn) the process by which water and wind wear away the land. (p. 28)

ethnic group (EHTH nihk groop) a group of people who share a language or culture. (p. 220)

expedition (ehk spih DIHSH uhn) a journey with an important goal. (p. 119)

famine (FAM ihn) a widespread shortage of food. (p. 217)

flow resource (floh REE sawrs) a resource that is neither renewable nor nonrenewable, but must be used when or where it occurs, such as running water, wind, or sunlight. (p. 7)

forty-niner (FAWR tee NY nur) a miner who went to California in 1849. (p. 206)

free state (free stayt) a state that did not permit slavery. (p. 144)

frontier (fruhn TEER) the edge of a country or settled region. (p. 187)

 G

geothermal (jee oh THUR muhl) related to heat from beneath Earth's crust. (p. 93)

gold rush (gohld ruhsh) when many people hurry to the same area to look for gold. (p. 206)

goods (guhds) objects that are capable of satisfying people's wants.

graphic organizers (GRAF ihk or gahn EYE zuhrz) shapes and pictures, such as flow charts, webs, Venn diagrams, and T-charts, used to organize information.

 H

heritage (HEHR ih tihj) something that is handed down from one generation to the next. (p. 288)

human characteristic/feature (HYOO muhn kair uhk tuhr RIHS tihk/FEE chur) an aspect of a place built by people, including cities, parks, buildings, and roads.

human resources (HYOO muhn REE sor sihz) a productive resource consisting of the talents, knowledge, intelligence, and skills of human beings that contribute to the production of goods and services. (p. 56)

hydroelectric power (hy droh ih LEHK trihk POW er) electricity produced from flowing water. (p. 94)

 I

immigrant (IHM ih gruhnt) a person who moves to another country to live. (p. 216)

independence (ihn duh PEHN duhns) freedom from being ruled by someone else. (p. 153)

inference (IHN fuh rehns) an idea that is not directly stated. (p. 228)

interchangeable parts (ihn tur CHAYN juh buhl pahrts) parts made by a machine to be exactly the same in size and shape. (p. 199)

interdependence (ihn tuhr dee PEHN duhns) depending, or relying, on each other. (p. 19)

interior (ihn TEER ee ur) a place away from a coast or border. (p. 61)

intermediate direction (ihn tur MEE dee iht dih REHK shuhn) the points of the compass that fall between north and east, north and west, south and east, and south and west, such as northeast, northwest, southeast, and southwest.

interpreter (ihn TUR prih tur) someone who explains what is said in one language to people who speak a different language. (p. 188)

irrigation (ihr ih GAY shuhn) supplying land with water. (p. 94)

 L

latitude lines (LAT ih tood lynz) imaginary lines drawn from east to west on a map or globe. (p. 72)

levee (LEHV ee) a high river bank that stops the river from overflowing. (p. 79)

line graph (lyn graf) a graph that shows changes in data over time. (p. 138)

location (loh KAY shuhn) the position of a point on Earth's surface expressed by means of a grid (absolute) or in relation to the position of other places (relative).

lock (lahk) a part of a waterway that is closed off by gates. (p. 79)

longitude lines (LAHN jih tood lynz) imaginary lines drawn north to south on a map or a globe. (p. 72)

Loyalist (LOI uh lihst) someone who was still loyal to the king and believed Britain should rule the colonies. (p. 156)

manufacturer (man yuh FAK chuhr ur) a person or company that uses machines to make goods. (p. 263)

map element (map EHL ih mehnt) a part of a map, such as a compass rose, legend, or scale.

maquiladora (mah keel ah DOH rah) a factory in Mexico near the United States border. (p. 280)

market (MAHR kit) the interaction of buyers and sellers exchanging goods or services.

market economy (MAHR kit ih KAHN uh mee) an economic system in which decisions on production and consumption are made by individuals acting as buyers and sellers. (p. 54)

mass production (mas pruh DUHK shuhn) making many identical products at once. (p. 199)

merchant (MUR chunt) someone who buys and sells goods to earn money. (p. 118)

meridian (muh RIHD ee uhn) a line of longitude that runs north and south and measures distances east and west of the prime meridian. (p. 72)

migrant worker (MY gruhnt WUR kuhr) person who moves from place to place to find work, mostly on farms. (p. 258)

migration (my GRAY shuhn) movement from one region to another. (p. 110)

minerals (MIHN ur uls) natural substances that lie deep in the ground. (p. 85)

mission (MIHSH uhn) a religious community where priests taught Christianity. (p. 125)

monarchy (MAWHN ahr kee) a system of government headed by a monarch, such as a king, queen, shah, or sultan whose position is usually inherited.

motto (MAHT oh) a short statement that explains an ideal or goal. (p. 289)

nation (NAY shuhn) a group of people bound together by a strong sense of shared values and cultural characteristics, including language, religion, and common history.

national park (NAHSH uh nul pahrk) an area set aside by the federal government for recreational or other uses. (p. 97)

natural resource (NACH ur uhl REE sawrs) a productive resource supplied by nature that people use, such as ores, water, trees, or arable land. (p. 6)

naturalization (nach ur uh lihz AY shuhn) the legal process of becoming a citizen by learning the laws of the country and the rights and duties of its citizens. (p. 268)

navigation (nav ih GAY shuhn) the science of planning and controlling the direction of a ship. (p. 119)

neutral (NOO truhl) not taking sides. (p. 156)

news article (nooz AHR tih kuhl) a piece of writing that describes a recent event. (p. 284)

nonrenewable resource (nahn rih NOO uh buhl REE sawrs) a finite natural resource, such as petroleum or minerals, that cannot be replaced once it is used. (p. 7)

nonviolent protest (nahn VY uh luhnt PROH test) a way of bringing change without using violence. (p. 255)

opportunity cost (ahp ur TOO nih tee kahst) the value of the next best alternative given up when a choice is made. (p. 10)

outline (OWT lyn) text that identifies the main ideas and supporting details of a piece of writing. (p. 196)

parallels (PAR uh lehlz) lines of latitude that run east and west and measure distances north and south of the equator. (p. 72)

Patriot (PAY tree uht) a colonist who wanted independence from Britain. (p. 156)

peninsula (puh NIHN suh luh) a piece of land surrounded by water on three sides. (p. 61)

persecution (pur sih KYOO shuhn) unfair treatment that causes suffering. (p. 218)

perspective (pur SPEHK tihv) a specific point of view that affects the way events are understood or evaluated. (p. 166)

physical characteristic/feature (FIHZ ih kuhl kair uhk tuhr IHS tihk/FEE chur) a natural aspect of a place, such as land formations and vegetation zones.

physical map (FIHZ ih kuhl map) a portrayal on a flat surface of the physical features of the earth, such as landforms and elevations.

pictograph (PIHK toh graf) a diagram or graph that uses pictures to convey information.

pioneer (py uh NEER) one of the first of a group of people to enter or settle a region. (p. 187)

place (plays) a location having distinctive characteristics which give it meaning and character, and distinguish it from other locations.

plantation (plan TAY shuhn) a large farm on which crops are raised by workers who live there. (p. 134)

plaza (PLAH zuh) an open square. (p. 280)

point of view (point uhv vyoo) the way someone thinks about an issue, an event, or a person. (p. 166)

political map (puh LIHT ih kuhl map) a portrayal on a flat surface of the political features of the earth, such as international boundaries, capitals, and political subdivisions.

pollution (puh LOO shuhn) anything that makes the soil, air, or water dirty and unhealthy. (p. 28)

prairie (PRAYR ee) a dry, mostly flat grassland with few trees. (p. 78)

prejudice (PREHJ uh dihs) an unfair, negative opinion that can lead to unjust treatment. (p. 250)

primary source (PRY mehr ee sors) an account of an event by someone who was present at the event. (p. 90)

producer (pruh DOO sur) a person who makes goods and services. (p. 67)

product (PRAH duhkt) something produced by human or mechanical effort or by a natural process.

production (pruh DUHK shuhn) the act of combining natural resources, human resources, capital goods, and entrepreneurship to make goods and services.

productive capacity (pruh DUHK tihv cuh PAS ih tee) the maximum output that an economy can produce without big increases in inflation. (p. 202)

productive resources (pruh DUHK tihv REE sawrs ehz) the resources used to make goods and services, including natural resources, human resources, capital goods. (p. 56)

productivity (proh duhk TIHV ih tee) the amount of goods and services produced in a certain amount of time by a person, machine, or group. (p. 199)

profit (PRAHF iht) in a market economy, the money left over after a business pays its expenses. (p. 54)

proprietor (pruh PRY ih tur) a person who owned and controlled all the land of a colony. (p. 133)

province (PRAHV ihns) a political region of a country that is similar to a state. (p. 276)

pull factor (puhl FAK tur) a social, political, economic, or environmental attraction that draws people to a new area. (p. 27)

push factor (puhsh FAK tur) a social, political, economic, or environmental force that drives people away from an area. (p. 27)

Q

quota (KWOH tuh) the maximum number of people allowed to enter a country. (p. 222)

R

region (REE jehn) an area with one or more common characteristics or features that make it different from surrounding areas. (p. 16)

refugee (REHF yoo jee) a person who has left his or her home country to escape danger. (p. 224)

relative location (REHL uh tihv loh KAY shuhn) the location of a place in relation to other places.

reliability (ree ly uh BIHL ih tee) the degree to which something or someone is trustworthy or can be depended upon.

renewable resource (rih NOO uh buhl REE sawrs) a natural resource, such as fish or timber, that can be replaced if used carefully. (p. 7)

research (rih SURCH) the search for facts. (p. 246)

responsibility (rih spahn suh BIHL ih tee) a task that a person has a duty to perform. (p. 269)

revolution (rehv uh LOO shuhn) an overthrow, or a forced change, of a government. (p. 152)

rights (ryts) freedoms that belong to a person by law, nature, or tradition. (p. 153)

S

scale (skayl) the relationship between a measurement on a map and Earth's surface.

scarcity (SKAIR sih tee) the lack of sufficient resources to produce all the goods and services that people desire. (p. 10)

secondary source (SEHK uhn dehr ee sors) an account of an event by someone who was not present at the event. (p. 90)

selective service (suh LEHK tihv SUHR vihs) a registry for possible military draft. (p. 269)

self-government (sehlf GUHV urn muhnt) a form of government in which the people who live in a place make laws for themselves. (p. 135)

service (SUR vihs) actions by a person or company to satisfy people's wants. (p. 86)

specialization (spehsh uh lih ZAY shuhn) the production of the goods and services that people are best able to produce with the resources they have. (p. 18)

spiritual (SPIHR ih choo uhl) an African American religious folk song. (p. 144)

suffrage (SUHF rihj) the right to vote. (p. 190)

suffragist (SUHF ruh jihst) a person who worked for the right to vote. (p. 249)

summary (SUHM uh ree) a short description of the main points in a piece of writing. (p. 116)

supply (suh PLY) the amount of a good or service that producers are willing and able to provide at various prices. (p. 32)

tariff (TAR ihf) a tax on imported goods. (p. 278)

tax (taks) money that people pay to their government in return for services. (p. 150)

tenement (TEHN uh muhnt) a rundown, poorly maintained apartment building. (p. 220)

thematic map (thee MAT ihk map) a portrayal on a flat surface of geographic topic such as migration routes, resource locations, or population densities.

tolerance (TAHL ur uhns) respect for beliefs that are different from one's own. (p. 133)

trade (trayd) buying and selling goods. (p. 19)

trade-off (TRAYD awhf) the sacrifice of one option for another when a decision is made.

treason (TREE zuhn) the crime of fighting against one's own government. (p. 154)

treaty (TREE tee) an official agreement between countries. (p. 159)

tributary (TRIHB yuh tehr ee) a river or stream that flows into another river. (p. 79)

Underground Railroad (UHN dur ground RAYL rohd) a series of escape routes and hiding places to bring slaves out of the South. (p. 242)

veto (VEE toh) to reject a law. (p. 164)

volunteer (vahl uhn TEER) someone who helps other people without being paid. (p. 270)

wages (WAYG es) the money people are paid for work. (p. 99)

wagon train (WAG uhn trayn) a line of covered wagons that moved together. (p. 205)

want (wahnt) a psychological or physical desire that can be fulfilled through the consumption of goods and services.

Glossary

Index

Page numbers with *m* after them refer to maps. Page numbers that are in italics refer to pictures.

Index

Index

Acknowledgments

For each of the selections listed below, grateful acknowledgment is made for permission to excerpt and/or reprint original or copyrighted material, as follows:

Maps
All maps by Spatial Graphics, Inc.

Photography Credits
iv–v © Panoramic Images/Getty Images. vi © Neil Rabinowitz/CORBIS. vii © Jeff Greenberg/PhotoEdit. viii–ix Andrew Sawyer, SunWatch Village/Archaeological Park. x–xi The Granger Collection, New York. xii AP/Wide World Photos. xiii © Joseph Sohm/Visions of America/CORBIS. xiv © Yann Arthus-Bertrand/CORBIS. xv © #539687 Index Stock Imagery, Inc. xviii Brown Brothers. xix The Granger Collection, New York. xx Courtesy of National Constitution Center (Scott Frances, Ltd.). xxi The Granger Collection, New York. xxii (bl) © Richard T. Nowitz/CORBIS. (bc) PhotoDisc/Getty Images. (br) © Jose Fuste Raga/CORBIS. xxiv (bl) © Mike Grandmaison/CORBIS. (bc) © Bohemian Nomad Picturemakers/CORBIS. (br) © Mark Karrass/CORBIS. xxvi (bl) © David Stoecklein/CORBIS. (r) © Krista Kennell/CORBIS. xxviii (bl) © Danny Lehman/CORBIS. (br) © Scott Sinklier/CORBIS. xxx © Joel Bennett/CORBIS. xxxi © Stocktrek Images/Alamy Images. nf–1 © Gunter Marx Photography/CORBIS. 2 (bl) © Gerolf Kalt/zefa/CORBIS. (bc) © Friedmar Damm/CORBIS. (br) © David R. Frazier Photolibrary, Inc./Alamy Images. 3 © William Manning/CORBIS. 4 © E.R. Degginger. 5 (l) © Mark Muench. (r) Alan Kearny/Getty Images. 6 © Jeff Greenberg/Alamy Images. 7 © Robert W. Ginn/Alamy Images. 8 Glen Allison/Getty Images. 10 © Jeff Greenberg/PhotoEdit. 11 © CORBIS. 12 AP/Wide World Photos. 13 (t) © Chad Ehlers/Alamy Images. (b) Greg S. Clark. 16 © Danny Lehman/CORBIS. 18 (tl) © Gunter Marx Photography/CORBIS. (tr) © Charles O'Rear/CORBIS. 20–21 © Daniele Pellegrini/Getty Images. 21 © Michael & Patricia Fogden/CORBIS. 24 (l) Mark E. Gibson/CORBIS. (r) Artbase Inc. 25 (l) Alan Kearny/Getty Images. (r) © Stan Rohrer/Alamy. 26 © Andre Jenny/Alamy. 28 (l) © Rab Harling/Alamy. (r) David R. Frazier. 30 © Stan Rohrer/Alamy. 31 © Andy Sacks/Getty Images. 33 © Blend Images/Alamy. 35 © MedioImages/CORBIS. 44 (bl) Michelle Garrett/CORBIS. (bc) Courtesy of Tennessee Valley Authority. (br) Garry Black/Masterfile. 45 Grant Heilman/Grant Heilman Photography, Inc. 46 (l) Miles Ertman/Masterfile. (r) Mark Richards/PhotoEdit. 47 (l) Ed Bock/CORBIS. (r) Ray Boudreau. 48 Grant Heilman Photography, Inc. 50 Reuters NewMedia, Inc./CORBIS. 51 Joe McDonald/CORBIS. 52 Kenneth Batelman. 53 Rudi Von Briel/PhotoEdit. 54 Elizabeth Hathon/CORBIS. 55 Tony Freeman/PhotoEdit. 56 (bl) Grant Heilman Photography, Inc. (bc) Arthur C. Smith, III/Grant Heilman Photography, Inc. (br) Roy Morsch/CORBIS. (cr) Photodisc/Getty Images. 57 David Young-Wolff/PhotoEdit. 60 J. Brian Alker/Getty Images. 62 Joe Skipper/Reuters NewMedia Inc./CORBIS. 63 Paul Conklin/PhotoEdit. 64 Paula Bronstein/Getty Images. 66 Courtesy of Tennessee Valley Authority. 67 (tr) © Inga Spence/Index Stock Imagery. 67 © LWA-Dann Tardif/CORBIS. 68 JonathonKatnor/Getty Images. 70 Ray Boudreau. 71 Ray Boudreau. 76 (l) Jake Rajs/Getty Images. (r) Myrleen Ferguson Cate/PhotoEdit. 77 (l) James A. Sugar/CORBIS. (r) Mark Richards/PhotoEdit. 78 Garry Black/Masterfile. 81 Steve Harper/Grant Heilman Photography, Inc. 84 © Al Fuchs/NewSports/CORBIS. 86 David Young-Wolff/PhotoEdit. 88–89 Artbase, Inc. 91 Ray Boudreau. 92 (bl) H. Spichtinger/Masterfile. (br) © Jan Stromme/PhotoEdit. 94 (b) Grant Heilman/Grant Heilman Photography, Inc. (br) © Eastcott Mormatiuk/Getty Images. 95 Grant Heilman/Grant Heilman Photography, Inc. 96 David R. Frazier Photolibrary, Inc. 98 Loren Stanow/Getty Images. 99 David H. Smith Photography. 104 Musee National de la Renaissance, Ecouen, France. 105 (tl) The Granger Collection, New York. (bl) Smithsonian Institution, National Numismatic Collection, Douglass Mudd. (tr) Massachusetts Historical Society, Boston, MA, USA/Bridgeman Art Library. (br) Photodisc/Getty Images (digital composite). 106 (bl) © Giraudon/Art Resource, NY. (bc) Time Life Pictures/Getty Images. (br) © Archive Iconografico, S.A./CORBIS. 107 (bl) North Wind Picture Archives. (bc) Photodisc/Getty Images. 108 (bl) Wood Ronsaville Harlin, Inc. (r) Bibliotheque Nationale, Paris, France/Bridgeman Art Library. 109 (l) © Archivo Iconografico, S.A./CORBIS. (r) Wood Ronsaville Harlin, Inc. 113 Cincinnati Art Museum, Gift of General M.F. Force, Photo: T. Walsh. 114 Courtesy of Victor Masayesva, Jr. 115 (tr) Los Alamos National Laboratory, Public Affairs Office. Photo: Leroy Sanchez. (br) Courtesy Leslie Marmon Silko. 118 © Reunion Des Musees Nationaux/Art Resource, NY. 118–119 © Lee Snider/Photo Images/CORBIS. 123 (t) © J. Garcia/photocuisine/CORBIS. (c) © Richard Cummins/CORBIS. (b) The Art Archive/Global Book Publishing. 124 © Archivo Iconografico, S.A./CORBIS. 125 © Jerry Jacka. 128–129 © Owen Franken/CORBIS. 128 © Ilene MacDonald/Alamy. 129 (tl) © SuperStock, Inc/SuperStock. (tr) © Perry Mastrovito/CORBIS. 130 © North Wind Picture Archives. 131 © Brownie Harris. 132–133 American Philosophical Society Library. 134 Metropolitan Museum of Art, Gift of Edgar William and Bernice Chrysler Garbisch, 1963. 136 © Richard T. Nowitz/CORBIS. 137 (c) © #539687 Index Stock Imagery, Inc. (b) Bob Daemmrich/PhotoEdit Inc. 140–141 © Joseph Sohm: Visions of America/CORBIS. 141 Colonial Williamsburg Foundation. 142–143 © Bettmann/CORBIS. 144–145 © Louise Wells Cameron Art Museum. 148 © Bettmann/CORBIS. 149 The Granger Collection, New York. 150 (bl) © Bettmann/CORBIS. (br) © North Wind Picture Archives. 151 Library of Congress. 153 Independence National Historical Park (detail). 154 Fenimore Art Museum, Cooperstown, New York. Photo: Richard Walker. 155 (tl) © Bettmann/CORBIS. (br) Metropolitan Museum of Art, Gift of John Stewart Kennedy, 1897. 156 (t) The Granger Collection, New York. (bc) New York Historical Society/Bridgeman Art Library. 157 The Granger Collection, New York. 158–159 SuperStock. 158 Courtesy National Park Service, Museum Management Program and Morristown National Historical Park. 159 Courtesy National Park Service Museum Management Program and Valley Forge National Historical Park. 161 (tl) © Reuters New Media, Inc/CORBIS. (tr) © Joseph Sohm/Visions of America, LLC/Picture Quest. 166 (cr) The Granger Collection, New York. (br) © Reunion des Musees Nationaux/Art Resource, NY. 170–171 Photodisc/Getty Images. 173 (t) Peter Gridley/Getty Images. (c) Andrea Pistolesi/Getty Images. (b) Photodisc/Getty Images. 174 © Dennis Brack/Black Star Publishing/PictureQuest. 175 (bl) © SW Productions/Brand X Pictures/PictureQuest. (br) Photodisc/Getty Images. 180 Independence National Historical Park. 181 (tl) Stock Montage. (tr) © Peter Turnley/CORBIS. 182 (bl) National Museum of American History, Smithsonian Institution, Neg #89-6712. (bc) Monticello, Thomas Jefferson Foundation, Inc. 183 (bc) Tony Freeman/PhotoEdit. 184 The Granger Collection, New York. 185 (l) Culver Pictures. (r) Denver Public Library, Western History Collection. 186–187 Mark Segal/Panoramic Images/NGSImages.com. 187 From the collection of Gilcrease Museum, Tulsa Oklahoma. 188 (tl) © Giraudon/Art Resource, NY. (cl) © Burstein Collection/CORBIS. 189 The Montana Historical Society. 190 © Smithsonian American Art Museum, Washington, DC/Art Resource, NY. 192–193 Steve Patricia. 194–195 Steve Patricia. 199 The Granger Collection, New York. 201 Baltimore County Public Library. 204 Whitman Mission National Historic Site. 205 Culver Pictures. 207 Courtesy of the California History room, California State Library, Sacramento, California Neg 911. 208–209 Peter Turnley/CORBIS. 210 © Ted Spiegel/CORBIS. 211 (t) © imagebroker/Alamy. (cr) © Louise Murray/Alamy. 214 (l) Donna Day/Getty Images. (r) © Laurie Platt Winfrey, Inc. 215 (l) New York Public Library. (r) © AP/Wide World Photos. 217 © M Stock/Alamy. 218 Photographs taken by MetaForm Incorporated/Karen Yamauchi of artifacts in the National Park Service Collection, Statue of Liberty National Monument, Ellis Island Immigration Museum. 219 Union County Historical Society. 221 © Laurie Platt Winfrey Inc. 222 Library of Congress. 223 Brown Brothers. 224 Robert E. Daemmrich/Getty Images. 225 © Tony Freeman/PhotoEdit. 227 Brown Brothers. 234 © Bettmann/CORBIS. 235 Mario Tama/Getty Images. 236 (l) Brown Brothers. (c) Hulton Archives/Getty Images. (r) Carl Iwasaki/Time Life Pictures/Getty Images. 237 (bc) AP/Wide World Photos. (tr) Hulton Archive/Getty Images. 238 (l) Schlesinger Library, Radcliffe Institute, Harvard University. (r) © Michael Herron/Take Stock. 239 (l) © AP/Wide World Photos. (r) © Tony Freeman/PhotoEdit. 240 Library of Congress. 241 AP/Wide World Photos. 242 Ohio Historical Society. 243 Library of Congress, USZCN4-49, G01231. 244 © CORBIS. 244–245 © CORBIS. 248 © Bettmann/CORBIS. 249 Ohio Historical Society. 250 © Bettmann/CORBIS. 251 Library of Congress. 252 © Stock Montage. 253 (tl) Hulton Archive/Getty Images. (tc) © Topham/The Image Works. (tr) © Wally McNamee/CORBIS. (bl) © CORBIS. 255 Robert W. Kelley/Time Life Pictures/Getty Images. 256 (tl) © Charles Gatewood/The Image Works. (r) © NASA. 257 (tl) © Wally McNamee/CORBIS. (tr) AP/Wide World Photos. 258 © 1976 Bob Fitch/Take Stock. 259 AP/Wide World Photos. 260–261 Francis Miller/Time Life Pictures/Getty Images. 260 (bc) © Bettmann/CORBIS. (br) Express Newspapers/Getty Images. 261 AP/Wide World Photos. 262 Ron Anderson; Courtesy Capital Square Review & Advisory Board. 263 Center for Archival Collections, Bowling Green State University. 264 Ted Polumbaum Collection/Newseum. 265 © AP/Wide World Photos. 266 © AP/Wide World Photos. 267 (t) © Katy Winn/CORBIS. (c) © Bettmann/CORBIS/The Houghton Mifflin Company. 268 AP/Wide World Photos. 269 Ohio Center for Law-Related Education. 270 © AP/Wide World Photos. 274 Alec Pytlowany/Masterfile. 275 Independence National Historical Park. 278 (t) © Will & Deni McIntyre/Photo Researchers, Inc. (cl) © Carl & Ann Purcell/CORBIS. 280 © Jeremy Woodhouse/CORBIS. 282 Alec Pytlowany/Masterfile. 283 (tl) © Danny Lehman/CORBIS. (tr) A. Ramey/PhotoEdit. 286 © Lawrence Migdale/Photo Researchers, Inc. 287 (tl) Carl Mydans/Time Life Pictures/Getty Images. (tc) AFP/CORBIS. (tr) Ohio Department of Health. 288 Richard T. Nowitz/Photo Researchers, Inc. nf–R1 © Yann Arthus-Bertrand/CORBIS. R1 © Photo Library International/CORBIS. R2–R3 © LWA-Dann Tardiff/CORBIS. R4 (cl) © Bettmann/CORBIS. (br) Arnold Michaelis/Pix inc./Time & Life Pictures/Getty Images. R6 The Pilgrim Society, Plymouth, MA. R7 (tr) Philip Mould, Historical Portraits, Ltd., London, UK/The Bridgeman Art Library. (br) Royal Albert Memorial Museum, Exeter, Devon, UK/The Bridgeman Art Library. R8 The Granger Collection, New York. R9 Royal Academy of Arts, London. R10 Anne S.K. Brown Military Collection. R11 Independence National Historical Park. R12 Benn Mitchell. R17 Dennis Brack. R18 Steve Dunwell. R20 Independence National Historical Park. R22 The Granger Collection, New York. R23 Hulton Archive/Getty Images. R24 Picture Research Consultants, Inc. Archive. R25 (tr) Museum of American Political Life, University of Hartford. (br) US Army Signal Core Photograph in the John Fitzgerald Kennedy Library, Boston. R27 Black Star. R28 Bob Daemmrich/Stock Boston. R29 Maryland Historical Society. R30 (tl) Fabian Bachrach/Hulton Archive/Getty Images. (cl) Hulton Archive/Getty Images. R31 © Flip Schulke/CORBIS. R32–35 White House Historical Association. R36 (tl) PhotoEdit. (c) © Bettmann/CORBIS. R37 © CORBIS. R38 © Bettmann/CORBIS. R39 © CORBIS.